Recreational Tourism

ASPECTS OF TOURISM 11
Series Editors: Chris Cooper (*University of Queensland, Australia*),
Michael Hall (*University of Otago, New Zealand*)
and Dallen Timothy (*Arizona State University, USA*)

Recreational Tourism

Demand and Impacts

Chris Ryan

Viva Books Private Limited
New Delhi • Mumbai • Chennai • Kolkata • Bangalore • Hyderabad • Kochi • Guwahati

First Indian Edition 2006
Reprinted 2010

VIVA BOOKS PRIVATE LIMITED

- 4737/23 Ansari Road, Daryaganj, New Delhi 110 002
  E-mail: vivadelhi@vivagroupindia.net, Tel. 42242200
- 76, Service Industries, Shirvane, Sector 1, Nerul, Navi Mumbai 400 706
  E-mail: vivamumbai@vivagroupindia.net, Tel. 27721273, 27721274
- Jamals Fazal Chambers, 26 Greams Road, Chennai 600 006
  E-mail: vivachennai@vivagroupindia.net, Tel. 28290304, 28294241
- B-103, Jindal Towers, 21/1A/3 Darga Road, Kolkata 700 017
  E-mail: vivakolkata@vivagroupindia.net, Tel. 22836381, 22816713
- 7, Sovereign Park Apartments, 56-58, K. R. Road, Basavanagudi, Bangalore 560 004
  E-mail: vivabangalore@vivagroupindia.net, Tel. 26607409, 26607410
- 101-102 Mughal Marc Apartments, 3-4-637 to 641, Narayanguda, Hyderabad 500 029
  E-mail: vivahyderabad@vivagroupindia.net, Tel. 27564481, 27564482
- Beevi Towers, First Floor, SRM Road, Kaloor, Kochi 682 018, Kerala
  E-mail: vivakochi@vivagroupindia.net, Tel: 0484-2403055, 2403056
- 232, GNB Road, Beside UCO Bank, Silpukhuri, Guwahati 781 003
  E-mail: vivaguwahati@vivagroupindia.net, Tel: 0361-2666386

Published by arrangement with

Multilingual Matters Limited
Frankfurt Lodge, Clevedon Hall,
Victoria Road, Clevedon BS21 7SJ
UK

ISBN : 978-81-309-0177-0

Published by Vinod Vasishtha for Viva Books Private Limited, 4737/23, Ansari Road, Daryaganj, New Delhi 110 002.

Printed and bound by Raj Press, R-3, Inderpuri, New Delhi - 110 012.

Contents

Preface

It is over a decade since *Recreational Tourism: A Social Science Perspective* first appeared. During the intervening years, tourism research has become better established and the volume of published research has continued to grow almost exponentially with, or so it seems, each passing year bringing forth more journals in the field. Nonetheless, throughout this intervening period I have continued to receive enquiries as to whether a new edition of *Recreational Tourism* would appear.

Finally, it has happened! I would like first to thank all those people who kept asking for a new edition. Second, I would wish to thank Mike Grover and his team at Channel View Publications for their good will (the manuscript was a month late in arriving!) and technical support. Among others I should thank Mike Robinson, Nigel Evans and Richard Sharpley for hosting me at the Centre for Travel and Tourism at the University of Northumbria. This edition was commenced while I stayed there in November 2001. I must also thank my colleagues at the University of Waikato in New Zealand for letting me stay at home more days than perhaps I ought in order to complete the text. And, of course, a big thank you to my immediate family, Anca and Mark, who left me alone in our garage while I typed away at the laptop. (They might have actually thought this was an improvement over normal home life!)

It has been interesting reviewing and further conceptualising tourism in the sense of assessing to what degree work undertaken in the 1980s still had validity in the early years of the twenty-first century. The first flush of enthusiasm about ecotourism has come and gone, with its advocates stating that that it has, in its form of sustainable tourism, impacted on the mainstream to the benefit of many forms of tourism. I tend to more cynical perspectives myself – most tourists remain holidaymakers, not lay biologists. If they are educated, it is through the emotions, not the intellect, and edutainment seems to have gained sway! I tend to agree with that school who might see ecotourism as part of the problem. In a review of the earlier version of the book, Eric Cohen picked up my espousal of purpose-built tourism destinations as being more environmentally friendly than permitting tourists to enter previously unspoilt places. If anything, I tend more to that view today. It seems to me that for tourism to be the 'saviour' of fragile places, species and environments, then that implies a failure of better methods. It is perhaps a weak argument for tourism when (eco-) tourism can be advanced only as the least worst form of development.

In other spheres, the quest for authenticity that dominated an important part of the literature in the 1980s has, or so it seems to me, dissolved into two concepts. First there is existential authenticity – which implies that the feelings of the tourist and the performer are the measure of 'reality'. It is the epitome of consumerism – segmentations are dead; the individual consumer is king! Second, the argument has, to my mind properly, been replaced by 'authorisation' – who authorises any display or interpretation? In short, the reality of power structures finally begins to be revealed.

As for the conceptual survivors – then surely Dick Butler's theory of the destination lifecycle still retains significant usefulness as a measure against which to measure resort development, even though today it is more than uniformly recognised that it does not apply in all cases, and is certainly not inevitable? It is also evident to me that the techniques of analysis have become more sophisticated, and that positivism no longer rules supreme.

In writing this book, I have tended to eschew the approach that reduces knowledge to checklists of 'key points' or to draw boxes around 'case studies' as seems to have become the fashion. Knowledge is not a matter of lists to be remembered – rather it is an issue of understanding and questioning inter-relationships between dynamic factors – and this is certainly true of tourism. I strongly suspect students know this, and that better students are actually dismissive of attempts to remove complexity from reality. Their own realities are difficult enough as it is, and thus they readily appreciate that the management of tourism is far from being certain or wholly scientific – and is certainly more than just a checklist of items. This has meant that, within the structure of the book, there are elements of repetition in some instances. It is not expected that everyone will read the book from start to finish; some will want to simply dip into individual chapters, and thus such chapters had to be relatively free standing. However, while some repetition exists, hopefully it is comparatively minimal.

This then raises the issue of what is the purpose of this text? The original text was motivated by a wish to structure the determinants of tourism demand, and to subsequently examine the implications of that demand at the destination. Consequently demand is examined from within a framework of the economic, social and psychological determinants. In one sense economic factors enable holiday choice to be exercised, while social and psychological variables help to shape the nature of the choice being made. In practice, though, it is not necessarily that simple, and the factors are inter-dependent. For example, one's economic conditions might well play a role in shaping one's life expectations, and thus economics possess psychological implications.

As a preamble to the consideration of these factors, a history of tourism is described as a means of indicating how the economic, social and indeed technological conditions of an age determine holiday patterns. History is, however, not simply a case study that illustrates how socially-determined factors shape behaviours, but is in itself both a precursor and a determinant to that which is currently taken for granted. Consequently it is not surprising that many of the holiday-taking patterns that are discernible today are shown to have long and well-established antecedents, in spite of the new technologies that might be employed in a contemporary age.

The final purpose of the text is to examine the effects of tourism, and to illustrate the nature of the challenge posed for destination planners. Any identification of problems is, however, but a first stage towards attempted solutions – but such solutions are often drawn from an arsenal of comparatively well-established techniques at an operational level. On the other hand, the extent to which these techniques are applicable is often dependent on a debate about that which is valued, and the resource that will be allocated to the achievement of desired ends. Consequently operational methods open to destination planning are not divorced from wider social considerations of desired ends, politics and the power to achieve goals.

Whether it will be another decade before another edition appears is, thus far, not even a question that has been formulated; but if this edition is as helpful as the first appears to be, then the book will have served its purpose.

Chapter 1

A History of Tourism in the English-Speaking World

Introduction

In order to better understand the nature of tourism at the commencement of the twenty-first century, a brief history may be of use. While the following description and interpretation is Eurocentric (if not indeed primarily British), it can be argued that Western thought and the modes of capitalism that emerged from Europe's past, when combined with the industrial strength of North America, have been the main drivers of contemporary globalisation. In its turn, tourism has been both a consequence of, and a contributor to, the global nature of business and travel networks that exist today. Indeed, it has become a cliché to argue that the current nature of these networks specifically owes much to the period that followed the Industrial Revolution. Naturally travel preceded the second half of the nineteenth century, and indeed had an importance because it provided a model of forms of travel that had been the norm until that period. Like all models, it was modified and adapted by later generations in the light of new technologies and needs. Thus the antecedents of contemporary tourism reflected prior histories, just as today's tourism industry reflects its immediate past. Consequently this chapter examines the history of tourism from the perspective that the past explains, in part, the present.

The purpose of this chapter is to develop a context within which contemporary aspects of tourism can be viewed as being first, an evolutionary process and, second, significantly different from the past in terms of a compression of space and time made possible by new technologies. The chapter will end with a brief discussion of some themes that can be identified within this history.

The Classical World

The history of travel as a leisure activity is often traced to the classical civilisations of Greece and Rome, if only because of the presence of written and archaeological evidence. The historian Herodotus, living in about 465 BC, is known for his travels as described in *The Histories.* His *Histories* are full of asides relating to travel. For example he notes of Solon, the Athenian lawgiver, that '...no doubt for the pleasure of foreign travel – Solon left home and, after a visit to the court of Amasis in Egypt, went to Sardis to see Croesus' (465/1954, 23).There is reason to believe that the higher-income groups of Rome maintained residences by the sea in order to escape the heat, and probably the smells, of Rome during the summer season. Indeed, Ovid in his ode to the arts of love writes: 'No lust of place or riches weighs us down, We love our shady couch and spurn the town' – practical advice during the height of the Roman summer (6/1965: 112). Moreover, they travelled further afield. Towner (1996: 96) comments that 'Wealthy Romans, for example, travelled to Greece in search of the culture to which they ultimately aspired and which reaffirmed and validated their own beliefs and practices'.

The Medieval Period

In spite of a re-appraisal of the period from the fall of Rome to the emergence of Renaissance Europe, it is still probably true to describe the travel of the Middle Ages as being dominated by motives of warfare and pilgrimage. Yet, as Chaucer describes, pilgrimage was not without its merry side as attested by the enduring images of his *Canterbury Tales* with their paradox of the profane amid the declared intention of pilgrimage to holy sites. Thus it is notable that the worthy woman from Bath had been three times to Jerusalem, to Rome and to St James of Compostella. In short, pilgrimage routes were well established and frequented, and the wife from Bath was far from being alone in her travels.

Yet, for most people of this period, life was hard and bound to the seasons, although the influence of the Christian Church generated holy days of rest from work. Indeed, the various Christian churches were to have an influence within Europe for much of the period until the early twentieth century. In the Renaissance travel for purposes of curiosity about a wider world became entwined with motives of commerce, religion and politics. The discovery of the Americas and the journeys around Africa by explorers like Columbus, Cabot and Da Gama opened up a new network of voyages where, from the early fifteenth century into the nineteenth century, explorers were followed in ever-increasing numbers by soldiers, missionaries, settlers and administrators. It is tempting to see the unbroken but increasing stream of humanity leaving the shores of Europe to conquer South America, settle North America and explore darkest Africa as part of the same exodus. While simplistic, there is some truth in the perception that this period maintained a sense of expansion, of new places to be discovered, and of growing economic wealth. Of course this was not a continuous, homogeneous stream of movement. Different people moved to different places in response to different dominant imperatives. For example, some moved to escape religious persecution, others moved to administer new colonial empires, while yet others were taken in slave and convict ships. Nonetheless, given these many and diverse movements of people, the period from the fifteenth century onwards becomes increasingly dominated by a new leisure class for whom travel was motivated by enquiry, sightseeing, hedonism, simple curiosity and a sense of self seeking. Parks (1951: 264) cites Justus Lipsius as writing in 1578, 'Humble and plebeian souls stay at home, bound to their own piece of earth, that soul is nearer the divine which rejoices in movement, as do the heavens themselves'. Indeed Towner (1996: 101) cites an early seventeenth century theory of travel derived from the work of Robert Dallington, *A Method for Travill* published in 1605. This had two main categories of travel motive, namely preservation of self and observation. But the preservation of self is dominated not by what Maslow (1943,1970) later was to term safety and physiological needs, but by 'keeping his religion' and 'bettering his knowledge'. Likewise 'observation' was not only of cosmological and geographic features, but also of how people lived and the nature of their governance.

The Period of the 'Grand Tour'

An early example of travel for educational and leisure motives that is often much quoted is that of the Grand Tour. In his history of the Grand Tour, Hibbert (1987) traces its antecedents to the earlier pilgrims and movement of students and young aristocracy of the Elizabethan era, but commences his main history from the 1750s onward. Certainly, while the Grand Tour may have involved at most about 0.2–0.7% of the mid-eighteenth century British population, the 15,000 to 20,000 who travelled overseas each year represented a significant part of the estimated 200,000 or so of the landed classes who lived at that period (Towner, 1985). As the elite within eighteenth century Europe, the landed and aristocratic gentry were to set both a fashion and a desire to which an emergent middle class aspired.

The significance of the Grand Tour is not to be underestimated. First, the need for information began to create a market for the new guidebooks that began to emerge. An early example was William Thomas's*The History of Italy,* which was published in 1549 . De Beer (1975: 1) notes that between 1660 and 1730 'books of travel provided the principal secular reading of a growing readership.' By the early eighteenth century, travel literature took on the form of a 'bestseller' with prominent titles such as Thomas Taylor's *Gentleman's Pocket Companion for Travelling into Foreign Parts* (1722) and Nugent's *Grand Tour Containing an Exact Description of Most of the Cities, Towns and Remarkable Places of Europe* (1749) being numbered among them. Nor was this solely an English phenomenon, as is evidenced by Duclos' *Voyage en Italie* (1766). Indeed, these early guidebooks (cited in Inglis, 2000) offered detailed information about conditions of travel and things to see, and avoid. Misson's guides published from the late 1680s into the 1720s provided, for example, details as to the conditions of roads and the aesthetic qualities of landscapes. Towner (1996) cites Addison, Brown, Smollet, Burnet and Howell as some of the authors and guidebook writers who provided information about cities, landscapes and churches in the late seventeenth and eighteenth centuries. In addition to books, the papers and magazines of the time often carried travel articles that were read not simply as travelogues but as potential sources of useful information. The links between newspapers and guidebooks are easily explained when one considers the journalistic careers of people like Addison.

While these early tourists were generally male and taking advantage of the extended family networks of aristocratic dynasties, there were some women of note who also journeyed abroad. Notable among these was Lady Mary Wortley Montagu. Indeed, the very fact that she travelled added to her notoriety amongst her contemporaries, although few then or since went to the lengths that she did to travel in modes not always thought fitting. For example, Hibbert (1987) notes her writing of taking the veil and *djubbah* at one stage, and subsequently dressing as a man in order to visit a mosque. And, like many a young aristocrat of her time, she was drawn to Venice, then known for its masque balls and easy women, where she for a time engaged in an affair with Count Francesco Algarotti who was half her age. Yet Lady Montagu was not the only woman who travelled in Europe. After all, society at Bath and the other eighteenth century spa towns of Europe was often frequented by ladies who had travelled there unaccompanied by husbands, who may have been detained by political, commercial or agricultural business concerns. However, it would appear that female travel from Britain to Europe became better established after the end of the Napoleonic Wars. For example, in 1820 Mariana Starke noted a growing popularity of walking tours in Switzerland. In 1821 Lady Morgan wrote of her travels in Italy, and also described a growing trend to visit not only the sites of classical antiquity but to also the countryside. No longer were mountains dark, brooding presences to be avoided, but sites of romance and freedom.

Thus a second reason for the importance of the Grand Tour was that it created a model of what it was that people did when travelling, and what was to be observed as having value. The young aristocrat wondered at the sites of classical times, collected works of art, created networks of friends and society, required travel arrangements and then regaled colleagues back home with stories of foreign travel. Indeed the routes described by Nugent in his 1749 Grand Tour books (Nugent, 1749) could still be described today as being major routes for tourists. But while travel in the early eighteenth century was strongly motivated by the maintenance of social networks, a curiosity in history of the classical period and an interest in art and architecture, from the 1770s onwards Towner (1984) discerns the emergence of a new, separate interest in scenery as a specific objective for travel. Thus, by the early nineteenth century patterns of travel were clearly beginning to change. The previous century had marked the Grand Tour as being part of an Englishman's education, in all its various forms. For example, for much of the eighteenth century, Venice, described by Hibbert (1987: 136) as 'the brothel of Venice', was a recognised destination within the Grand Tour for all young bucks, and often was the culmination of their travels. Indeed, such was the state of affairs that Hibbert (1987:134) comments that 'Nuns were considered to make delightful lovers' and, from the evidence he provides, seemingly quite willing ones. An example of the Englishman's education is provided by the diarist James Boswell (the son of Alexander, Lord Auchinleck) who in 1766 wrote:

> At Rome, I ran about prostitutes till I was interrupted by that distemper which scourges vice in this world. When I got to Venice I had some small remains of disease, but strange, gay ideas which I had framed of the Venetian courtesans turned my head, and away I went to an opera dancer and took Lord Mountstuart with me. We both had her and we both found ourselves taken in for the punishment I had met with, at Rome. (Boswell, 1766/1955: 109)

Indeed, one obtains the impression that such behaviour, if not supported, was expected; but what was definitely not condoned was the thought that one of the young British gentry should seek to marry a European lady. Black (1992: 202) notes that 'Problems were created when impressionable young men fell in love. Venereal disease was bad, but so was *mésalliance.*' Careful plans of dynastic considerations were rarely put at risk. But, in spite of the, at times, quite sexually explicit outpourings of young British aristocracy as is illustrated by Black (1992) in his chapter entitled 'Love, Sex, Gambling and Drinking', most young men returned home perhaps wiser, but unmarried.

The Nineteenth Century: From Middle to Working Class Tourism

By the beginning of the Victorian period such behaviour, while it no doubt continued in different settings, was no longer publicly approved of in polite society. Over time, the society of courtesans in the United Kingdom gave way to the *bon mots* of fashionable society that was to be later described by Oscar Wilde, although in France courtesans still continued to host the younger sons of the aristocracy and to contribute in part to their education, as evidenced by the novels of Zola. For the English traveller, and for many of his or her continental counterparts, the late eighteenth and early nineteenth centuries were a period of rediscovery of the natural as a source of inspiration, as already noted above. This emergence of emphasis on the picturesque is often associated with the Romantic movement and poets such as Wordsworth. Yet its antecedents are clearly found before the establishment of the large conurbations brought into being by the Industrial Revolution and the establishment of factories surrounded by terraced, high-density housing occupied by the workforce within walking distance of the mills, mines and factories. For example, in 1768 William Gilpin published *An Essay upon Prints: Containing Remarks upon the Principle of Picturesque Beauty*. By the 1780s a number of guides had been published on the Lake District of England, and a long heritage links Carke's *Survey of the Lakes* (1787), Wordsworth's *A Guide through the District of the Lakes* (which had its fifth edition in 1835) to the contemporary guides of Wainwright. In fact Inglis (2000) attributes the popularity of the watercolour to a combination of tourism and the discovery of landscape:

> The charm of the watercolour is not only its readiness – painting in the open air is swift and easy; it is also that the watercolour so gracefully encompasses a quick glimpse of things or the sort of slight but pretty scene for which the grander effects of classical oils would simply be too much. In other words, it is the tourist's best medium. Its mobility, its modesty, its pastel colours and its quick effects made it into the tourist's own art form and especially the tourist who simply didn't have the money to commission the big names, as Boswell did Hamilton, for 200 guineas a time. (Inglis, 2000: 27)

In a sense, the watercolour was the camera of the early eighteenth century and, like photographs, watercolours came to be hung on the walls of the new houses of the middle classes that were being built in the new suburbs of English and Continental European towns. Indeed, the very size of cartridge paper, being usually 20 by 15 inches, 'was a size to fit happily on the walls of middle-class drawing rooms in the tall terraces of Bath, Brighton and Scarborough' (Inglis, 2000: 27). This emphasis on natural beauty might be interpreted as in part a response to the growing grime of the new industrial cities, but it was first adopted by classes not usually resident in the over-crowded slums of places such as Manchester, Sheffield or the other new industrial cities of northern Europe. Hence Wordsworth was to write of Tintern Abbey in 1798:

> These beauteous forms
> Through a long absence, have not been to me
> As is a landscape to a blind man's eye:
> But oft, in lonely rooms, and 'mid the din
> Of towns and cities, I have owed to them,

In hours of weariness, sensations sweet,
Felt in the blood, and felt along the heart:
And passing even into my purer mind,
With tranquil restoration...
(*Lines composed a few miles above Tintern Abbey*,
Wordsworth, 1888/1999)

The countryside was a balm to ordinary life. Trips to the countryside were to be remembered as sources of recompense and strength in future days; an emotional souvenir was being articulated that has become part of the importance of modern-day tourism. The modern tourist travels not for curiosity alone, but to enrich him or herself so as to develop psychological strengths that inform and reinforce for future life. Travel has become the creation of memory of past better times, and a promise of future good times. The sanctity of the medieval holy day became 'the holiday' – the sanctuary of the modern man.

Crawshaw and Urry (1997) have written about the importance of the Lake District in formulating a new way of looking, of creating new sets of relationships between that gazed upon and those that gaze. In their thesis the landscape became imbued with new meanings that served, and serves still, a positive purpose for the onlooker. In this very manner the guidebook writers like Wordsworth became gatekeepers, pointing out that which is to be observed, and by their silence condemning other aspects to the status of the non-observed. While as Inglis (2000: 31) notes, there came to exist a correspondence between the attributes of landscape (wildness, tranquillity) and 'the inarticulate but expectant feelings we bring to it', such an observation raises the question, how did these expectations arise and through what means were they being fostered? However, while Wordsworth was, no doubt, pleased to receive monies from those who purchased his guidebooks, he nonetheless opposed the extension of the railway line to Windermere, 'fearing that it would bring large numbers of people more intent on simple pleasures than admiring the sublime beauty of the region' (Sharpley, 1994: 68). Indeed, as will be seen in Chapter 3, Ruskin anticipated the arguments of Boorstin a century later by noting that the train 'transmutes a man from a traveller into a living parcel' (cited by Buzard, 1993: 33).

There is little doubt that growing literacy, an emergent middle class and increased income all played a role in developing a demand, and that that demand was based on the model established by the aristocratic Grand Tour. The Industrial Revolution not only generated the horrific conditions described by various Committees of Enquiry that are so carefully encapsulated by Thomas Carlyle in *Past and Present* (1843/1981), but also created a managerial, administrative class that had not really existed before – at least, not in the numbers being required by the new modes of production.

Equally, associated with this was a growing civil service that offered new, administrative middle-class occupations at both national and municipal level as the reforming zeal of town planners and a meritocracy based on success in public examinations began to replace the networks of social connections based on birth. In short, combined with the new transport technology of rail by the latter half of the nineteenth century, ease of travel (which addressed the issue of constrained time for the emergent middle classes), higher incomes, and the growing numbers of people with the income and urge to travel overseas, the conditions were right for the emergence of new forms of travel. And entrepreneurs like Thomas Cook in the United Kingdom and Reisen in Germany responded to the changing market conditions to lay the foundations of the package holiday companies and mass tourism that exist today. The story of Thomas Cook and his rail excursion for signatories of the Temperance Pledge between Leicester and Loughborough on 5 July 1841 is oft told, but it was four years before he commenced on his real operations of note. In 1845 he started arranging trips to the seaside, the first being an outing from Leicester to New Brighton near Liverpool. In 1846 he was packaging tours to Scotland that included not only travel by rail but also by the new steamers. In 1851 he arranged tours for 165,000 to the Great Exhibition at Crystal Palace. Four years later he took visitors to the Great Paris Exhibition, and by 1863 he had established tours to Switzerland and Italy using the new tunnels driven under the Alps. By the end of that decade he was taking visitors to Cairo and in 1872 by booking space on the *SS Oceanic* he inaugurated trans-Atlantic package travel. Very soon after he opened offices in Broadway and in 1894 introduced the concept of travellers' cheques. By then his company's expertise had been enlisted by the British Government and his son, John Cook, was making arrangements for the transportation of troops to the Middle East and India. By the 1880s not only were the British travelling across the Atlantic, but so too a growing number of higher income Americans were travelling to England and Europe to repeat the travel paths of the aristocratic Grand Tour. Such travels were not unknown to those who became readers of novels by authors such as Henry James, who in *Portrait of a Lady* (1908/1988) describes how Isabel Archer travels through Europe with her companions, Mrs Touchett and Madame Merle. Similarly E.M. Forster's novel *Room with a View* (1908/1088) tells its story within the context of an Edwardian family's trip to Italy and specifically Florence.

The American visitors to Europe brought with them not only their thirst for the sites of classical civilisation and a desire to visit the historic places of the home country, but also their expectations of first class hotel accommodation. To the interest of place was to be added the desire for luxury. Not that Europe was without its luxurious hotels. The railway age brought not only ease of transport but also a growing number of people requiring accommodation at the same time in the same place, and thus the great railway hotels were built by many of the railway companies. All over the United States and Europe, almost simultaneously in the mid-nineteenth century, large numbers of mock Gothic or Italianate hotel buildings with several hundred bedrooms were being built. On November 6, 1872 Thomas Cook, when accompanying a group on the steamer, *Colorado,* wrote:

> In American hotels, great attention is paid to the privacy and comfort of ladies, for whom large and elegant drawing rooms are provided, with separate entrance and staircase, available also for gentlemen with ladies. The first floor is generally appropriated to dining and breakfast saloons and drawing rooms, for which no extra charge is made. (Cook, 1872/1998: 21)

Thus Thomas Cook unerringly noted a combination that has stood the holiday industry well over the intervening years, namely that of affordable luxury. Equally, 22 days later, in Yokohama, he highlighted another promise of the industry, that of being able to see that which was previously not available to visitors, and thereby offered a promise of the 'authentic'. So he wrote:

> Until very recently it was not permitted for foreigners to enter the precincts of the Temple of Shiba and the surrounding and gorgeous tombs of Tycoons and their wives of the past 250 years. Yesterday my party walked freely through and round these indescribable buildings at Yedo, which for richness in carving, gilding, and decoration surpass all that I have seen in any land. Only a year ago an escort would have been required to conduct a party like mine through Yedo. (Cook, 1872/1998: 28)

It would appear that Thomas Cook was also aware of the role of promising exoticism in the development of his tours to the Far East.

For the middle classes Cook offered an identification of those sights said to be worth seeing. Unlike the aristocracy of the eighteenth century who could spend years on their travels, the new management and administrative classes were more time constrained. In addition they did not often possess the family connections that the aristocracy possessed, and thus required accommodation that was both affordable and at the least imposed no hardship, and preferably offered comfort not available in the suburbs of Bolton, Preston or London. Moreover, Thomas Cook offered the security of travelling with experienced, English-speaking guides in foreign countries, and the company of like-minded English people with whom to share experiences. As already noted, the novel, *Room with a View* by E.M. Forster with, as a focus, a trip to Florence, captures many of the nuances of the trips organised by Cook and similar companies of this era.

But just as the railways and hotels were catering for the upper and middle classes, so too the same assets began, over time, to meet the needs of a working class who too sought escape from the towns. Additionally, while elements of this market sought to duplicate the travel patterns and demands of the more affluent markets, others sought more immediate pleasures in song, dance and 'having a good time'. With reference to this market it might be said that an older theme within recreation was rediscovered, and that was a sense of carnival. Just as Chaucer's tales contained husbands who farted into the faces of their wives' lovers at the top of ladders (as in the *Wife of Bath*), and Fool's Days of the Medieval Courts represented a temporary reversal of authority, so too at seaside resorts the working classes were to create an escape. This escape was not only from the physical crowding of the city, but also from the rules and regulations imposed by the Victorian bourgeoisie – albeit at times it was an escape within which one set of rules was substituted by the rules of the tyrannical English seaside landlady.

At first this development was not immediately apparent. Just as the Romantic movement discovered value in the lakes and mountains, so too the coastal landscape came to be valued for its own contrasts. Additionally, the Prince Regent had popularised Brighton as a resort in the latter part of the eighteenth century and it might be said that this action on his part was an extension of the spa as an inherent part of the milieu of the then fashionable society. Towner, however, is at pains to point out that sea bathing was already an accepted practice, not only in the warmer climates of the Mediterranean where it would have been seen by various visitors to that part of the world, but also in northern England. Towner (1996: 171) cites Walton (1983: 11) when he writes: 'Further north, in Britain, a popular sea-bathing culture existed on the Lancashire coast, not emulating the rich but having a "prior and independent existence"'. Thus, Towner (1996: 171) observes, the usual attribution of the growing popularity of the seaside to the initial actions of fashionable society may yet again be a case 'where those who dominate the historical record are assumed to have been the innovators of the custom'.

Perhaps one of the more detailed histories of the seaside resort is that of Walton (1983). What is shown clearly by Walton's study is that working class demand for seaside holidays was constrained by regional working practices and wage rates, not to mention prevailing patterns of leisure and recreation. Thus differences occurred in regional practice and adoption of the seaside holiday. The Lancashire textile towns tended to be the early adopters, partly due to quicker access by the rail network to the coastal resorts of Blackpool, Morecambe and, as already noted, New Brighton. The Yorkshire woollen industry tended to lag some 10 years behind, and of course tended to be based on areas such as Whitby and Scarborough. Walton also notes that seaside holidaying by those working in Birmingham did not really commence until as late as the 1880s, when a few extra days were added to the August Bank Holiday.

The advent of the railways had similar impacts in other countries. When, in 1860, Nice was annexed by France from Savoy, the extension of the railway meant a rapid increase in population from 48,000 in 1861 to 143,000 forty years later. Visitor numbers increased from 5,000 to 150,000 in the same period (Rudney, 1980). Soane (1993), however, indicates another important reason for the development of seaside resorts such as Nice, namely the willingness of outside financial sources to act as suppliers of capital investment. Indeed, the availability of that capital and the desire to engage in property development created very different types of seaside resorts around the world. Some like Nice, became and remained embedded in a tourism of the higher-income groups, others like Blackpool became associated with short stays and low-cost accommodation and developed a culture based on working-class hedonism. Other areas were discovered by artists, writers and travellers: locations like Brittany or specific villages like St Ives in Cornwall provide examples of this. In these cases development tended to be slow, and often it was not until the twentieth century and the greater geographical freedom permitted by the motor car that these locations entered the domain of tourism more fully.

Tourists were also helping to create new product. Perhaps one of the better examples of this was the development of Alpine tourism. By 1857, there was sufficient interest for the Alpine Club to be established, with 300 charter members. While the club was dominated by middle-class professionals from Oxford and Cambridge universities, it was not unique to the United Kingdom. In 1862 the Austrian Alpine Club was formed, followed by those of Switzerland (1863), Germany (1869) and France (1874). While these clubs were male dominated, female mountaineers were present almost from the early days. Withey (1998) mentions the names of Marguerite Breevort (an American), Lucy Walker and Mrs Stephen Winkworth among others, and comments that 'what to wear was a problem for the female mountaineers' (Withey, 1998: 209).

Faulkner and his colleagues have suggested that the development of seaside resorts cannot always be logically explained by the broad economic forces of capital, population movements or technical forces such as the building of railways. Advocating the use of chaos theory to help explain broad changes in tourism, Russell and Faulkner (1999) specifically draw attention to the 'movers and shakers' who, while at times motivated by profit, nonetheless were often eclectic in their choice of location and nature of attraction, or had histories of business failure or eccentricity prior to making their contribution to the development of tourism resorts. For their part, Russell and Faulkner select the development of Australia's Gold Coast in the 1960s as an example. Thus they note:

> The men…responsible for the emergence of Surfer's Paradise as the focus of tourist activity were in varying degrees colourful, flamboyant, innovative, driven and often reflecting in their personal relationships the attributes of Chaos and Complexity. (Russell and Faulkner, 1999: 419)

One example they provide is that of Bernard Elsey. An English immigrant with little formal education who worked as a plumber in Toowoomba, he arrived on the Gold Coast in 1949. He earned money by simultaneously selling cruises to Tippler's Passage on Stradtbrooke Island during the day and selling Singer Sewing Machines on a door-to-door basis in the evening. Eventually he was to build three hotels, including the Surfers Paradise Beachcomber, and with pyjama parties and Hawaiian nights 'pushed the edges of law, filling national newspapers with copy and his establishments with patrons' (Russell & Faulkner, 1999: 421).

Indeed the very title of 'Gold Coast' seems to have come about by accident. Initially the area held the unglamorous name of 'Town of the South Coast', and then in 1958 it became 'Gold Coast Town'. Richardson (1999) recounts the story that it became the 'Gold Coast' in the 1950s after a pictorial editor on the *Brisbane Courier Mail* changed a reporter's story and then continued to use the term. The developing seaside resort deliberately built on its image when, in 1965 (a period when bikinis were still frowned upon at Sydney and Melbourne beaches), the meter maids of Surfer's Paradise, clad in little more than gold bikinis made what could only be described as an appearance in a blaze of national publicity. Their function was ostensibly to feed coins into expired parking meters, but their real value lay in the publicity that the Gold Coast acquired.

Similar parallels might be drawn with the development of Coney Island in New York State. Initially consisting of mud flats, in the 1870s the area was infamous not for its scenic features but for the zone known as 'The Gut' – a ramshackle area of places of ill-repute, brothels and drinking dens. As hotels like the Manhattan Beach became established, the juxtaposition between these and 'The Gut' led to entrepreneurs taking various actions. Foremost among these entrepreneurs was John McKane, an interesting gentleman whose personal history included being Chief of Police for Coney Island, but without formal salary as 'licences' were paid by gambling and other shady businesses. Power based on land deals made McKane an establishment figure with both Democrats and Republicans, yet he was to finally end his career by serving four years in Sing Sing prison.

By the 1920s Coney Island had become a melting pot where immigrant groups met with earlier immigrants, and all cavorted in the sea or stood amazed at the lights of Luna Park. Blackpool too had its own Luna Park, as did other places in the world such as Sydney, and in all cases they became locations of difference. Surrounded by funfair delights, they represented places of escape, where the achievements of modern science were put to use as play things or items of wonderment, where boys met girls, and normal restrictions did not apply. At Coney Island, for a long time one of the most popular attractions was one where draughts of air were blown up female's skirts to expose ankles and legs and where a clown prodded gentlemen's behinds with an electric stick. Underwear was revealed and shocks administered. The very presence of the clown maintained a tradition back to the jester of medieval courts, and the role of holidays as a time of reversal and denial of normal strictures continued to be confirmed.

Equally, the seaside, as indicated above, was associated with new freedoms that set aside a prurience that existed side by side with Victorian sexual interest, and brought the unspoken into the open. The bathing hut was invented to hide the modesty of females, but was at best, of limited success in achieving its objective. Sprawson (1992: 29) remarks that the women were encased in waisted, bloomered, skirted swimsuits, but they were made of 'woven cotton, which, when wet, tended to become transparent and cling to the body, revealing more than they concealed'. He continues:

> But whatever the restrictions, they (bathing huts) failed to prevent women from becoming objects of the greatest curiosity. In the Victorian coastal resorts, when the sea was normally 'black with bathers', the females did not venture beyond the surf but lay on their backs, waiting for the approaching waves, with their bathing dresses in 'a most degage style. When the waves came', commented one onlooker, 'they not only covered the bathers, but literally carried their dresses up to their necks, so that, as far as decency was concerned, they might as well have been without any dresses at all'. (Sprawson, 1992: 29)

But while the carnivalesque was present, not all working-class recreation could be characterised as being unrestrained extensions of the bawdy music hall. In the 1890s the bicycle became the first means of mass transport and there was, as Rubenstein (1989) came to call it, a 'cycling boom'. Not only did the bicycle bring a personal spatial freedom, but it was also indicative of the new freedoms slowly being accorded to, and gained by, women. The 'new woman' was often personified as being some one riding a cycle. Alderson (1972: 85) illustrates this by citing the *Complete Cyclist* of 1897 – 'now women, even young girls, ride alone or attended only by some casual man friend, for miles together through deserted country roads'. In Britain the Cyclists' Touring Club was founded in 1878, and between 1894 and1899 its membership rose from 14,000 to 60,000 (Rubinstein, 1977). The foundations of the Raleigh company in Nottingham were being laid at this time as many took to the country roads, either singularly or in groups. Associated with this movement was a new attitude towards the countryside, as fresh air, exercise and good companionship became part of the English psyche. The Youth Hotels Association, Rambling Clubs and the Boy Scouts all emanated from common roots of an enjoyment of the countryside not for so much its aesthetic beauties (as had informed early nineteenth century thinking), but as a backdrop to 'healthy exercise'. Later, in the twentieth century the same motives came to be present in the novels of Arthur Ransome (albeit with small boats) or in the adventures of Enid Blyton's Famous Five (with wooded copses to be explored and rabbits to be chased by family pets).

This new enthusiasm for the 'great outdoors' as a place to be explored was not confined to the United Kingdom. Tobin (1974) notes the rapid growth of the cycle industry in the United States, and its similarities with Britain in a number of respects. First, it was popular with women. Second, its popularity was greatest in the major urban areas of the east and mid-west as populations sought an escape from urban areas into the country-side. Additionally Tobin notes a precursor to the motor car age, as published routes led to higher usage of these routes, and in turn to the establishment of shops, hotels and inns that were attracted to these cycle ways. In short, an infrastructure came into being, thereby creating the paradox that the escape from the city brought the resources of the city to support the new activities. It might be said that the commodification and industrialisation of leisure have long antecedents.

The Twentieth Century

In the period prior to the First World War there was, on the whole, a continuation of trends that had commenced thirty years earlier. The tours of Thomas Cook and its competitors continued to spread ever further and in greater numbers, but still primarily using steamers and trains. The seaside resorts on the whole continued to flourish, whilst clubs and outings of various sorts remained a feature of leisure and holidaying. Much of the holiday industry was thus dominated, if not by mass movements of people using the same resources, certainly by group movement. However, in the period after the Great War this was to begin to change. In short, a movement towards greater individualisation of holiday taking commenced, albeit at first slowly, but with increasing rapidity as the twentieth century grew to a close. A number of factors accounted for this. First was the advent of the motor car and its increasing availability to growing numbers of the population as prices fell. Second, the emergence of air transport became increasingly important. Third, at least for a time, there was a reduction in the working week and, although for many at the end of the century the promise of more leisure time began to sound like a hollow promise, the changing nature of work and the blurring of boundaries between work and leisure for many people meant more travel and less-structured ways of working. As always, though, these broad social movements and changes can be found to have precursors. But, as is often the case, the initial instances of any given form of activity tend to be individual, and often associated with wealth. Nonetheless it would be a mistake to believe that non-mass recreational and holiday taking did not exist prior to the 1920s. Inglis (2000), for example, highlights the role of the holiday home. But he comments:

> The past of these places is... surpassed and mythologised. Such simplicity comes damned expensive. But it matches a taste in which Emerson and Thoreau over there are compounded over here with Wordsworth, William Morris and the Arts and Crafts movement, to say nothing of the noble Lord Armstrong who made millions out of machine guns and built the wildly Romantic, lavishly simple Craigside in Northumberland. (Inglis, 2000: 63)

But around the coast of Britain summer homes began to emerge, more modest affairs perhaps than Craigside, but comfortable, middle-class summer cottages began to intermingle with the fishermen's' homes in places like Southwold and elsewhere in coastal Britain. Similar but even more modest summer homes were established elsewhere in the world, albeit perhaps a little later. For example, in Canada lakesides came to be dotted with wooden and tin shacks that offered children the great summer delights of messing in boats, getting wet and other simple, playful pleasures while fathers fished at the end of jetties and mother fussed over insect bites. Thus, for example, at Lake Waskesiu in the Prince Albert National Park, Saskatechewan, by the 1940s such shacks were already an established part of the summer holiday lifestyle and over 200 existed (Waiser, 1989). However, it is perhaps in New Zealand most of all that the informal, wooden and tin holiday home achieved its greatest heights. The summer 'bach' has entered into the sensibility of idyllic, and perhaps past, summers of long, warm, sunny days spent by the beach or lakeside. Indeed in New Zealand the 'bach' has become an established architectural form of varying degrees of optimism, professionalism and skill, and access to different types of building materials redolent of self sufficiency and eccentricities, as is amply demonstrated by Wood and Treadwell (1999) and by Male (2001).

The motor car opened up the countryside and the potential for independent travel in a manner previously unknown. In the United Kingdom, in 1920, there were 200,000 private cars, in 1939, 2 million, while in 2001 there were 24.5 million licensed vehicles. The train, as Inglis (2000: 100) observes 'powerful, vastly over-capitalised, gradually turned into a stalwart icon of the industrial family: it became Thomas the Tank Engine and Gordon the Express Train'. With, in the 1960s, the commencement of motorway building in the United Kingdom, holidaymakers could travel from places like Birmingham to South or North Wales, or to Cornwall and Devon within the day. Yet, just as these places began to develop new infrastructures to cope with increasing demand, the growing number of domestic holidaymakers turned their attention to the warmer climates of the Mediterranean. The impact of mass air transport was soon to make itself felt in a way that came to dominate the holiday industry in Europe.

The same pressures were felt also in North America. While Hollywood has romanticised the road even late into the twentieth century with road movies such as *Easy Rider* and *Thelma and Louise*, the golden age of interstate highways like that of Route 66 was comparatively short-lived. Route 66 was the designation awarded to the Chicago to Los Angeles highway in 1926. In his novel, *The Grapes of Wrath*, Steinbeck proclaimed US Highway 66 the 'Mother Road', and Route 66 came to represent the 'road to opportunity' as those affected by the dust bowls of the mid-west travelled to California in the 1930s. Route 66 spawned the architecture of modern highways like motels and auto camps, and the evolution of the filling station, and finally entered US folklore. In the 1950s Route 66 increasingly became superseded by a new interstate highway, and by the 1970s this and air traffic meant that it was falling into disrepair. Today, however, 'the love of the open road', and a growing interest in America's history has meant a renewed interest in the stories and architecture of the Route, and the International Route 66 Mother Road festival attracts thousands in a mix of nostalgia, history, car enthusiasts and lovers of John Steinbeck's work. Together different groups of enthusiasts are seeking to retain the edifice of the Route and many different tourism products are being constructed around it.

In its turn air transport was to advance significantly as a result of the two World Wars. While attracting newspaper headlines, flight remained an interest of only the few in terms of actual participation. Rae (1968) noted that in 1914 only 49 aircraft were manufactured in the United States, although this figure increased significantly after America's entry into the First World War. In the UK, after 1919 the Northcliffe Committee developed a plan for civil aviation. However, in those early days it might be said that flying as a passenger was a form of adventure tourism! An important marker of developments were the achievements of Amy Johnson. With her flights to Australia she proved the reliability of aircraft, and gave flying a romance and newspaper headlines that induced others to follow. Incidentally, the name of her aircraft, *Jason* is still echoed in the very successful *Jason's Guides* with which most visitors to New Zealand will be familiar. In 1925 airlines flew about 21,000 people to and from Britain (Dyos & Aldcroft, 1969), and even by 1935 Imperial Airways still carried only 66,000 to all parts of the globe, albeit in somewhat extravagant luxury but at no or little profit (Higham, 1960). Nonetheless, in the United States events with significant implications for the future began to unfold. The Douglas Aircraft Corporation began to move from the production of fighter planes to the development of passenger aircraft, and in 1933 the vice-president of the newly formed TWA (Transcontinental and Western) flew the first production DC2 from Los Angeles to Newark in 13 hours – a new record. Within two years, the DC3 was introduced with a cruising speed of 190 mph and a load of 21 passengers. At the same time William Boeing had commenced aircraft production, although at that time it was generally thought that the Boeing 247 was outclassed by the products from Douglas.

For countries like the United States, Australia and New Zealand, the development of air transport was of vital importance because of their size and, in the case of Australasia, its distance from the main centres of population in the northern hemisphere. In 1922, the Queensland and Northern Territory Aerial Services Limited (QANTAS), was founded by two former Air Force pilots, W. Hudson Fysh and Paul McGinness. In 1936 Ansett Airways started in Australia. In 1939 the forerunner of Air New Zealand was established, namely the Tasman Empire Airways Limited (T.E.A.L.), of which QANTAS had a 30% shareholding.

Just as the First World War gave an important impetus to the development of aircraft and the formation of airlines as currently understood, so the period after the Second World War was to usher in the age of cheap air transport. In 1946 there were many discharged airmen who still liked the fun and pleasure of flying, and sought a means of combining pleasure with earning a living. Many tried to live off mail-run contracts, and many were on the verge of failing in places like the United Kingdom. Salvation came from an unlikely source, namely the Russian blockade of West Berlin. That city was sustained by the continuous airlift. Nor was it simply Berlin that was sustained – so too were a number of embryonic airlines including that of one Freddie Laker. In 1947 Laker was working for London Aero Motor Services, and buying and selling war-surplus trucks, aircraft radio and electrical surplus at government sales. Additionally, to raise extra money he and his wife were selling seedlings from the back of one of these trucks. In October 1947 he set up his own company, Aviation Traders, and within three weeks had exhausted his capital. The Russian blockade of Berlin changed all of that within a matter of months. As Eglin and Ritchie (1981: 16) were later to record in the book *Fly Me, I'm Freddie!* there was considerable cash flow and they were all drawing regular wages. Indeed:

> The generous charter rate and the huge number of hours flown produced enough cash flow for the independents to set up complete organisations with flying crews, ground staff, UK bases, plant and equipment. And the unrelenting tempo of the airlift, with month after

> month of round-the-clock flights, taught the independents a lot about how to run continuous air operations. (Eglin & Ritchie, 1981: 16–17)

Equally important was the political situation of Franco's Spain. Left alone in 1946 as the last of the Fascist regimes, Spain was marginalised from the mainstream of European economic recovery. There was no Marshall Aid to Spain, nor an external impetus for a regeneration of investment and capital. Yet Spain had something to offer to the northern European countries (other than perhaps France), and that was sunshine and a Mediterranean coastline. Using a mixture of grants and tax breaks, the Franco regime encouraged the development of hotels and hotel chains which, in turn, were to enter into an alliance with the new entrepreneurial airline companies of the United Kingdom, Scandinavia and Germany. Whereas but a few years earlier British pilots had flown to bomb cities under Fascist regimes, they now flew holidaymakers into Franco's Spain. Given the later reputation of some British holidaymakers, the cynical might make wry comments about this comparison. Yet nonetheless the political implications of bringing Spain out of isolation were significant, and it can be argued that tourism played a major role in the eventual democratisation of Spain.

By the end of the twentieth century, tourism had significantly grown throughout the world. The World Tourism Organisation (WTO, 1998) recorded that, in 1950, arrivals of tourists from abroad, excluding same-day visits, numbered about 25.2 million. By 1997 the figure was 612.8 million. In 1950 receipts from international movements were $US2,100 million, in 1997 they were US443,770 million. While at the end of the twentieth century Europe still dominated international tourism movements with over 58% of those movements (WTO, 1998), the East Asia/Pacific region had the fastest annual growth rates and was accounting for about 15% of all travel movements. In short, the twentieth century had witnessed a democratisation of travel and the duplication of a wish for mass travel and tourism by non-European nations on a scale that had not been previously achieved.

Lessons from History?

Thus far this has been a description of history – indeed a generally uncritical and selective history that has traced growth and the democratisation of tourism. With tourism no longer a preserve of the aristocratic few, Uncle Norman, Auntie Edith and all their children, nephews, nieces and siblings can now seek the sun. So what can be learnt from this review?

Several implications can be drawn from this summary of tourism history, and they follow in no particular order of priority. First, Coney Island, the seaside holidays, the use of railways, theme parks, and air transport – all show a very close connection between tourism and advancements of technology. Travel, technology and tourism create a close triumvirate that fed off each other and reinforced the development of each. The travel of Victorians to new resorts for tourism created the demand that furthered the technical advance of the railways so that within a short period of time the tracks and trains became capable of higher speeds. Today, travel needs have been an important impetus in the development of the Internet and, by 2003, while difficult to ascertain, it has become a cliché that tourism and travel needs have displaced pornography as the single major use to which the Internet is put. eDestination marketing has become a commonplace. Some airline businesses in the no-frills sector have totally bypassed the travel agent, while full service airlines have been catching up with their online provision. Many other types of tourism organisations have been tracing increases in online bookings, and it is common for visitor surveys to include questions about the usage of the Internet.

Indeed, it is not perhaps too much of an extension to argue that tourism has played an important role in the development of many technologies. Today the camera-toting tourist is being replaced by the digital camcorder tourist, who therefore requires the video editing software incorporated into an operating system like that of Windows XP in order to edit his or her holiday film. There is evidence that the relationship between image and tourism goes back a long way. As already noted, the popularity of the watercolour was associated with a growth of travel. Miller and Robbins (2001: 20) note that, included among the 200 'calotype' prints of the Edinburgh Calotype Club taken in the early 1840s, were holiday snaps from trips to the Continent. Crang (1999) has noted the almost instinctive desire of people to make a permanent record of the places that they have visited, and hence it is not too far fetched to argue that tourism demand may have helped to further the technological advances seen in the photographic and image-capture industries.

Second, a key feature related to technology is the importance of the role of access in the development of tourist destinations. With each successive improvement in transport technologies, travellers have ranged further away from home. Today that process continues, and indeed limitations imposed on access have become one way of protecting natural areas. The denial of a runway restricts access. The development and extension of a runway permits wider-bodied jets to access airports, thereby disgorging more passengers per flight. The provision of accommodation is often associated with any easing of access. Space tourism is just becoming a reality and not simply a dream, and as such is helping to financially sustain further space exploration. The tourism periphery, it might be observed, now extends into space (Smith, 2000).

A third lesson to be learnt from history is that technological change and improvements to access are not perhaps sole determinants of demand – motive and an ability to fulfil desire are also prerequisites for tourism development. The theory of the moving periphery – that is, of destinations over time meeting the needs of different social classes (in a European context, usually from upper to middle to lower social groupings) has implicit within it changes in the distribution of disposable income and available leisure time. Simply put, over time more people have had both the time and income to travel. Of interest is that divisions between work and leisure were eroding at the end of the twentieth century. The social certainties of the mid-century were breaking down to create less homogeneity in motives and travel patterns, with the subsequent development of individualistic marketing strategies on the part of product and service providers. These issues will be explored in later chapters.

Implications and New Directions

What are the implications of these lessons? It is possible to claim that if, in past centuries, changing technologies created 'outward-directed' touristic developments in terms of creating new destinations and new places to visit, then current changes in technology are more 'inner directed'. Today the creation of new product and the duplication of old product are becoming more independent of geography, history and culture. The Eiffel Tower and King Tutankhamun's tomb are both to be found in Las Vegas, while Mickey Mouse cavorts in both Paris and Tokyo. The past is daily re-enacted at places that are some times divorced from their original locations, so that, for example, medieval banquets with knightly jousting are popular with visitors to Los Angeles. The time–space compression of modern tourism is motivated by a wish to profit from the entertainment of the tourist, and the satisfaction of curiosity about place and culture at places that are convenient to the tourist. In many senses this is little different from London being thrilled by the exploits of Buffalo Bill's Wild West show in part celebration of Queen Victoria's Golden Jubilee in 1887. But the difference today is that the simulacra are more frequent, more pervasive and more convenient to the point where the discovery of new places is almost being conveniently delivered to the consumer's living room through the Internet and digital television set.

If therefore the simulacra of travel itself are present at home, then does not the nature of travel itself pose an alternative – the experience of the real as distinct from the experience of the 'fake'? Certainly within the academic literature there has long been a juxtaposition of the authentic with the inauthentic. Implicit within such comparisons has been the legitimacy of the former over the latter, with earlier writers such as Boorstin (1961) being particularly critical of the new forms of tourism as emasculated forms of travel devoid of the sense of 'going'. Thus Boorstin (1961: 102) wrote of air travel 'My passage through space was unnoticeable and effortless. The airplane robbed me of the landscape.' For him the air stewardess was 'the Madonna of the Airways, a pretty symbol of the new homogenenised blandness of the tourist's world' (Boorstin, 1961: 103).

Boorstin identified six characteristics of the 'image'. These were:

(1) It is synthetic – it is planned, created for a specific purpose.
(2) It is believable – it serves no purpose unless it has this appeal.
(3) It is passive – by which Boorstin meant that the consumer of the image was expected to accept, and fit, the image – but such 'fitting' is a change of face, not heart.
(4) An image is vivid and concrete – it therefore abstracts from complexity to present only a few specific qualities.
(5) An image is thus simplified – and therefore contains within itself its own decay, as it inevitably loses meaning.
(6) An image is ambiguous – it floats between expectation and reality.

For Boorstin the image replaces the ideal in contemporary society. Yet there remains the ideal, always present – ready to expose the fallacy of the image. His book ends with a call to awake from illusion, to rediscover the real from the self-deceptive dream. The issue for many at the commencement of the twenty-first century is whether the image has become the reality, has attained its own legitimacy wherein the need for continuous reinvention is the norm and constancy is the sign of failing systems. However, modernity (or post-modernity) is made more complex by the consumer's realisation that it is an image that is sought. The image, while fuzzily separate from the ideal, by reason of its existence adds richness, playfulness and new meanings to the original at the bequest of the tourist as consumer of place, culture, event and history. The implication for tourism is that there exists a challenge both to tourism and to our means of conceptualising it. The arguments of the authentic versus the inauthentic were a discussion of more than forty years past – today there exists a new generation of the mass-media age whose realities are those of the ephemeral, the fad and the short-lived fashion. If there is a consistency it is that of the satisfaction of whim. The continuous display of imagery designed to satisfy and the changing roles that the tourist can adopt are all inter-related. The current reality is that tourism mirrors the desire for a world of adventure, heterogeneity of experience, new sensations and a rejection of sameness, conformity and received knowledge. From one perspective this can be interpreted as akin to the situation described by Michael Moorcock's characters in his trilogy *The Dancers at the End of Time* (Moorcock, 2000); namely, it is boredom that is to be avoided and, if boredom can be negated through whimsy, reinventions of the past and desired roles, then tourism successfully meets the needs of its participants. If this sounds like nothing more than self-indulgence, then it needs be admitted that self-indulgence may be an outcome of such processes. But equally it can be seen as part of a process of life enrichment wherein new technologies, opportunities for travel and differing products at destinations combine to present current generations with ranges of choice previously unknown.

What roles can be discerned? Gibson and Yiannakis (2002) in a reprise of earlier work, list a number of identified roles that tourists adopt. These include 'sun lover', 'action seeker', 'anthropologist', 'drifter' and 'educational tourist' among others. However, in this study they contend that their research 'provides statistical support for the contention that tourist roles serve as vehicles through which vacationers may satisfy or enhance deficit or growth needs (*sic*)' (Gibson & Yiannakis, 2002: 378). They further provide evidence that these roles are far from consistent, possess varying importance for different life stages and genders, and assume different meanings over time. The current situation is possibly both a culmination of past trends, and the start of something that is qualitatively different from the past. To perceive history as no more than an antecedent of the present is to imply a progress from simpler to more complex times, and that is probably just as much of a trap as were the earlier interpretations of history as a process from the less to the more civilised. Nonetheless, the current volume of tourism is new and the infrastructure to which it has given birth is truly global in a manner not previously seen. Equally, the world of the twenty-first century as it is known by those with access to computer-driven technologies is one of more complex stimuli and choice. Some, in previous generations, expressed the view that the fast speed of rail transport would induce nausea to such an extent that rail-based travel was doomed. Today space tourism beckons. The only certainty is that the future will find antecedents in its past, but equally will generate its own expression and product in ways that it is not possible to predict with any degree of accuracy.

Chapter 2

The Economic Determinants of Demand

Introduction and Definitions

To paraphrase the great English playwright, William Shakespeare, if indeed all the world is a stage, and men and women have their exits and their entrances, then perhaps in the early twenty-first century the tourist is a participative audience. Perhaps tourists do not always comprehend what it is that they see, perhaps at times the tourist enters upon the stage as either the figure of fun or the catalyst of change, but increasingly the tourist cannot be ignored. Certainly, in a period of increasing customisation of product to meet the particular needs of consumers, tourists are increasingly used to exercising individual choice, preference and interaction with the suppliers of purchased products and services. As already noted in Chapter 1, the numbers of tourists continue to swell, as if in response to some pressing need to see the world, to view it as if it contains some truth that would otherwise be denied to them. As in Chapter 1, appropriate questions to be asked include what is the nature of this phenomenon, and what is it then that leads to this need? In Chapter 1 a historical, descriptive approach was adopted and, while such an approach is of help, it can be argued that description is but a first stage towards analysis. In analysing the nature of tourism, a number of approaches may be taken. One approach is to view tourism as an economic activity, and thus recognise that tourism may be defined as possessing the characteristics of an industry. Those characteristics include the production of a service and the establishment of a structure of business relationships with the prime motive of satisfying wants associated with travel and the resulting accommodation needs for the purpose of achieving profit. Such an approach is inherent in a definition that refers to tourism as:

> The demand for, and supply of, accommodation and supportive services for those staying away from home, and the resultant patterns of expenditure, income creation and employment.

If this type of approach is adopted, it in turn creates a need for specific definitions that permit measurement. The history of technical definitions of tourism is very much a post Second World War phenomenon as governments in the 1950s accepted a range of economic and social responsibilities not previously adopted. With the growth of international tourism, it was not surprising that standards of measurement common to all countries were sought. In 1963 a United Nations Conference on International Travel and Tourism recommended to national governments that the following definitions be used:

> ... for statistical purposes, the term 'visitor' describes any person visiting a country other than that in which he/she has his usual place of residence, for any reason other than following an occupation remunerated from within the country visited. (United Nations, 1963)

As well as proposing a definition of 'visitor', the Rome Conference in 1963 also proposed that the term 'visitor' should cover two distinctive classes of traveller: tourists and excursionists. Tourists were defined as temporary visitors staying more than 24 hours in a country visited and the purpose of whose journey can be classified as (1) leisure, i.e. recreation, holiday, health, study, religion or sports, (2) business, (3) family, (4) mission or (5) meeting. Over time, additional meetings were held, for example the meeting of the United Nations Statistical Commission in Rome in 1976, and that of the World Tourism Organisation (WTO) in 1991. Distinctions have been drawn to ensure, for example, that tourists are counted separately from other groups such as migrants, members of armed services, refugees or embassy personnel. At the conclusion of the 1991 WTO conference the accepted definitions were those shown in Table 2.1.

For some countries the definitional components of domestic tourism might still differ from those given in Table 2.1 in that a spatial component is added. For example a domestic tourist might be expected to travel at least 40 kilometres away from his or her home and stay overnight in order to qualify for the status of 'tourist'.

While such definitions as these are important (they are definitions based on observed travel behaviours), they say little about the nature of, or reasons for, those behaviours. They begin to quantify without explanation. Therefore alternative definitions of behaviour might be conceived. For example, the psychological impacts of recreational tourism may be recognised. Given that the prime motivations for such travel are ones of rest, discovery and pleasure, holiday tourism may be defined as:

> The means by which people seek psychological benefits that arise from experiencing new places and new situations that are of a temporary duration, whilst free from the constraints of work, or normal patterns of daily life at home.

Ryan (1991a) also argued for a fourth approach to be adopted in any definition of tourism, one that was more holistic and incorporated what he saw as being important, namely the 'fun' component of the holiday experience.

Table 2.1 World Tourism Organisation definitions of tourism

	International tourism	*Domestic tourism*
Visitor	A person who travels to a country other than that in which he/she has his/her usual residence, and which is outside his/her usual environment, for a period not exceeding one year, and whose main purpose of visit is other than the exercise of an activity remunerated from within the country visited.	A person residing in a country, who travels to a place within the country, but outside his/her usual environment, for a period not exceeding six months, and whose main purpose of the visit is other than the exercise of an activity remunerated from within the place visited.
Tourist	A visitor who travels to a country other than that in which he/she has his/her usual residence for at least one night but not more than one year, and whose main purpose of visit is other than the exercise of an activity remunerated from within the country visited.	A visitor residing in a country, who travels to a place within the country, but outside his/her usual environment, for at least one night but no more than six months, and whose purpose of the visit is other than the exercise of an activity remunerated from with the place visited.
Excursionist	A visitor residing in a country who travels the same day to a country other than that in which he/she has his/her usual environment for less than 24 hours without spending the night in the country visited, and whose purpose of visit is other than the exercise of an activity remunerated from with the country visited.	A visitor who travels to a place within the country but outside his/her usual environment, for less than 24 hours without spending the night in the place visited, and whose main purpose of visit is other than the exercise of an activity remunerated from within the place visited.

Source: WTO (1991)

However, it is here maintained that the definition then proposed failed to be holistic in the important sense that it was demand-derived and made no inclusion of the hosts, their culture, heritage or place that was a home and not simply a location to be visited. Holistic definitions thus become difficult, but the 'economic' definition previously postulated can, it is suggested, be extended and thus tourism is:

> The demand for, and supply of, accommodation and supportive services for those staying away from home, and the resultant patterns of (1) expenditure, income creation and employment that are created, (2) the social, cultural and environmental consequences that flow from visitation and (3) the psychological changes that result for both visitor and host.

Whilst this definition might lack the 'fun' that was thought important (and indeed it is recognised that fun and pleasure associated with tourism are important), it must be recognised that the psychological consequences of tourism cannot all be categorised as being pleasurable. At some times tourism might pose cathartic experiences that are life changing, or indeed, on fortunately rare occasions, travel may induce death or injury. It thus becomes possible to define tourism from at least four viewpoints: economic, technical, psychological and holistic. In turn these considerations can be used to analyse the nature of tourism. For the remainder of this, and the next two chapters, the demand for tourism will be considered and for this three separate, albeit related, approaches can be undertaken.

The first approach is to view tourism as a service or a product like any other, its demand determined by economic variables, and hence subject to the economic 'laws' of demand. Any economic study can be undertaken at both a micro- and a macro-level of analysis.

A second approach might be to view tourism and the nature of its demand as a reflection of social change. Indeed, this approach has become very popular with some commentators. For example, Urry (1990) considered tourism to both reflect and contribute to changes in the ways in which people 'gazed' upon society. In their analysis of tourism associated with issues sexual, Ryan and Hall (2001) argued that attempting to isolate what is called sex tourism not only from mainstream tourism but also from the socio-economic structures of society implies a failure to understand what sex tourism is about, or what motivates its current structures. The same comment can be made about tourism more generally.

A third approach is to attempt to understand what motivates visitors. In short a socio-psychological framework might also help to understand the demand for tourism, what it is that tourists seek, and to offer a context and explanation for the patterns of demand that emerge.

Thus this chapter is concerned with the economic determinants of demand for tourism, and will identify the variables thought important by economists, and the nature of the relationships between these variables. One important purpose of analysis is to enable prediction to occur, and so reference will also be made to the econometric literature that has sought to forecast tourism flows. Chapter 3 will subsequently examine how social trends interact with income distribution to help create new market segments, and Chapter 4 will examine how psychological motives also help to define patterns of demand.

The Economic Determinants of Demand for Tourism

While in themselves economic factors such as higher levels of income, levels of prices and exchange rates are not motivating factors for undertaking leisure travel, they are nonetheless important enabling variables. Additionally, there is a link between income and motivation because any higher income removes some of the uncertainties of life, thereby freeing people from the need to continually concern themselves with the need for shelter, warmth and food. Instead, people can then seek to enrich their lives not solely with the material but also with the experiential, and travel becomes an important means of experiencing and engaging with the new. From an economist's perspective, it is the enabling function of variables such as prices and income that are important as being both measurable and of predictive use. If a correlation can be shown between income and the amount of travel that will be undertaken, this permits a prediction that if income increases by x% then travel will increase by y%. From the pragmatic stance of those wishing to build roads, hotels, attractions and infrastructure, the potential use of such information is of obvious importance.

In conventional micro-economic theory, the demand for any product or service can be defined in terms of:

(1) $D_t = f(P_t, P_1 \dots P_n, Y, T)$

where D_t = the demand for tourism
P_t = the price of tourism
$P_1 \dots P_n$ are the prices of other goods
Y = income
T = taste.

These variables will be considered in turn, beginning with the role of income.

The role of income

It can be hypothesised that, as incomes increase, so the demand for tourism is also likely to increase. However, studies show that, for the developed world and for most of the second half of the twentieth century, the demand for tourism increased faster than the growth of National Income (Cooper *et al.*, 1993). For example, expenditure on tourism proved remarkably resistant to the recession in the early 1970s that followed the oil crisis, and it would seem that the demand for tourism is income-elastic and, to a degree, price-inelastic. In other words, for any given percentage increase in income, tourism demand grows proportionately faster. On the other hand, if income moves in a downward direction, tourism demand appears to be relatively income-inelastic; in other words, if there is a reduction in income (or, more likely in a practical sense, incomes rise less quickly than expected), the demand for tourism does not diminish to the same degree. Equally, it can be claimed that the demand for tourism continues to grow, even if prices increase. This is not to say that there has been an unbroken pattern of ever-increasing demand for travel overseas; but in many instances the causes of a reduction in demand for travel to and from any group of countries has been due to non-economic, exogenous factors. Examples that come readily to mind include the reduction in American travel overseas during the Gulf War of 1991 and in the aftermath of the hijacking of aircraft on September 11 2001 by Al-Qa'eda terrorists and their use to destroy the World Trade Centre in New York and to damage the Pentagon. Other examples of terrorist action include the 1997 attacks on tourists at Luxor, which resulted in the killing of 71 people and adversely affected subsequent tourism flows to Egypt. Equally the foot-and-mouth epidemic in the United Kingdom led to a 30% reduction in overseas visitors to the United Kingdom in the summer of 2001 because of perceptions that travel through Britain was severely restricted and many attractions were closed (Sharpley & Craven, 2002).

In October 2001, the British Tourist Authority (BTA, 2001) sought to examine the relationships between these types of exogenous impacts and general economic factors. It noted that, with reference to Middle East conflicts, it is extremely difficult to disentangle broad economic factors from the nature of the exogenous event – indeed, one can comment that in the immediate short-term the exogenous event itself impacts on those economic variables that influence travel. For example, currencies may change value, fuel prices usually react upwards, and of course confidence can be affected, which may be demonstrated by economic variables such as changes in share prices that impact on holdings of wealth. The BTA noted significant geographical and travel-segment sensitivities to such external shocks, noting for example that holiday-independent travel and holiday-inclusive travel tend to bounce back quickly, but geographical factors are also important. The USA outbound holiday market is very sensitive in the short term; but possibly one of the surprising results from the September 11 2001 attacks was not that the USA outbound travel market dipped very sharply, but that by February 2002 it had bounced back for overseas travel, especially to 'safe' destinations like those of New Zealand. This 'bounce back' was generally quicker than many commentators had predicted only five months earlier.

In a study of the impacts of the 1997 earthquakes on central Italy, Mazzocchi and Montini (2001) concluded that it was domestic flows of tourism that were the slowest to resume, and that international tourism was adversely affected only for quite a short period of time. On the other hand, tourism flows to Egypt were significantly affected when the 71 tourists were shot at Luxor; an event that received significant worldwide reporting in the media (see www.cnn.com). The speed of 'bounce back' can be determined by many apparently different things, including the type of media reporting, the degrees of knowledge about (and familiarity with) a destination that major markets in tourist-generating countries have, the type of marketing campaign and pricing adopted by tourism organisations, the attitude adopted by insurers both of individual tourists and of airlines, the ability of channels of tourism distribution to quickly access information about destination conditions, and the types of tourists that are being attracted to the destination.

However, as with all generalisations, care needs to be taken when considering such events and variables. It can be concluded that attempts to forecast the future growth of tourism by using economic models prove that, in practice, income alone explains little of the variance in changes in tourism flows. Partly this may arise for technical reasons. From a macroeconomic viewpoint, in the use of national income data, average wage rates and their movements, the analyst will often use what is in effect a long-term tourist demand function. For example if the growth in total tourism expenditure (or some other measure of tourism activity such as the number of trips or the number of tourist nights) was plotted against income over a number of years, the Figure 2.1 might result. What this shows is that as income rises, so too does the level of spending on tourism – so line AB represents a tourist consumption function.

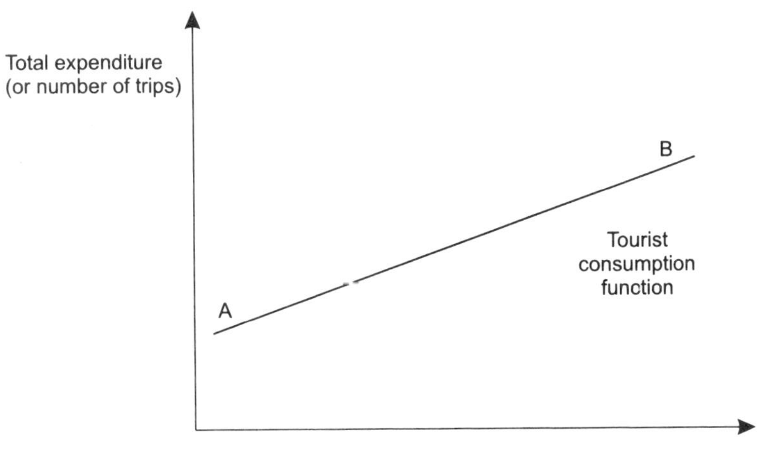

Figure 2.1 The tourist consumption function

However, within each of these different years, a cross-sectional analysis would show that of course not everyone earns the average income figure, and people with different levels of income might have different propensities to spend any increase in income on travel and tourism. Therefore, there is a need to impose on the original diagram the annual cross-sectional distribution of incomes within a society as is illustrated in Figure 2.2.

Thus the long-term tourist consumption function AB consists of the points where the midpoints of the annual consumption functions (CF^1, CF^2, CF^3) form the long-run consumption function, AB. A number of questions arise about such 'consumption functions'. For example, as lower-income groups attain higher income levels, how does this influence their spending patterns? Do they spend all their additional income, and at what time do they begin to increase their savings? Other similar questions might relate to the use of credit. This distinction between longitudinal income patterns and cross-sectional distribution of income may in part help to explain why studies that concentrate on annual movements of income and tourist expenditure do not always show the expected high correlation, or may even prove disappointing in their predictive capabilities. Indeed, Witt (1992) has argued that naïve models of demand forecasting, where either (1) the previous year's level of demand is the forecast for the current year or (2) where last year's demand plus a trend growth line is used, can provide viable usable forecasts, especially perhaps where generally non-dynamic situations exist. On the other hand, when Davies and Mangan (1992) specifically studied data derived from the British Family Expenditure survey they considered a simple model where expenditure was a function of income, but undertook some of the cross-sectional analysis discussed above by considering whether or not a family had children. They found that

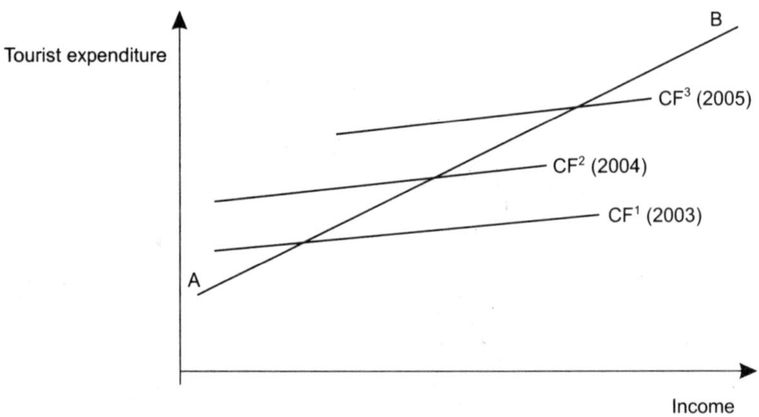

Figure 2.2 The long-run consumption function and cross-sectional analysis

income elasticity had values greater than one, but there were differences between income groups. For example, for lower-income groups a 1% increase in expenditure led to a 4% increase in spending on hotel and holiday expenditure, whereas for higher-income groups a 1% increase in expenditure resulted in only a 1.5% percent increase in hotel and holiday spending. Davies and Mangan conclude that increases in income for low-income groups would result in greater holiday expenditure, but the presence of young children certainly restricts the market in the short term.

From the viewpoint of tourism analysis, a further question relates to the definition of income. It might be that the relationship between tourism expenditure and gross personal income is indirect, and the links between 'discretionary' income and tourism spending are more pertinent. The relationship may be defined in the following manner:

$$(2) \qquad E_t = f(Y_{dis}) = f[(Y_d) - (E_b), S]$$

where E_t = expenditure on tourism
Y_{dis} = discretionary income
Y_d = disposable income
E_b = expenditure on non-leisure activities
S = savings

and $Y_d = f(Y - T)$

and $E_b = f(P_{1 \dots n}, i)$

where Y = gross income
T = taxation
$P_{1 \dots n}$ = prices of non-leisure items
i = interest rates.

From this viewpoint disposable income is equal to gross income minus taxation. However, every householder has to meet certain bills and expenditures. For example, there is the need to pay for food, heating, lighting, travel to and from work, and mortgages on household properties or rents. Only then is there sufficient money left for either saving or spending on leisure pursuits. These costs have to be deducted from disposable income to arrive at the income that remains for spending on leisure items and activities. This can be called 'discretionary spending'. It can therefore be seen that such discretionary income can be affected by variables such as increases in the cost of food and travel to work, and other inflationary pressures. Interest rates may also have an important role to play. For example, in the late 1980s and early 1990s many economies faced high inflationary pressures. On the proposition that this was caused by excessive levels of demand, governments sought to reduce consumer spending by increasing interest rates. This has two effects. First it increases the cost of debt and, in societies with high levels of home ownership being purchased with mortgages, this can mean significant increases in mortgage repayments, thereby reducing discretionary income. Second, higher interest rates might make savings more attractive by increasing the rate of return on savings, thereby again dampening consumer spending. If inflation is also raising house prices (which may hold out a promise of capital gain on property and so feed the inflationary spiral) the increased mortgages will be on higher house prices for recent borrowers. The consequence is significant reductions in discretionary income. Such, for example, was the situation in the United Kingdom in 1989. Therefore, when looking at the level of demand for overseas travel in that period, one finds that there was a reduction in demand for foreign package holidays from approximately 14 million in 1988 to 12 million in 1989. However, other variables intrude in such an analysis, for 1989 also saw a significant increase in holiday bookings by the British within Britain – holidays that were not necessarily cheaper than the holidays offered by the British Tour Operators. Hence this may have also had elements not of a reduction in demand *per se*, but of demand switching as a result of disillusionment with the overseas package holiday. For many Britons, 1988 had been an experience of long delays in airports on both outward and return flights – a feature that had been reported widely by both press and TV media. Ten years later, with a period of economic growth, low inflation and generally low interest rates on mortgages, overseas travel had continued to grow in volume and expenditure. The WTO (2001a) report that, in the period from 1995 to 1999, outbound travel from the UK increased from over 41 million to 50.8 million departures.

The degree to which such an analysis can continue to be applicable will also vary over time. Much, as has been noted, may depend on the patterns of home ownership. Therefore if mortgage interest rates are to be an effective determinant of holiday demand, then it must be assumed that large numbers of people are fairly recent home buyers (so mortgage repayments represent a high proportion of disposable income), or are primarily financing such purchases by mortgages rather than by past savings, by realising family assets (such as selling homes of equal value) or by using inherited wealth. With an ageing population that increasingly has access to inherited wealth, as is symptomatic of many Western developed nations of North America and Northern Europe, such assumptions may become less valid, and mortgage interest rates will have a weaker effect on determining the demand for tourist expenditure. That there are significant demographic changes with serious implications for both wealth and income distribution and future patterns of holiday demand is evident, and will be discussed in more detail in Chapter 3.

From the above it can be argued that any attempt to relate tourism flows to income movements must therefore take into account not only gross income changes, but also changes in taxation, general inflation and interest rates. In addition, it might also be noted that increasing interest rates may not only affect leisure expenditure by increasing the price of necessities either directly or indirectly, but may also encourage a shift in the savings ratio (savings/income), which in turn impinges on possible expenditure on leisure. It must also be noted that expenditure on tourism also competes with expenditure on other leisure pursuits, a factor that is further examined below.

The cost of travel

Expression (1) also indicates that a possible economic determinant of demand for tourism is the price of the holiday. The price that the tourist pays for the holiday might be said to cover three components:

- cost of travel;
- cost of accommodation;
- cost of the activities undertaken by the tourist at the destination area.

Each of these three components will now be examined in turn. With reference to an ITC (inclusive tour charter), or independent travel requiring a flight, the main components of the cost of travel could be hypothesised as being:

(3) $C_t = \mathrm{f}(F,O) + \mathrm{f}(R)$

where C_t = cost of travel
F = cost of fuel
O = other travel costs, including administration
R = profitability of airlines.

In the case of holiday costs, approximately 37% of the price of a package holiday offered by British tour operators arises from the flight, with a further 37% being accounted for by hotel costs (Flook, 2001). Of the flight costs, an important variable is the price of fuel. Fuel costs are subjected to significant causes of uncertainty because of two factors. The first is that past history has shown that petroleum product prices are far from stable in spite of efforts by the OPEC countries to control oil prices, and fluctuations can occur not only from year to year but also from month to month. Attempts to use a futures market in aviation fuel to overcome the risks involved for airlines and tour operators do smooth out some of these fluctuations, but still leave airlines subject to the risks of either buying at the wrong time or of buying insufficient fuels at the right time. For example, it was generally understood that in 1999–2000 part of the differential profit performance between Air New Zealand and Qantas in the Australasian/South East

Asia/Pacific markets had been due to Qantas's better (or more fortunate) fuel purchases. A second uncertain variable is that aviation fuel is priced in US dollars, and thus prices are affected by exchange price movements. In practice, this may in fact be a simplifying and stabilising element, as any alternative position could pose major problems for airlines. The thought of having to pay for aviation fuel in the currency of the country of embarkation would create a highly complex movement of prices, and could affect the willingness of airlines to fly to any given destination. Nonetheless, even the current situation can mean that, as currencies move against the United States dollar, costs for fuel may fall or rise for any given airline.

Under these circumstances, it may very much be a matter of 'swings and roundabouts'. In some cases favourable movements in exchange rates may be offset by increases in prices of fuel, in other cases both variables may move together, either favourably or unfavourably. In some situations they may be less influential than might otherwise be the case. For example, in the period 1982–1984, neither currency nor fuel price movements were particularly favourable for British tour operators, yet the costs of holidays and flights were highly competitive. This was a reflection of the market place, where an expansion of supply dictated a need to fill aircraft, and the utilisation of marginal pricing techniques, where discounted seats meant that the sale of a seat obtained at least some revenue, whereas empty seats of course meant no revenue. Thus in formula (3) above, profit (as reflecting organisational difficulties) is the variable that may reflect this situation. Certainly the structural state of the airline industry and the marketing exigencies it gives rise to are very important determinants of the prices being charged by airlines. In the de-regulated markets of North America and Europe, a number of factors outside of cost structures become very important. Arguably, in the United States over the period 1999 to 2001, increasing losses were being sustained by airlines because of a reluctance to give up take-off and landing rights on routes with significant volumes of traffic. For example, one might have found four airlines all wishing to depart from New York to Washington DC in the morning at the same time, all competing to obtain the same business traffic. All four might be making losses on the flights, but none would wish to give up that potentially profitable slot – 'potentially profitable' if one airline withdrew its service. It was almost a case of knowing that, even if the one airline was making a loss, so too were the others. That was seen as more acceptable than cutting losses by rejecting that route, if, by that rejection, it meant the remaining three airlines moved into profit. The consequences of such actions included:

(1) Increasing problems of air traffic control in the USA because of the sheer numbers of flights.
(2) An increasingly poor record of time keeping because while, in this

example, all four airlines might advertise an 8.30 am departure time, it is evident that not all four aircraft could depart simultaneously. As flights early in the morning were delayed, the knock-on effect meant further delays later in the day and more headaches for air traffic control. The end result was poorer service for clients.

(3) Increasing losses for the airlines meant costcutting exercises, which again meant poorer service for clients as, for example, the quality of in-flight catering and other services was reduced.

(4) Reduced service meant less brand loyalty and more switching by customers, who would then become more price sensitive.

(5) Price-sensitive clientele resigned themselves to lower levels of service and therefore became more likely to patronise 'no frills' airlines when they became available (which of course further increased the problems being faced by air traffic control).

Therefore, even prior to the attack on the World Trade Centre, US airlines were plunging deeper into loss. The post-September-2001 decline in numbers flying was the final catalyst that led to the abandonment of routes, and in some cases to the demise of respected airlines. This situation was not confined to North America, although there the position was arguably made worse by the lack of any central authority in the allocation of take-off slots and landing rights at airports. Europe saw similar problems, with massive losses being announced by airlines like Sabena, major reductions in profits by companies like British Airways, and even significant restructuring in the package holiday market as companies like Airtours attempted to revitalise themselves by creating closer links with internet-based operations and reinventing themselves (in Airtours case, as MyTravel). Interestingly enough, Airtours had announced an increase of 57% in operating profits prior to September 2001. But, in the aftermath of the September 11 attack and the disruption it caused to airline services, Airtours had had to spend £11.4 million on the repatriation of stranded passengers (BBC News, 2001). In other parts of the world, both long-established airlines like Ansett Australia and newer airlines like Impulse ceased trading. Indeed, in 2001–2002 many governments had to decide whether or not to offer financial support to national carriers and other airlines as profits plunged into losses. On the other hand, RyanAir, EasyJet, Virgin Blue, Freedom Air and other no-frills, basic services airlines seemed to continue successfully trading, and indeed placed orders for more jets. Aided by high levels of price sensitivity by the holiday market, low fares attracted high loadings, with cost savings being achieved by a combination of little pre-paid in-flight service and direct internet bookings that saved the travel agents' commission. Profitability was then aided by customers' willingness to purchase extra food and drink on flight. In November 2001 British-based companies like EasyJet began new marketing campaigns aimed at further eroding the market share of the long-established 'high service' carriers like British Airways. EasyJet commenced an advertising campaign seeking to extend beyond its traditional market with advertisements asking 'What do you want from a business airline?' It cited frequent flights between UK airports and major business cities, flexible fares, 'no rip-off' day returns, good punctuality and a long-term relationship with its customers. This last point was supported by reference to EasyJet being a FTSE250 public company with a capacity growth of 25% per annum; and the numbers of passengers carried having increased by 40% in 2001.

In short, structural and competitive paradigms in the world's market places had significant impacts on patterns of flying, and the words 'volatile' and 'dynamic' became almost over-used in describing the airline industry in the early twenty-first century.

The cost of accommodation

An important consideration in any holiday is the accommodation, its standard and price. With reference to the cost of accommodation, exchange rates can yet again play an important role. The possible extremes of price/exchange movements can be demonstrated both historically over the long-term and in the immediate short-term. For example an American tourist may have visited Britain in 1964, and paid £10 for a hotel room. At that time the exchange rate was $2.79 to the £1, hence from the American's viewpoint the price was $27.90. If it is assumed that the American returned to Britain 20 years later and that hotel prices had increased three-fold to £30 per room, the American was not in fact faced with a 300% increase in costs. In 1984 the exchange rate was only $1.23 to the £1, and the American tourist would therefore have seen the room as costing $36.90, an increase of only 32%. Our American would then probably conclude that Britain was a 'cheap location'.

Consider the effects of the more short-term movements of the United States dollar against the New Zealand dollar in the period 1999–2000. In that case the New Zealand dollar fell by about 20%, thereby making New Zealand a cheap destination for Americans, and the United States a more expensive one for New Zealanders. Such was the fall of the New Zealand dollar against the currencies of major tourism-generating countries like the USA and the United Kingdom that these mature markets showed a consistent growth in tourist numbers going to New Zealand of over 7% per annum for the three-year period ending in June, 2001. The importance of exchange rates, especially in the case of package-holiday deals, is difficult to overestimate. The accommodation relationship can be written as shown in equation (4).

(4) $C_a = f(H, X)$

where C_a = costs of accommodation
H = hotelier's costs
X = exchange rate.

The hotelier's costs are potentially very dynamic, and profitability can be affected by price movements that have nothing to do with actual trading conditions or perhaps direct operating costs. For example, in 2000 the Australian hotel industry had to increase prices to its international market to take into account the government's introduction of a Goods and Services Tax. Again, interest rates have potentially serious implications for those hoteliers for whom loan repayments are a high component of their fixed costs, as a 0.5% increase in interest rates on, for example, a £500,000 loan means a need to sell perhaps as many as 250–500 extra rooms per annum depending on rack rates. Over the period 1998–2000, many businesses in the United Kingdom faced quite significant increases in costs of business because of government policies on business reporting; and in the 2001 British election, an *Election Manifesto for Tourism* was published with a request that the amount of 'red tape' faced by the industry be reduced.

Conventionally hoteliers's operating costs are determined by variable costs relating to labour, housekeeping, catering and refurbishment. However, the ratio of variable to fixed costs is important to the industry and to individual hotels. In any period when the industry faces major investment expenditure, increased property taxes and rates and increased business reporting costs, then for many hotels the ratio of variable to fixed costs will swing towards fixed costs. This requires, as noted before, more sales to cover those costs, but additional sales are associated with additional variable costs. The hotel industry has thus faced difficult times, particularly in Britain where the industry had to recover from a loss of international business due to the onslaught of foot-and-mouth disease and the decline in trans-Atlantic traffic in 2001 after the destruction of the World Trade Center on September 11 of that year.

Cost of activities

Once at the location, and having settled into his or her accommodation, the tourist will, after a time, wish to travel around the area and 'see the sights'. This requires further expenditure on his or her part, and the number of trips taken and activities enjoyed will again depend on a balance of tourist income and the prices being charged. These prices, and the costs on which they may be based, are shown in equation (5).

(5) $$C_{ac} = f(X, \delta P_h \delta t P_g)$$

(6) $$C_{ac} = f\left\{X, \frac{\delta P_h}{\delta t} \Big/ \frac{\delta P_g}{\delta t}\right\}$$

where C = cost of tourist's activity in the tourist destination
X = exchange rate

$\frac{\delta P_h}{\delta t} \Big/ \frac{\delta P_g}{\delta t}$ = rate of inflation in the host country divided by the rate of inflation in the tourist-generating country: a measure of the differential inflation between host and generating countries.

In the late twentieth and early twenty-first century, many of the countries of the developed world have experienced comparatively low rates of inflation and thus the differential rates of inflation have been of less importance than was the case in the early 1980s. In that period, there were quite significant changes. For example, in the period 1982–1983, British tourists would have received 10% more pesetas for their £1 sterling; but with, in the same twelve months, a 15% rate of inflation in Spain, much of that gain was wiped out by higher Spanish prices. By 1984 a reduced pound/peseta exchange rate and continuing inflation in Spain made the Spanish Costas even more expensive for UK citizens. Just how much less affordable this made Spain to the UK market was determined, in part, by levels of wage inflation in the UK. However, as stated, inflation has fallen significantly since then, and exchange rate movements have come to dominate the picture. In the aftermath of the Asian financial crisis of the late 1990s, some destinations such as Bali and the rest of Indonesia became very attractive financially to the Australian market, yet by 1998 some of this advantage was then eroded by the political troubles that Indonesia experienced as the Suharto regime declined into its final days.

Discussion

The previous paragraphs can be summarised as stating that the economic determinants of demand for tourism are:

(1) total income;
(2) levels of taxation that determines personal disposable income;
(3) prices of other goods that determines discretionary income;
(4) interest rates that affect mortgage and credit repayments and the attractiveness of savings;
(5) economic structure of industries relevant to tourism and their profitability;
(6) inflation in the host and tourist generating countries;

(7) rates of exchange;
(8) cost of travel;
(9) exogenous factors like an oil crisis, pilots' strike, foot and mouth disease or terrorist action.

Of course, such an approach says little if anything about the perceived attractiveness of the destination, and it leaves unstated the supply side of the equation other than through the indirect pressures on their costs that destinations may experience. There is some evidence that the market structures have more influence than might otherwise be thought. For example, in a study of Mallorca, Aguiló, Alegre and Riera (2001) argued that, in the case of German package holidays, the hotel category, type of board and location were significant explanatory determinants of price. They went on to comment that '...the inclusion of the identity of the tour operators as an explanatory variable is also statistically significant' (Aguiló *et al.*, 2001: 72). To some extent they were confirming the earlier and similar findings of Sinclair, Clewer and Pack (1990) in their study of Malaga. However, a demand-side economist would object that the success of any operation is still determined by the acceptability of the price to sufficient market segments that are large enough to generate the required volume necessary for profitability. In short, demand is the important component.

A Review of Evidence

This contention raises the question, what is the evidence? It has been shown that a series of potentially testable economic relationships can be hypothesised, and indeed the literature contains many examples of attempts to explain tourist flows by the use of econometric modelling. While there is a consensus that income, exchange rates and travel costs are important, there is a lack of consensus about the contribution that each makes to determining demand, and under what conditions one might be more important than the other. For example Witt and Martin (1987) conclude that income is an explanatory variable in 38 out of 39 cases, but note differences between nationalities. For example lagged income was important in explaining British holiday-taking behaviour, which contained a degree of destination loyalty that was missing from the German market; i.e. the British continued to undertake holidays at the same destinations in spite of adverse income movements. However, in his original doctoral thesis, Witt (1978) warns of the enormous difficulty of undertaking such work because of the significant inputs of data that are required. Thus, in examining British visitor numbers to Italy, he found that the statistics from the Italian 'Centro per la Statistica Aziendale' were incomplete. Witt (1978) also concluded that a 1% increase in real personal disposable income per capita resulted in a 0.518% increase in the number of foreign holiday trips per capita.

This compares with later findings that show that tourism is income elastic (Witt & Martin 1987; Martin & Witt 1988). More recently Sinclair and Stabler (1997) reviewed the evidence and found considerable variation in income elasticities (some as high as 7.01) but most were in excess of 1. They conclude that such a wide range is not surprising, given the different time periods, countries and tourism flows being studied. But they go on to remark that '.. a number of the estimated values may be inaccurate, owing to inappropriate specifications of the demand equations on which they are based' (Sinclair & Stabler, 1997: 38). One factor that they feel contributes to this is the lack of modelling of consumer behaviour. Ryan (1991a) seemed to agree with this when he argued that people are reluctant to forgo their annual holiday and, in periods of recession or when economic growth has slowed down, the holiday will be financed either from changes in spending patterns or, more probably, from a reduction in savings. Consequently, during such periods, tourism will appear to be income-inelastic as falls, or reductions in economic growth, do not cause any diminution in tourism demand (the lagged-income effect remarked upon by Witt and Martin in 1987). However, in periods of economic growth characterised by feelings of confidence, tourism demand may be income elastic in that, for any given increase in growth of income, there may be a faster percentage growth in tourism demand. To add to these findings, Sinclair and Stabler (1997) also record a range of relative price and exchange rate elasticities, and conclude from this that there needs to be more discussion as to whether these should be regarded as separate or as linked variables. Witt and Witt (1994) also noted that, in the case of UK outward-bound travel to France and Austria, airborne holidays were more price sensitive than holidays by surface transport. This raises not only the question of degrees of substitutability of one form of transport for another within modelling, but the issue that different forms of transport actually create different travel experiences. It is also evident that significant cross-elasticities of pricing exist with reference to the package-holiday industry. Flook (2001), the Secretary General of the International Federation of Tour Operators (IFTO) noted that, if prices to one destination increase in relation to its competitors by 1%, then bookings to that destination will fall by 3–5%. He went on to observe that 'This price sensitivity means that the entire industry has to take great care not to upset this very delicate balance. We all ignore the basic economic laws of supply and demand at our peril. Tourism to a country is relatively fragile' (Flook, 2001: 2).

Certainly that debate has long existed in the literature, aided now by a greater use of the technique of cointegration. Economists and statisticians have for long been aware of the problems associated with multicollinearity that arise when seemingly independent variables are in fact or in theory linked. For example during a period of wage-induced inflation, prices, expenditure and income are arguably not entirely separate variables.

Equally, however, there may be strong reasons to disaggregate the variables as some sections of society (pensioners, for example) may not be wage earners. These issues are discussed below in a little more detail.

For his part, Morley (2000) has argued that, if any better understanding is to be gained, it is necessary to look at approaches other than conventional econometric ones. He suggests means of measuring and incorporating diffusion effects into the economic modelling of demand. The diffusion model is based on the concept that visitors to any area include repeat visitors and also those who are attracted to an area owing to the recommendation of friends who have visited the region in the past. Consequently the numbers visiting an area are a function of the numbers of past visitors as well as new 'adopters'. The percentage of the total that each category accounts for is itself an indicator of future tourism flows. On the other hand, this approach implies that other than economic variables may be of importance. Indeed Huybers and Bennett (2000) propose choice modeling based on UK visitors' perceptions of North Queensland's environment as one method of forecasting flows of visitors to that part of the world. This approach creates a synthesis between demand and supply models. On the one hand the economic variables determine the ability to make a visit. On the other, the physical properties of the place and their evaluation by the tourist on the basis of past experience creates a predisposition to visit one location in preference to another within the existing economic parameters.

The problems of econometric forecasting are compounded further when tourist demand functions for smaller areas are attempted. For example, Quayson and Var (1982) consider demand functions for tourists visiting the Okanagan in British Columbia, and suggest that a 1% increase in income will generally be associated with a less-than proportionate increase (0.623) in tourism receipts in the Okanagan. However, for visitors from California, tourist trips to British Columbia were in fact income-elastic, implying that tourist trips to destinations that are further from home, and hence by implication more expensive, are more readily determined by income. For their part, in a study of an even smaller area, Cheddar Gorge, Downward and Lumsden (2000) found that visitor spending was not fundamentally related to various attractions. Rather, it was '... related to the duration of a group stay on the day of travel, and the size and composition of the group' (Downward & Lumsden, 2000: 259). Consumer behaviour may also be swayed by ethical or environmental issues. For example Huybers and Bennett (2000: 37) found, using questionnaires based on a willingness-to-pay technique, that 'green' tourists were 'willing to pay an extra premium for a holiday at a destination if authorities protect the current unspoilt state of the environment'. For a trip from the UK to Queensland, this premium was calculated as being £738.

In the past a possible confounding factor in modeling demand was that in many cases the price paid comprised different components of travel, accommodation and activities. As noted, it might be claimed that different currencies acted as a veil through which costs might be disguised or not fully understood. For example, a tourist might feel that the price paid at the travel agent represented good value but, on arrival at the destination, found it to be expensive owing to currency exchange rates. Mazanec (2002) points out that, at least within the European Union, that veil became more transparent with the introduction of the common currency (the Euro) across much of Western Europe. He concluded that, during the period of transition, 'travel consumers react to Euro versus local-currency pricing receptively enough to adapt their preferences for trip packages' (Mazanec, 2002: 252). In the longer term, the easier comparison of inter-destination pricing would, according to classical economic laws of demand, further increase demand for lower-priced zones, everything else remaining the same.

Technical Difficulties in Econometric Tourism Forecasting

A number of the issues discussed above relate partly to technical problems involved in forecasting. These may be classified as being three-fold: namely, issues about the data, statistical techniques and how the model is defined. First, data concerns are ones of both quality and volume of data. For example, while the cost of travel is thought to be important, actual airfares paid by passengers on any one flight may vary from nothing for employees using travel passes to maximum rate for first-class passengers. Again, within Europe the geographical proximity and range of alternative airports and the resultant complex flight patterns and airfare structures mean that considerable volumes of data are required (Witt, 1978). Another difficulty identified by Witt is the derivation of data about promotional effort by National Tourism Offices. Witt argued that:

> ... promotional expenditure is expected to play a role in determining the level of international tourism demand and thus should feature as an explanatory variable in the demand function. (Witt & Witt, 1994: 517)

but noted that it was often difficult to obtain data that specified levels of promotional spending in different countries. There is some evidence to suggest that this may be a factor, for example, in the increase of tourism arrivals in South Africa following the dismantling of apartheid. In this case overseas arrivals increased from 2,703,191 in 1992 to 4,944,430 in 1996 (WTO, 1998). This was considerably in excess of the 18% growth rate in world tourism (as measured by arrivals) that took place in the same period.

No doubt much of this was due to special factors, but equally it is true that the South African tourism authorities took every opportunity to promote themselves, particularly in the markets of Northern Europe and North America. Subsequently tourism inflows into South Africa have increased at significantly much slower rates, and by 2002 the growth was not much more than 2% owing, it is suggested, to an image of urban violence.

The second group of difficulties is those related to statistical techniques. For example, regression techniques assume the independence of variables. In practice, particularly perhaps in inflationary periods characterised by high cost-push inflation that is associated with increasing labour costs, the relationship between incomes and prices is obviously one of action and reaction. Equally, when considering travel costs in areas of major land-masses, then there may be substitutability between air and surface transport. Accordingly, under these conditions *multicollinearity* (the existence of high degrees of correlation between variables) will exist, and may invalidate the forecasting model. A second common issue is that of *heteroscedasticity*, namely the violation of the assumption that all residuals maintain a constant variance over time. This violation is common if the data cover long periods of time, and this is particularly the case with tourism, which in many instances has experienced fast rates of growth. Patterns of variance are easily identified by charting the residuals. Frechtling (1996) suggests the use of data transformation to overcome this problem, for example the use of logarithmic scales or the use of squared roots. The former is often related to the use of the Cobb-Douglas production function (Wynn & Holden, 1974). A third problem that may be encountered is that of *autocorrelation* (where a variable correlates strongly with its own past values). One reason for its existence may be the continuing effects of specific events. Thus, for example, the Asian crisis might have created a high correlation between tourist expenditure in periods t and $t+1$ even though income in period $t+1$ has increased. This might be because a change has taken place in the income/tourist activity relationship. This change could theoretically occur because behaviour is being affected more by recent past experience than by expectation about future increases in income, with the result that tourism expenditure remains a constant between periods t and $t+1$, thereby generating the observed correlation between expenditure in both periods. Kane (1974) observes that, because regression models will often evidence some degree of stochastic dependence between successive values of the error term, it is important to test patterns of residuals to determine if the relationship is too large to attribute to chance, or whether an omitted variable accounts for the observed autocorrelation.

The above discussion highlights another problem, and that is how the relationships are modeled. It could be argued that the introduction of lagged variables relating to expenditure variables would overcome some of the potential problems, and that really the problem is not autocorrelation but one of defining relationships. Therefore the nature of the regression is based on the modeling process. This requires first a selection of the variables thought to determine tourist demand, and second, a determination of the relationship between them. As just noted, one common question is whether a lagged relationship might apply where demand in period t is partially dependent on the existence of a variable in the period t–1. It might also be thought that the relationships are not linear ($Y = a + bT$) but, say, quadratic ($Y = a + bT + cT^2$).

A further problem faced by forecasters is that a forecast of tourism flows in the future may itself be dependent on the accuracy of forecasts relating to the economic variables of exchange rate movements, fuel prices and so on. One response to this is to develop alternative forecasts based on different scenarios. In Australia in 2001 the Tourism Forecasting Council developed a model, ISMIDOT (Integrated System Model of Inbound, Domestic and Outbound Tourism), that incorporated assumptions relating to GDP (Gross Domestic Product), income and exchange rates for source markets. The forecasts were then adjusted for qualitative factors that included airline capacity, oil shocks, the marketing effort made by Australia, and an Olympic effect. The forecasts were then developed for three scenarios: one where the real exchange rate for the Australian dollar was 55 US cents, a second where it was 58 US cents, and the third for a rate of 60 US cents, with appreciation to 65 US cents over the remainder of the forecast period to 2009. The consequence was that the forecast level of inbound arrivals varied between about 9.8 million and almost 12 million by 2009 (Tourism Forecasting Council, 2001).

The Use of Time Series and Other Developments in Forecasting

A common method of forecasting that ignores issues of determination by economic variables is the use of time series. This, essentially, is the extrapolation of past trends into the future, and thus to a large degree its validity rests on the assumption that the underlying relationships between determining variables remain constant over the period being tested. As Lim and McAleer comment:

> Predicting future movements of tourism demand based solely on the past behaviour of (proxy) variables such as arrivals or tourist expenditures, rather than relating them to other variables in a causal framework, is simple but straightforward. (Lim & McAleer, 2001: 966)

'Raw' time series data may, however, consist of four constituent parts:

trend, cycle, seasonal and irregular component parts. In tourism applications seasonality of data is, of course, common, and economists and statisticians have developed widely-known smoothing techniques to cope with these problems. The simplest of these is the single moving average (SMA), while other techniques include single exponential smoothing, double exponential smoothing, autoregression, Box-Jenkins, ARMA (autoregression/moving average combined) and ARIMA (autoregression/integrated/moving average). One of the comments often made about these approaches is that they are essentially atheoretical in that they extrapolate from a known set of data (such as visitor numbers) without examining the underlying determinants of the data. On the other hand they work from easily-accessible data, which (as described above) is not always the case for regression-based methods.

Both regression and time series approaches need to consider the 'non-smooth' patterns of tourism flows. A tourism arrival series is said to be stationary if the mean and variance values of the series remain constant over time. This is uncommon, and statistically means that the mean of the series does not converge to some constant as the number of observations increases. However, exponential smoothing methods based on recursive techniques have been developed whereby smoothed estimates become the weighted average of actual arrivals between period t and t+1, and are continued into estimates of future flows. Hence, in a study of tourism flows to Australia from Hong Kong, Malaysia and Singapore, Lim and McAleer (2001) were able to use computer software based on five different methods to conclude that the Holt-Winters exponential smoothing method produced the best fit between forecasts and final outcomes.

One of the issues that has continually exercised the mind of econometricians is the accuracy of the resulting forecasts. It has already been noted that naïve models are not without value. However, to conclude that forecasting is simply a statistical process of little value is to miss one of the points of forecasting. If forecasting has, as its strategic aim, the development of desired outcomes and the avoidance of undesirable ones, then acting on the results of the forecast may change the relationship of the variables on which the forecast was based. For example, if a downturn in tourist arrivals is expected, and a government then increases the promotional budget and provides tax incentives to companies, a subsequent increase in tourism arrivals is not the proof of poor forecasting.

Nonetheless, statisticians continue to seek new ways of improving forecasts. One comparatively recent introduction is the use of *cointegration analysis* in tourism forecasting. This arises in part from the observation of the relationship of variables, for it has been found that, although many economic time-series may trend up or down together in a non-stationary way, *groups* of variables may drift together. Underlying this is the assumption that theoretically there may be good reasons for believing that such groups may adhere over time in a linear fashion. A growing number of studies is emerging based on this approach. For example Seddighi and Shearing (1997) used co-integration to assess the relationship between price and demand for tourism in the North-East of England. They concluded that, in the long run, for every 1% increase in relative prices, a 9% fall in demand would result; but a 1% increase in real incomes would create a 19% increase in demand. Subsequently Seddighi and Shearing generated an error-correction model that produced good predictions for the period 1972–1992. Their results again point to high levels of price and income elasticity, arguably affected by the existence of highly substitutable destinations. While today it might be thought that these sensitivities are very high, the period covered included some periods of very high inflation with, at the beginning of the 1990s, the beginning of a period of quite stable prices. Consequently a further issue is identified, and that is the degree to which stability exists within any given economic system over any period of time. Any lack of stability in a system makes forecasting that much more difficult.

For their part Kulendran and Witt (2001) review data relating to forecast flows of visitors to eight countries, and discuss the comparative strengths of moving averages, least-squares regression models, error-correction modeling and those that use cointegration techniques. They question the degree to which poor forecasting might have been due to poor model formation, or whether it has been due to ignoring the advances made in methodologies. The results are those of a series of contradictions within the literature, but conclude that an approach combining error correction and model/cointegration appears superior to the time-series methods. Interestingly the 'no change' model that is used for comparison still fares relatively well, and it is suggested that this might be because the other models fail to capture changing demand elasticities. For his part Crouch (1992) reviews 44 studies of price and income elasticities and notes the difficulties in determining a tourist price index, and that the expedient use of consumer price indices tends to dominate. What becomes very evident from the studies is the high level of variability in estimates, and Crouch (1992: 660) observes that 'the price definition used was found to be one of the few factors that seemed to be at all significant in accounting for any variation in the estimated elasticities'. It can be suggested that this observation poses a major issue for forecasting and restores to a place of primacy a need for consistency of definitions and usages in statistical series as they relate to tourism. As will be discussed with reference to satellite tourism accounts in Chapter 7, this is something that international bodies such as the World Tourism Organisation have started to tackle; but currently it is an issue that particularly bedevils forecasting.

Conclusions

This brief review of the issues and evidence as they relate to econometric forecasts might lead to a number of potential conclusions. The first is that economic forecasting may be able to indicate, within constraints, potential demand for tourism activities, but may be poorer at predicting actual flows in terms of where people go within countries or destination zones. Secondly it might be contended that economics is based on a concept of the 'rational economic man', and tourism is concerned with motivations other than rationality. Guitart (1982: 37) comments that:

> The Briton is essentially, a great traveller; he retains his old habits even in an unfavourable domestic economic climate... It might have been expected that ... relating numbers of passengers using ITC flights to per capita private direct consumption in constant terms would provide a high correlation coefficient. But this was not the case in the UK's case. One might equally have expected a certain amount of economic rationality by UK tourists, changing or modifying their decisions in the election of their destination as the prices changed in the Mediterranean areas. But this was not always true. (Guitart, 1982: 37)

Thirdly it might be concluded that econometric techniques are not perhaps appropriate in analysing tourism patterns of expenditure. Rebecca Summary in discussing a demand function for Kenya's sun-lust tourists concludes that:

> ... typical multivariant demand functions estimated by the ordinary least squares regression may not represent the optimal technique to use in all tourism studies ... perhaps the best solution as Uysal and Compton suggest is to use qualitative and quantitative models to provide the best possible tourism-demand analysis. (Summary, 1987: 322)

It should be noted that a number of alternative forecasting techniques exist. The use of time series is one such technique and, while it has been traditionally argued that such techniques assume a continuation of current trends, it has become increasingly possible to model both for broad social change and for the exceptional event. Morley (2000) discusses a number of these issues. Indeed, the literature comprises many examples of researchers using increasingly sophisticated methods to model flows of visitors. For example, Turner and Witt (2001) have argued that linear structural equation modeling represents one approach, while, more from a consumer behaviour approach, new modeling techniques that incorporate neural network modeling are beginning to appear in the literature. For a discussion of this and its applications see, for example, Law (2000) and Ryan (2000a).

It must be admitted that, amongst policy makers and entrepreneurs, there is sometimes a sense of exasperation that forecasts are not more accurate, and a perception that econometrics is an arcane art form little better than attempting to read the future in the tea leaves left in a cup. While this is understandable, it should be said that at times one would wish to avoid that which is being forecast. As already stated, if it is thought that there will be a decline in tourism demand to a certain location, then corrective actions may be sought through more promotion or destination upgrading. Consequently if numbers of visitors are retained or perhaps increased, does that invalidate the original forecast? Often there seems to be little discrepancy analysis undertaken; that is, there is little examination of the reasons for the difference between forecast and actual outcomes. Much of what is done seems to be attempted by econometricians or statisticians seeking to achieve a better fit between their models, and so the literature tends to be dominated by discussions of a technical nature. Rarely does there seem to be a discussion that analyses such discrepancies from a policy perspective, and a number of reasons can be advanced for this. First, in terms of the structures of the public sector, there may be changes of personnel over time that inhibit any sense of policy continuation. For example, elections often bring, if not changes of government, then changes of ministerial direction. Second, there may not be a wish to re-examine what may have been overly-optimistic forecasts from the past because of a perceived association with policy failure (thereby implying that there is nothing to be learnt from failure – a possibly expensive notion). Thirdly, over time social conditions might change, and it is this last possibility that is discussed in Chapter 3.

Finally, given the complexities of forecasting, there appears to be a need for a rigorous procedure of peer review and continuous monitoring, especially for those forecasts being released into the public domain by formal forecasting bodies. Here practices seem to vary. For example, in Australia the Tourism Forecasting Council (TFC) has conducted a review of its work and, as noted, in 2001 it introduced its model ISMIDOT – mainly to overcome problems revealed by the review. These latter usually assume a single direction of determination – from the determining economic variable to the determined observable response of tourist flows. ISMIDOT recognises feedback mechanisms within any tourism system. For example, the determination of new tourist flows by, for example, the introduction of new airline schedules, will involve the creation of new patterns of demand because the supply of new routes will often create further demand, especially if accompanied by a strong promotional effort. Such demand changes may subsequently cause either an increase or decrease in fares, which in turn will further impact on patterns of flow. The TFC has sustained a continuous dialogue with consultants and academics active in econometric forecasting.

On the other hand, in New Zealand the first forecasts used single-equation models because of their simplicity, and there was a limited process of peer review that included no academics among the four reviewers (Fairgray, 2001). To a large extent, this reflects a process of maturation. In 2002 the TFC celebrated its twelfth year of existence, while in 2001 the New Zealand Tourism Research Council was still an embryonic organisation.

What can be concluded is that there exists a rich literature of both tourism forecasting and comment on techniques. Indeed there is now a specialist journal, *Tourism Economics*, that carries many of the articles within which this debate is progressed. For the moment, perhaps the final words in this chapter can be those of Lim and McAleer, who comment:

> Data analysis has become increasingly more straightforward as a result of the proliferation of computer software packages.. Consequently, the analyst and the forecaster are now in a position to evaluate and improve upon the quality of forecasts. (Lim & McAleer, 2001: 976)

This author would add the caveat that, like statistical packages, the increased ease with which calculations can be carried out does not remove the requirement for an understanding of the processes engaged upon, otherwise such packages simply become 'black boxes' where inputs produce outputs without any understanding of the assumptions that underlie the modeling.

Chapter 3

The Social Determinants of Demand

Introduction

It has been noted that discrepancies often exist between forecasts and realities, particularly over longer periods of time. Equally it often appears that history is a succession of changes, and that the pace of change has increased throughout the last hundred years. In 1900, cars had just made an appearance and flight, literally, was only just taking off. In the 1950s computers were physically large, and limited in capabilities. By 2000 the world was spanned by the Internet, Sony was producing robot pets, and a wired global village was being created even while ethnic killings had occurred not only in Africa (Rwanda) but in Europe in the former Yugoslavia. Our world is changing, and some of the broad trends as they affect the major tourist generating and receiving countries of the western world can now be discussed. Consequently, the social consistency required by economic forecasting over the longer time period may no longer be assumed, especially when forecasting is over a period of decades. There is a need, therefore, to examine more closely some of the changing patterns of work and leisure in order to better understand the demand for tourism.

An Overall Framework for Analysis

In the early 1980s it was suggested by Guitart (1982), Pearce (1982b) and Mayo and Jarvis (1981), amongst others, that attempts to explain determinants of tourism demand without reference to motivations or social change can at best yield only incomplete forecasts of tourism movements. This observation remains true at the commencement of the twenty-first century. The implications of social change can be discussed with reference to the tourism/work and tourism/leisure ratios. These can be defined as being:

$$\text{Tourism/work ratio} = \frac{\text{Percentage change in hours spent on tourism}}{\text{Percentage change in hours spent on work}}$$

$$\text{Tourism/leisure ratio} = \frac{\text{Percentage change in hours spent on tourism}}{\text{Percentage change in hours spent on other forms of leisure}}$$

As already discussed above, the growth of tourism demand has been fuelled by an increase in income, but another important factor is the increase in leisure time permitted by, in the earlier part of the twentieth century, increments in paid holiday time and free weekends. In addition, the introduction of flexible working patterns permits people to plan and to take extended weekend breaks more easily than in the past. Thus the tourism/work ratio swung towards tourism as the number of hours of taken holidays increased, and the number of hours worked decreased. However, as the number of hours of leisure available to people increased, so too, arguably, the tourism/leisure ratio also changed, as other forms of leisure began to compete with tourism. There are also linkages with economic factors in a micro-economic sense. People may obtain increases in leisure time but, if those increases in leisure time are not accompanied by proportionate increases in income, then the available discretionary income per unit of available leisure time will fall, thus restricting a greater use of leisure time for holiday purposes. To take a clear example: the worker made redundant has obvious increases in leisure time, but not necessarily the income that permits expenditure on increased travel. Equally, the person who receives additional holiday entitlement from work without an increase in pay also has less available income per unit of leisure time, and thus the additional holiday time might be spent on leisure pursuits within or around the home. The factor of discretionary income and available time might therefore indicate potential inhibiting factors on the growth of tourism. In 1979 the Economist Intelligence Unit sought to assess growth in tourism to 1990 by assessing the changes in leisure time and in population to estimate the total weeks available for tourist activity. The study concluded that, whereas for a country such as the UK, 87% of the potential market was already being penetrated, different habits in other countries such as Canada meant that only 39% of the possible tourist market had been capitalised on there. The tourism/leisure ratio can also be determined by other factors:

(1) There might be a growth in the popularity of other leisure activities that rival tourism in competing for the valuable hours of leisure time. It is true that the holiday always offers one thing that other forms of activity based at home do not possess, and that is the chance to experience a new environment; and the motive to experience novelty is strong in us all to a greater or lesser extent. However, if people are finding significant degrees of fulfilment in their hobbies and interests practiced in their home area, then the escape motivations that prompt travel are weakened.

(2) There may be diminishing satisfaction per additional unit of tourism experience consumed. This is an application of the economist's

concept of diminishing marginal utility. Can it be argued that continued increases in personal travel produces yet further wants or needs to travel, or does there occur at some point a form of world-weariness that makes the traveler appreciate if not actually yearn for the peace and luxuries of home? If holiday travel becomes synonymous with experiences of delays at airports, traffic jams, queues for entrance, being subjected to abuse from drunken fellow travelers, and the transfer of the ills of the city into the countryside, then indeed the tourist may feel that 'home is best.'

(3) The motives of our forbears in seeking holidays may be less valid in the last part of the twentieth century. Amongst the factors that induced a growth in travel was the wish of working people to escape from the everyday noise and bustle of work and large cities. The countryside not only offered peace and tranquillity, or scenic beauty, but also a chance to recover from daily toil. But if the nature of the daily task changes, perhaps our requirements of the holiday also change.

In examining this relationship between work and leisure four hypotheses can be examined (Zuzanek & Mannell, 1983). These are:

(1) The trade-off hypothesis, where people choose between work and leisure time.
(2) The compensation hypothesis, where holidays and leisure compensate for the boredom or troubles of everyday life.
(3) The spin-off hypothesis, where the nature of work produces not contrary but similar patterns of leisure activity.
(4) The neutralist hypothesis, where there is no relationship between work and leisure.

Each of these will be commented on in turn.

The trade-off hypothesis

From this viewpoint there is an inverse relationship between work and leisure time. Consequently there is a choice between working longer hours and generating more income, or working fewer hours and having less income. This situation is demonstrated in Figure 3.1.

Here it could be argued that a choice has to be made somewhere between the points OA (maximum income) and OC (maximum available hours of leisure). However, the concept can be refined further. Curve I^1 represents a series of options that might be available to an individual, and in which all yield the same level of satisfaction. The curve is known as 'an indifference curve'. The choice made would be the point where the coefficients are Oa of income and Oc of leisure time, because this combination represents the highest indifference curve that the individual can reach. Other indifference curves can be hypothesised to lie to the right of I^1, but they lie beyond the constraint imposed by the line AC. Any indifference curve to the left of I^1 would represent a lower level of satisfactory alternatives. However, economies have tended not to stand still, but to progress, and with increases in productivity made possible by increased investment, for any given amount of hours worked, over time the income per hour worked will increase. Therefore the constraint line, AC, will pivot about the point C, for at point C, if no hours are worked, income will remain at zero. This now produces a new combination of hours worked and hours taken in leisure. This enables us to derive a demand curve for leisure as is shown in Figure 3.2. In the first instance, if the combination selected is Oa of income, and Oc of leisure, then the 'price' of that leisure is the income lost whilst taking that leisure, i.e. Aa. Hence the 'price' of the leisure is Aa/Oc per leisure time unit (hour). As the constraint line changes, so too does the price of the leisure time taken. What happens now is that a new, higher indifference curve is engaged by the pivoted budget line, XC. Now the choice made is to retain Oz of income (which is higher than before) and Ox of leisure time (which in this example is slightly less than before). Economists would refer to the income lost as the 'opportunity cost', that is in this instance, it is the income forgone in order to spend time on leisure. The original point of Aa/Oc can be joined to the subsequent point of Xz/Ox, and by joining these points a demand curve for leisure time can be derived.

The above analysis has a number of technical problems associated with it. One major one is that the pivoting of the time-constraint curve around point C may not be as smooth as it is drawn. As drawn, it implies that the

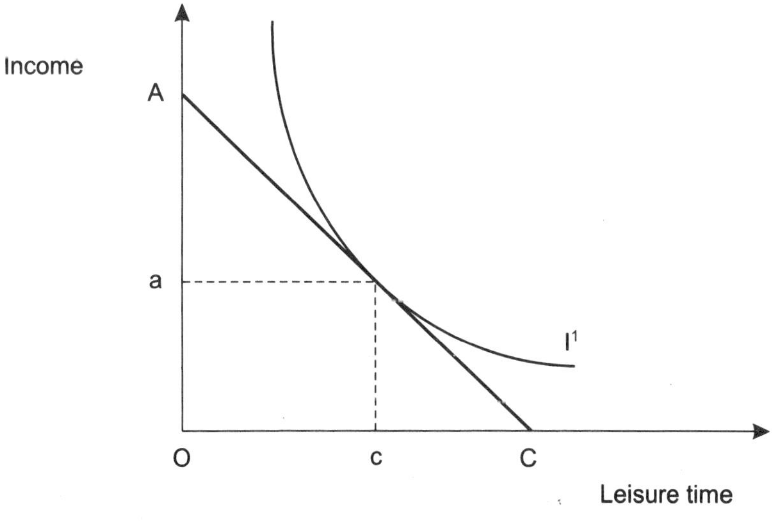

Figure 3.1 The work/leisure 'trade off'

increase in productivity leads to increases in income whereby those selecting a higher income receive larger increases than those selecting an option of lower income and more leisure time. This might appear plausible, but such factors may actually change the shape of the initial indifference curves. This particular example illustrates a not-too-uncommon relation-

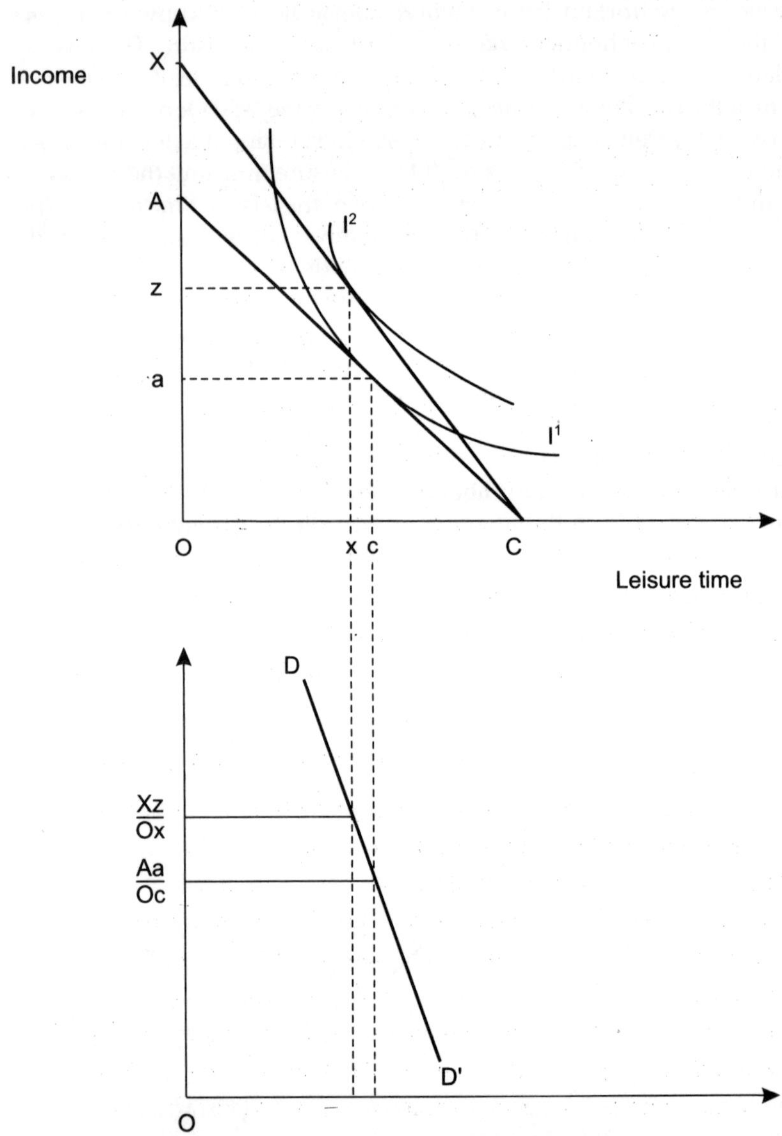

Figure 3.2 The derivation of a demand curve for leisure

ship where those earning more income may end up with less leisure time and pay more for it. Indeed, a whole series of curves and diagrams may be drawn that show different sets of relationships, and a number of issues arise. For example, to what extent are there movements along the curves taking place as distinct from moves of the curves and budget lines themselves? What in effect is occurring may be degrees of substitutability of income for leisure time and vice versa; and a key determinant is the actual price of the leisure or holiday product. In a sense Figure 3.2 illustrates indirect relationships between income and leisure and shows the 'cost' of leisure in terms of income forgone; but in practice the monetary value of the leisure or tourism product will have a significant influence on the leisure/ work time ratio.

It is quite possible that the demand curve, DD' in Figure 3.2 may be upward sloping (i.e. sloping upwards left to right) implying a hypothesis that the demand for tourism/leisure actually increases the greater the cost of that leisure in terms of forgone income. A few comments may be made about this hypothesis. The first is that there is some evidence to suggest that this may indeed be the case, in that, as has already been argued, there is evidence that the demand for tourism is income-elastic. In other words, as incomes increase, the demand for tourism increases at a faster rate. Even when incomes grow less slowly, the demand for tourism may increase faster than disposable incomes. Thus, for example, in 1990 the Conference Board of Canada predicted that, for 1991, even whilst Canadians' disposable income would increase by 1%, tourist expenditure on foreign travel would increase by 3.2% (Conference Board of Canada, 1990). Therefore, the real cost (or opportunity cost) of the holiday increases in that, to finance a 3.2% increase in expenditure when disposable income increases by 1% means that other items are not being consumed, or interest earned from savings is being forgone. Hypothetically, as society moves into a post-industrialised world characterised by the flexible working patterns that may be enjoyed by high-income groups, as described by writers like Toffler (1970), the decision to take time off from work is financially costly. But, because high pay is earned during time spent at work, the cost can be borne. It is important to remember that the upward-sloping demand curve results from the constraint line pivoting because of increased productivity. Hence the professional person who in effect contracts out his or her skill to an employer or client during the time spent working is able, because of that experience, to charge a higher fee on subsequent periods of work. The decision not to work thus implies a higher opportunity cost for leisure/tourism. It can be postulated that this scenario becomes more common in the emerging post-industrial world, and is not restricted to young urban professionals.Finally, it should be noted that within economics it has long been recognised that any movement along a demand curve derived from indifference-curve analysis comprises two components: an income effect and a substitution effect. Any reduction in price of a product, service, holiday package, destination, etc. will possess a substitution effect in that more of a given product is purchased than before. But equally any reduction in price, assuming that income remains static, implies an increase in income (the income effect). This is demonstrated by most introductory textbooks in economics. Within tourism there always exists the possibility that the income effect may be such as to reduce purchases of the lower-priced item in favour of the more expensive, given the fact that the determinant is discretionary income and duration of stay is flexible. As Ryan (1991a) demonstrated, it is possible to generate upward-sloping demand curves. While economists (e.g. Koutsoyiannis, 1975) have long held to the view that Giffen Goods (goods where increases in demand are associated with increases in price) are uncommon, this may not necessarily be true of tourism, although empirical evidence is required to support this contention. However, for the purposes of the current argument, it can be noted that changes in price generate not only changes in purchases, but also changes in income.

The compensation hypothesis

The compensation hypothesis argues that leisure is the means by which people compensate for the deficiencies in their work. If work is boring, repetitive, dictated by the speed of the machine or subdivided into smaller tasks so that the worker never sees the whole, then leisure is the means by which the worker *recreates* the sense of being human. This theme of the worker as an appendage of the machine is common both in films and in literature. One example is Charlie Chaplin's *Modern Times* (which he filmed between 1932 and 1936) and in one scene Chaplin's tramp character is almost literally fed into the cogs of the machine. The historical social evidence for such a thesis is provided by examples derived from the late nineteenth and early twentieth centuries, when the mining communities of South Wales and Yorkshire developed their traditions of choral singing and brass bands, and the textile workers of Lancashire and Yorkshire were founder members of hiking and cycling clubs. The implication for holidays is that the desired holiday is determined by the motive to *escape*. The holiday becomes a means of escaping the daily routine of toil not only of work but also of the home. In consequence, the holiday offers fulfilment of a fantasy, perhaps based on a concept of the life of the 'idle rich'. The holiday is where the daily chores of cooking and washing need not be done. The hotel offers a standard of accommodation higher than that experienced at home, and is a place where waiters come to serve drinks as the tourist takes his or her place in a sun lounger by the side of the pool. Also, in a work environment where communication with fellow workers becomes well nigh impossible over the din, cacophony and noise of machinery, the holiday offers communication with like-minded people. The resulting holiday becomes hotel based, and actual destination is of secondary importance.

However, if the hypothesis is consistent, it must also work in the opposite direction. In other words, those with interesting work will seek peace and monotony at home and at leisure. Whilst there is some truth in the caricature of managers who return home to converse with their spouses only in grunts as they collapse in front of the television set, it would appear from the evidence (Parker, 1971; Pennings, 1976; Zuzanek & Mannell, 1983) that this is generally not the case.

The spill-over hypothesis

The spill-over hypothesis shares with the compensation hypothesis a recognition of the importance of work, and an assumption that it affects the way in which we spend our non-work time. However, unlike the compensation theory, it argues that there is not a contrast between work and leisure, but rather a complementary relationship. For the worker who fills a role subservient to machine-dictated routine, leisure becomes a passive affair. Thus a major leisure pursuit might be watching television, and the role normally adopted is that of spectator rather than participant. It might be argued that the traditional package holiday, as designed in the 1960s, represents a continuation of this process. The holidaymaker is taken from aircraft to hotel, from hotel to day trip and back again. Decisions about where and when, and indeed what, to eat are removed from the holidaymaker. The holiday itself becomes as much a production-line process as the industrial work left behind. Holidays become industrialised in form and format. On the other hand, for those involved in interesting work, leisure also is characterised by participation in doing things. People are generators of action, be it do-it-yourself, amateur dramatics or playing sports.

The above situation descriptions are caricatures, but for a purpose. By the late 1960s futurologists were identifying a number of emergent trends that they thought would be self-sustaining. For example, Alvin Toffler (*Future Shock*, 1970; *The Third Wave*, 1981) argued that, as developed societies move into a post-industrial period, the nature of work and consumption changes. In his original work, *Future Shock*, Tofler argues against the concept that technology creates standardisation and indeed calls one of his chapters, 'The Origins of Over Choice'. One aspect of this is the growth of a service sector characterised not by human/machine relationships, but by personal relationships supported by the machine (computer). Such work patterns, it was argued, have a potential to create more self-fulfilment. Emery (1981) added to this argument. Not only does the work/leisure relationship change, but so too does the home/travel relationship.

As people adopt more fulfilling work patterns, then owing to increasing incomes, their home patterns of life offer more opportunities for leisure. People have their windsurfers and boats; they have accessibility from home to their golf, leisure and sports clubs. Pursuits previously undertaken perhaps only whilst on holiday become a normal part of home life. In addition, increasingly hotels no longer offer a style of accommodation that is more comfortable than home. When a hotel advertises it has satellite or cable television it is not a boast that it is offering more than the holidaymaker is used to, but rather a reassurance that normal home television viewing will not be interrupted due to a loss of facilities. In short, increases in participation levels in various leisure and recreation pursuits might be expected. However, various constraints have emerged (Jackson & Dunn, 1987, 1988) and it has also been noted that one characteristic of modern society is an apparent lack of time. Shaw (1990) used the expression 'time famine' to describe this phenomenon. However, it was noted that those with the highest participation rates tended to note the constraint of time most (Kay & Jackson, 1990), whilst Shaw's findings in part depend on the definitions of leisure that are used. For example, is engaging in a three-mile jog a leisure activity, or part of a keep-fit programme that the respondent sees as an essential? Equally, as Toffler (1970) observes, transience becomes a feature of social life, and a feeling of impermanence infiltrates with differing levels of appeal. For some, the fast pace of life is an excitement they seek, while for others it represents an anathema.

There is emergent evidence of reduced leisure hours and perceived constraints on time. The Henley Centre in the UK has been tracking this issue through its Leisure Tracking Surveys. In 1992 the number of non-working hours in a week were estimated as being 67.3; in 1996 they were 65.2, and more recent estimates would indicate a further reduction to about 64 hours (Edwards, 1998/1999). Edwards also notes the erosion of the weekend, with about 57% of employees in the UK and Italy stating that they worked either sometimes or always on a Saturday, while in France, the Netherlands, Spain and Germany the figure was about one-third. Of course one reason for this is the very extension of the leisure and tourism industries themselves which, in order to provide their facilities, require employees to work on weekends. The Henley Centre also tracks levels of agreement with statements such as 'I never seem to have enough time to get things done'. Those agreeing with this statement in the early 1990s were about 50% of respondents, by the end of the decade the figure was over 60%. Edwards (1998/1999) also suggests from the Henley surveys that 25% of respondents fail to take their full holiday entitlement. Additionally it can be observed that as more people feel 'time famine' then they also, if married, attach more importance to family relationships, especially if children are present. In consequence, the pressures on holiday time to be 'perfect' become substantial, and equally the industry has to be aware that this has a tendency to generate even more demanding clientele.

Further examples of these are to be easily found in the press. For example, in an article on 'the relaxation business', Pamment (2001: 47) quotes a life coach at 'The Energy Bank' in London as saying 'Due to the pace at which we live, it is hard for us to relax on our own. Our clients see the value of having someone to coach them into relaxing and who can guarantee that, in the time they've set aside, that's exactly what they are doing.' In major cities around the world central business districts are increasingly not only offering gymnasia, but a whole range of relaxation centres offering massage, meditation, autogenic training, acupuncture and other techniques designed to bring 'instant' relaxation upon payment of a fee.

It can be said that the early optimism of the 1980s in respect of holiday entitlements and leave gave way to significant alternative working practices, particularly from the early 1990s. For example, the World Tourism Organisation (WTO, 1999: 30) notes that, even though between 1986 and 1994 the working week in Canada declined to 37 hours, this was misleading. It is noted that this apparent decline was due to the growth of part-time employment, while between 1990 and 1995, average real incomes declined by 6%. The same report noted that, even in the instance of the United States, which in the 1990s enjoyed almost a decade of economic growth, working weeks tended to remain long, holiday entitlements still remained poor compared with many other countries, and economic success was being purchased at a high cost. Equally though, for many the demarcation between work and leisure became blurred. For example, household tasks such as shopping were being increasingly established as a partial leisure experience with eating out, combining shopping with cinema visits and/or combining daily household shopping requirements with leisure-interest shopping. In other instances the World Tourism Organisation (WTO, 1999) points to specific increases in weekly and annual working hours, as was the case of Australia in the review period.

While this trend seems to be common across many of the English-speaking countries and Europe, do the same issues apply to the emergent tourism-generating countries of Asia and South America? It is generally well known that the Japanese Government has introduced legislation at different times to reduce the working week, and by 1995 the 40-hour working week had been achieved at 95% of establishments employing 300 or more (WTO, 1999). However, many Japanese work in much smaller companies, and in practice it appears that about 40% of paid leave in Japan is not taken. However, while the Japanese economy has languished in the 1990s, that of China has progressed to the point that both domestic and overseas travel have become significant economic drivers (Zhang & Heung, 2001; Cai *et al.*, 2001). In other Asian countries, the same trends towards shorter working weeks of 40 hours are occurring. Moreover, while the Asian economic crisis toward the end of the 1990s adversely affected travel patterns, the signs are that, at the commencement of the twenty-first century, the economies of countries such as Hong Kong, Korea, Taiwan and Singapore will achieve some economic growth, albeit less than in the 1980s. Some uncertainty exists as to the possibility of, and length of, a world recession, but the various forecasts still indicate that South East Asia will continue to be a growing source and recipient of tourism flows (WTTC, 2001).

The consequence of these changing work patterns, and changing leisure opportunities around and within the home environment, is a change in what is sought from the holiday. The holidaymaker becomes more selective in his or her choice. Escape motives are undermined, and pull factors become more important. The pull factors include not only the nature of the destination and accommodation, but also the activities undertaken whilst on holiday. Some evidence for this is represented by the growth of demand for self-catering holidays. This is not motivated by a wish for cheaper accommodation, but for the freedom that it represents. Indeed, self-catering accommodation may be more expensive than 'all-in packages' because there is a tendency to eat out rather than spend time cooking. But the eating out, the choosing of restaurants and the tasting of different cuisines become an appreciated part of the holiday experience. Similarly the 1980s and 1990s provided evidence of the growing popularity of 'seat-only' flight sales. Indeed this opened the opportunity for a whole range of no-frills airlines (from EasyJet operating from the UK to Freedom Air in New Zealand) all repeating a formula of low fares and internet sales with people increasingly make their own independent arrangements. Arguably the concept has matured beyond the point initiated by People's Express (in the USA) in the 1970s to become an accepted part of airline services. Tour operators also picked up on the new trends, offering smaller, more personal hotels, and holidays based on an extension of hobbies. Many now require of their holiday that it extends the mind, and hence holistic holidays such as the *Skyros Experience* can attract holidaymakers. Ryan and Groves (1987) found, for example, that high-income holidaymakers valued flexibility and independence within their holiday arrangements. In countries like New Zealand, bookshops sell guides to holidays based on retreats founded on concepts such as self healing or Zen. For a commentator like Boniface (2001) a spirit of Zen informs new modes of tourism. Emery (1981) argues that in the future the relationship between the home setting and that of the holiday destination will change, with the result that tourists will be more selective about their choice of destination. However Emery warns against laying too much stress on the concept of self-actualisation as a holiday motivator, writing:

> Self-actualisation and self-expression are too limited to the era of self-liberation in the sixties and seventies. In the longer haul, and over the broad reaches of human society, I do not think that self-actualisation will be found adaptive if it is not also an active concern to nurture the self-actualisation of others. (Emery, 1981: 66).

Thus, for many seeking 'time out' from the angst of modern lifestyles, travel associated with holidays is becoming to resemble the old concept of a pilgrimage, except that today the pilgrims may not holiday on their way to Canterbury or Rome, but to places like the Hoffman Institute on the Sussex Coast. There participants engage in processes of seeking personal harmony of their own psyche, and as Jenkins described the process:

> I found it very therapeutic to just let go and give myself over to the ride ... I found the process more of a holiday than any beach. I loved the fact that I never knew what was going to happen next, and even though we were at it 11 hours a day, I was almost never bored. (Jenkins, 2001: 38)

This type of comment raises interesting questions about the nature of holidaying. If holidaying is about time out, but the therapeutic processes being offered by a retreat of this nature are found to be more relaxing, does the commodified, commercial holiday give way to the old concept of the retreat, albeit perhaps in various secular forms, in order to achieve the purpose of the holiday?

There is an argument that, if the nature of work changes and there is indeed a growing freedom from the self-denying labour of the past, then one possible outcome of this 'nurturance of others' is the possibility that tourists may become more concerned about the impact that their tourism has on host societies and cultures. This may, in turn, change the nature of tourist activity. Boniface (2001: ix) strongly argues that a new dynamic tourism is emerging that means 'doing tourism differently'. The characteristics of this new form of dynamic tourism include:

> prevailing spirituality, a taste for more intangibility to products, individual inclination, imagination and responsibility pertaining, though in a matrix of world-wide awareness, global consciousness, and efforts directed toward sustainability ... (Boniface, 2001: 156)

For his part, Ryan (in press, a) criticises Boniface's thesis as being far too selective and thereby ignoring many other forms of tourism that, while perhaps being less spiritual, are nonetheless an important component of modern tourism. He points to the continued popularity of theme parks, package holidays in the sun, disco dance parties in Ibiza and the like as being far more representative of the majority of holiday-taking activities than those of quiet contemplation or litter collection in the name of ecotourism.It can be said that tourism increasingly faces increased competition from other uses of leisure time.

Some of these uses simply erode time that might otherwise have been spent on tourism. It has been suggested that some future leisure patterns based on virtual reality will prove to be substitutes for tourism. Thus far the reality of this technology has lagged behind the perceived potential (see Cheong *et al.*, 1995; Hobson & Williams, 1997). However, it is expected that the first of the new 64-bit chips will soon be appearing in personal computers that increasingly are just parts of the home-entertainment system of television, DVD and the Internet, while by 2025 it is possible that chips based on quantum theory will be available, creating as-yet-unthought-of modes of entertainment and experience. If, as Ryan (2001a) argued, tourism is part of the entertainment business, then one implication is that degrees of substitutability exist between the entertainment that occurs within or near one's place of residence, and the entertainment that takes place away from home. If, as one thesis suggests, globalisation generates homogeneity between places, then the individual control permitted by new entertainment technologies may become, by comparison, more attractive.

The neutralist hypothesis

Both the compensation and spill-over hypotheses have a common viewpoint in that human behaviour has an underlying entity. The work experience either drives people to seek compensatory action, or drives us to adopt leisure patterns similar to our work experience. It assumes an ascendancy of work, and implies a causal relationship with work being the determining factor. It is true that the arguments of Emery (1981) and Toffler (1970, 1981) can be re-interpreted to imply a reversal of this last contention. If, in post-industrial societies, not only does work become interesting, but it also becomes possible to opt into and out of work in flexible working patterns as dictated by the wish to adopt different positions on the leisure time/income indifference curve postulated by the trade-off hypothesis, then it can be argued that the leisure component of the desired lifestyle will begin to determine the work pattern to be adopted. Some signs of this are demonstrated in software development companies where young programmers and games developers have their skateboard zones, just as in more conventional companies the gymnasium and coffee shop are part of the expected facilities. Nonetheless, even these examples still maintain a work/leisure relationship either of comparison and contrast, or of deliberate complementarity. The neutralist hypothesis rejects such linkages, arguing that there is no relationship between work and leisure – both are separate components of our lives, and people can distinguish between the two, and act differently in each. Ironically, this separation is made possible by the very same processes that Toffler and Emery describe. As Bacon (1975: 180) recorded, 'Work has lost its former hegemony and centrality in most people's lives and has become a much more marginal experience'.

If this is the case, then the emergent holiday trends referred to above are not so much a product of work changing and becoming more fulfilling. Rather, with work becoming less demanding, individual choice over the use of non-work time becomes increasingly more a reflection of individual needs and inherent psychological drives. Hence there is a need to assess the psychological motivations for tourism.

However, before leaving the general social framework that may dictate the demand for particular types of holidays, and indeed the overall demand for holidays, it can be noted that to some extent all four hypotheses are not mutually exclusive in the sense that only one must explain all behaviour at any one time. Just as when discussing the role of income it was suggested that both a longitudinal and a cross-sectional analysis needs to be conducted to assess the role of income, so too, the same may be true of the social forces. It is tempting, albeit dangerous, to see a temporal progression in society from the compensation to spill-over hypothesis, and hence to possibly the neutralist stance. Rather it can be stated that within society different social segments or groups might adopt different patterns of work/leisure/holiday relationships, and that these need not be consistent over time. Zuzanek and Mannell (1983) discuss the evidence for each of the theories and in approaching this topic comment that, whilst there are methodological and operational deficiencies, it can only be concluded that the work/leisure relationship is multi-faceted and multidimensional. What certainly must not be forgotten is that work in itself can be a source of satisfaction, and the workplace is an important source of social interaction for many people. A survey of 3,600 men and women conducted by the University of Michigan found that work rated as the fourth most preferred activity out of a list of 25 (Rodale 1989). From the viewpoint of tourism, what is of interest is that there appears to be some ceiling to continued growth of demand that is operated by social factors. For example, examination of the data for holiday-taking activities of British tourists, as published in the English Tourism Board/British Tourist Authority's *Tourism Intelligence Reports*, indicates that consistently about 15–20% of AB social group do not appear to take a holiday of four or more nights away from home. For such a group it is not a lack of income that affects this decision. Part of the result may be accounted for by ill-health, and for some members of the group intensive work schedules may also account for not taking such holidays, but it can be contended that for some there is a deliberate choice not to take a holiday. Equally, for others within the AB social grouping, whilst they tend to take more holidays than their C1/C2 counterparts, there has not been a drastic growth in additional long-stay (more than four nights away from home) holiday taking. In other European countries, there seems to be the same slow down in the growth of numbers of people taking holidays. For example Mazanec (1981) examined the German holiday market and, using factor analysis, postulated a number of lifestyles, some of which were conducive to tourism, some of which were not. He concluded:

> ... the leisure type mapping endorses the view that leisure life style barriers to continuous market penetration of travel and tourism are real: some incompatibility exists with certain leisure life styles. It becomes particularly pronounced if home-orientedness combines with low cultural/educational aspiration level. (Mazanec, 1981a: np)

Another factor in assessing the changing relationship between leisure and tourism is a growing desire for a quality of tourism experience that may actually reduce the total amount of tourism travel below that which would otherwise take place. Sarbin (1981) records a survey of American tourists where:

> ... the proportion of respondents who stated they like to travel but were engaging in other activities instead because of the 'hassle' of travelling had recently increased from 13% to 24%. Forty percent of respondents to a national survey said they did not visit parks and recreation areas because of crowding, and 25% said the areas were too polluted. (Sarbin, 1981: np)

Changing Demographics and Resultant Implications.

In the final resort the demand for tourism is determined by populations, and not only by their size but also by their composition. In 2001 the UK National Office of Statistics released a report on population trends. Table 3.1 is extracted from that report, and illustrates just how high is the dependence on migration for any sustaining of current population size. It can seen that, for many of the European countries, the decline in population will be more than 20% in the period 2000 to 2050, unless there is immigration. In a country such as Britain, in 2000 the average number of children being born to a woman was 1.74. Equally, while in many of the European and English-speaking nations the proportion of those of working age to those over the age of 65 is about 4 to 1, by 2050 the ratio will be about 2.5 to 1. These trends are also to be found in other OECD countries, and in places like Australia and New Zealand a new debate is occurring as to what sizes of population are required to sustain economic growth but retain the lifestyles associated with their comparatively low population density.The long-term implications of this for tourism are many. First, it indicates a growth in the numbers of older people who are likely to want to continue travelling, but a need for the industry to have to compete for a declining number of potential employees, thereby implying a need to pay higher wages and thus drive up

Table 3.1 Trends in demographics in Western Europe (population size)

Country	*2000 (000s)*	*2050 (000s) without immigration*	*Difference (000s)*	*% Difference*
Austria	8,080	6,113	-1,967	-24.3
Belgium	10,249	8,652	-597	-15.6
Denmark	5,320	4,623	-697	-13.1
Finland	5,172	4,511	-661	-12.8
France	59,238	59,870	632	1.1
Germany	82,017	59,504	-22,513	-27.4
Greece	10,610	8,130	-2,480	-23.4
Holland	15,864	13,802	-2,062	-13.0
Ireland	3,809	4,818	1,009	26.5
Italy	57,630	40,525	-17,005	-29.6
Luxembourg	437	418	-19	-4.3
Portugal	10,016	8,555	-1,461	-14.6
Spain	39,910	30,029	-9,381	-24.8
Sweden	8,842	7,328	-1,514	-17.1
UK	59,415	54,479	-4,936	-8.3

Source: National Office of Statistics (2001)

costs. If markets comprise older people on fixed incomes, how might this affect their ability to pay for such holidays? To what extent would older markets wish to explore new destinations and activities?

One of what may be described as the conventional wisdoms of marketing in the 1960s and 1970s was that an older person's market represented a market with high levels of disposable income. More specifically, older people in their 50s had significantly high levels of discretionary income. This was an age group who had generally paid off its mortgages and whose children had left home to start their own families. These 'empty nesters' as they were termed, were also probably at the height of their earning in terms of wage levels. Such empty nesters continue to exist today as a section of society, but it would be a mistake to assume that all of those in the 50+ years age bracket enjoy high discretionary incomes. Families are today far more mobile, and home ownership changes are much more frequent. For those less than 50 years of age in the USA it appears that the mean length of home ownership before moving is seven years. Consequently such people are likely to have mortgages to pay. Second, divorce rates are significantly higher in the early twenty-first century than 40 years ago, with, in many European countries, about a third of all marriages ending in divorce. Consequently it is not uncommon for 50 year olds to have children, sometimes quite young children, still living at home. Third, the age at which women are bearing their first children has been delayed over the past five decades. This is due to more people spending longer in education and so delaying their entry into the work force, and then seeking to develop their work careers. Additionally the mean age for first marriages is moving from the early to later twenties. Also if, as has been noted, work is more fulfilling, particularly for females, then motives for having children are, if not weakened, then at least put aside for longer periods of time. The end result again is that those aged 50 years of age or thereabouts are likely to have children still at home. Equally, there is evidence that the longer periods being spent in education (and especially as the costs of that education rise as university fees increase and governmental grants are eroded or ceased) result in a tendency for children in their early twenties to still be financially dependent on parents. Therefore, for couples having children in a second marriage, this means that the demands on the family income may well continue into the prime wage earner's sixties. Additional financial burdens might also exist if the income earners have a need to support elderly parents. In the English-speaking world with a past tradition of social welfare support, changing demographics are increasingly imposing strains on the health services dedicated to the elderly. Public health services are less able to cope, and so families are increasingly paying for private care. The squeezed middle class middle-aged generation facing the need to support both children and elderly parents are less able to take holidays. It might be argued that self-interest dictates an increased willingness to pay higher taxes to support better health care, as is being argued in Britain following the Chancellor's predictions on November 2001 for future budgetary spending until 2003 and the actual increases in taxation announced in the 2002 budget.

On the other hand, a growing market segment is that of the unmarried and those choosing to enter relationships but not have children. These two market segments are growing both in numbers and as a proportion of the total population. But, unlike the elderly, late family starters or divorced people, they will in all likelihood have high disposable and discretionary incomes. From this perspective they are akin to the gay and lesbian markets in terms of their ability to spend on leisure pursuits. Further evidence of the changes in holidaying patterns and the demise of homogeneity in the holiday market is provided by Ryan (Ryan, D., 2001). She cites the growing trend towards women-only holidays, and quotes Charlie Hopkinson of Dragoman holidays as saying that, compared with 1999, his company experienced a 77% increase in pairs of women booking, a 280% increase in trios, and a 400% increase in groups of four. This phenomenon is not restricted to that company. Scott Dunn is quoted by Ryan as observing similar increases and suggests a three-fold category, the young, single career woman travelling with a friend, the retired woman, and mothers travelling with daughters. In her survey of companies it is evident that the type of holidays being taken by such women correspond, not unnaturally, with the type of products being offered. But what is evident is that the phenomenon of women travelling with other women has become a discernible trend since the mid-1990s. The novelist, Joanna Trollope (2001) wrote that:

> More and more women are choosing to holiday alone. It seems that as the traditional stigma of the impropriety and pitifulness of it fades, so more than two-thirds of women according to a recent survey, can say openly that they would actually prefer to holiday without men and without children. They use phrases such as 'revitalise' and 're-evaluate' and 'self-define' and, of course, 'rest'. (Trollope, 2001: 1)

Given the demographic trends referred to above, and the growth of career single women, this is not surprising. Arguably what has been more surprising is the comparative tardiness with which the industry has recognised this trend, and the slow development of product that is specific to this market.

This has not been the case with the gay and lesbian markets. For example, in January 2000 the British Tourist Authority (BTA) published brochures specifically aimed at the gay American market. The BTA's research had found, for example, that while the national average for the USA population holding a passport is 18%, for the US gay market in the targeted areas and cities it was 82%. In 1991 Disney World hosted its first 'Gay Day'. In the period May 30 to June 1 2002 more than 100,000 gays and lesbians attended 'Disney Gay Day. Events such as Sydney's Mardi Gras have been assessed as contributing over $A12 million to the local economy (Lyon, 1999). Nonetheless, while it is true that today the mainstream industry is showing greater sensitivity towards the gay and lesbian communities and creating commercial product that meets their needs, it can be argued that initially it was homosexual people themselves that initiated their own products to meet their own requirements. The mainstream industry reinforced, but did not initiate, this trend.

Given societal trends and working patterns, it might be observed that for many the need for a holiday might be greater than before. However, if, for many heterosexual families, there is a reduced real discretionary income, then the implications for holiday demand in terms of destination and accommodation switching becomes evident. First, it might be hypothesised that there will be a reduction in demand for holidaying, at least in terms of expenditure, albeit perhaps with a lesser reduction in nights spent away from home. However, this is thought unlikely at the aggregate level, as generally incomes are expected to continue growing – but the patterns of growth of discretionary income will be very uneven. The result of this will be a continued demand for value for money. Clients will continue to expect improvements for the same price as before. As members of a technological age that has seen computing power per dollar, euro, yen or pound paid, consumers have grown accustomed to large-expenditure items continuing to offer new, improved, better variants. Holidays could be said to fall into this category. Second, as noted, the ageing of the population will create a demand for holidays associated with a quieter pace of life. As a consequence, the growth of demand for activities like adventure tourism may be threatened, while the demand for family-oriented holidays involving children will also be less important. On the other hand, products more oriented toward culture, or at least nostalgia, might become more important, at least within the markets dominated by Euro-North-American patterns of demand.

However, it is possible that more significant trends than these might arise. First, as just noted, the market will be even less homogenous than it is with reference to discretionary income, thereby creating a greater number of market segments and more product differentiation as entrepreneurs determine which market they wish to target. There is the opportunity of greater fragmentation in the market place. From one perspective this will be akin to the fragmentation that has occurred in countries with comparatively low mean incomes that have developed a thriving tourism industry that attracts large numbers of overseas tourists. While this would be quite common in developing countries, it is not unknown in developed countries too. For example, at rates of exchange prevailing in 2001, the mean household income in New Zealand was about £9,500. In 1999 the new Labour Government increased income tax on the top 10% of income earners, which was defined as those earning in excess of about £20,000 ($NZ60,000) at the then-prevailing rates of exchange. Many middle- to higher-income groups in New Zealand will tend to travel overseas for their holidays to Australia or the South Pacific Islands, taking advantage of packages put together by tour operators or airlines. Domestic tourism in New Zealand is thus dominated by beach holidays and low-cost accommodation such as camp and caravan sites. The mainstream structure of New Zealand tourism, as reflected by annual tourism award winners, is very much dominated by businesses catering to the overseas market and charging prices accordingly. Indeed, in 2002 at a 'road show' in Wellington, George Hickton, Tourism New Zealand CEO, made a call to the New Zealand industry to increase prices to obtain better yield and take better advantage of the low exchange rate (Coventry, 2002). Hence it might be said that a two-tier market has resulted in New Zealand, and increasingly that market geared to the overseas market is beginning to dominant not only total tourism earnings, but also government tourism policies. Where that leaves a domestic, lower-income market is unclear.

Another trend that will probably be confirmed by its continuance is the movement toward shorter holiday periods. For example, the report *Tomorrow's Tourism* (Department for Culture, Media and Sport, 1999: 71) noted that in 1997 75% of the British population took holidays of less than 4 days duration in the United Kingdom, and that the mean length of domestic stays was 3.6 nights as compared to 4.1 nights in 1989. Equally it was noted that the mean length of stay of overseas tourists had fallen from 10.9 to 8.7 nights over the same period – a decline not wholly attributable to tourists selecting to visit other destinations in addition to the United Kingdom when on holiday. It is consistent with the thesis of 'income rich, time poor' that such declines in holiday duration should be observed, although the corollary is towards there being more short holidays than in the past.

Within this scenario of social change based around an older, smaller and more differentiated population lies at least one significant assumption, and that is an absence of immigration. Such an assumption cannot be left unexamined. The growing number of illegal migrants across Europe and South East Asia or of Mexicans to the United States points to a demand for entering the wealthy countries of the West. More relaxed policies could certainly impact on both the age profiles of populations and subsequent birth rates, given a historical tendency for migrant groups to have larger families (at least initially), than the host population. However, considerable problems arise from such policies. First, the recipient countries usually prefer migrants with higher educational qualifications. Depriving societies from which migrants come of their better-educated and highly-skilled people does little to solve their problems. It can be additionally argued that, unless something is done to aid such countries more directly, then the world will see more instances of desperate boat people. This is evidenced by the incidents surrounding Australian waters in 2001, when the Australian government reacted by effectively 'exporting', at least temporarily, refugees who were seeking admission to Australia to places like Nauru. From a tourism perspective, migration does have an impact on the visiting friends and relatives (VFR) market, resulting in more international travel. VFR travel often presents opportunities for specialist travel agencies and tour operators. But over time such companies almost inevitably seek to build on their expertise of arranging travel with what are generally less developed countries to offer product to the non-immigrant market within the tourism-generating host country.

Other assumptions can be questioned. For example the scenarios assume that people will continue to retire at about 60 or 65. Some countries, such as New Zealand and Australia, have already introduced legislation so that workers cannot be required to retire at 65 if they are still capable of meeting an employer's requirements. Many would wish to continue working. For some, financial motives would dominate because of family commitments; for others, as already noted, work provides a sense of identity and social networks. Another issue is that of government population policies. Gove (2001) cites evidence to indicate that, within the UK, increasing the fecundity of women from 1.74 to 2 children would be akin to an annual inflow of 500,000 migrants in terms of changing the ratio between those of working age and the elderly. Additionally, such an increase in birth rate would not generate the same demand for additional housing with, therefore, less damaging environmental consequences. If governments resorted to 'family friendly' policies and benefits, as the French Government did in the inter-year wars, then this would subsequently have some impact on patterns of tourism demand.

Broad social trends are therefore very important in determining patterns of demand. Additionally, what might be termed micro-social movements can also be important. Fashions in interest can be observed, and this is exemplified by the way in which locations can experience significant increases in tourism following the release of a popular film. For example it has been argued that Scotland received a boost to its tourism industry after the success of the film *Braveheart* even though much of the action was filmed in Ireland. Certainly the Tourism Intelligence Reports record a significant increase in visitation to Scotland in the year following the release of the film, when the number of visitors increased by 14% compared to a 6% increase the previous year (BTA, 1996, 1997). Riley (1994) records the impact the earlier films *Deliverance* and *Field of Dreams* had on American locations, and of course tourism promotional bodies build upon these themes. Ryan and Harvey (2000) note the continuing high recognition factor of *Crocodile Dundee* among visitors to the Northern Territory, although in this case the film creates a confirmation factor in the 'authenticity' of the visitor experience rather than attracting visitors in the first place. Popular television series have also produced new tourism products, from tours of *Inspector Morse*'s Oxford to Granada Television Studio tours of *Coronation Street*. Popular culture and tourism are thus closely entwined in many ways. The importance given to films by tourism promotional bodies is evidenced by the attempts made by Tourism New Zealand to build visitor numbers after the release of the *Lord of the Rings* cycle of films. Not only were images carried over into the board's website, but specific product associated with the film such as 'Hobbiton' was developed at places like Matamata in the Waikato, North Island New Zealand.

Image, Consuming and Social Process

To discuss the importance of film as a determinant of tourism flows is not without a wider significance. Since the 1970s there has emerged an argument that a fundamental change in society has occurred. From the period of the Industrial Revolution in the nineteenth century, modes of production generated higher levels of output based on standardisation of product. Called by some a Fordist period because Henry Ford introduced conveyor-belt production methods to generate a standardised product (namely the black Model T Ford), it represented the logical extension of scientific management to working life. Comparisons could be made against a measured standard, and found wanting or not. The breaking down of tasks into smaller components removed not only judgement and the exercise of individual skills, but inconsistencies in performance. Furthermore, by removing the need for judgement, it allowed the use of lesser skilled (and lower paid) labour to be used. However, the subsequent development of computer-controlled production methods, wherein individual preferences could be programmed without any increase in costs, permitted a considerably greater range of product to be produced. Moreover, for many products, larger markets came to exist because of economic growth and the general increase in incomes. Thus purchases became increasingly dominated not by function and performance of products, but by aesthetics, appearance and personal preference on the part of the consumer. This process was reinforced by a growing advertising industry for whom branding became exercises in establishing lifestyle and self-image reinforcement in order to distinguish between one product and another. With the advent of television and the greater ease of presenting images, consumers became, so it is argued, selectors of image that they felt were congruent with their own. But consumers were not the simple, passive consumers of image that was envisaged by commentators like Boorstin (1962). Rather, according to Urry (1990), consumers, and in his thesis of *The Tourist Gaze*, tourists, could engage in play and indeed be 'post-tourists'. In short, people are able to see through the advertising flummery and promises and choose either to play the 'consumer role' as envisaged by the advertising agency, or to subvert the role at whim or as part of a more sustainable purpose.

These tendencies, which include sophistication and selective participation in the use of image, are allied to a fragmentation and reconstruction of social stories. It has become almost a cliché for tourism academics to point out how peoples' culture, history and folklore are subverted into commercial products, or packaged into 30-minute presentations for the tourists. Through this process of re-interpretation, arguably different stories are being authorised by those doing the packaging. As will be discussed in a later chapter, it is argued that the authenticities associated with history and culture are being changed and, according to critics like Boorstin (1962), becoming more superficial and shallow. Equally, in the telling of the stories, the demarcation between myth and fact, between past and present, become merged. For many commentators (e.g. Hollinshead, 1999; Jamal & Hollinshead, 2001), Disney exemplifies many of these trends, but they can be found in many other places. For example, do visitors to Alnwick Castle in Northumbria visit it as the historic home of the Percy Family, or for its role as Hogwarts School in the film of the popular fantasy novels, *Harry Potter*?

Tourism is often seen as the epitome of the forms of consumer behaviour that are associated with a post-modern world of individualism, fantasy, time-space compression, de-differentiation, commodification and the playing out of fragmented power constructs. Whether any reader fully subscribes to the notion that a significantly different way of seeing the world is required to better analyse contemporary society, what cannot be denied is that the social forms created by new technologies pose challenges that are different in quality if not in type from those faced by past generations. Information flows faster through satellites and the Internet, and a sense of a global cosmopolitanism if not of the global village intrudes on our thinking and frames of references (Urry, 2000). As such, these social changes create an ambience within which we frame our reactions to the demographic and other changes noted above, just as those changes contribute to the environment within which we live.

Chapter 4

The Psychological Determinants of Demand

Brief mention has been made of the fact that tourism as a 'product' represents either an escape from daily reality, or a means of self-fulfilment. Whilst tourism can offer more than this, it does highlight one particular characteristic of the 'product' that differentiates it from many other purchases. Essentially tourism is not a purchase of the physical, but a means by which the holidaymaker acquires experiences and fulfils dreams. It possesses the very essence of intangibility, for at the end of the holiday the purchaser has little in the way of physical possessions. And those that do exist, the souvenirs and the photographs, have as their main purpose the evocation of memory. There are further 'odd' aspects that distinguish the holiday from other purchases. There is a substantial outlay without, in many cases, a previous sight of the destination. Even if the tourist has previously visited that destination, there is no guarantee that the second experience will replicate the first. The holiday is looked forward to – it is seen as the culmination of a year's work. People make purchases 'for the holiday'. New swimsuits and beachwear are purchased. Indeed Ryan and Robertson (1997) found that of their sample, 25% went so far as to include condoms within their holiday baggage. Anticipation becomes part of the product. After the holiday, it becomes part of experience that can be evoked to help the tourist through the dark days of winter, and past memories are refreshed by the anticipation of new holiday experiences. The holiday is often not a spontaneous decision. It is perhaps a joint decision between family and friends. Part of the pleasure is the comparison of brochures and/or of places. It can be seen that the holiday experience is not simply an experience of place; it also has a temporal dimension that commences before the vacation and may persist afterwards to the end of a person's life.

This chapter will not develop a model of tourist demand. Such models tend to be located within specific domains of psychological theory, and as might be imagined there are a number of these. Indeed, within the literature of consumer marketing there exists a number of models, ranging from simple attention attraction, intention creation, decision making and action (AIDA) models to more sophisticated models of heuristic learning. Equally, within the tourism and recreation literature, there is a recognition that the nature of the tourism experience contains elements specific to itself. For example, within the service situation it is recognised that the tourist possesses significant opportunities to be proactive and manipulate the environment owing to the duration of stay and the destination learning that takes place – variables not always present in other services marketing situations (for an example of such a discussion see Ryan, 1999a). Ryan (2002a) has also noted that much of the psychological literature pertaining to tourism is based on a tradition of humanistic psychology. This is partly because, unlike other psychiatric concerns, it is a study of 'normal' people, not a study of those who are psychologically dysfunctional. Given the emphasis that humanistic psychology lays on self esteem, self respect and self actualisation, and the potential that holidaying provides for people to reflect, it is not surprising that many commentators have drawn on the work of psychologists like Maslow and Rogers as a foundation for their models (e.g. Pearce, 1982a, 1982b, 1988). Given the complexities of modeling that exist, this chapter will primarily undertake a task of identifying variables that writers believe to be important in determining reasons for holiday taking.

Motivation for Holidaying

Certainly it can be argued that holidaying meets a series of deep psychological needs. Cohen (1974), Crompton (1979), and Mathieson and Wall (1982) identify a number of motivations.

The escape motivation

This has already been described in some detail, and is essentially a wish to get away from a perceived mundane environment.

Relaxation

Partly related to the escape motivation, this is a wish for recuperation.

Play

This is a wish to indulge in activities associated with childhood. Play on holiday is culturally sanctioned. Adults indulge in games not otherwise permitted (except perhaps on TV gameshows!). There is a regression into the carefree state of childhood.

Strengthening family bonds

In the common situation where both partners are working full time, the holiday represents a time when they can renew their relationship. However, there is a reverse side to this. Relate, the British Marriage Advisory Council, has reported that holidays are an occasion when both parties realise that they have grown apart. Daily life has been led with each doing their 'own thing', and the enforced sharing of each other's company for 24 hours a day puts too great a strain on the marriage. More happily, holidays can provide a time when fathers in particular can spend time with their young children, and so strengthen paternal bonding (Ryan, 2003).

Prestige

Status and social enhancement amongst one's peers can be temporarily gained on the basis of the destination chosen for the holiday. Certain destinations are fashionable, whilst others are not. The selection of a fashionable, or unusual (and hence perceived as exotic) destination will serve to confirm an impression about the holidaymaker. Holiday destination choice becomes yet another statement about 'lifestyle', a confirmation of self-identity and role amongst one's peers. It is also not simply a question about destination, but also about the form of accommodation and activity. To stay at a hotel on the Costa del Sol says one thing about you, whilst to stay in your own villa makes a different kind of statement.

The desire for status enhancement need not necessarily be confined to one's peers back home. It can also be met by creating a role within a given group of holidaymakers, or by the group creating a group identity whereby they perceive themselves as being superior to other groups of tourists, or the members of the host society.

Social interaction

The holiday represents an important social forum for individuals where the normal conventions can be disregarded. For a fortnight group members meet to share a common experience, and without past knowledge of each other's backgrounds. The dynamics of such groups can be a powerful determinant of the success or failure of the holiday. Holiday companies who specialise in holidays based on outdoor activity centres or on hobby or leisure interests such as painting or sailing, recognise that one of the major determinants of the success of their holidays is that it creates a group of like-minded people with a common interest all sharing the same experience. Other holidays are designed for single people so that they can become part of a group and not feel isolated on the traditional family-orientated package holiday.

Sexual opportunity

One aspect of social interaction is the opportunity for sexual relationships. This can be overt or implied, physical or romantic. One of the traditional appeals of the trans-Atlantic ships of the 1930s was the possibility of a romance. The popular characterisation of the 18–30 holiday as sometimes displayed by the tabloid press is that it represents an opportunity for 'bonking', or whatever is the current pseudonym. However, in certain cases the rationale of the holiday is simply an opportunity for sexual activity, as is demonstrated in the sex tourism of the Far East in Thailand or the Philippines. To some extent there is both in this case and in the opportunity of play a common theme in that the holiday offers an opportunity to be free from the normal constraints of home. The holiday may be a period of a loosening of a sense of responsibility. The clerical workers on the 18–30 holidays who drink too much, eat too much, create too much noise in rowdy games and disco all night long, do actually return home to their 9-to-5 jobs and their respectability. Behaviour that at home might threaten a loss of job, on holiday, far from home, becomes, if not excusable, tolerated to a degree. Indeed, it is in part anticipated by hosts, and perhaps even encouraged by representatives of the holiday companies as part of ensuring that clients have 'a good time'. An example of such holidays are those provided by Superclubs Hedonism II and Hedonism III in Jamaica where the website states:

> Not for the faint of heart, Hedonism II exists for one sole purpose: Pure, unadulterated self-indulgence for the mind, body, spirit and soul. Anything goes (almost). Shocking, stimulating, always sexy, never stuffy – Hedonism II has become legendary among pleasure-seekers worldwide. With its relaxed attitude and endless activities – the good times just keep going. (Website for Hedonism clubs)

Educational opportunity

At the heart of tourism is the concept of travel; a chance to see new and strange sights, to learn about the other places of the world, and to talk to others with different cultures and viewpoints. No matter that the cynical may agree with Ogden Nash that 'Travel does not broaden the mind, only the bottom' or that in the process of creating the global village the Coca-Cola sign is found everywhere or that one hotel complex looks like another, there still remains an opportunity to discover differences. Equally there is a chance to see the sites of history, or the original great works of art instead of the reproduction. It would certainly seem from the evidence that an intellectual or cultural exchange is desired by some for at least a part if not the whole of their holiday (see Craik, 2001 for an introductory description of cultural tourism).

Self fulfilment

The voyage of discovery may not be simply a discovery of new places and people, but also the opportunity or catalyst for self-discovery. In the medieval world it may have been called the pilgrimage to the holy places. A secular age permits individuals to create their own holy places, which may be places of natural beauty, or areas where they challenge their own sporting skills or bodies. The search for self-discovery may be directed and purposeful as the tourist specifically seeks a type of holiday experience, or it might come unsuspecting as a thief in the night. It is not unknown for people to return from holiday with either a changed life or a changed perspective. It might be the knowledge, as indicated above, that the marriage is now sterile, or indeed reborn. It might be that some respond to the siren call of summer sun and return to give up their jobs and become sailing instructors under Mediterranean skies. Others may return to their previous existence, but with some experience that gives an inner strength. For such people the full sense of the word, recreation, is indeed a reality. If this is read as being poetic licence, then the promoters of holidays based on events such as outdoor activities, sailing or hiking can generally cite examples of such conversions. This theme is certainly found in contemporary literature and strikes a chord with readers, as can be seen by the success of Willy Russell's *Shirley Valentine* and David Lodge's *Paradise News*. Both novels are about processes of self discovery, romance and sex while on holiday.

Wish fulfilment

For some, the holiday is the answer to a dream – a dream that has perhaps sustained a long process of saving. The naturalist may feel a thrill as he or she visits the Galapagos Islands and has prepared by reading about Charles Darwin's visit aboard the *Beagle*. Increasingly the experience may be the translation of a pretence into a reality. How else can one explain the popularity of theme parks, except that they are an escape into a fantasy? It can be objected that the fantasy is commodified, encapsulated into carefully engineered moments of time dictated, in part, by the need to ensure crowd control whereby queues are minimised, but that does not mean that there is no sense of enjoyment. The film, *WestWorld*, in which holidaymakers travelled into a themed existence where robots permitted them to act out their fantasies, was but an extension of the common experience of the theme park carried through to a logical conclusion. Indeed in the 'Western villages' of theme parks such as the American Adventure or Warner Brothers Movie World it is possible to have your photograph taken in cowboy garb and placed on a 'wanted' notice. Some holiday on 'dude ranches' in locations across Montana and other parts of North America, while Japan has a thriving Western Riding Association. Already one can 'journey' on the Shuttle Missions by attending the IMAX cinema, or use nature as the themed experience by hunting with historical weapons in North American parks, or replicate the pioneer experience by travelling by wagon train or raft. History provides us with many themes that permit a realisation of the dream of time travel as visitors mix with the costumed inhabitants of Colonial Williamsburg or the Beamish Museum. Some of the fantasies are turning into reality. The world's first space tourist, Dennis Tito, paid $US20 million in 2001 to journey into Earth orbit, and a Space Tourism Promotion Act was introduced into the House of Representatives in July 2001. A cursory search for 'space tourism' on the Internet revealed, in April 2002, more than 610,000 references.

Shopping

Although this may seem a prosaic reason for holidaying, shopping is not only one of the most common tourist activities, but it can also, at least under certain circumstances, be a motivating factor for travel away from home, and indeed for international travel. An example is provided by the aftermath of the signing of the free-trade agreement between Canada and the USA, combined with, in 1987, the growing strength of the Canadian dollar. The firm of accountants, Ernst and Young, recorded in 1988 a 31% increase in automobile traffic over the year at 31 Canada–US border points, and at Pigeon River alone an increase of $CN19 million of goods were brought into Canada in the year ending July 1988. The number of custom filings for imported goods rose by 133% in the same period for Canadians buying goods in the USA and bringing them back home. The same phenomena can be observed at many other border communities, for example, between Eire and Northern Ireland, or between Switzerland and Italy. As all these trips are cross-border trips, they may be counted in the official statistics as tourist trips.

Within some cultures, shopping is very important. Hobson and Christensen (2001) provide a full description of, within Japanese culture, the giving of *senbetsu* to the traveller upon departure from Japan, and the reciprocal giving of *omiyage*. *Omiyage* has two components: first it must be a culturally acceptable symbol of the place visited, and second it must equate to about half the value of the *senbetsu*. While not providing any empirical evidence, the authors argue that this explains the very high proportion of total Japanese tourist spending that is accounted for by shopping. It has also been maintained that, within other cultures, the cultural symbolism of the souvenir is a factor that influences purchase. But Kim and Littrell (2001), perhaps not surprisingly, found that the one consistently important variable in determining choice of souvenir shopping for the shopper's own use was the aesthetic qualities of the item being considered. It should also be noted that shopping can be used for the generation of profit through the changing of tours whereby the tour operator, guide or driver obtains a 'kick-back' or commission from sales resulting from tourist spending. Ko (1999) describes how Korean Inbound Operators in Australia would change schedules, and that prices in Korean tourist shopping centres in Sydney could be 20% more expensive than in other outlets. Therefore, while shopping may at first sight appear to be a not-overly-important motive when compared with the others, and indeed may perhaps be more properly described as a subset of the above motives, its practical implications are important.

These, then, are some of the psychological motivations that may initiate the type of holiday chosen. Whatever type of holiday is selected may in fact be a statement about a person's self-identity; or simply a statement about a set of priorities felt at the time of decision taking. However, in the diversity of both choice and needs, it would be dangerous to read too much into the actual choice, for many people will undertake more than one type of holiday over time, perhaps delaying the meeting of one particular need in order to meet another.

Types of Tourist

Built on the concept that different motivations differentiate between categories of tourists, a number of profiles of tourist types have been created. One of the earliest, and still much quoted, was that of Cohen in 1972. Cohen described four types of tourist based on the degree of institutionalisation of the tourist and the nature of the impact on the host community. Briefly stated his four categories were:

Organised mass tourists

These are the least adventurous tourists. On buying their package holiday, they remain encapsulated in an 'environmental bubble', divorced from the host community as they remain primarily in the hotel complex. They adhere to an itinerary fixed by the tour operators, and even their trips out of the complex are organised tours. They make few decisions about their holiday.

The individual mass tourist

These are similar to the organised mass tourists in that they utilise the facilities made available by the tour operator, but they have some control over their own itinerary. They may use the hotel as a base and hire a car for their own trips. However, many will tend to visit the same places as the mass organised tourist in that they will visit the 'sights'.

The explorer

The explorer arranges his or her own trip alone, and attempts to get off the beaten track. Yet such tourists will still have recourse to comfortable tourist accommodation. However, much of their travel will be associated with a motivation to associate with the local people, and they will often speak the language of the host community. Nonetheless, the explorer retains many of the basic routines of his or own lifestyle.

The drifter

The drifter will shun contact with the tourist and tourist establishments, and identify with the host community. Drifters will live with the locals and adopt many of the practices of that community. Income is generated by working within the community, but often through low-skilled work, which creates a tendency to mix with the lower socio-economic groups.

One problem with this categorisation is that, while it creates easily-recognised pictures, it may not reflect the complexities of tourist behaviour. The categories are observations of behaviour without reference to the reasons that cause that behaviour to be adopted. Many behaviour patterns may be the result of constraints rather than specific preferences, as the tourist indulges in a series of exercises to optimise the return on limited time. Equally, as previously observed, with several sectors of our society taking more than one holiday each year, holidaymakers may adopt different styles of holidays. In short there is no consistency of behaviour. Pearce (1982b) reviews many of the categories of tourists as described by Chadwick (1981), Cohen (1974), and V.L Smith (1977b). Indeed he advances his own categorisation based on factor analysis in which he distinguishes between 15 types based on 5 role-related behaviour patterns. Witt and Wright (1990) argue that multi-motivational models are necessary to understand tourism motivation.

Allocentric vs. psychocentric

One way in which these tourist classifications have a value is to relate them to the destinations that any given tourist type will prefer. Plog (1977) was one of the first to do this. Essentially Plog argued that there was a continuum between types of tourists from the allocentric to the psychocentric tourist. The allocentric tourists are akin to Cohen's explorers in that they seek new destinations, and are prepared to take risks in searching for new cultures and places. On the other hand psychocentric tourists seek the familiar, and are happier in an environment where there are many like-minded tourists. They are not risk takers and adhere to the proven product, being conservative in choice. Plog hence identified that these types of tourists would be drawn to a particular destination. This is illustrated in Figure 4.1, which indicates the destinations as originally identified by Plog. It thus represents an American perspective of tourist destinations as it existed more than thirty years ago.

As will be discussed with regard to the social impact of tourism, this has some important implications in terms of the types of tourists that destinations attract. An additional implication is that there is a time element associated with links between tourist type and destination. Destinations are originally 'discovered' by allocentrics, but subsequently they seek other destinations as they are followed by the near-allocentrics, and so on through the tourist types until a destination becomes a psychocentric destination. For example Palma de Mallorca is now a psychocentric destination and is in danger of being perceived as a downmarket destination, whereas in the 1950s it could have been typified as a near-allocentric or midcentric destination as far as British tourists were concerned. This process has been identified as the 'shifting periphery of tourism', and is closely related to Butler's lifecycle theory, which is discussed in Chapters 6 and 9.

The classifications advanced by Cohen and Plog have both been debated in the literature over the intervening years. For example in the early 1990s Smith (1990) criticised Plog's model arguing that, in applying questions designed to elicit responses on the allocentric– psychocentric continuum, no such categories emerged. For his part Plog responded that the questions being used were invalid, and in 2002 he criticised many psychographic descriptions as having no conceptual foundation, and suggested a concept of 'venturers' and 'dependables'. However, Plog does not, in that article, propose a psychological basis for this division of buyers, and equally continues to contend that 'psychographics has received little attention either in the world of business ...or among academic researchers' (Plog, 2002: 249). To the mind of this author this appears to be an untenable position, given the great frequency of articles based on market segmentations that appear in the journals. Indeed a search of CABI's leisuretourism.com database quickly identified 140 such articles, without any sophistication being used in the search terms. Segmentations based on motive are far from infrequent in the tourism literature.

Cohen's categorisation has also been adopted by some and modified by others. For example, within the arena of ecotourism, drifters and explorers

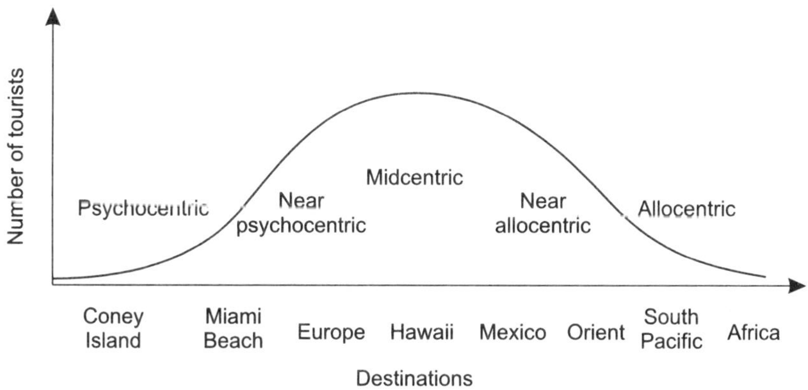

Figure 4.1 Plog's categorisation of tourist types and destinations
Source: Plog (1977)

have been identified with environmentally-aware tourists who wish at least to maintain if not to enhance the natural environment. But as a destination becomes better known it begins to attract a wider range of tourists and thus independent mass tourists arrive at the site. Finally, mass organised tourism occurs (e.g. Richins, 1996). A similar model is proposed by Higham (1998), who adapted the concept suggested by Duffus and Dearden (1990) of destinations initially being attractive to a small, specific group of visitors based on a highly-focused area of interest, but over time developing to become attractive to a more general audience. Figure 4.2 illustrates Higham's argument with reference to the albatross colony at Taiaroa Head in New Zealand.

According to Higham, at first a destination like that of Taiaroa Head attracts only those specifically interested in the nature of the attraction. Therefore, as shown in Figure 4.2, the numbers of tourists are comparatively few and are oriented toward the 'expert' (E) – in this particular instance, the specialist ornithologist. Over time, though, the destination begins to attract an equal number of experts and those having more of a general or novice's (N) level of knowledge, and of course the total numbers of visitors grow. Subsequently, the number of novices (N) is greater than the number of 'expert' visitors. For each of these stages, Higham (1998) and Duffus and Dearden (1990) argue that there are differing levels of accept-

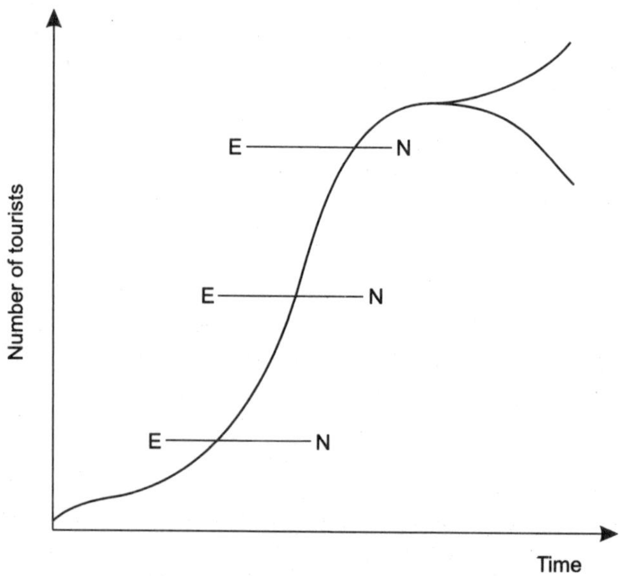

Figure 4.2 The changing pattern of tourist demand

able change in the design of the destination. The level of acceptable change refers to impacts on natural environments that result from recreational or touristic activities, and the concept is more fully explained in Chapter 8. However, as each succeeding visitation stage is reached, it is accompanied by increasing levels of visitor management. Each of these management intrusions possesses greater implications for environmental change as management seeks to preserve the original focus of the visit. For example, at Taiaroa, increasing numbers of visitors negatively impacted on albatross behaviour through a lack of controls. So there is now a visitor centre with access to viewing areas. While this has been established to protect the nesting areas, the physical existence of the buildings has also created a change to which many might originally have been opposed on the grounds that it is an intrusion on a natural landscape. Second, as it is promoted, the centre in itself attracts more visitors with, as Higham (1998) notes, some evidence that consequent noise from the centre negatively impacts on the behaviour of albatross chicks. In short, some evidence exists that the albatross is now selecting suboptimal nesting sites further away from the centre. Briefly, what this case study illustrates is that there is relationship between motive and site design, and this relationship will be further explored in Chapter 8.

It can be observed that the structure of the tourism industry has changed significantly since the 1970s when Cohen was first developing his model. First, Cohen seems at least in part, to have derived his model from research undertaken among, for example, backpackers in locations such as Phuket; and the late 1960s was also a time when 'hippie trails' were being established to places such as Nepal. The 'drifter' classification was therefore based in part on a specific description of a tourism that arguably has changed. While, no doubt there are still 'drifters' in the Cohen mode, it can be argued that backpacker tourism itself has definitely changed and has split into various subgroups (Loker-Murphy, 1996). Thus, arguably many backpackers follow a well-defined trail characterised by infrastructures and support services for backpackers; this means, in effect, that they do little but meet other backpackers. Echoes of history might be heard! Hibbert (1987: 235) notes John Moore writing in 1792 that young men on the Grand Tour ' ... go to France and Italy and there converse with none but English people, and merely to say that you have been in these countries is certainly absurd.' The same criticism is heard of backpackers, and there is some truth in the accusation that those constrained by time and using services like *Kiwi Experience* do little but meet others of the same ilk. Equally, at the other end of Cohen's scale, the nature of mass tourism has changed. There are few today who either directly, or through the Internet, do not use the services of the organised tourism industry to book travel and accommodation, and indeed create their own packages. Therefore, while the destinations being visited may be those of the package-holiday industry, people will hire cars and make their own arrangements. There has, arguably, been a blurring of the mass and the individually-organised package holiday, while even today the adventure product has become commercialised, commodified and packaged. Climbers book years ahead to climb Everest with professional guides, office clerks become day-long white-water rafters – adventure and exploration abounds. And for those who still seek adventure by, for example, crossing Antarctica by foot, there may still be the comfort of GPS, television back-up crews and radio communications with base. In short, as shown in Chapter 1 and as is further examined in Chapter 5, the nature of tourism and the experiences it bestows have changed considerably over time. Nonetheless, the Cohen model still evokes recognition and provides the basis from which to develop more complex structures and understandings of the 'tourist experience'.

Motivations

In many cases these descriptions of tourists are based on observed behavioural patterns, and motives are subsequently attributed to them. It might also be that in many cases the lists of motivations have perhaps two essential drivers. These may be described crudely as a 'push' motivation, that is a wish to get away from a place, and a 'pull' motivation, a desire to see some other area. Iso-Ahola (1982) clarified this latter motivation as 'a desire to obtain psychological (intrinsic) rewards through travel in a contrasting world'. The 'pull-push' factors can also be held to operate on humans in two dimensions, man as the social animal seeking interpersonal relationships, and man as the solitary person seeking either refuge from others or solitude. Accordingly a matrix of four segments is suggested by Iso-Ahola (Figure 4.3), in which it becomes possible to locate the series of different motivations that other writers have identified.

Figure 4.3 represents Iso-Ahola's classifications wherein the 'push' factor is represented by the desire to leave behind the home environment, and the 'pull' variable is represented by the search for intrinsic reward. Each motive can itself be divided into two: first, where the motives and rewards gained are primarily personal, and second, where they have value by being related to other people. Thus, the desire to leave home may be a personal wish for a change of environment, but is directed towards another person in terms of strengthening personal relationships and thus the pull factor is interpersonal. To provide a second example, someone may wish to go to an exotic location to achieve a sense of prestige – so the desire to leave home is to create the opportunity to achieve the personal goal of 'prestige' associated with the exotic pull of a place. The strength of the model is that it recognises that 'pull' and 'push' possess an interactive dynamic. They simultaneously exist as opposites and as complementary forces; as being both isolated and as conjoint. It is possible to separately identify both motives, but the full meaning is derived only from the synthesis of the two. On the other hand the model says little about the reasons for such motives; they are almost taken as 'being given' and nor is there any relationship postulated as to behaviour, satisfaction and choice of place. The processes of choice are not really considered.

While it can be argued that the primary motives for tourism are well understood, as indicated in the above list, what is less well understood is the timing of purchase decisions, and the constraints that exist on any purchase of a holiday. Dellaert, Ettema and Lindh (1998: 314) present evidence that travel-choice decisions take into account 'restrictions because of time and money budgets and coupling constraints caused by work, family and friendship relationships'. Their study clearly showed that life stage characterised by the presence of young children certainly imposed restraints on choice of travel dates and travel duration because of schooling needs. Equally, income was a differentiator in terms of the numbers of trips being made, although both high-income and low-income groups made similar choices as to destinations visited. In short, the economic and social factors discussed in the earlier chapters influence the actual psychology of decision taking.

The classification of tourist types and motives listed above possesses some advantages, but the evidence increasingly shows that tourists are not consistent in their wants, and hence in the type of holiday selected. Gyte (1988) found in his survey of tourists in Majorca that some perceived their package holiday as a second holiday not only in terms of numbers of holidays taken, but also in type. In Plog's terminology, the holidaymaker may engage in allocentric behaviour at one time, and in psychocentric behaviour at another. Given increased incomes and travel opportunities, people can increasingly meet a series of needs. Iso-Ahola's model recog-

		Seek intrinsic reward	
		Personal	***Interpersonal***
Desire to leave behind home environment	***Personal***	Ego-enhancement Escape from responsibility Aesthetics	Strengthen kinship
	Interpersonal	Status enhancement Prestige	Meet new people in new places Play

Figure 4.3 Motivations of holidaymakers

nises the dialectical process that exists between a wish for escape and the desire for intrinsic reward. It is thus becomes possible that, not only over different holidays but indeed within the same holiday period, people will switch from one cell to another within the suggested matrix (Figure 4.3). This is a recognition that, although a holiday may satisfy a prime need, a 'good' holiday also has the ability to satisfy a series of secondary needs. These secondary needs may become more pressing when the primary need is satisfied. For example, if the primary need is for relaxation, a few days of idleness might well meet that requirement, and the holidaymaker will then indulge in other forms of behaviour, such as seeking out new places and new activities, thereby becoming far more proactive.

This suggests that holiday taking is goal driven, and that the goals are attained through the adoption of specific forms of behaviour. It also implies that holidaymakers are just that, holiday*makers* and not simply holiday *takers*. Given this proactive interpretation of tourism, it becomes possible to perceive a series of potentially alternative tourism roles. Yiannakos and Gibson (1992) identified three main motivational dimensions that underlie tourist roles. These were a desire for more or less structured itineraries or activities, a wish for either a stimulating or a tranquil environment, and finally whether the tourists wished to visit a familiar or an unfamiliar environment. Based on these dimensions Yiannakos and Gibson were able to identify fourteen different tourist roles: 'sun lovers', 'action seekers', 'anthropologists', 'archaeologists', 'organised mass tourists', 'thrill seekers', 'explorers', 'jetsetters', 'seekers', 'independent mass tourists', 'high class tourists', 'drifters', 'escapists' and 'sports lovers'. For example, action seekers would often seek a structured adventure tourism product in a stimulating environment in unfamiliar surroundings. With reference to life stage, the same authors subsequently examined whether these roles were associated with any specific demographics (Gibson and Yiannakos, 2002). They concluded:

> ... gender and life-stage linked psychological needs (push factors) 'drive' the selection and enactment of tourist roles ... Further (the study) provides statistical support for the contention that tourist roles serve as vehicles through which vacationers may satisfy or enhance deficit or growth needs. (Gibson & Yiannakos, 2002: 377–378)

Ryan and Huyton (2002), although writing with specific reference to tourism based around the culture of indigenous peoples, raise another point. They argue that the identification of a tourist as a 'cultural tourist' actually says little about the depth of that interest, and suggest that within each classification of tourist type there may be a continuum from 'serious leisure' to superficial interest. One interpretation of their research findings would be at least three types of cultural tourist in the context of Australian Aboriginal tourism. First, the serious, who would stay overnight in an

Aboriginal community (in their study, about 3% of visitors). Second, those who have an interest of varying levels, including those for whom an interest in Aboriginal culture is located in a context of an understanding of the 'Outback'. Finally there are those with just a simple wish to obtain a little understanding, albeit through a medium of 'edutainment'. However, from the viewpoint of official statistics, since all are recorded as having attended an Aboriginal event, there is a danger that all would be classified as 'cultural tourists'. Whilst, intellectually, the idea of links between motivation, holiday types and destinations is attractive, in practice the linkage may be subtle, exposed as it is to a lack of consistency of behaviour as the tourist changes holiday types from one holiday to another. Additionally, for many, family holidays may in fact be compromise decisions that attempt to reflect the differing interests of family members. One must also again refer to the nature of the holiday decision. As previously stated, it is the purchase of, in most instances, a previously-unseen intangible, and it might be that false images created by the marketing departments of tour operators actually lead the holidaymaker to make a wrong decision. Crompton (1979) makes this warning statement:

> ... to expect motivation to account for a large variance in tourist behaviour is probably asking too much since there may be other inter-related forces operating. (Crompton, 1979: 424)

These other forces have been identified as being economic and social as well as psychological. In isolation each seems unable to forecast tourist behaviour; together the variables are perhaps too many to permit an easy explanation of complex behaviour patterns. However, together they point not simply to a growth of demand for tourism, but to a realisation that such growth cannot simply be taken for granted. The very increases in income that made tourism possible now generate opportunities for an improved quality of life within the home environment that undermines the escape motivation. Concern with quality of life may make people wonder if travel is necessary. The tourist may travel, but each takes his or herself. Escape from daily routine is possible, escape from self is not. If there is a relationship between income, recreational opportunity and concern about quality of life with the attributes of self-actualisation as described by Abraham Maslow, then the question can be asked, does self-actualised man require travel? Certainly there have been occasions when, at least in the very short run, people have chosen not to travel. One such example was after the suicide attacks on the World Trade Centre on September 11, 2001, by members of Al-Qa'eda; for several months after, American citizens delayed or cancelled travel plans both domestically and internationally. Ironically, however, such an example illustrates the very opposite end of the Maslow hierarchy of needs, when fears for safety overcome other needs that motivate travel.

Urry (1990) has provided an alternative thesis – that the changes in our society have created the cosmopolitan rather than perhaps the global citizen. Such a citizen, it might be argued, collects experiences, and is sufficiently sophisticated to slip into various roles and indeed is more than capable of role-playing. This ludic tourist can also effect detachment, can capably split him or herself from place and action even while performing the ritual associated with place. It is possible for the sophisticated tourist to wryly smile at his or herself as while pounding the table at the bequest of some 'jester' at the medieval banquet. This they say, is fake: 'I know it to be authentically fake, and I can enjoy it for what it is'. The motives for travel thus become quite complex. In part people travel because that is what people do on their holidays. It is the norm, it is what is expected. Yet the motives outlined earlier also have their role to play – travel is still prompted by curiousity, by relaxation needs and by purposes of social interaction. But the tourist is able to play out different roles at the destination, can adjust and adapt, change motives, and might be said to be a chameleon traveller, able to absorb not only that which is sought, but that which is provided. In short, while on the one hand general economic, social and psychological themes may be identified and analysed as potential determinants of demand for tourism in general, and indeed for specific categories of tourism product, the individual's choice and experience has still yet to be explained. It is possible to separate, at least theoretically, the context within which holidays are demanded, and the specifics that pertain to any individual his or her choice of place. In short, questions arise as to what is the nature of the tourist experience that is so strong as to induce people, time after time, to engage upon travel and leave behind the comforts of home.

It has been argued that the tourist is a collector of experiences who provides meaning to the spaces through which he or she passes (Wearing & Wearing, 1996; Ryan, 2001a). If the experiences are gained through transitional space and ephemeral periods, to what extent can it be said that the tourist is 'satisfied'? This seems to imply a whole range of experiences, ranging from the shallow to the profound, and it can be argued that tourism does provide all of these. That tourists are satisfied is shown directly by studies of tourist evaluations of places and indirectly by the high level of repeat behaviours shown by tourists. For many, holidaying is more than simply an annual event. Within the services marketing literature, the debate over satisfaction in the 1980s gave rise to models of service quality as offering measurable determinants of satisfaction. The model of service quality that for much of the last two to three decades has dominated the literature has been the ServQual model suggested by Parasuraman, Zeithaml and Berry (1985, 1991).

The Expectation–Evaluation, Confirmation–Disconfirmation Paradigm

The conceptualisation of service quality initially suggested by Parasuraman, Zeithaml and Berry (1991) is based on a simple notion, namely that service quality can be measured by the gap that exists between scales that measure client expectation and evaluation of a transaction (or, in this case, a holiday). Thus if on a seven-point Likert type scale (where 7 is the highest score) a holidaymaker has an expectation of 6, and evaluates the experience as being 6, then it might be said that as expectation is met, service quality is high. The literature relating to ServQual quickly raised a series of questions, among which were:

(1) If expectation (E) is 1, and evaluation or satisfaction with the holiday (S) is also 1, (i.e. $E = S = 1$), in what way can a gap of zero measure service quality? What if $E = S = 5$? In short, was the value of the gap a constant in meaning, or did it differ depending on the part of the scale from which the gap emerged?

(2) If expectation is, say 5, and evaluation equates to 7, how does one interpret this in terms of a measure of service quality if confirmation of service quality is said to exist when expectations are met? Is this some form of 'super satisfaction'?

(3) How are expectations formed? It might be said that expectations can be formed with reference to past experience, what are thought to be acceptable levels of service, or against some model of the ideal. If this is the case, is there commonality in any of these measures of expectations, or do these three sets of expectations relate to different concepts?

(4) It was quickly found that the gap was primarily determined by the level of evaluation (satisfaction) in that this measure showed greater degrees of variance. What role, therefore, did the expectation scale play? Was it not simply possible to measure service quality by a measure of satisfaction alone?

Given these and other criticisms (which are, in the context of tourism, reviewed by Ryan, 1999a), the actual measures of satisfaction being adopted by researchers might be said to fall into one of a number of classifications. These include:

(1) The *atheoretical*, ad hoc scales. Basically these can be described as scales based on no psychological theory; they are simply assessments of a list of attributes possessed by a location or attraction.

(2) *Importance–evaluation* modeling, where it is argued that two components of satisfaction might exist. First there is an evaluation of attributes, but this is thought to be insufficient without reference to an assessment of what is important to a visitor. There is a difference

between a high rating of satisfaction on an attribute of lesser importance and the same rating on an item of higher importance. It might be said that there exist two measures of satisfaction – the absolute measure of the evaluation (or satisfaction) scale alone, and the relative measure, when the gap between importance and evaluation is measured. However, as yet this approach is, from the perspective of satisfaction measurement, poorly conceptualised, and it is open to some of the same criticisms made of the ServQual scale above. Here, though, the theory is derived from attitude measurement (e.g. Fishbein, 1967) and the belief that attitude comprises three components: the cognitive, the affective (or emotional) and the conative (the predisposition to action).

(3) *Non-positivistic* approaches, where it is argued that satisfaction is a shifting entity dependent on the presence or absence of many variables, and is not consistent. It can be found only through qualitative research methods where the actual words and language of the participants are the raw data. Interpretation is thus dependent not only on the language use of the respondent, but also on the stance and role adopted by the researcher. These issues of researcher–respondent relationships are part of the considerations voiced by Denzin and Lincoln (1994).

(4) *Motivational* approaches, where satisfaction is explored on the premise that it is based on the presence of varying needs. These needs include self esteem, a need for society, a desire for knowledge, a wish for prestige and the desire to relax. From a psychological perspective they are, within the tourism literature, derived primarily from humanistic psychology, with which the name of Maslow is closely associated. Thus, as explored in the next chapter, theories of tourist action have been based on Maslow's hierarchy of needs (see Pearce, 1988 and Ryan, 1998a, for an analysis of the tourist career ladder). However, other schools of motivational importance exist, and Ross (1994) offers a review of these theories within the context of tourism. These include McClelland's need to achieve, and Skinner's theory of operant conditioning.

Finally, before completing this section, it needs to be stated in fairness to the ServQual model that it goes beyond a simple consumer gap between expectation and evaluation. The full model examines in more detail four other relationships that pay attention to management expectations and evaluations also. This full model has been applied much more fully within research related to the hospitality industry than tourism, and of some interest have been recent findings that, perhaps because of the globalisation of the hotel industry, the model possesses value for management even in non-Anglo-Saxon based cultures. For example, in preliminary research, Tsai, Ryan and Lockyer (2002) argue that, for five-star business and resort hotels based in Taiwan, there was little evidence that Chinese cultural values of *kuan-hsi* and *mien-tsu* intruded on guest, staff and management evaluations of service quality. *Kuan-hsi* is regarded as a set of connections that secure business and personal interests; *mien-tsu* is loosely translated as a sense of importance or, colloquially, 'face'. Essentially Tsai *et al.* concluded that the derivation of satisfaction came from the service expected from a multinational hotel chain mode of operation, and thus the ServQual dimensions were operational. These dimensions relate to tangible signs of service, reliability, responsiveness, empathy with customers and reassurance; but respondents did not utilise traditional Chinese concepts when relating to service.

On the other hand, Seaton (2000) raises another issue about the nature of tourism that is not well catered for in the models discussed, and that is what might be termed 'emotional intensity'. In a description of different groups of tourists touring the battlefield sites of Flanders, Seaton describes the sense of ownership felt by an expert group of hobbyists. Their research led them to identify with individual fallen and sites, and they became, in their eyes, part of the drama. They 'talked of the battlefields in affectionate, proprietorial terms, as if it was a kind of homeland (Seaton, 2000: 70).

Summary

The demand for tourism is determined by a number of economic, psychological and social factors. These include variables such as income, taxation, interest rates, attitudes to saving, available time, prices of holidays, and other factors. In consequence, the potential holidaymaker has a discretionary income that permits holidaying behaviour, but the type of holiday to be taken is decided not in isolation, but within a set of behaviour patterns that reflect allotted values to competing demands on leisure time. People may wish to use holidays as a means of escape, or of fulfilment, but in many cases holidays are prompted by more than one motive, whilst being subjected to income constraints and the demands of other family members. Simple unicausal theories are inadequate to explain holiday-taking behaviour, and complex models incorporating economic, psychological and sociological factors would be required to develop more meaningful explanations.

Chapter 5

The Tourist Experience

Introduction

Chapter 4 finished with an introductory discussion of service quality and its relationship to satisfaction with the tourist experience. It is a commonplace that the holiday requires several components to work effectively before a satisfactory holiday is generated.

Cost

The first component is the ability of travel agents and other initial intermediaries to make the appropriate arrangements at prices suitable to the tourist. Given the increasing degree of choice and the at times bewildering patterns of airline pricing, any tourist requires a travel agent with a high degree of knowledge of ticket availability. While it is true that, for many passengers, direct booking through websites creates some price savings, it is not yet true that perfect knowledge of a transparent market exists. Some airline websites are simply inadequate. For example, while Air New Zealand had introduced web-based ticketing some years earlier, it was only in 2002 that they introduced an ability to purchase children's fares on the website. In this they were not alone. In other cases, return tickets are cheaper than one-way prices. In some cases flights via an intermediate destination and onward to a third destination are cheaper than a direct flight from the origin of the trip to the intermediate destination. Wily passengers simply end up buying a full ticket and throwing away the final part, or buying return tickets and either not using or, in some cases, on-selling the return part of a ticket. For their part, airlines over book expecting 'no-shows' and sometimes they get it wrong, so some passengers miss their flights. On the other hand airlines then offer hotel accommodation and upgraded seats in compensation. It is easy to feel that logic and airline pricing are not always compatible. Recently the author found that a fare from Auckland to Seoul was $NZ1700, while a continuation of that same flight to London was only $NZ100 more! However, airlines seek to carefully control and allocate seating and pricing to obtain the most profitable loading through the exercise of yield-management techniques. Airlines juggle booking between First, Business and Economy classes; between employees flying for free, other privileged clients such as politicians, and others seeking to use air points for free or upgraded flights. Such is the situation that one feels that optimum loadings are not always achieved. For these reasons, plus the convenience offered, it is of little surprise that package and all-inclusive holidays continue to hold major portions of some markets. In addition to the convenience, there also exists, on the part of the consumer, a greater degree of certainty in the purchase decision. This is because not only is there knowledge of the destination and holiday type, but this is reinforced by expectations associated with brand. Package-holiday companies increasingly seek to capture loyal clients through relationship marketing based on databases of past purchases. This creates a symbiotic relationship of mutual advantage. The client gains certainty as to enjoyable outcomes through the avoidance of unpleasant surprises, while the company gains repeat business. From the tourist's perspective the fulfilment of expected outcomes is an optimal solution to risk taking within limited periods of leisure time that involve significant financial outlay. Not all tourists have the opportunity to experiment with holiday types, particularly, for example, if they are constrained by the presence of young children. Additionally the safeguard exists that failure to deliver the required services renders the travel company liable to legal action. Certainly within the USA and European Union the use of the package-holiday industry sector simplifies the gaining of redress for accidents and other unfortunate outcomes that might occur overseas.

Travel

The next component for many people is that of travel. Land travel often involves the use of cars or other forms of road transport. Car hire companies often provide a sense of security through the provision of new vehicles with little mileage, offers of cell phones, temporary membership of automobile associations and, today, the provision of Geographical Information Systems and mapping systems that continually monitor progress. In addition, car rental companies provide other services such as advanced bookings through the Internet, and minimal paperwork for customers belonging to their schemes so that they can walk directly to car parks to pick up their vehicles when they arrive at airports. Similarly, airlines seek to provide loyalty schemes, club lounges and check-in points at city centres and hotels. In short, there is again an emphasis on customer reassurance and convenience.

Accommodation

The next stage in the holiday experience might be that of commercially provided accommodation. This sector is also now characterised by pre-booking, loyalty schemes and yield management and, over time, by an upgrading of facilities and services. Equally, however, a range of types of accommodation has come into being to suit client needs. There are campsites, huts, budget motels, luxury motels, hotels, deluxe hotels, eco-lodges and luxury lodges – a range of accommodation from the most basic to those with full suite services, private spa pools and baths, a choice of restaurants or no restaurants. Hotels can be distinguished by location. They range from airport hotels located within a few minutes of an airport offering limousine or shuttle services for their clients, to those serving central business districts, beach resorts, islands, mountainous areas or indeed floating hotels – for example on the Great Barrier Reef off Australia's eastern coast.

Facilities

Once at a destination, the tourist might take advantage of a range of services, attractions and facilities dependent upon the type of holiday being sought. The choice is enormous; from tours of cultural and historic sites, to night club entertainment, from the most active of pursuits to the most passive.

From this brief review it can be seen that to discuss the nature of the tourist experience is to enter a minefield of exploration. However, and bearing in mind the content of previous chapters, a series of issues can be identified for consideration. These include:

(1) To what extent is satisfaction with the holiday an evaluation of the whole experience, or of a series of events? During the holiday, to what degree is there a tolerance of disappointment with some aspects that can be offset by above-expected levels of performance or experience in other parts of the holiday? Are there critical incidents of such magnitude that they have the potential to literally make or break a holiday?

(2) Given, as seen in Chapter 4, a number of different roles that tourists can play, can there be any portfolio of roles that tourists are able to adopt given any range of circumstances? Does the 'ecotourist' who books into what is described in the brochure as an eco-lodge on a safari holiday adopt another role quite easily when it is found that the lodge actually services the needs of perhaps well over a hundred short-stay tourists on package tours? In other words, do individual tourists possess social skills to readapt in order to achieve the main goal – which might be defined as having a 'good holiday'? Or do they demonstrate less flexible skills that lead to situations of disappointment and perhaps conflict?

(3) Just how important is the issue of authenticity in tourism? For many writers tourists are characterised by a wish to sample the unfamiliar, but such sampling should occur within what are seen as 'authentic' locations.

The Issue of Authenticity

There has been significant discussion within the academic literature about the need for authenticity and the nature of the product that is being offered to tourists. The roots of this debate can be discerned in a number of writings. First, there was the feeling that modern tourism emasculated the experience of travel. As already noted, this was a view advocated by Boorstin (1962), who saw in the development of advertising, branding and the speed and ease of modern transport systems, a removal of the *travail* associated with travel. The packaged holidaymaker was then being served with time-constrained presentations abstracted from the original context of meaning associated with the culture from which the performance was lifted. So, it was argued, tourism lacked the rigour of travel of the past and served up a pastiche of culture. Greenwood's study of the Hondarribian Alarde (Greenwood, 1977) was then often cited (e.g. by Mathieson & Wall, 1982) as an example of host communities themselves seeking to meet tourist's needs by separating spectacle in culture from original meaning. The implication was that this too represented a degradation of the host culture in exchange for profit. In this particular case, a re-enactment of a past siege in 1638 had been attracting increasing numbers of tourists to the extent that the local municipality decided to hold a second performance, on the same afternoon, to meet tourist demand. For Greenwood this represented a diminution of a tradition based on the celebration and reinforcement of local community, and he felt that outsiders should not intrude.

The word 'authenticity', with its associations of adherence to an original, when compared to the commercial values associated with the word 'commodification' that came to be used to describe this process, appeared, somehow, morally superior. Certainly a number of criticisms came to be voiced. MacCannell (1976) adopted the view that Boorstin was incorrect in his view that the tourist was satisfied with this process. For MacCannell, the irony of tourism is that many tourists achieve the highest levels of satisfaction when they feel that they have ceased to be 'tourists'. They do not necessarily want to be full members of the host society, for to do so means they lose the privileges accorded to a guest. Rather, they seek the status of guests, because as such they are welcomed into what MacCannell (1976) called the 'back stage', the area not normally seen by the outsider. MacCannell wrote:

> Tourists are not criticised by Boorstin and others for leaving home to see the sights. They are reproached for being satisfied with superficial experiences of other peoples and other places ... (but) touristic shame is not based on being a tourist but in not being a tourist enough, on a failure to see everything the way it 'ought' to be seen. The touristic critique of tourism is based on a desire to go beyond the other 'mere'

> tourists to a more profound appreciation of society and culture, and it is by no means limited to intellectual statements. All tourists desire this deeper involvement with society and culture to some degree; it is a basic component of their motivation to travel. (MacCannell, 1976: 76–77)

A second criticism of this perspective of Boorstin (1962), Fussell (1982) and MacCannell (1976) himself was that their perspective was based on traditional elitist values that often obscured other sets of values no less important. For example, it was pointed out that holidays traditionally had been periods of disjuncture in social processes. Rojek (1993) indicated a history of tourism that included 'fool's days' and the carnivalesque, where settled order was deliberately set aside. Ryan (2002) pointed to a working class history of holidaying where a celebration of solidarity was often an important consideration, whether in the walking clubs or the hopfields of late nineteenth century England. The work of historians of tourism also demonstrated that concerns with the authentic culture had often been mediated in various ways, by class values, by guidebooks that were selective in what deemed sightworthy, and that in many cases motives for travel were not always the best (e.g. see Towner, 1996).

A third critique of the importance of 'authenticity' is that cultures are dynamic and change, and that these processes are often an evolutionary process created by change agents, adaptation to change by those affected and the choice of both viewer and viewed as to what is considered to be acceptable. MacNaught (1982) pointed out that host societies were not empty sponges that simply and without question absorbed the influences of the visitor. The nature of the demonstration effect began to be questioned more critically and, as will be considered in Chapter 9, the complex interactions between some types of visitors and some types of hosts came to be better understood.

Fourth, it was recognised that almost any experience offers the reality of an emotive and cognitive reaction. Wang (2000: 49) has argued that there are different interpretations of authenticity, including existential authenticity. In effect, this distinguishes between the level of congruence that a replica or performance has with the original, and the nature of the experience that the participant feels. Therefore while, for example, the performance of a dance with poi by Maori performers in Rotorua, New Zealand, may not exactly replicate the original performance and meaning of that dance, for the overseas visitor it provides an insight into Maori culture that is new and never before experienced. Such a visitor can genuinely enjoy the dexterity of the performers and the spirit in which the performance is given. In short, existential authenticity lies in a state of 'being'. However, there exists, too, the existential authenticity of the performance. This example has, however, several levels of analysis. The Maori people of

Rotorua have been involved with the tourism industry for more than 140 years, and have established their own traditions of performance and guiding (Ryan, 1997). Former guides are remembered and honoured by the *Te Arawa* people, and thus the tourist performance has come to take on its own authenticity as being part of an unbroken tradition of several decades. In short, the meanings of 'authenticity' have been re-examined and found to be complex. Heron (1990) argued that any interpretation creates its own selections and choices, some of which are associated with the norms of professionalism adopted by guides, interpreters and others associated with the sustenance and presentation of cultures. Wang (2000) therefore suggests two other forms of authenticity, objective authenticity, which is conformity with the original, and constructive authenticity; which is the authenticity projected on to the toured objects by the tourists and producers of tourism images.

Fifth, there has been a re-investigation of the evidence. For example, V.L. Smith, in her investigations of Inuit people and the skinning of seals modified her interpretations of practices of public and non-public seal skinning between the first and subsequent editions of *Hosts and Guests* (V.L. Smith, 1989; Smith & Brent, 2001). Similarly Aramberri (2001) revisits Greenwood's work and asks, where is the proof of the claims made? Additionally Aramberri advances the example of a similar Alarde held at Irún, where, in 1997, the mayor cancelled the march because of disputes between the traditionalists and those supporting feminist claims to permit women to be involved in the march. What, he asks, is the value of authenticity when it is based on division, dubious ancestry, and who is selling what to whom? By its nature, culture is vibrant, changing, and exists in world of commerce.

Ryan (1997, 1999c, 2003) and Ryan and Huyton (2000, 2002), in a series of studies of tourism associated with Maori and Australian Aboriginal people, question the use of the term 'authenticity'. In the case of tourism based on the culture of indigenous peoples, they argue that its use has hindered analysis of the key issues. Cultures, it is argued, are continually subject to change, and to seek compliance with some perceived 'original' raises the issues of stultifying a culture, creating stereotypes, and indeed of passing initiatives to the promoters of tourism product. The key issue is, they argue, who authorises the performance, and it is suggested that the term 'authorisation' rather than 'authenticity' should be the subject of analysis. Is the performance within the control of the indigenous people? Where does the power lie? Who receives the income and what levels of income ? These are more meaningful questions than whether a performance is 'authentic'?

The Tourist as 'Outsider' or as Guest

While wanting to delve into the backroom, to experience that which is perceived to be close to the original, the tourist may be defeated by a combination of factors. The first is that, while the tourist may have this wish to understand the host society, it is but one of a number of wishes, and relaxation and other motivations may have priority. Second, the tourist usually has only a limited amount of time, and hence must use the intermediaries available to him or her, and such intermediaries may promise understanding of the host society and culture, but may themselves be tangential to it. Third, the tourist is caught up in what Pearce (1982a, 1982b) has termed, a 'tourist environment.' Pearce argues that the characteristics of the tourist environment are that it has a highly transient population, has been physically modified to facilitate inspection of the locale, and has a structure to control visitor accessibility. These physical attributes foster the feeling of being 'a tourist'. Essentially what is this feeling? It can be argued that it consists of sensing that one is an 'outsider', and of being immediately recognised as such. Arguably the sense of being a tourist is not strongly felt in mass tourism centres such as Torremolinos or Benedorm, but is in fact more keenly sensed in the less-crowded areas, in the areas perhaps visited by few tourists. Perversely, in the areas of mass tourism, especially those popular with one's own nationality, the sense of being an outsider may be only marginally felt. The shops, places of entertainment, and accommodation are filled with people with whom communication is easy, and with whom there are shared conventions and sets of expectations. In such cases the tourists experience the sense of being 'outsiders' only if something goes wrong and they come into contact with the legal or medical systems of the host community.

It can be argued that there is a continuum that moves from being a 'tourist' to being a 'guest' and potentially a 'friend of a local resident'. This is demonstrated in Figure 5.1. A sense of being a tourist can be engendered within the context of 'The Mass Tourist' (Cohen, 1974, 1979). The tourist is but one in a coach party, just one of many staying in a hotel. Often tourists seek to establish their identity, as is evidenced by the need to strike up a relationship with the waiter who usually serves their table. But the waiter has seen such attempts every week of the summer. Accordingly identity is often established with other members of the holidaying group, and thus the sources of satisfaction are found in communication with fellow holidaymakers and not from contact with the host community. The desire, if it was at all strong in the first place, to relate to the host society is displaced by this activity to meet the needs of belonging. Dann (2000) in his study of older British tourists staying on the island of Mallorca, provides ample evidence of these people creating their own spirit of community and resistance to the structures imposed upon them by the holiday package. Indeed, Dann's comments on the treatment of these visitors make one wonder about the nature of the holiday experience. Thus he writes:

> Reference has already been made to the clinical features of *La Paloma Blanca*. The admission procedures tend to substantiate this impression. On admission .. all-inclusive customers have plastic bracelets affixed to their wrists similar to those applied to hospital patients. The bands have expiry dates on them and are generally worn on and off the premises. (Dann, 2000: 85)

Given the institutional arrangements of this 'holiday', it is little wonder that guests revert to playing a role of 'us against them' – and indeed Dann proposes an extension of Ryan's (2002d) analysis of time on holidays by asking whether 'these senior tourists ... (are) having the time *of* their lives, time *for* their lives or are simply doing time?' (Dann, 2000: 91).

From the viewpoint of those who serve the tourist, the tourist is but part of an anonymous, amorphous mass. The situation begins to improve when the tourist manages to establish some personal identity with the supplier of a service. In this process the tourist becomes a customer; there is a recognition of individuality, albeit on a formal basis. Some tourist environments permit this. The hotel waiter can get to know those he serves, the receptionist can recognise the hotel guests and call them by name. Those who serve in local shops can recognise their customers. On the other hand those who receive tourists at tourist attractions by the busload will have little opportunity to relate to their visitors in such a way. Indeed, a criterion for

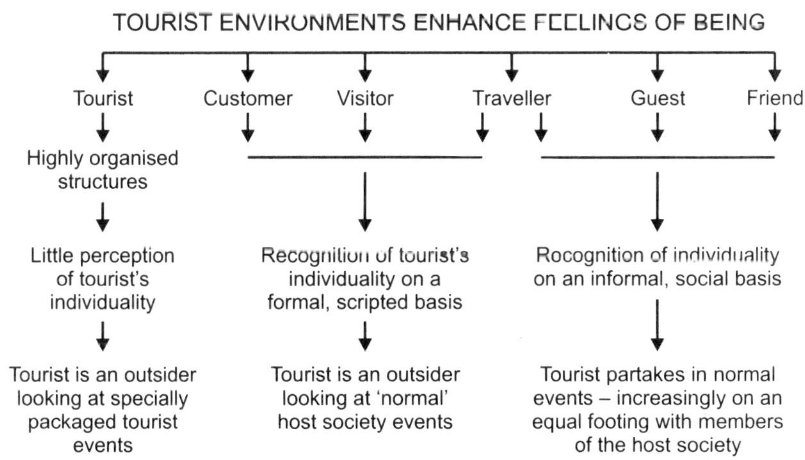

Figure 5.1 The tourist–guest continuum

the success of such visits is whether the tourist feels that a relationship has been created by the tour guide. At the same time, as the tourist goes shopping, uses local transport, perhaps goes to the local theatre or cinema, or uses a restaurant, he or she engages in the same type of activities as many of the host society. In consequence, those that serve these activities, whilst they may treat tourists differently from local people, have constraints imposed upon them by the fact that both tourist and local person intermingle more closely by sharing the same physical space.

For many tourists, a reason for continuing to return to a given destination is that they have established a relationship with local people and a friendship has developed. Increasingly they become part of a local community, even if for a short time. It might be said they are part of, but not from, the host community. For many tourists a highlight of the holiday is talking with 'local people'. A perverse phenomenon may be observed about such contacts. The middle-class tourist frequents a bar and is drawn into conversation with a 'local', who often is a manual worker. Upon returning home, the tourist will talk of the conversation and the insights that it gave him or her into the host society, and perhaps even into 'life' itself. The irony is that whilst at home that tourist would not normally frequent the company of manual workers.

Aramberri (2001) objects to the emphasis that tourism scholars have placed on host–guest relationships on the premise that a romantic nonsense is being perpetuated and the realities of most tourism encounters are being ignored. First, most tourist encounters are not with indigenous peoples. They are, quite simply, with other tourists or with the intermediaries of the tourism industry. Aramberri also argues that most tourism is about visits to locales of similar nature to those from which tourists come, and thus:

> The host-guest paradigm cannot be used to account for most types of what is called tourist behaviour. Excluded from the visual field are all the interactions that do not take place between members of pre-industrial communities and denizens of developed societies. (Aramberri, 2001: 745)

However, Aramberri's own observations are not beyond criticism. First, it might be doubted that the notion of tourist–host interactions of the kind described by Smith (1977) was being advanced as a theory to explain tourist behaviours. Rather, they were instances of specific types of circumstance relating to impacts on host cultures, not a general theory of holiday experience. Second, Aramberri's critique seems peculiarly blinded to the very things that he wishes to espouse, namely the nature of everyday interactions between tourist and host. Instead he seems to concentrate on a selective reading of a supposed academic position, which to this author is not representative of most of what written about tourism.

It might be said that, as with any experience, events do not take place in isolation from other events. The tourist experience results from a set of behaviours, which themselves may be dictated by a set of antecedent conditions interacting with intervening variables. The tourist arrives at a destination with a set of expectations and motivations shaped by socio-economic variables, and his or her knowledge and perception of the area. The location itself is an information transmitter with an infrastructure of facilities, transport networks and contact points that influence an individual's wishes, desires and subsequent behaviour. Equally, the time constraint and the abruptness of changed circumstances have their role to play in determining the tourist experience. The holiday may have been long anticipated, and there might be an excitement about the travel and the arrival. This may be tempered by tiredness on arrival. Therefore, on arriving at a new location there is a process of recovery from the journey, followed by learning, discovery and an exploration of the immediate vicinity. Whilst this process of learning and discovery may last the whole of the holiday, it tends to be at its greatest during the initial holiday stages, and thus subsequently the latter part of the holiday might involve repetition of favoured behaviours. Towards the end of the holiday, thoughts of the return home occur, while other emotions such as regret that the holiday is drawing to a close might also be felt.

Tourist Learning and Behaviour

From this simple description, a number of hypotheses can be constructed about patterns of behaviour:

(1) there is a pattern of exploratory behaviour by the tourist;
(2) stress may be associated with the process of adjustment;
(3) environmental learning of that thought to be important by the tourist occurs relatively quickly; and
(4) behaviour is determined in part by anticipation of enjoyment.

The first observation to be made is that initial anticipation about the nature of the destination and the existence of a time-constrained holiday period on the one hand can create an eagerness to learn and explore, while on the other hand it can generate an intolerance of what is perceived as inferior service. Both perhaps are aspects of a desire for immediate gratification of wishes. The first couple of days of the traditional package holiday are often characterised by certain sets of behaviour. The first day is spent in both recovering from the journey and checking the immediate environment. During this checking a process of comparison takes place. The expectations about the actual hotel and resort derived from past experience, hearsay or the travel agent's brochure will be used to measure the perceived reality of what is found. Expectations may be met, surpassed or disappointed. Often the first night of the stay is characterised by a group of tourists discussing initial impressions, and these might not always be favourable compounded, as they might be, by the remnants of tiredness from the journey and the process of adjustment. This adjustment process is not simply one of a change of venue, but a change, however temporary, of life-style. During the second and third days, it can be hypothesised that in many cases a misplaced confidence can occur. It is during this time that the holidaymaker may lie in the sun too long, and so become sunburnt, or eat or drink too much, and therefore suffer with upset stomach or a hangover. Past travel experience can of course inhibit such negative practices, but such behaviour patterns would be readily recognised by many travel couriers. After a few days, exploratory behaviour takes the tourist further afield and, by the beginning of the second week of the typical two-week or ten-day holiday, favourite venues are being established, whether they be tavernas, scenic spots, restaurants or discos. Thus by the end of the holiday, a greater predictability of travel patterns might be established.

Is there evidence to support this type of observation? Evidence of the predisposition for minor illnesses comes from Pearce's (1982a, 1982b) study of Australian holidaymakers on the islands of the Great Barrier Reef. The study sample was asked to record minor illnesses for the fortnight prior to the holiday, and then those that occurred during the holiday. These Pearce divided into three categories. 'Tension symptoms' (feelings of anxiety, headaches, nervous irritability and the like) were felt by a third of the sample prior to the holiday, but these symptoms declined through the holiday so that by the fourth, fifth and sixth days only 8.6% of the sample of 300 recorded such feelings. On the other hand there was an increase in 'viral symptoms' (colds, coughs, stomach upsets etc.) so that by the same period a third complained of these. And just over 60% complained about stings, insects bites, skin rash, sunburn and similar 'environment shock symptoms' by the end of the first week's holiday. The nature of such illnesses will be in part determined by the age and social characteristics of the tourist, and the degree of difference between the physical components of the holiday environment and that of the tourist's home. Nonetheless, the reality for many holidays is that they are indeed characterised by minor complaints (usually associated with food, sun or drink) that can mar enjoyment. However, in recounting the story of their holiday to friends and peers upon return (which process is itself part of the enjoyment of the holiday), such illnesses are either conveniently forgotten, or become part of the story of adventure. Few will actually admit to not enjoying their holiday.

Evidence for the exploratory patterns of tourist travel also exists. For example, Cooper (1981) mapped the travel patterns of a sample of tourists to the island of Jersey. Within the first day the great majority of visits (75%

approximately) were of St Helier, the capital and the hotel. Only a small proportion went touring on their first day. On the second day St Brelade's Bay became a popular destination, and it was not until the fifth day that the tourists were reaching Plemont. Also by this stage of the holiday travel patterns were becoming more dispersed. Similarly Elson (1976) traces the 'recreation activity space' of visitors to the south coast of Sussex in England. The coastal resorts of Brighton and others account for 90% of the reported visits, whilst only 20% visited the northern parts of the county. In consequence travel patterns by visitors can be established, and it does appear that there are temporal aspects to such travel activities.

Guy and Curtis (1986) studied the speed with which tourists make perceptual maps of the holiday destination by observing tourists visiting the town of Wurzburg in West Germany. The results were scored on four variables, the number of items mentioned, the correct identification by name and the correct function and location. The researchers concluded that:

> Overall, the results of the exploratory research parallel expected patterns. First, it appears that environmental learning takes place relatively quickly. Fewer tourist sites were added to maps over time than business or retail items suggesting that perhaps most touring activities occurred early in the visit. Shopping and retail commerce activities evidently remain stable or increase as the tourists' stays lengthened.
>
> Experience did indeed function as the primary correlate of environmental learning in terms of scope, accuracy and detail. (Guy & Curtis, 1986: 163)

In another study of tourist learning about place, this time of Coffs Harbour in Australia, Walmesley and Jenkins (1992) asked tourists to draw maps of the resort zone. It was found that the longer the stay the less detailed became the maps as the longer-stay tourists tended to concentrate on those landmarks that were of specific interest to them. Those who had not been in the resort so long tended to identify more geographical locations as they were still engaged upon a process of site discovery. As might be expected, the maps drawn also reflected the main types of holiday activities being engaged in. For example, there was a higher incidence of locating certain fast-food outlets among holidaymakers accompanied by young children as compared with those without such companions. Many of these types of studies are heavily dependent on the initial analysis offered by Lynch (1960), one of the first modern geographers to look at perceptual mapping. He found that five elements dominated such maps: paths (channels of movement), edges or boundaries, districts (zones of identifiable character), nodes or foci of travel and landmarks. Pearce (1981) also found that the experience of travel had an important impact on the creation of perceptual maps. For example, drivers had a better and more detailed recall of routes than did their passengers.

One of the factors that may influence travel patterns in terms of determining the number of sites visited is social class. Cooper (1981), in an analysis of numbers of sites visited, found that professional classes were more likely to visit a greater number of sites on a holiday trip. In his sample, over 40% of social group AB visited more than 9 sites, compared with 34% of group C1C2 and less than 28% of group D. Various hypotheses can be put forward as to why this is the case, but the travel pattern is partly the result of an interaction between motivation, expectation, accessibility and promotion. Moreover, the recording of such travel behaviour is not in itself a measure of the strength of any one of these individual factors, but rather of the synergy arising from combining these variables. Social class plays a role as education shapes an awareness of site possibilities and income generates the means to access those sites.

During the 1990s there was a growing interest in health and accident studies relating to tourists and their experiences of place. Initially much of the interest in travel medicine stemmed from an interest in the epidemiology of diseases, motivated in part by the relationship between travel and the incidence of AIDS (for example see the work of Cossar *et al.*, 1990, and the subsequent publication of the books edited by Clift & Page, 1996, and Clift & Grabowski, 1997), but subsequent work has analysed the causes of death and accidents amongst tourists. The growth of these interests is signified by the establishment of a *Journal of Travel Medicine* and the Centre for Risk and Tourism Management at the University of Queensland under the directorship of Professor Jeff Wilks. For example, Wilks, Watson and Faulks (1999) reviewed evidence and their own past research into the causes of motor accidents involving tourists in Australia and made a number of recommendations as to ways in which such accidents could be diminished. Many of these would require quite significant changes in practice on the part of customers and car rental companies, and being pragmatic the authors changed some of their original proposals. However, some possible practices are simple to carry out – for example providing a tape or CD that can be played in the car and provides useful information on patterns of driving and rules of the road in the host country. That car accidents are a leading cause of mortality amongst tourists is confirmed by the work of Page *et al.* (2001), who also provide a useful summary of the literature on this issue for the period 1985–1999. Unfortunately, although estimating that the costs of accidents involving overseas tourists from 1992–1996 came to about $NZ21 million in New Zealand, the authors conclude that 'there appears to be little interest from the public agencies and the tourism industry' that tourist road accidents are a real problem' (Page *et al.*, 2001: 522). In another New Zealand study, Irving (1999) estimated that accidents involving tourists accounted for a work load equivalent to about 27 general practitioners. The nature of these accidents has also been analysed. For example, Bentley, Page and Laird (2000) comment that, while the risk of serious injury is very small, higher incidences of minor injuries such as sprains and bruising are not uncommon, and tend to be associated with activities that involve the risk of falling from a moving vehicle or animal. They cite activities such as cycle tours, quad biking, horse riding and white-water rafting as being those most likely to result in injuries to participants. Observation at any ski-field will also show that broken limbs are a measurable risk with this form of tourism. Other studies have looked at tourists as victims of crime and at the nature of insurance claims that are made (e.g. Ryan, 1996).

Espiner (2001, 2002) has suggested that one of the paradoxes of the contemporary age is that, while on the one other hand society increasingly reduces the risk that individuals assume through a range of measures including insurance, safety legislation and the need for tourism operators to adhere to standards of good practice and risk minimisation, and the more explicit messages of warnings that are required by legislation, on the other hand, adventure tourism has been growing in popularity. It can be observed that, like the term 'ecotourism', the term 'adventure' has been appropriated for marketing purposes, and covers a range of activities from 'soft adventure' to the hard core extreme activities requiring high levels of skill and expertise. Espiner (2002) suggests that more regulated societies give rise to a compensatory need for risk. Ryan (In press, b) nonetheless suggests that:

> ...what is required is the certainty of achievement – of being able to achieve within their limits a feeling of surmounting challenge. In consequence the commercialism of the adventure leads to the construction of an experience where both company and client play a game of shared disbelief. The company promises adventure and its accompanying risks while trying to ensure that risks for any given level of ability are minimal and that satisfaction is the outcome. Nature is 'coerced' into being a resource to satisfy the wants of escape, achievement, challenge and physical release required by the tourist. The tourist on the other hand wants to believe in that presence of challenge, but equally entrusts the company to deliver the means toward achievement. (Ryan, in press b)

In seeking to explain the paradox proposed by Espiner, it might be suggested that a mutual process of reciprocal responsibilities is being assumed by individuals and current society. The regulatory forces of legislation, concerns over worker safety, safe practices and the extension of those practices to tourists are designed to protect the provider of services from legal liabilities in the event of things going awry, subject to the caveat that the provider of services can show that all reasonable care was taken. This protects the interests of tourists, and in turn their responsibilities towards their dependents. On the other hand, the tourist assumes the responsibility to take due care and act responsibly by complying with the instructions given. In situations known to involve risk, then the tourist knowingly assumes those risks – that is, it is the duty of the operator to clearly convey and clarify those risks, but having done so the tourist excuses the operator from further liability. The paradox is more apparent than real; and is simply a recognition of more clearly defined positions of responsibility, albeit within a context that there is a need for higher degrees of explicit warning and consent than existed previously.

The Role of Expectations

Expectation and perception can be powerful determinants of satisfaction, but the direction between these two variables and satisfaction is not entirely predictable. Saleh and Ryan (1990: 327) observe with regard to guests' perceptions of hotels that '... it is imperative that guests' expectations be realistic and possible for the firm to deliver, otherwise an obvious gap in service quality is created'. The question arises as to how the tourist deals with the gap. The tourist may either feel dissatisfied by the shortfall between reality and expectation, so that the holiday or trip experience is perceived as having negative components, or a process akin to cognitive dissonance occurs. What takes place in many cases is a re-evaluation of aspects of the location, and changes of behaviour result from such re-evaluations. For example, holiday destinations have spatial components, and hence the holidaymaker can escape the immediate cause of dissatisfaction in two ways. The first is simply a geographic move away from hotel, beach, resort or source of dissatisfaction; the second is an associated activity change. Coupled with cognitive dissonance whereby the unsatisfactory hotel may now be perceived as being unimportant in the holiday mix because compensating activities have been initiated, the holiday may still be perceived as being successful. The determining factor as to which path is selected may be the commitment to the success of the holiday. As Kelly (1955) comments, behaviour is an anticipatory as well as a reactive factor. An example of this is given by Adams (1973) in a study of beach users in New England. When the weather forecast was one of 60% chance of rain, this information was interpreted differently by separate behavioural groups. Of those actually on the beach, 46% interpreted the forecast as meaning that it was likely or almost certain to rain. Of those that cancelled their trip, 86% interpreted the same data as being likely or very likely to rain, as against two-thirds of a control group who similarly interpreted the forecast. One interpretation of these findings is that the level of commitment to a given course of action (in this instance, going to the beach) meant reinterpretation of data. The reluctance to let unsatisfactory factors interfere with the enjoyment of the holiday is perhaps reinforced by the process of anticipation of enjoyment prior to departure. The anticipation shapes the behaviour, the behaviour changes the perception. Equally, therefore, the findings can be interpreted as meaning the actual behaviour was subsequently justified by offering a specific interpretation of the data. No matter which interpretation is accepted, what is operating is that actual behaviour is linked to selective interpretations of probabilities; that is, it is linked to expectations. Nonetheless the implication of any theory of adaptive behaviour in the light of destination- and interaction-specific variables, is that subsequent sources of satisfaction may have little to do with initial sets of expectations.

Furthermore, the above discussion implies at least two broad roles for expectations: namely that there are predictive and normative expectations. The former relate to what consumers believe will happen in the forthcoming consumption experience, while the latter relate to what they believe *should* happen. Given this distinction, the sources of expectation are important. Ryan (1999a) has argued that a reiterative relationship exists between past and current satisfaction, which in turn implies that the normative can be tempered by past consumption that influences the predictive. In short, while it is easy to conceptually make the distinction, the actual measurement of each one is very difficult. Yuksel and Yuksel (2001) argue that consumers use multiple interpretations in the same question set when responding to questionnaires and, indeed, may also be highly dependent on biased sources of information in the absence of others. Examples of such biased sources include information disseminated by service providers, or by informal sources such as friends.

The Interpretation of Experience: Cultural Capital and Preference

European, and particularly British, package holidaymakers might be said to have a love–hate relationship with the tour operators. They love the low-cost holidays when things go well, but hate the consequences when things do not go according to plan. In different years (for example in 1988, 1989, 2000 and 2001) issues have arisen over holiday airline schedules and their disruption. Strikes by air traffic controllers, or by Spanish coach drivers, have meant long delays at airports with little compensation being offered other than perhaps a meal voucher; meanwhile embattled airlines did the best that they could with aircraft in the wrong place at the wrong time. For several holidaymakers this caused high levels of dissatisfaction at two key points in the holiday process. First there was a delay at the very onset of the holiday. Expectations of an immediate departure were simply not being met. On the other hand, the very press coverage of the issue actually meant holidaymakers arrived at the airports expecting a delay, and hence 'small' delays of up to two hours were regarded as 'acceptable'. For those experiencing longer delays, it can be expected that encroachments were being made on valuable holiday time and hence higher levels of dissatisfaction were being created. This was particularly the case if only one week's holiday had been booked. However, upon arrival at the holiday destination, the pattern of the holiday would mitigate the initial bad impressions. But at such times the return home was also characterised by the same delays, and in many cases these were worse because return flights from overseas airports are often undertaken later in the day. This permits 'knock on effects' to lead to accumulated delays. It can be suggested that one requirement of returning holidaymakers is certainty of arrival time in order to meet family, the need to travel perhaps for several hours back home from the airport, and a requirement to get back to work. If delays are long, the very benefits of the holiday in terms of relaxation are undermined. However, one difference between events in the late 1980s and those of the early 2000s was that holidaymakers had better modes of communication with family and work colleagues back home through the use of cell phones. So there were fewer problems of worried relatives awaiting the return home of their loved ones.

The risks run by holidaymakers go beyond those of simply delay and inconvenience. Holidaymakers may be shot in 'exotic' destinations such as Thailand or Kenya, 'mugged' and have their bags stolen from their shoulders by young Mediterranean males on scooters, run the risk of being assaulted by fellow holidaymakers, or taken hostage by rebel groups as in the Philippines. Throughout 1988 and 1989, the trade press reported new airline policies of refusing to carry drunken passengers. By 2000 many airlines had put into place hard-line policies of suing passengers for any extra costs incurred by having to depart from schedules or for disruption to in-flight services and annoyance to other passengers.

At the other level, sources of annoyance simply include other tourists. Davison (1989, cited by Ryan, 1991a), reporting on the 40th anniversary of the British Package Holiday, saw fit to repeat Eric Idle's observations from a Monty Python sketch that:

> Herded into endless hotel Miramars, Bellevues and Continentals with their modern international luxury roomettes and Watney's Red Barrel and swimming pools full of fat German businessmen pretending they're acrobats ... Adenoidal typists from Birmingham with flabby white legs and diarrhoea trying to pick up hairy bandy-legged wop

> waiters called Manuel. So-called typical restaurants with local colour and atmosphere and you sit next to a party from Rhyl who keep singing 'Torremolinos, Torremolinos' and keep complaining about the food. (Ryan, 1991a: 42)

The truth of such observations is that the resorts that attracted the initial expansion of the Mediterranean package holiday came to be perceived by many, in the late 1980s, to be drifting down market, offering tacky accommodation and risks of interruption by boisterous if not drunken 'lager louts'. In resorts such as Torremolinos, at the height of the tourist season, it was not uncommon for 200 British youths to spend the night in a Spanish jail because of drunkenness and creating disorder (*Sunday Times*, 30 July, 1989; cited in Ryan 1991a) and over the intervening decades the pattern has become established. By 2002 several different 'reality television' programmes (particularly British ones) had followed the antics of hedonistic holidaymakers in locations such as Ibiza, the Caribbean and the Canary Islands. The fortunes and misfortunes of holidaymakers had become the established fare of several television series based on airlines, airports, coach line operators and specific locations. That such programmes were not only being made but also proving popular testifies to the images and importance of holidaying, certainly amongst the British. It is interesting to speculate why this has been the case. On the one hand there is the recognition factor among audiences, and a modeling or demonstration effect that holidays are periods of escape from norms of respectability; they are sanctioned periods of irresponsibility. Yet the image that comes across has a moralistic tone – for often these holidaymakers are shown as foolish, as clowns seeking a few minutes of fame. The holiday time is one of hubris; and shadows of carnival hang over the proceedings where respectability is overthrown. Arguably though, there is now a difference. The cultural values are those of 'laddism': live for today, hangovers are the norm, chicks or blokes are for bedding, and exuberant behaviour is the norm. The carnivalesque described by Rojek (1993) and other like commentators has now been commodified, packaged and sold to an audience for whom the holiday has become an extension of the Saturday night out with the lads and lasses – it is adolescent pub culture gone to the Mediterranean. However, there is another side to this particular coin. New, more serious television programming about holidays where comments are made about environmental impacts and a need to respect local cultures have emerged from the holiday review programmes of the 1980s.

There is perhaps a wider explanation based on Bordieu's (1978) concept of 'cultural capital'. By this term Bordieu meant that all consumption, including sports and leisure consumption, requires appropriate tastes and preferences as well as skills and knowledge. Cultural capital is a consequence of a socialisation process of upbringing and education, and thus varies by social class. He came to this conclusion when comparing the sporting activities and preferences of the French social classes, arguing that there existed 'prole' sports such as boxing in which the upper classes were not interested. An alternative explanation is that access to various sports, recreations and indeed types of holidays is determined by income, in other words by economic rather than cultural capital. Thus the more expensive types of holidays are accessible only to higher-income groups. However, such is the pace of social and technological change, that the world of the early twenty-first century is different from the more structured world of the French social class system of the 1970s. Package holidays can be found for almost all types of holiday, the hedonistic and the cultural, and arguably the price differentials are considerably less than was once the case. Second, the working classes are not necessarily lower-income groups, given the squeeze that has occurred since the 1960s on the incomes of many traditional middle-class occupations (for example, teaching in schools and universities). The growth of the entertainment and IT industries has also created high-income jobs based on skill, while the widening of access to higher education has meant that more people can gain those skills. Additionally the models of pop stars, soccer players and other entertainers, who are not notable consumers of 'high' cultural product (or at least, not as so reported by the popular media), legitimise more hedonistic ways of spending leisure time. Therefore, paradoxically, cultural capital in terms of preferred norms, becomes more important than economic capital in determining holiday choice and experience – yet the economic forces of the contemporary world commodify all types of experience, making, in terms of time and price, all types of holiday more accessible to all. Consequently, as discussed in Chapter 4, it is personal preference that becomes the most important determinant of holiday choice, and of the selection of criteria by which holiday experiences are assessed.

Bordieu's concept of cultural capital originated in a comparison of class structures and values, but it can be argued that culture has a specific role when holiday patterns are examined across different ethnic groups. There is a growing literature about cultural differences between cultures, particularly with reference to the differences between Western and Asian cultures. It has been observed for example, that Chinese culture places more emphasis on group travel, the importance of gift giving, and the different ways of interpreting courtesy and empathy (e.g. see work by Reisinger & Turner, 1997, 1998; Becker *et al.*, 1999). On the other hand, it has been observed that there are inter-generational differences between Asian groups, and that the younger ethnic Japanese and Chinese are more likely to share many of the same values as their western counterparts (e.g. in studies of backpackers, see Ryan & Mohsin, 2001). On the basis of interviews undertaken in hotels in Taiwan, Tsai, Ryan and Lockyer (2002) also suggest that the culture of service shared by hotels that aim at the models of best service as demonstrated by multinational chains, combined with the expectations of staff, management and guests, creates its own culture of service norms. Thus they found little reference being made to traditional Chinese values of *kuan-hsi* (personal relationship) and *mien-tsu* (face) in the service situation. For their part Master and Prideaux (2000) found no linkage between culture and holiday satisfaction in the case of Korean holidaymakers, while McCleary, Choi and Weaver (1998) found many commonalities between Americans and Korean business travellers in their assessments of hotel services. It is also evident from different studies of the Chinese market (e.g. Ryan & Mo, 2001; Yu & Weiler, 2001) that, in ranking various motives for visits to overseas destinations, the reasons given are close to those provided by other overseas nationals. Thus, for example, in visits to New Zealand, the scenic and 'fresh, green' values rank as highly with Chinese visitors as with Europeans and North Americans.

The Privileged Outsider

It can be suggested that there is an additional facet to culture and cultural capital – the culture of being 'a tourist'. Yiannakis and Gibson (1992) and Gibson and Yiannakos (2002) have suggested that tourists assume roles, while Ryan (2002a) has argued that holidays possess the potential for cathartic experiences. In short, the temporary exile from home and all that is associated with these temporary periods of freedom from the usual responsibilities creates a different set of norms by which people act. If, indeed, culture comprises sets of assumed values, behaviours and artefacts, then the paraphernalia of hotels, beaches and tours are the visible signs of a culture that is different from the norm. It is not new to suggest that tourists are marginal people (e.g. Cohen, 1982a; Ryan & Hall, 2001). In 1987 Cohen explored the relationship of tourist and the law by pointing out that the tourist is in an ambiguous position. The tourist is not simply a stranger, but is a *temporary* stranger. To a greater or lesser extent the tourist is a guest, but an impersonal guest. The result is that, given the context of the state of tourism development in the host community and the types of tourists being attracted, the tourist may be victimised as being a highly visible stranger ignorant of laws and customs. Alternatively, the tourist may be given preferential treatment, with ignorance being treated as an extenuating circumstance for minor infringements of the law. Cohen (1987) also argues that the mass organised tourist will be less exposed to local criminals and will enjoy the protection of the tourist establishment and the law-enforcing agencies. The drifter may be more exposed to the local criminals but enjoy protection from the local community, even whilst, however, subjected to suspicion from the legal agencies.

An important component of the tourist experience is the quality of the encounter with the provider of a service, and in other industries this has increasingly been studied. Bitner, Booms and Tetreault (1990) explore the 'service encounter' through the use of critical-incident analysis in three situations: hotels, restaurants and airlines in the United States. They concluded that degrees of satisfaction and dissatisfaction arose within three groups of incidents, namely, employee response to service delivery failure, employee response to customer needs and requests, and the nature of unprompted and unsolicited employee actions. There were industry differences between the incidences of each of these incident types – for example most of the incidents in the restaurant industry were of the third type (unsolicited actions). Arguably, within tourism as a whole, it is this third type of incident that will be the greatest source of satisfaction or dissatisfaction, as tourists find what is to them out-of-the-ordinary concern for them as individuals, or possibly the opposite, marked rudeness because the tourist is perceived as an 'outsider'. Parasuraman *et al.* (1985, 1991, 1994a, 1994b, 1994c) draw attention to the gap between expectation and perception of the reality of the service as a source of satisfaction or dissatisfaction. The model they proposed, the ServQual model, was based on the dimensions of tangible components of the service, reliability, responsiveness, assurance and empathy. Additionally it comprised various gaps that determined the consumer gap wherein the quality of the service provided was assessed by a gap between client expectations and client evaluations of the experience obtained. The other gaps that needed to be assessed included the gap between management perceptions of what clients wanted and the client expectation, the gap between management expectation of service delivery and actual service performance, and the gap between service promised (for example, by the marketing messages) and the service performance. Such gaps shaped the consumer gap, or at least indirectly highlighted the operational constraints under which management would operate. For example, management might desire a given level of service performance based on its perception of what its customers wanted, but have to accept lower levels of service performance because of restrictions on supply capabilities.

This mode of thinking has had an important influence on the literature of services marketing generally, and has been widely adopted as a framework of analysis within both tourism and hospitality management. It possesses real value as a means by which management can identify areas of operational concern, but nonetheless there are conceptual issues that imply some limits on the practical use of the instrument. First, in its application to tourism it must to be noted that the tourist has more discretion over the nature of the service provision than in other service industry situations. Tourists can simply use other restaurants, visit other attractions and change their patterns of behaviour within a resort zone if they do not get the level of service they initially expect at one bar of restaurant. They can also switch into different roles. In short, the state of being a tourist permits a more proactive role over the period of the holiday than does the time-specific service encounter at any one retail store, bank, garage or restaurant. Second, what is meant by expectation and evaluation? How, it is asked, is an expectation being formed – is it against an 'ideal' level of service, an 'acceptable' level or a level determined by past direct experience (Ryan, 1999a; Oh, 2001)? Third, it has been noted that much of the variation in the consumer gap is due more to the evaluation scale than to the expectation scale. The gap correlates highly with the assessment of service, thus raising the question as to whether the gap is needed at all as a measure of service quality (Teas, 1993, 1994; Ryan & Cliff, 1996, 1997a). Indeed, in 1994 Parasuraman, Zeithaml and Berry amended their initial scale by increasing it to 9 points to increase discrimination and by re-allocating some of the items to different dimensions (Parasuraman *et al.*, 1994a, 1994b, 1994c). Possibly most important of all, they attempted to measure 'a zone of tolerance' by introducing a third measure – that of 'expected service'. Unfortunately, the questionnaire became much more cumbersome and time consuming for respondents.

An alternative approach can be recognised in the work of Csikzentmihalyi (1975) and Csikzentmihalyi and Csikzentmihalyi (1988) and Voelkl and Ellis (1990), who argue that in recreational pursuits the degrees of satisfaction to be obtained are determined by the dimensions of challenge and skill. If the challenge exceeds the level of skill, dissatisfaction results, with a reduction in participation. If skill exceeds challenge, then boredom results. However, if both the nature of the challenge and the level of competency an individual possesses are congruent, then a condition of flow occurs, as represented by the diagonal line in Figure 5.2. While initially designed to explain the nature of intrinsic motivation and satisfaction where individuals such as painters could work as hard as any high-earning executive, but for much less financial reward, the concept has been utilised by researchers in the fields of leisure, recreation and sport. Within the touristic setting it has been used in examples such as white-water rafting in adventure tourism to explain the role of guides in shifting the competency levels of participants so as to better ensure a flow situation without engendering highly risky situations (Ryan, 1997b). From another perspective it might be argued that the flow situation is one of optimal levels of arousal, where enabling stress occurs. The person has a heightened sense of being, is in tune with the environment, and is reacting positively to any challenge. This model has immediate application not only to certain types of holiday

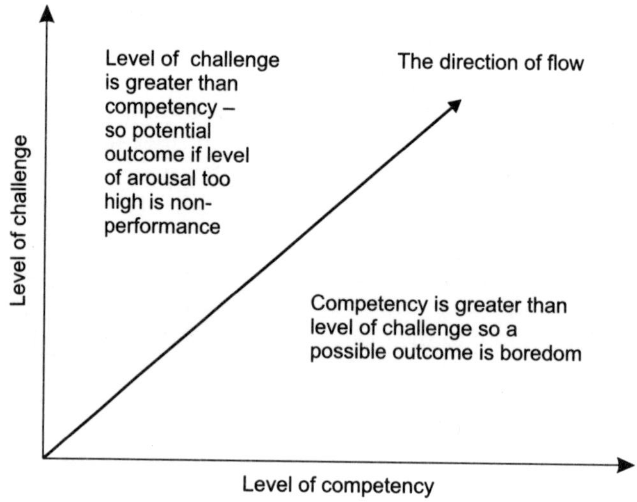

Figure 5.2 The condition of 'flow

activities based on hobbies and sports, but could also be adapted to cover certain components of the travel experience. For example, passengers delayed in air terminals might be observed to pass through a process of arousal to anxiety to worry to apathy as they are initially frustrated by delays but eventually reach apathy because of an inability to control events (i.e. their 'skills' are not appropriate to the situation). Certainly these approaches open new avenues for research into the nature of the tourist experience.

The Quality of the Tourist 'Event'

One of the major activities undertaken by tourists is sightseeing. The quality of this activity has attracted criticism from a number of writers such as Boorstin (1962), Turner and Ash (1975), and Fussell (1982). Thus Boorstin writes:

> The multiplication, improvement and cheapening of travel facilities have carried many more people to distant places. But the experience of going there, the experiences of being there and what is brought back from there are all very different. The experience has become diluted, contrived, prefabricated. (Boorstin, 1962: 88)

To some extent these and other writers such as Rivers (1974a, 1974b) and

Morris (1987) decry the current tourist experience as not having value compared with the days of 'travel'. As has already been noted, adverse comparisons are made with the past, where the motivation for travel is perceived as being one of education and self-enlightenment. To some extent this view of the past may be a misconception. As Christopher Hibbert (1987) shows in his history of the Grand Tour, for many young men the highlight of the tour of Europe was not the culture of Classical Rome, but the adventure, spice and thrill of Venice, the brothel of the eighteenth century. The emptiness of the modern tourist experience is reputedly shown by what Boorstin (1962) termed the 'pseudo-event'. Thus it can be asked, what is the value of the visit to, for example, the 'Spanish Fiesta', where coaches bring several hundred guests from high-rise hotels to eat chickens barbecued and served with chips, to sing the anthem of the package holiday, 'Viva Espana', and to carouse with fellow holidaymakers of their own nationality. The Spanish influence is served and packaged without risk as dancers meet the desired stereotype, and the long wail of the *saeta* is not heard. For Boorstin this is a 'pseudo-event', a drama packaged for the tourist with little reference to reality. But, just as Boorstin perceives that it has little to do with a cultural experience of Spain, so too do many of the tourists. It has much more to do with different sets of values and norms, the norms of group consciousness and relaxation. The occasion is a pretence designed not to meet educational purposes, but to generate a 'good time', which parts the tourists from their money but leaves them feeling euphoric and good tempered. Perhaps more of a 'pseudo-event' are some of the very items celebrated by the middle-class tourist in their search for 'reality.' As MacCannell provocatively states:

> Modern museums and parks are anti-historical and unnatural ... not in the sense of their destroying the past or nature because, to the contrary, they preserve them, but as they preserve, they automatically separate modernity from its past and from nature and elevate it above them. Nature and the past are made a part of the present, not in the form of (an) unreflected inner spirit, a mysterious soul, but rather as revealed objects, as tourist attractions. (MacCannell, 1976: 76–77)

It can be argued that the value of the tourist experience is not that of the academic writer imputing a set of normative judgements to the situation, but what is felt by the tourist him or herself. In short, it is an issue of 'existential authenticity', as described above. The tourist brings to the situation and the site a set of expectations that interact with the site. The site itself is also not a constant with reference to the physical attributes of the situation. Part of the site is the weather and other conditions within which the tourist sees it. Thus, for the visitor to, say, the Alhambra in early spring on a clear morning early in the day, there is a magic that the visitor would not find in the month of August at 5pm when there are large numbers of other visitors present and the sun beats down mercilessly. Equally, the busiest hotel on the popular Costas can create different experiences for the tourist depending on the mix of people present, or the time of year.

Cohen (1979a) sets out a model of interaction between scene and expectation with reference to the authenticity of the event viewed. Essentially there are two dimensions, the tourist who views the event as either being staged or real, and the nature of the event itself, as being staged or real. Given the debate above about whether this concern over authenticity should possess the importance once attributed to it, the model may appear to have little current applicability. However, it might yet still have importance for specific types of tourism and tourists. If, as would appear to be the case, there is a minority of tourists (about 5–15% depending on definitions, see Chapter 9) for whom compliance with required norms of cultural or environmental legitimacy is important, it is possible to revert back to Cohen's model within this context. The model provides a four-cell matrix, as shown in Figure 5.3. Tourists with an expectation and need for authenticity or legitimisation as they perceive it will be dissatisfied if they find an 'inauthentic' event and perceive it as being such. Equally, if they feel an event to be staged, even where this is not the case, then low levels of satisfaction will occur. Cohen then develops the model for the tourist with a low need for authenticity/legimitisation, and indeed such a tourist, it may be cynically observed, has a higher chance of moderate degrees of satisfaction. But what are the clues that lead to these perceptions being formed, either correctly or incorrectly? Indeed, it has been argued that, as expectation shapes behaviour, tourists may indeed find themselves in the situation of obtaining high levels of satisfaction through having failed to identify the proceedings of a 'pseudo-event'! And what if the tourists, although

The tourist's impression of the scene

	Real, authentic	***Staged, inauthentic***
The nature of the event	Authentic and recognised as such. Result – high satisfaction	Suspicion of staging. Result – low satisfaction
	Failure to recognise the event as staged. Result – high satisfaction	Lack of authenticity is recognised. Result – low satisfaction

Figure 5.3 The link between authenticity and satisfaction

requiring authenticity/legimitisation, perceive the event to be false, but suspend disbelief and enjoy the spectacle on its own terms? This form of behaviour is found in many other areas of human behaviour, so why should it stop when a person becomes a tourist?

It is right to be concerned with quality of tourist experience, but the quality of that experience is not dictated by whether or not the event has an elitist meaning, as seems to be implied by writers such as Fussell, Boorstin and others. Nonetheless, historically, their viewpoint has had a significant impact on the literature of tourism, and to discuss the 'authenticity' of the tourist experience is in itself a reflection of their impact, for it discusses the issues on the terms they espouse. It is perhaps only in the period since about 1990 that commentators have been more critical of the terminology, and it might now be argued that a new orthodoxy has been established that perceives the issue of authenticity as requiring considerably more sophistication than was once the case. Today, it is a cliché to argue that the quality of the experience is dictated by the needs of a tourist, the quality of the provision of the service and the management of the tourist area. There is nothing intrinsically wrong with a desire for relaxation. The tourist can enjoy the experience of the fantasy as portrayed at theme parks, and can equally enjoy the packaged insight into native culture as carefully sanitised by native groups performing in the bars of multinational hotels. In both cases the tourist does not leave behind his or her critical faculties, and recognises that both are forms of 'show business'.

This approach permits more realistic appraisals of the problems of tourism. As Krippendorf (1987) observes, the holiday experience itself exhausts. The holiday resort is just a backdrop, often the reality of package-holiday tourism is that the tourist is surrounded by the familiar – the same people, the same nationality. More importantly ' ... we drag with us the problems of our towns and present them to our hosts – the traffic problems, air pollution, noise, metropolitan architecture, alienation' (Krippendorf, 1987, cited by Ryan, 1991a: 46). Whilst the packaged show of culture can be rationalised in that its objectives are limited to simply those of entertainment and generating an awareness of the traditions of a culture, it arguably fails to achieve the latter limited purpose when it distorts the culture of the hosts to fit tourists' stereotyped images. For example, Pettifer (1987) argues that to show bare-breasted African female dancers in Muslim areas of Africa is a reflection of the culture of the tourists, not that of Africa.

In the 1980s it was increasingly being argued by academics that this was a perverse presentation on the part of the tourism industry. Enthused by the emergence of a middle-class broadsheet press and television media that adopted a tone of 'responsible tourism', and partly in recognition of the growing popularity of a 'green' environmental movement, it was argued that tourists simply did not want this form of 1950s Hollywood style clichéd presentation of an exotic other. That view can still be found today, in for example, the claims being made by Boniface (2001) that a new spirit of tourism exists. Yet even as organisations such as *Tourism Concern* were being created to voice this way of thought, some criticised the perspective as ignoring the realities of the success of package holidays, and of advocating inappropriate solutions. Notable among such critics was Wheeller (1990, 1993). In 1993 Wheeller coined the expression 'ego-tourist' in an analysis of ecotourism as simply the taking of tourism to previously unspoilt areas, and as being inappropriate as a solution of mass tourism by simply ignoring the nature of that tourism. For Wheeller, ecotourism was simply an additional form of tourism designed to smooth the fragile social sensitivities of readers of the left-oriented press who wanted holidays with like-minded people in destinations where they would not feel packaged or guilty. The irony, of course, is that these tourists still used many of the services of the distribution chain, used polluting means of transport and then initiated the process of the destination lifecycle, which meant many previously small communities would become engaged in tourism growth.

Many claims were made about an emerging new sophistication on the part of tourists, and it can be argued that that is indeed true, but not perhaps in the manner understood by academic commentators of the late 1980s. It was true that tourists were experienced at being tourists. They had seen the peep shows and the imitations and, especially as they were not limited to one holiday a year, were clearer in their expectations and wants. In particular they wanted well-managed tourist resorts that permitted choice and flexibility of arrangements. The need for such management was, and continues to be, a two-sided need, for the host environment also needs similar care if it is to maintain the qualities that attracted the tourists in the first place. However the situation today is that the tourist, as Urry was to note in 1990, is such a sophisticated animal that he or she could engage in game playing. The modern (or should that be post-modern?) tourist is a collector of places and experiences, and can happily collect both the peepshow and the natural, unspoilt place that is offered by the ecotourist. The tourist is a willing participant in the creator of meanings devoid of their original context. The impact of films and their relationship to tourism is of specific interest. Do, it might be asked, the tourists who visit Alnwick Castle in Northumberland visit the home of the Percy Family (a significant family in English history), or do they seek to familiarise themselves with the original location of the game of quidditch from the film of the mythical *Harry Potter*? The castle, which incidentally has been used in many different films (including *Elizabeth* about the sixteenth-century English queen of that name), offers, legitimately, both stories – and both can be enjoyed by the tourist. The meanings of tourist space are not simply those associated with the history and structure of a place – meanings are not simply dominated by the 'supply' side of the equation. Meanings are the consequence of human thought, and such consequences are the outcome of a dialogue between message signifier, sender and recipient. The recipients, in this instance tourists, therefore bring to the place their own perspectives, interpretations and experiences, and use these to direct both the search for and the interpretation of messages for their own purposes in what they see, hear and do. Accordingly, tourists are capable of utilising both the 'older forms' of tourism and the 'new, alternative' products. Both types of products are simply 'experiences' created by capitalist systems into which the tourist as consumer buys, adopts, modifies and uses as he or she sees fit.

Generating Tourist Satisfaction

Are there any possible links between the elements of the above discussion? What is being implied is that there is a process between initial perceptions of destination image, consequent expectations, subsequent behaviours, and derived satisfactions. This link is contextualised through interaction with and between the intervening variables presented by the location, and the way the tourist responds to these variables. The response is a two-stage process. There is initially a series of conscious and unconscious adaptations to the destination that are subsequently expressed through sets of behaviour. These behaviours are generally directed by a wish to achieve satisfaction, but the ability to adapt to the gaps that might exist between the original perception and the actual experience becomes a determinant of eventual satisfaction or dissatisfaction. The antecedents of expectation creation prior to the trip are based on an interaction of personality and other attributes of consumer behaviour as tourists respond to the images that are created of the destination, their own past knowledge and experience and their assessments of the marketing efforts of the destination promoter. The nature of travel to the destination may, at least in the initial stages of the holiday, colour perceptions. Was it, for example, a trouble-free journey? During the first days of the holiday, the tourist will learn about the resort and what it has to offer. Gaps may then exist between expectation and reality, but the nature and seriousness of the gap depend both on the perception of the problem and the internal processes of adjustment. Part of this process depends on the possession of certain skills, for example social and adaptive skills. The result is that a series of behaviours are engaged upon that have has their objective the creation of a satisfactory feeling about the holiday. The level of satisfaction achieved in turn becomes feedback in the system in that it shapes knowledge for the next holiday.

This process is reflected in Figure 5.4, which highlights the role of the personality of the tourist. Personality is a factor that helps formulate motivation and sets of expectations, as indicated on the left of the figure. The

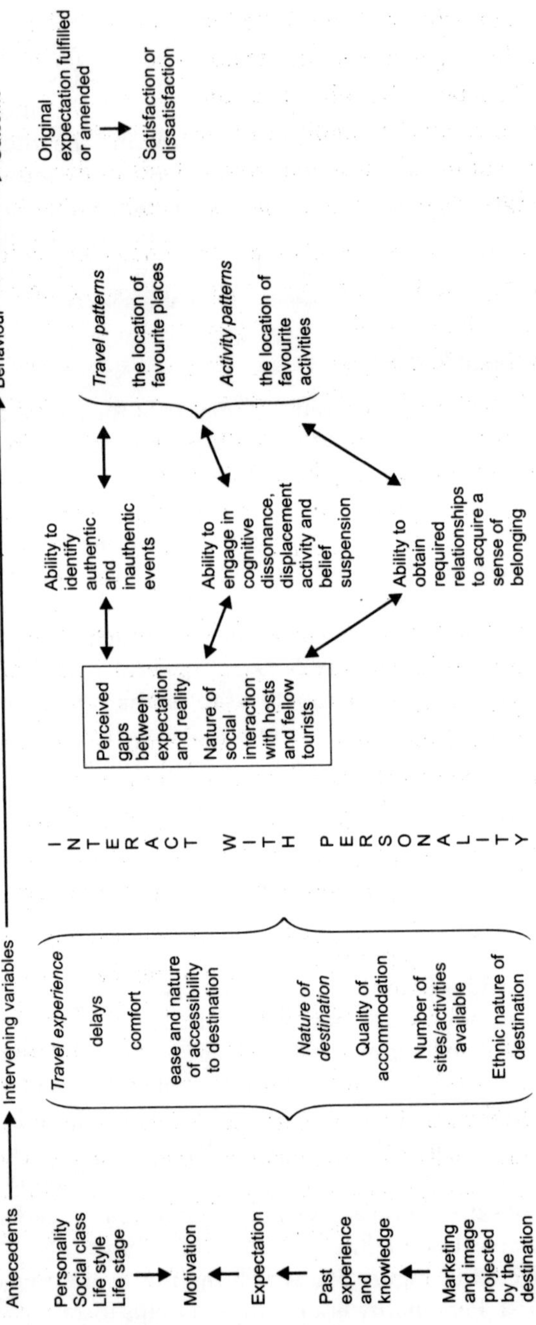

Figure 5.4 The link between expectation and satisfaction

interaction of the personality with the travel experience and the nature of the resort area both generates perceptions of gaps between the resort zone and expectations, and also governs the nature of interactions with others. But then certain social and psychological skills also come into play in the sense of being able to perceive authenticity, suspend disbelief when required, and conduct positive sets of relationships. These attributes help shape travel and activity patterns that permit the fulfilment of the original or amended expectations, and hence create satisfaction. Tourists do not therefore assume a passive role, but utilise all the social and psychological skills that they normally exercise within their home setting, and actually engage in goal seeking, purposive behaviour – the goal being the generation of a satisfactory experience. (Those who are interested can read a fuller explanation and derivation of this model in Ryan, 2002e.) Indeed, the cynic might say that it is this ability to generate a 'good time' out of the sometimes substandard accommodation provided by tour operators in the past that has in fact produced the high satisfaction rates recorded by Lewis and Outram (1986). Thus, they record that the flight was on time only in 27% of cases, in 23% of cases good food was not available, and the courier was not readily available in 30% of recorded cases. On the other hand, the weather was good on 95% of occasions! In total, 54% of the respondents agreed that there were some disadvantages to their holiday, and yet 69% also agreed with a statement that they would advise their friends to go on the same package holiday. The authors conclude that the data analysis indicated a high level of overall satisfaction among the respondents with regard to their package holidays. To which it can only be observed that, in view of late flights, a high chance of poor food, and experiences of some drawbacks, this indicates a high value placed on convenience and, it may be argued, a strong level of determination to enjoy the holiday.

Chapter 6

The Tourist Resort Zone

In seeking to analyse the tourist resort area it can be said that four approaches exist. These are:

(1) *The descriptive approach.* Essentially this consists of creating an inventory of facilities and assets possessed by the tourist area, and describing them. The description might also extend to a description of the tourists' perceptions of the area.
(2) *The explanatory approach.* This considers the patterns of travel and rates of usage of facilities within the area, and attempts to explain them. It notes the nodal points within the area, the routes taken by tourists between these points, and the mode of travel used. It seeks to establish the patterns of tourist travel and behaviour within the area.
(3) *The predictive approach.* If it becomes possible to establish patterns of usage within the tourist area, then by definition it could become possible to make predictions as to not only future patterns of use, but also the future shape of the tourist zone. The predictive studies of an area are thus concerned with trend analysis and the spatial interaction between attractions within the zone.
(4) *The prescriptive approach.* Forecasts in themselves are of little purpose unless used for management strategies in establishing priorities of use. In the case of tourism, the establishment of priorities requires a series of normative judgements, for the assets that are being used are natural habitats and social groups and, possibly fragile, non-renewable assets with limited carrying capacities. In consequence, the structure plans of planning authorities contain prescriptions as to use in terms of zoning levels of activity within the tourist resort.

In practice these are often overlapping approaches, for the descriptive should lead to the explanatory, and so on, and thus any given technique may serve more than one purpose. It will be argued that analysis of tourist resort areas is a complex task, for the tourist zone is not static in either spatial or temporal terms, and in addition there exists an inter-relationship between the attributes of tourist attractions and the types of tourists being attracted.

In describing the tourist area there is commonly a need to undertake an audit of the attributes of the area, and Gunn (1979, 1982a, 1982b) suggests a cartographic approach in his studies of Texas and Canada. Nine variables were identified; water resources, flora distribution, climate, topography, history, aesthetics, visitor attractions, service centres, and route network. Each of the nine variables was mapped, and the relative importance for an area of each aspect was assessed by distributing 100 points between the variables. The process can be simply completed by creating a series of overlay maps which then highlight areas or features with the scores indicating greatest importance for tourism. Two immediate problems arise with this approach. The first is the boundaries of the area. Usually a political or administrative area is studied, but of course tourist use does not always recognise such boundaries, and the tourist zone may overlap different administrative regions. In consequence, a second approach may be adopted, and that is to undertake some perceptual or cognitive mapping that consists of asking tourists to draw maps indicating the tourist attractions as they seem to them, and the spatial relationship between these facilities. Whilst both approaches establish boundaries, the problem of the stability of those boundaries still remains. However, to ask tourists to undertake perceptual mapping of an area does begin to quantify an answer to the question of how strongly the area is perceived. The detail and accuracy of answers become a measure of how clearly delineated the area is, and by implication, how 'mature' a tourist attraction it is.

Today, the mapping of such features and the tracing of tourist movements are much easier than in the past. Advances in geographical mapping and information systems combined with maps derived from satellite images and positioning now permit much more detailed cartographic analysis than in the past. Some industries have become heavy users of such facilities, including the utility industries that need to map gas pipes and electricity lines. Within tourism-related industries, different national parks systems around the world have quickly adopted the use of such technologies, which are used to plot changes in zones of vegetation, fire damage, geomorphological features and so on. It is evident that such mapping permits zones to be delineated much more accurately than in the past, and thus there are implications for tourism where zoning is used as a form of visitor control. For example, Delaney (1999) uses the situation of a proposed new marina development as an example of GIS (geographical information system) predictive modelling. If there is a raster grid cell layer for land values, it becomes possible to mathematically derive the changes of land values by using a distance decay curve. (A raster grid is simply a zonal analysis where the final grid is the sum of the previous grids, and is illustrated in Figure 6.1. So, for example, in the bottom grid the value of any one cell is the sum of the previous overlays.) Additionally, a common use made of cartographic modelling is where overlays of different land uses are developed to identify zones within which permitted or non-permitted activities might be allowed.

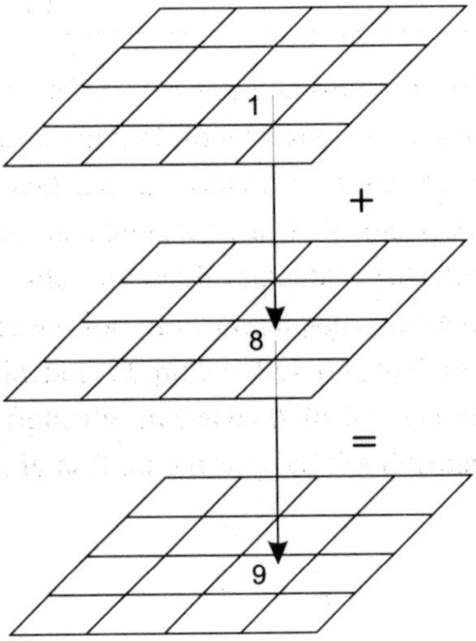

Figure 6.1 The development of raster grids for zonal analysis

One of the examples of current GIS applications in tourism has been that of Forer and Simmons (Simmons & Forer, 1996). In a series of papers, they applied GIS to data derived from New Zealand's domestic and international visitor surveys which request, among other data, lists of destinations visited. They have used these data in the mapping of New Zealand tourism flows with computerised maps that include more than 2,400 different place names. The analysis is, it is argued, of practical use for both government and industry. For example, the maps clearly show that German tourists in particular are being drawn to the west coast of New Zealand's South Island. Given the country's regional economic policies and the wish to develop new sources of employment for the area as employment associated with logging declines, policies designed to extend the stay of such tourists could have economic benefit. From an industry perspective, it is possible to interrogate the GIS database to find where visitors travel immediately prior to visiting any given destination. It is argued that this might have practical implications for a more optimal distribution of marketing literature to tourist information centres; more optimal in terms of deriving advanced bookings for accommodation and activities. The potential benefits of such earlier booking include not only possible increased revenue, but also better planning and more cost-effective allocation of resources to tour groups.

The Changing Nature of the Tourist Destination

Young (1983) and Miossec (1976), amongst others, have indicated how the tourist attraction may change over time. Young, writing of the development of a Maltese village into a tourist resort identifies a six-stage process, as shown in Figure 6.2. Initially the village is in its early 'traditional stage', and its traditional economic functions still provide the main sources of income for the village. Second, comes the 'late traditional' stage, which is characterised by the arrival of some summer homes and, in Young's model, by the arrival of a police station, which represents a need for higher levels of security, perhaps for the winter period when the summer homes may be empty. In many of these models, as will be discussed in Chapter 9, on the social impacts of tourism, there is often a supposition that one is considering the arrival of foreign tourists, but this is not necessarily the case. Indeed in many instances tourism is first developed by nationals of the country where the tourist resort is located, these being the first to identify the tourist potential of the location. Thus, for example, in the island of Majorca, it was the wealthy classes from the capital, Palma de Mallorca, who built their villas in the north at Alcudia and Porto de Pollensa. In Young's model therefore, it can be hypothesised that these summer homes might belong to fellow Maltese escaping from Valetta.

The third stage in Young's model represents the period of 'initial tourism exploration', where tourist rooms and guest houses are being established. The tourist area is now slowly beginning to change its shape and area. The summer homes have been built on the perimeter of the village, thus extending it. The guest houses may be creating a process of change of use of village buildings. This is certainly the case in the fourth stage, the period of 'early tourism involvement'. The village might now be showing some signs of the wealth accruing from tourism. In Young's example, a new church has been constructed; this is not only a symbol of new wealth, but is also a continuation of traditional priorities. But the tourist complex has also arrived, based on a new modern, luxury hotel. The original homes that faced the harbour are being purchased, and their original use has changed as they are used for souvenir shops and other enterprises based on the tourism trade. Hence into stage five – 'expanding tourism development'. A 'planning zone' has by now been created to cope with the increasing demands on land. This demand comes from at least two sources. There is continued expansion of hotels and villas, and the village is also expanding as it needs accommodation, schools and medical facilities to meet the demands of a larger population; the tourist industry will either have attracted migrant labour, stopping the past patterns of outward migration, or will have attracted back those who previously had left their village in the search for work. Finally, there is the stage of 'intensive tourism consolidation'. By now there is little that resembles the original fishing village. The very harbour itself will have become subject to a 'redevelopment plan' and is now a marina where luxury yachts have replaced the wooden fishing boats of the past. It is, nonetheless, a past rediscovered and packaged for

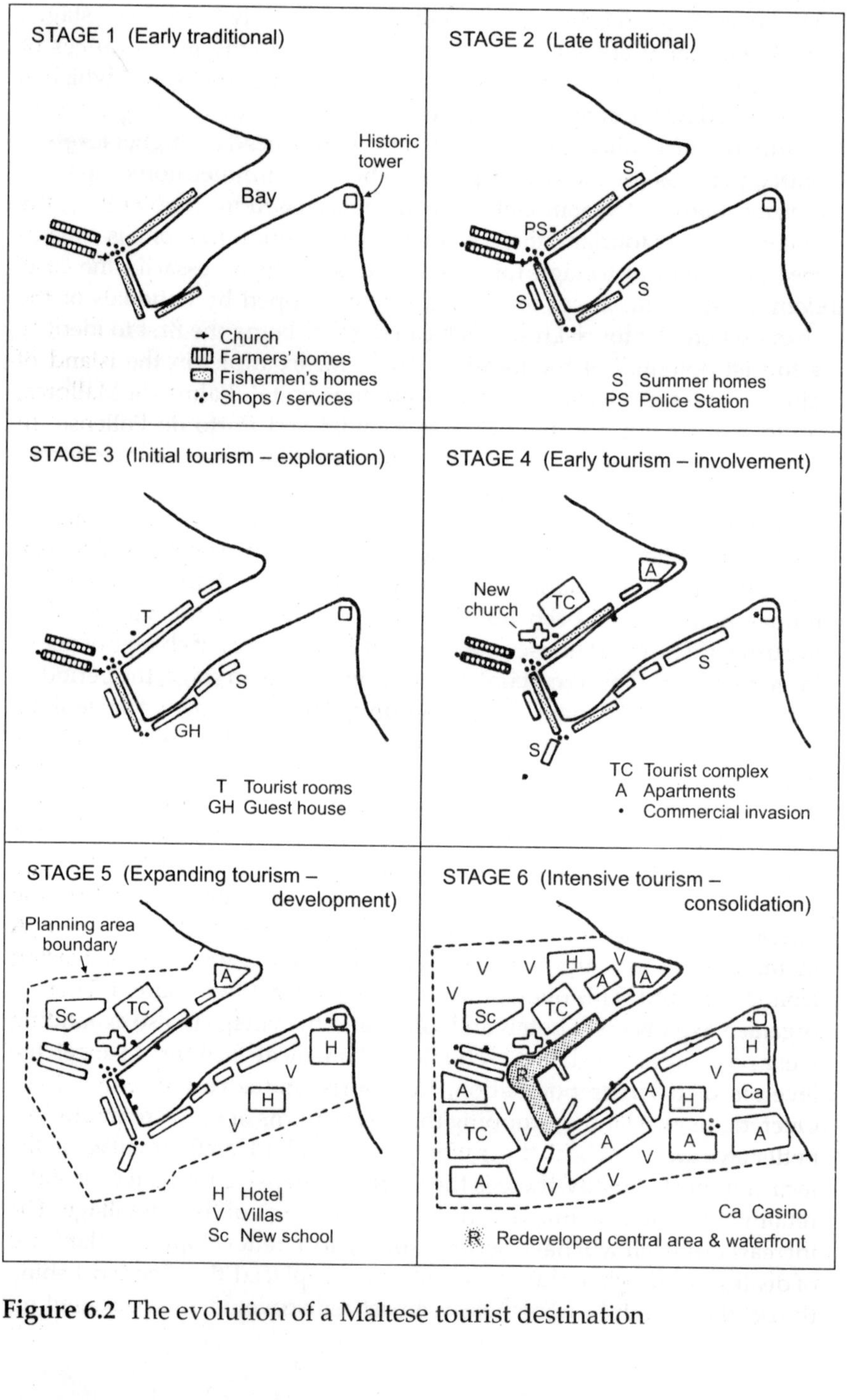

Figure 6.2 The evolution of a Maltese tourist destination

tourists through the celebration of a 'fisherman's day' and the establishment of a marine museum. A casino helps to attract an international jet set, and the rationale of the whole complex is tourism; it has no other purpose. Thus the tourist resort has developed, and as Miossec (1976) points out, the resort now has an image of its own. It is no longer perceived as being part of, in this case, Malta, with the images that tourists would associate with Malta, but now is clearly delineated in the mind of the tourist as being an area in its own right. Thus, for example, Benidorm or Torremolinos are no longer 'Spanish' in their image, but rather something else. The tourist resort area thus undergoes a change in terms of its area, its prime functions, and even its image.

In essence what has been described is 'a lifecycle' of the tourist resort area, and associated with each stage of the resort's development are different numbers and types of tourists. In the early stages, the supposition could be that if foreign tourists are involved they are not only few in number, but tend to be explorers as defined by Cohen (1974), or Plog's allocentric tourists (Plog 1977, 2002). As the numbers grow, so the early explorers leave, to be replaced by perhaps mid-centric tourists, until in the stage of maturity these too are being replaced by psychocentric tourists. There are many changes associated with the resort lifecycle. For example, it is possible to distinguish a changing pattern of business ownership and the intrusion of external capital over time. Initially the tourist industry is likely to be dominated by small, local businesses. Local families will hire out their rooms in bed-and-breakfast style accommodation, perhaps the wealthier will speculate by purchasing land and building holiday homes for let. A need will emerge for publicity material and perhaps the local authority will respond by helping to establish and fund a local tourism association. However, the association will soon find that it is dependent on external bodies to disseminate its material to the tourism-generating markets, and it will begin to find itself immersed in a system of commissions, inbound tour operators and overseas holiday companies. Should it be successful it will increasingly need to access more capital, which will require borrowing from financial intermediaries or establishing partnerships with outside organisations. There can come a point where those outside companies will feel a need to exert more direct control so as to better ensure service quality levels for its own clientele, or to maximise their profit from local operations. Over time, the better-financed external business organisations will be better able to buy the prime spots of land or indeed to change the whole local focus of business and geography by building larger hotels, complexes, retail malls and the like. Local businesses, according to this scenario, are increasingly marginalised, spatially, financially and operationally in terms of dealing with visitors that come from outside the region. The marketing of the destination now lies in the hands of businesses that are primarily non-local; and it is they who manipulate and manage the image of the destination and decide those types of visitors to whom they will market the destination. Of course, some local businessmen will have done well from this process, but even they will, for the most part, be dependent on the marketing effort of others.

A significant issue is that, if a resort becomes dependent on external sources of finance, marketing and resort development, then it can effectively become a prisoner of market forces that are oriented toward gaining a rate of return on investments made. Part of Butler's (1980) original thesis of a destination lifecycle was that resorts can experience a slowing of the rate of growth of visitor numbers, and indeed reach a position where these numbers consolidate, and then stagnate. If the numbers of visitors become static, and this is associated with constant numbers of bed nights and expenditure, then the implication is one of declining profitability as entrepreneurs need to finance refurbishment and enhancement from steady, but non-growing, revenue flows. There exists the danger that cost-reduction policies will be followed, and this can take the form of a declining level of service or a delay in refurbishment and non-delivery of product enhancement. The resort then faces the possibility of decline, particularly if new competitors emerge. Indeed Buhalis (2000, 2001) has suggested that, in the Mediterranean, package holiday companies have deliberately engendered competition between existing and emerging resorts so that as tour operators they can both indulge in product enhancement and keep accommodation costs down by threatening to switch demand through their own marketing efforts. One implication of this scenario is that, if external private sector finance is withheld from a resort, the public sector might well have to finance development, or manage the issues associated with resort decline. Accordingly local authorities will often adopt pro-development policies (e.g. permitting the development of marinas, casinos, resort complexes) to sustain the economic advantages that accrue from tourism, yet such policies inevitably create changes in the nature of the resort and the types of visitors being attracted.

There are certainly a number of studies that have examined changing patterns of locations and businesses over time. For example, Smith (1992) traced the changing land use of Pattaya in Thailand, to develop a beach resort model that has many commonalities with that described by Young. In short, initially buildings are clustered around the beach, perhaps around some key focal assets such as a jetty or a place suitable for the beaching of boats. Eventually buildings are built in a linear fashion along the beach front, and possibly service areas (for example, retail units) are then built back from the beach. In due course, a greater intensity of building occurs and there might even emerge a satellite business core that is built on the approach road to the emergent resort.

For their part, Kermath and Thomas (1992) analysed the geographical relocation of tourism businesses in Sosúa in the Dominican Republic and found that over a period from 1979 to 1986 almost half of the informal vendors had relocated. By 1987 foreigners owned approximately 75% of all tourism formal sector businesses. Similarly Debbage (1991) found evidence of growing degrees of oligopoly in the Bahamas with a spatial concentration of accommodation in the Nassau/Paradise Island area. In response to observations made by Haywood (1992) Debbage indicates that financial stagnation of the resort complex was very evident, as might be expected from the formulation of the resort lifecycle described by Butler (1980), which is described in Chapter 8. Haywood (1992) argues, for his part, that large multinationals often wish to encourage business diversification within a tourist zone, for a number of reasons. First, it represents some diversification of financial risk, and second, it permits complementary diversification of assets that add to the overall attractiveness of the tourist zone by creating new activities and attractions of a nature in which the multinationals have little business experience or interest. Haywood (1992) also suggests an ecological model of the destination lifecycle, arguing that it is one of the birth, death and changing numbers of businesses, each of which evolves different strategies for survival. Destination zones are dynamic entities, not simply systematic ones.

Further evidence for this is provided by Hovinen (2002), who examines one of the first applications of Butler's lifecycle theory. This states that destinations proceed from an exploratory stage to one of involvement with tourism to subsequent growth, consolidation and then possible decline or rejuvenation. In 1981 Hovinen applied this to Lancaster County, the site of the Amish communities in Pennsylvania. Returning twenty years later, Hovinen (2002: 227) concluded that 'Although Butler's proposed later stages of consolidation and stagnation do not fit well with the empirical evidence of Lancaster County tourism trends ... his model still provides a useful framework for description and interpretation in this case study'. Hovinen also comments that he found some evidence for the assertion by Russell and Faulkner (1998, 1999) that resort development cannot be explained solely in terms of logic and curvilinear relationships . There is a need to conceptualise the unexpected and the serendipitous in terms of the presence of 'movers and shakers', i.e. entrepreneurs who seek to break the mould in developing entirely new enterprises.

One debate about the concept of the destination lifecycle has been to what extent is it purely a descriptive process? Can it be used for management purposes – is it possible to make predictions based on past flows of visitor numbers? Haywood (1986) argues that an obvious method is to examine the change of visitor numbers from one year to another, and to plot such changes as a normal distribution with a zero mean to distinguish the stages of growth and decline of the resort. Wilson (1989) adopted this technique in her study of Scarborough, a mature seaside destination in Yorkshire, England, and she was able to distinguish, as Haywood suggested, six clear historical periods from 1761 to 1988, with stagnation commencing in the early 1950s. The same resort was studied by Cooper and Jackson (1989) and by Lundtorp and Wanhill (2001). Lundtorp and Wanhill develop a demand model of the resort cycle. In part they borrow from Morley's (2000) model of tourist demand by attributing an importance to previous visits, tourists' predisposition to return to the zone, and the word-of-mouth effect in recommending the site to others, so inducing them to visit. In consequence, at a period *t*, the market (*M*) will comprise those with knowledge of the destination (M_t) and those without ($M–M_t$). If *h* represents the velocity of dissemination of knowledge about destination D, then information will spread to $M_t \times h \times dt$ in the period *dt*. As more people get to hear of D, so the number represented by $M–M_t$ declines and the number who do know is represented by the relationship $(M–M_t)/M$. Therefore the total increase in the numbers knowing about D during a time, *dt*, will be:

$$dM_t = M_{th} \frac{M - M_t}{M} dt \, M_t < M$$

The solution of this differential equation is:

$$M_t = \frac{M}{1 + e^{-ht+c}}$$

where *c* is a constant. Lundtorp and Wanhill then assume that *c* can be defined as the velocity of information dissemination in the previous period, and this assumption permits the derivation of logistic curve, which replicates the normal curve associated with a destination lifecycle, as is shown in Figure 6.3 (which is simply a replication of Butler's original 1980 destination lifecycle). The curve is then applied to data about visitor numbers to two locations, namely the Isle of Man in the United Kingdom and Bornholm in Denmark. Lundtorp and Wanhill conclude from their studies that the destination lifecycle model fits observations fairly well in situations where there are high levels of repeat visitors. Otherwise it is an approximation to what actually happens, and furthermore 'becomes increasingly distorted ... to a point where the model collapses (Lundtorp & Wanhill, 2001: 962).

For her part, Agarwal (2002) approaches the issue from the perspective of supply of facilities, and emphasises the structuring of accommodation stock. Using the English seaside resorts of Minehead, Scarborough and Weymouth, she traces changes in accommodation stock, visitor numbers, visitor nights and expenditure. In her thesis she notes two forms of restructuring, namely product transformation, which is concerned with new product, and product re-organisation, which concentrates on enhancement of core product. Associated with each of these forms of restructuring are eight related strategies: product quality enhancement, diversification, repositioning, adaptation, professionalism, preservation, collaboration and product specialisation. Agarwal argues that these policies have been successful in the case of Spanish resorts, but, particularly in the case of Minehead, these strategies are failing because of a lack of finance. Additionally she suggests that in these instances restructuring is not occurring in ways that best create competitive advantage. It can be noted, however, that the conceptualisation of a rejuvenation phase in the destination lifecycle does not necessarily imply success. As Agarwal notes, but does not pursue in her article, the English seaside resort is now having to compete in a world of greater consumer choice, including short breaks in cities and longer holidays in warmer climates.

It can be argued that the model of the tourist destination lifecycle is but a model of what might happen if proactive resort planning, reinvestment and refurbishment policies are not adopted. A failure to engage in such approaches can lead to a decline in the resort – a decline that leads to a deteriorating asset structure that can attract visitors only by continuous price reduction, thereby impeding further the investment necessary to commence resort rejuvenation. Yet, equally, it is obvious that the changes being described here must have significant impacts on the social and natural environments, and these are discussed in subsequent chapters.

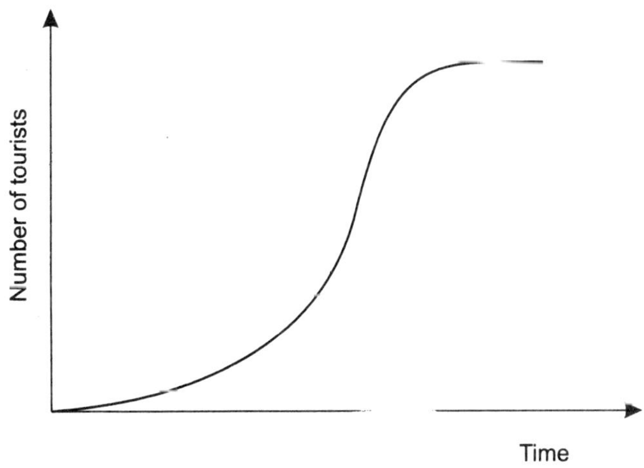

Figure 6.3 Possible pattern of visitor numbers to a destination
After Butler (1980)

The Role of Destination Image

To state the obvious, for a resort to develop, it must be attractive to existing and potential visitors. For those who have yet to visit the resort zone, the destination needs to project a positive image. The literature of tourism contains many studies of tourist place image because such images are important sources of information to potential visitors. Baloglu (1999) suggests a model of 'visitation intention formation' and argues that eight key factors exist: the variety and amount of information available, professional advice, word of mouth, advertisements, non-tourism books/ movies/news, escape/relaxation motives, knowledge and prestige. These eight factors impacted on visit intentions both directly and indirectly. They indirectly impacted by being utilised by visitors within a framework of past experience and evaluations of attractions, environment and values. It is evident that many of these factors can be summed up as having importance because they help the tourist formulate an image of the place. Gallarza, Saura and García (2002) review the literature relating to destination image, noting, for example, the different definitions of 'image' used by past researchers. For example, Lawson and Bond-Bovy (1977) referred to image as being an expression of knowledge, impressions, prejudice, imaginations and emotional thoughts that an individual has of a specific place. Reynolds (1985) defined image as a mental construct developed by the consumer on the basis of a few selected impressions among a flood of total impressions that comes into being through a creative process of elaboration, embellishment and ordering.

It appears that the image of any destination is (1) dynamic because it is subject to change, (2) often relativistic because generally a process of comparison is involved, is (3) multiple in nature, because it involves many different attributes and their evaluation, and consequently (4) generalisations about place do little to help in the promotion of any given resort. Two linked questions emerge. First, does any 'place image' *per se* possess degrees of commonality with other 'place images'? If image is relativistic and comparative, then this implies that common 'sets' exist within destination images, otherwise how else is image to be created and compared? Second, does the search for destination uniqueness mean, on the other hand, that in the final resort the image of any one place is solely unique to that place? If this is the case, then it implies that image of any one place cannot be assessed solely by the summation of, or product of, individual destination attributes, and that individuals perceive places as being both unique and sharing commonalities with other places. One of many such studies that sought to identify underlying dimensions was that of Russel, Ward and Pratt (1981). They found that four continua underlay affective images of place: arousing vs. sleepy, pleasant vs. unpleasant, distressing vs.

relaxing and exciting vs. gloomy. In a sense, therefore, this work predates, and reverses, the much-cited work of Echtner and Ritchie (1991), who discussed the issue of common functional attributes versus unique and psychological features. Certainly, as they and others have subsequently pointed out, most studies of destinations and places emerge with lists of attributes specific to the destinations being considered. For example, it is evident that seaside resorts will induce different sets of images from those associated with cities. It is also evident that images of the same place can differ among different sets of tourists, depending on the referential framework of the individual visitor. For example, in work commissioned by Tourism Auckland, Ryan and Cave (2002) adopted a process of open-ended questioning of English, Japanese and Chinese tourists to New Zealand and of New Zealanders from Wellington and Christchurch about their perceptions of Auckland. Using content analysis aided by textual analysis programs, they found that the different groups of respondents had quite different images of the same city. Additionally, even though there were commonalities between the Wellington and Christchurch visitors, nonetheless differences also existed. To summarise these differences the authors stated that for the overseas samples Auckland represented a comfortable urban escape from the world, while for the New Zealand sample Auckland represented the outside world being present in New Zealand.

That image can comprise a long list of attributes was shown by Seakhoa-King (2002) in the pilot study for his research into the quality of tourist destinations. Based on three methods of data capture (in-depth interviews, focus groups and open-ended questionnaires) he sought to capture what tourists meant by 'a high quality tourist destination'. The final list of attributes mentioned numbered over 100 and ranged from the vague ('all the activities offered at the destination are good') to the very specific ('the destination has a cheap taxi service', 'the destination has rubbish bins easily accessible to the tourist'). Echtner and Ritchie (1991) actually question whether it is possible to fully analyse and understand destination image as a concept. That it is possible to elicit lists of attributes of image from respondents is, however, demonstrated by a large number of studies in the literature. However, such lists may be time, place and respondent specific, which would raise the question of the durability of any image. In a sense, however, durability of image has as much to do with the dissemination of information about place, and the credibility attributed to the sources of information, as it has to do with the actual attributes of place. Issues of image have to recognise the potential for, at least in the short-term, the lack of congruence between place and image. For example, new destinations may seek to promote a certain image, but that image is unlikely to persist if the tourist experience is other than what is expected. One can only conclude that, while image of destination is important, it is also complex. It results from an interaction of visitor experience, promotional messages and actual physical and service attributes, the evaluations attributed to those attributes by actual and potential visitors, and is multi-dimensional, referential and subject to change.

Measures of Physical Attractiveness

One of the factors that follows from the above discussion is that, in describing the resort area, it is not sufficient simply to undertake an inventory of attractions. It is also necessary to have some measure of visitor perceptions. Some simple measures concentrate on the numbers of attractions that have a degree of 'uniqueness'. For example, within an area, however defined, if there is only one of something, then it might be that its uniqueness will call tourist attention to it and thus it becomes a heavily-visited attraction. Uniqueness can therefore be measured as:

$$U = \frac{1}{\text{Number of items having listed features}}$$

where U = measure of uniqueness.

The truly unique feature thus has a value of 1 (i.e. 1/1). It is possible to create a composite or aggregate uniqueness score where:

$$U = \frac{1}{F_1} + \frac{1}{F_2} + \frac{1}{F_3} + \frac{1}{F_4} \ldots + \frac{1}{F_n}$$

where $F_1 \ldots F_n$ are the features being listed.

The features listed may be separate features (e.g. the number of historical homes, churches etc.) or they may be aspects of a particular attraction. For example Leopold (1969) tried to create an index of uniqueness of rivers based on 46 variables representing physical, biological and human usage of rivers. A number of problems exist with this type of approach. First, there is the definition of the region, the numbers of competing regions, and the actual definitions and classifications of attractions to be adopted. The numeric value ends up as simply hiding a number of evaluative judgements. The second problem is the difficulty of interpreting the numeric scores that have in effect, been comparing the proverbial 'oranges' and 'lemons'.

For these reasons the uniqueness approach has been falling out of favour, overtaken both by better methods and by new technologies. Nonetheless it retains some value as a quick, 'back of the envelope' type of calculation. Another approach that has sought to quantify subjective assessments of geographical features has been the use of landscape photographs where respondents have been asked to 'measure' on various evaluative scales, the attractiveness of the landscape features (Fines, 1968; Smith, 1983). The result of such measures is that the derived scales can then be applied to other landscapes, thereby assessing the potential attractiveness of the landscapes or other tourist features. Amongst recent researchers who have adopted this approach are Fairweather and Swaffield (2001). In their work respondents sorted 30 photographs of landscape views of Kaikoura (New Zealand) on a scoring scale that ranged from –4 to +4. They were also asked to explain their choice. The scores were also used as data for a factor analysis, and from this it emerged that five themes underlie people's perceptions of landscapes and land usage: ecotourism, maritime recreation, the picturesque, family orientation and traditional coastal activities.

The problems associated with these approaches are self evident in terms of interpreting results, but there is a purpose to the exercise. As described below, one of the ways of predicting travel patterns within, or between, tourist areas is the use of spatial modelling, or gravity models, and such models require measures of 'attractiveness'. These measures of uniqueness etc. can therefore be used within the gravitational models. These are discussed in more detail below. Another approach, so far little used in the tourism literature, is that of hierarchical analytical techniques, as described by Saaty (1980). The premise behind hierarchical techniques is that it is difficult for tourists to rank or scale a series of features of attractiveness; but it is possible for people to make comparisons, and to say that one feature or facility is more attractive than another. Thus the respondent is presented with a series of pair-wise comparisons and asked to state whether the two items are of equal attraction, or one is more attractive or very much attractive than the other. It is as a result of these comparisons that a scale is developed. In his book, Saaty(1980) shows how the technique worked when respondents were asked to assess the distance of cities one from another. When used to quantify a variable, distance, where respondents did not possess an exact knowledge, the technique produced an answer that highly corresponded with measured distance. By inference, therefore, in cases where known measured scales do not exist, the technique produces a value that possesses 'objective' meaning. It is these scores that can then be utilised in spatial modelling. Unfortunately, the nature of the questioning required to use this technique becomes tedious for respondents, who are continually asked to make pair-wise comparisons between locations, and to assess, using given scales, just how much more attractive one may be over another. Once the list of destinations being compared is more than six, the numbers of such comparisons where all destinations have to be compared, one with another, means that respondents have to be well motivated to continue such assessments.

Other problems pertain to this approach. The image of a place, arguably (following Fishbein, 1967; Ajzen, 1988), consists of two components. The first is the belief about the place, and it is this that scales of attractiveness may be measuring. The second component is the importance of the belief. For example, it may be found that tourists rate an area as being very attractive, but still do not visit it because it is attractive on the basis of criteria that are unimportant to them. This may seem to be a perversity of human nature, in that the premise of attractiveness is that it 'attracts' people to it. But, to use Plog's (1977) typology, a psychocentric tourist may agree that the Amazonian Basin is indeed 'attractive', meaning beautiful, but would not wish to visit it. Equally, an allocentric tourist may agree that Banff National Park is 'attractive', but again would not visit it. It may be that the very word 'attractive' poses problems, and hence researchers need to be careful to distinguish between properties that actually 'attract/pull' tourists to them, and those that are perceived as being 'beautiful' but do not 'pull' the tourists.

It might be thought that the constructs of attitude towards what makes an area attractive or otherwise are complex, but researchers utilising the methods espoused by the American psychologist George Kelly have generally found that they are in fact comparatively few in number. Both Kelly (1955) and Allport (1961) argued that people attempt to make sense of the situations in which they find themselves, and in doing so create a list of elements (such as holiday destinations), and then seek to differentiate between them. This process of differentiation, the way in which two or more things are alike and thereby different from a third or more things (Kelly, 1955), thus forms a series of 'constructs'. Each construct is bi-polar, for the process of affirming something means that simultaneously something is denied. The third component of the attitude is the 'linking mechanism'. This requires a judgement of each element by the use of the construct. This 'linking element' is essentially revealed by the form of a 'grid' that might be measured through ranking, or as a list of dichotomous attributes.

Utilising the method is comparatively straightforward. Respondents are asked to indicate whether they like, dislike or feel unsure about certain holiday destinations. From each of the 'like' and 'dislike' lists, four destinations are selected, and to these is added one destination about which respondents might be 'unsure' or indifferent. The respondent is then presented with a group of three (a triad), compiled in such a way that they contain either two 'likes' and one 'dislike', or two 'dislikes' and one 'like', or one 'like', one 'dislike' and one 'unsure'. The respondent is then asked to select which is the 'odd' one out, and then to state why. The factor selected is the construct. Generally it is found that respondents will repeat themselves after a comparatively short time; equally, any given sample will generally produce a comparatively small number of constructs. The responses can be analysed by statistical techniques to find the underlying themes. From the viewpoint of practical research, comparatively small numbers of samples are required, approximately two dozen. Gyte (1988), in a study of British tourists to Mallorca, found that criteria being used to assess the attractiveness of the destination included: how good the beaches were, the variety of sites, host attitudes, whether the holiday was active or peaceful, the cost of the holiday, the scenery, the history and culture of the area, facilities, whether the destination was spoilt by tourism, food and drink, and the degree to which the culture was familiar or unfamiliar. Denis (1989) using a sample of Canadian students found similar constructs, with culture, climate, the degree of commercialism, scenery and familiarity accounting for most of the responses.

In another study, Pike (2001, 2002) applied Kelly's Triad to differing samples to better identify those variables thought important in short-break holidays. Among these were driving time, ability to visit more than one destination/attraction, beaches and other facets familiar to New Zealanders such as wineries and walking tracks. Bowler and Warburton (1986) utilised Kelly Grids to assess attitudes towards water resources in Leicestershire, and found that the attractiveness of the resource was assessed by scenic quality, leisure facilities, level of use, accessibility, size and the resource's 'naturalness'. The actual 'attractiveness' of the site to any given tourist will, however, depend on the type of tourist, and the requirements of the holiday. Thus, with multiple holidaytaking occurring, the tourist may want an urban setting for one type of holiday, and an unspoilt rural setting for the next. The same destination can therefore be both 'attractive' or 'unattractive' depending on the type of holiday that is required. In short, models that utilise measures of attractiveness cannot necessarily regard 'attractiveness' as an objective value without reference to the context of use. Nonetheless, such a measure is required when seeking to explain travel patterns.

Patterns of Travel Between and Within Resorts

Spatial models

One means of 'explaining' travel between locations and within locations has been spatial modelling, which owes its origins to Newtonian physics. The law of gravity can be rephrased to state, 'Two tourist areas attract trade from an intermediate (tourist generating) point in proportion to the size (attractiveness) of the centres and in inverse proportion to the square of the distances from these two tourist areas to the intermediate place.' Initially developed in the 1930s by Reilly (1931) to trace retail patterns in the southern USA, it can be expressed as:

$$\frac{T_a}{T_b} = \frac{P_a}{P_b}\left[\frac{d_a}{d_b}\right]^2$$

where T_a = the proportion of trade attracted by location *a* from the intermediate point
T_b = the proportion of trade attracted by location *b* from the intermediate point
P_a, P_b = populations of locations *a* and *b*
d_a, d_b = distances from the intermediate point to locations *a* and *b*.

From the viewpoint of initial work in assessing retail location, size of population was a sufficient criterion of attractiveness, but subsequent studies began to replace this with other criteria such as floor space or retail mix. Following, therefore, the redefinition of the concept by Huff (1966), the basic model became:

$$T_{ij} = \frac{A_j^a / d_{ij}^b}{\sum_{n=1}^{I} A_j^a / d_{ij}^b}$$

where T_{ij} = the probability of a trip from origin i to destination *j*
A_j = the attractiveness of destination *j*
d_{ij} = the distance between origin *i* and destination *j*
a and *b* are parameters to be empirically determined.

There are both practical and conceptual difficulties involved in the use of such models. The first is, what measurement of attractiveness is to be used? For example, in the case of Canadian tourism, Smith (1989) uses populations of areas on the basis that much Canadian tourism is prompted by visiting friends and relatives. Ryan (1999b), in a study of New Zealand conference centres, used the ratings of an expert panel to assess the attractiveness of such centres. In many cases the criteria of attractiveness are quantitative, and rarely attempt to utilise measures of subjective attractiveness, although in tourism one would expect images of places to play a role in determining travel. A second practical problem is determining the values of the parameters *a* and *b* to be used. One method is essentially a curve-fitting exercise, whereby the variables are applied to known data on travel movement, and the values of parameters duly determined. These values can then be transferred to a new situation. In undertaking this, reference can obviously be made to past studies, and with a computer the process becomes relatively easy. The conceptual problem can be essentially summarised as whether a law of physics, which has no reference to human behaviour or its motivation, can really be applicable to a subject such as tourism? Even if one does incorporate subjective assessments into the criteria used for measuring 'attractiveness', the question remains. Smith (1989: 113) refers to this question, and argues:

> This criticism was historically correct but is irrelevant, and is no longer true. Stewart (1948) and Zipf (1946) ... based their formulations explicitly on an analogy to Newton's law of gravitation. Although their models had no theoretical basis, it has been shown empirically that their models and various modifications that developed were successful or more successful in forecasting travel patterns than models derived directly from theory. Further, Niedercorn and Bechdolt (1966) have derived the gravity model from existing economic theory. They demonstrated that the gravity model is a logical and theoretically sound solution for the problem of maximising individual satisfaction subject to time or budget constraints. (Smith, 1989: 113)

Ryan (1999b), however, points to the significant amount of data that such models use, as the New Zealand study required travel time estimates between a comparatively large number of competing centres, and had to take into account car, ferry and air transport. Again, however, advances in computer technology and cartographic systems that incorporate travel times make such systems easier to use than in the past. A further point that needs to be borne in mind about the technique is that it has a tendency to over-predict short trips and to under-predict long trips (S.L.J. Smith, 1989; Ryan & Richardson, 1983). This tendency can be adjusted by using various weightings.

Mayo and Jarvis (1986) have some useful comments about the spatial/ psychological dimensions of space as they relate to gravitational models. The usual assumption is that distance is an inhibiting factor in travel, but this is obviously not necessarily the case. Mayo and Jarvis enumerate six factors that will influence inter- and intra- tourist destination travel:

(1) gravity – a force that stimulates travel, 'pulling' people to a destination;
(2) friction of distance – a force that deters travel;
(3) start-up inertia – a force acting to impede travel of any length, no matter how short;
(4) inertia of movement – a force acting to reduce the effect of friction of distance (i.e. momentum);
(5) subjective distance – a force stimulating travel beyond a certain point because each additional mile is perceived to be less than a measured mile; and
(6) the attraction of the far-off destination – some travel to a destination simply because it is far off.

They argue, on the basis of studies of perceptual mapping, that subjective distance increases proportionately less than objective geographic distance does, but that, as subjective distance increases, the attraction of the destination grows for the tourist. An example of this is Fiji. For many British tourists, Fiji would be an exotic destination, and they would not realise that it is in fact a built-up tourist destination catering for the Australian market. One of the possible implications is that, if gravitational models are being used to study movements between tourist areas, then perhaps the distance component within the formula may have to reflect the subjective distance as described by Mayo and Jarvis (1986). Another variable that may influence the pattern of travel, both within tourist areas and between tourist destinations, is that of travel time. If, as appears to be the case, in large urban areas that are also tourist attractions (such as London), the average speed of travel is 10 mph, then time becomes a consideration. It is also one of the perversities of modern flight that the time taken to travel from home to actually sitting in the aircraft may be longer than the time actually taken to fly several hundred if not thousands of miles. Travel time rather than distance *per se* might thus be the friction in the gravitational model.

Nearest-neighbour models

A related question is whether, in looking at a tourist area, the attractions are clustered or randomly distributed. Arguably random distribution is an inhibiting factor in tourist travel. A planning authority might therefore be seeking to locate new attractions in places that create logical travel patterns. The word 'logical', in practice, obviously requires careful definition. For the current purpose it might mean the location of attractions in positions that help engender tourist visits, alternatively they may be in positions that help protect fragile areas. Accordingly various measures of dispersal have been created. Ten patterns of dispersal can be identified; each of the ten in turn being based on combinations of patterns on linear, uniform, clustered, dispersed or randomly arranged formations. Figure 6.4 illustrates this.

Associated with each pattern is a range of values derived from various techniques such as nearest-neighbour analysis. This approach has been used for a number of problems as diverse as measuring distribution of flowers in a field (Clark & Evans, 1955; Pielo, 1959), shopping patterns in Nottingham (Whysall, based on cartographic analysis, 1974, 1989) and the provision of urban recreation facilities (Lovingood & Mitchell, 1978; Rolfe, 1964). When applied to tourism, the technique seeks to assess whether or not there is any order in the location of facilities.

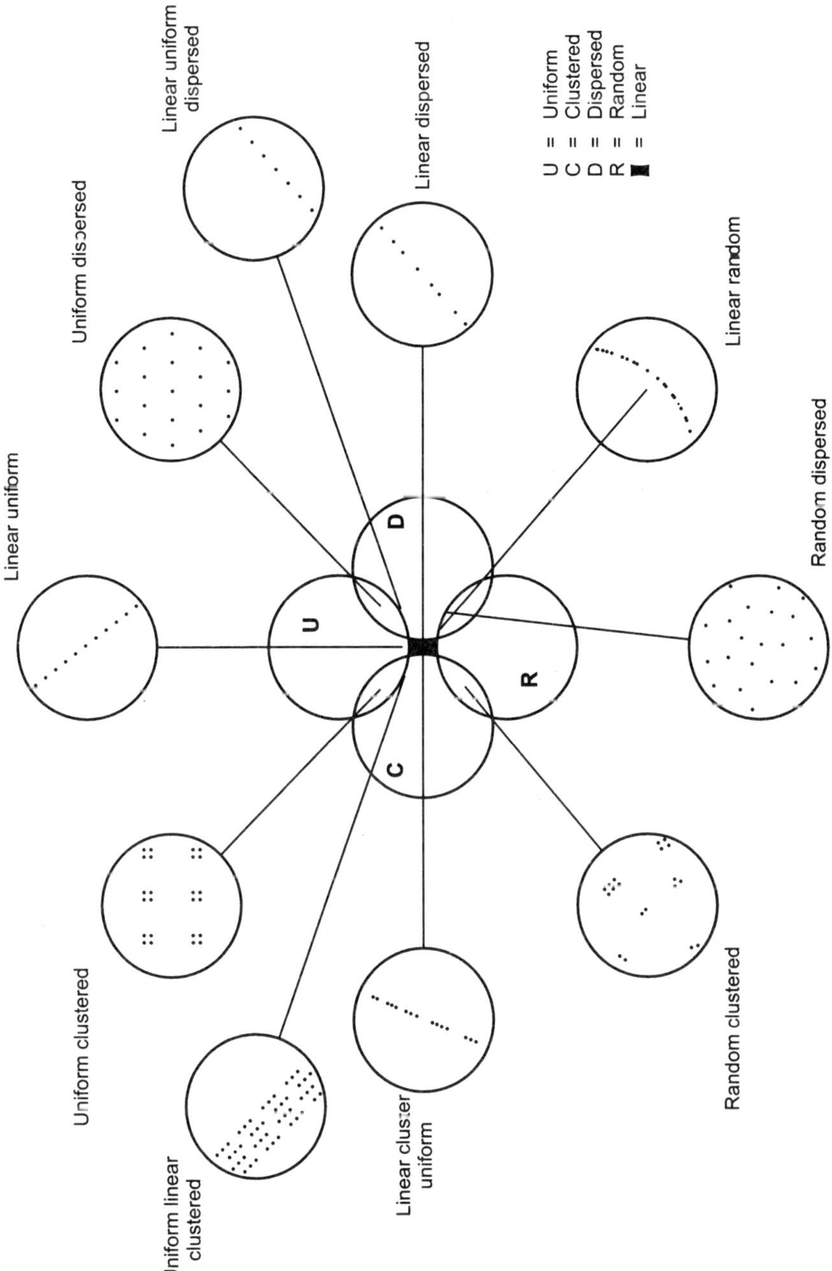

Figure 6.4 The distribution of spatial patterns
Source: Kariel & Kariel (1972)

Essentially the nearest-neighbour statistic is a ratio between the actual mean distance between neighbouring features, and the expected mean in a randomly distributed pattern of equal density. It can be expressed as:

$$R = \frac{R_a}{R_e}$$

where R = nearest neighbour statistic
R_a = actual mean distance to neighbour
R_e = expected mean in a random distribution of equal density

and R_e in turn is the reciprocal of the square root of the density of points multiplied by 2, i.e.

$$R_e = \frac{1}{2\sqrt{D}}$$

The calculation of density will in part depend on the nature of the shape of the area being considered. In looking at linear shapes, R_e has the value of $0.5(L/n\text{-}1)$, where L is the length of the line and n is the number of points or attractions being considered. Smith (1983, 1989) provides examples of calculations. The resultant value of the calculation can be compared to a series of known values. Thus for example, if $R = 1$ then there is a random pattern, if $R = 2.14$ there is a hexagonal pattern of Christaller's central place theory (1964). Should R have a value of less than 1, then a cluster is emerging, but above a value of 1, more uniform spacing is occurring. There are some criticisms of the approach. For example, in interpreting the result, some different patterns may be associated with the same value of R. Smith (1989) raises the point that it is important where the boundaries are drawn, as this changes the value of R_a. One might also question just how satisfactorily the technique deals with vacant or empty sectors. In addition, the technique is essentially concerned with pair-wise relationships within the area. Morisita (1957) and Whysall (1974) further refine the approach to overcome these objections by imposing quadrants on the area in question and looking at clusters within the quadrant. Morisita's Index of Dispersion is thus given as:

$$\text{Id} = qx$$

where $$x = \frac{n_i(n_i - 1)}{N(N-1)}$$

where q = number of quadrants
ni = number of quadrants containing i units
N = total number of units in the pattern.

Nearest-neighbour analysis thus becomes a planning tool in that it can be combined with gravitational models. The planner can not only look at the forecast probability of trips between locations or between attractions within the same tourist area, but can assess the logic of the location of the new site according its spatial relationship with others. In short, nearest neighbour analysis might help in locating a 'logical' location for a new attraction, and gravity models will predict the probability, and the magnitude, of flows of tourists to the new site.

It has to be admitted that the numbers of applications of such tools being reported in the tourism literature are few and, given the current direction of human geography and geographers' seeming obsession with post-modernistic interpretations of space, then it is unlikely that this situation will change. Indeed, even such a conventional geographer as Doug Pearce (who makes reference to gravitational modelling in his book, *Tourism Today: A Geographical Analysis*) confines nearly all of his examples to studies undertaken before 1990. Stephen Williams (1998), in his analysis of tourism geography, makes no reference to such modelling. Norton (2000) analyses the decline of spatial modelling, arguing that it was founded in a positivistic tradition, and was important in the 1960s and 1970s to the point where it dominated much of geographical thinking. From the perspective of the English-speaking world, it can also be noted that this was a period of rapid expansion in retail development with a need for studies relating to store and warehouse location, and was also a period of establishment of 'new towns' (particularly in the United Kingdom) with needs for spatial planning. Such models also lent themselves to the new computer-based modelling that was emerging. However, Norton states that in the final resort it contributed little to cultural geography, partly because it was perceived as dehumanising, and indeed Norton concludes that 'cultural geography has not been able to retrospectively single out any aspects of spatial analysis that might be of value' (Norton, 2000: 193). Hall and Page (1999) provide a detailed discussion of the contribution made by geography to the study of tourism, and in their own book *The Geography of Tourism and Recreation* (1999) provide examples of spatial patterns of distribution both of infrastructure and of visitor use of space. Yet, in the latter case, the most detailed case they provide is derived from the work of the late Sue Glyptis and her published study of visitors to Westwood Common near Hull, in the United Kingdom. Glyptis (1981), by her use of nearest-neighbour analysis, was able to demonstrate that visitors used only about 20% of the space available to them, that specific patterns of site usage could be discerned, and that carrying capacity was not a fixed entity. It might also be observed that even in the journal, *Tourism Geographies*, articles on gravitational modelling and its derivatives are notably infrequent, and thus it might be concluded that geographers are increasingly being seduced by new forms of analysis. Yet these new forms of analysis would appear to require a greater analysis of sociological, psychological and economic trends than those associated with traditional geography. It might also be asked why geographers want to deny their own traditional concerns with spatial relationships, geology and geomorphology where their skills have much to offer.

Econometric models

Nonetheless, the use of gravitational and related models, particularly if allied with GIS, makes it possible to forecast the effect of various changes on visitor flows. For example, any change in one of the variables within the model that relates, say, to attractiveness of the resort because of an enhancement to the visitor attractions, to a diminution of travel time because of increased accessibility or to changes in population can be assessed with reference to numbers of visitors to that resort. However, such modelling initially implies that the coefficients *a* and *b* are constant, which may not necessarily be true over longer periods of time. While these coefficients can be changed, there must be good reasons for alternative values. Additionally, if the forecasts are to be valid, it is probably necessary to disaggregate visitor numbers into different sectors based on variables such as interest, ethnicity, age and income, thereby again requiring very high levels of information. While not wanting to diminish the practical issues that surround the use of such models, examples of possible applications exist. For example, in 1992 the English Tourist Board introduced a computer-based model for examining flows of visitors to recreation centres and potentially to other sites (ETB, 1992). Based on gravitational modelling, the software permitted not only an estimation of clients' movements, but also, by incorporating revenue and cost estimates, extrapolated the numbers of visitors into revenue and cost flows.

Yet, in spite of such advances, the numbers of such applications are few, particularly when compared to the use of econometric modelling in forecasting international visitor movements. Reference has already been made (in Chapter 2) to some of the studies by Witt and Martin (1985) and Quayson and Var (1982). To briefly reprise their arguments, the validity and reliability of econometric models in tourism rest on a number of requirements. Technically problems such as multi-collinearity may have to be avoided, i.e. the variables perceived as determining variables will need to be independent of each other. This will be difficult to achieve. If, for example, exchange rates and real incomes are perceived as potential determinants of demand for tourism, there is a need to recognise that exchange rates and real income may in fact be linked variables in terms of their economic relationship. Adverse exchange-rate movements may increase the rate of inflation within a country by increasing the price of imports including consumer durables and raw materials, and increased inflation reduces real incomes, even whilst increasing the cost of overseas holidays. In the absence of countervailing processes, *ceteris paribus*, the demand for tourism would be expected to fall. But what proportion of the reduction in demand is due to adverse exchange rates or falling real income? Apart from these problems, for which there are statistical techniques to help, it has to be recognised that econometric models for tourism require large amounts of data. Even comparatively simple models might require data on the costs of transport, travel time and departure frequency (important for business travel), the characteristics of the destinations, the relative costs of activities at the resorts, socio-economic data about consumers, income data, exchange rates, and differential inflation rates between competing tourist destinations and the tourist generating countries. All these data will be required for each of the years under examination. A further problem then emerges, and that is the quality of the data. There are well-known problems with some tourism data. Hotel occupancy rates are a particular problem if the sample needs to be representative, because smaller hotels in particular may make returns infrequently. Regulations on the need to register guests may vary from one country to another. Theoretically the quality of this data should improve with an increasing adoption of computerised reservation systems that will print out tables of occupancy rates on demand. Data on international travel are also, in some cases, prone to what is in effect double counting. British tourists who land at Calais and proceed to drive into Belgium, then through Germany on their way to ski in Austria may be counted four times, even though the duration of their stay in France and Belgium may be quite short. Figures of cross-boundary movements may include shoppers who, living in the locality, may simply cross the border to take advantage of lower prices or tax differences. They nonetheless may be counted amongst the arrivals. The sampling points of cross-border traffic may be comparatively few in terms of not simply counting tourists, but seeking further data, eg on the purpose of the visit.

Implications for Planning

The above discussion has centred on such questions as, what tourist facilities exist, how they are to be described, what their components are, how attractive they are, what numbers of people are likely to come, what patterns of transport might emerge, and similar tactical questions. But it is vitally important to ask the strategic questions, how many tourists do we want and how many can the host environment sustain, both physically and socially? This requires a concept of carrying capacity, and a recognition that management of tourist areas is not simply a question of tourist promotion. There is little to be gained from increasing visitor numbers if the result of such numbers is an increasing hostility to tourists, and a downgrading of the very factors that attracted the tourists in the first place. The management of tourist resort areas requires that the tourist experience is enhanced even while the benefits to the host area are maximised and the 'dis-benefits' minimised. The product lifecycle of the tourist resort area as initially described would appear to have an in-built logic to growth and inevitable decline. The process is not automatic. The host community may in fact choose not to permit tourist development beyond a certain point. This is, however, difficult to achieve. It requires that the host community has some other sources of economic wealth that permit employment and income, or that the community has a strong cultural and organisational bond whereby it is able to dictate the terms on which it permits tourism, and is able to control its own members (some of whom will want to encourage tourism development). In many instances the cycle is not completed for reasons beyond the control of the community, for example tour operators might find other resort areas more willing to permit the developments they wish to foster. These questions will be discussed in more detail in the following chapters. They do, however, add another dimension to what is meant by the tourism area. The tourist resort area is not only a geographical entity that may change spatially over time, it is also a reflection of norms and attitudes that become expressed through the type of tourist development that is permitted. It is a cultural entity. The nature of the culture it reveals is a reflection of the strength of the host community norms and aspirations. Yet, even this truism, as Murphy (1978) shows, needs careful assessment, for it cannot be held true that the host community is homogeneous, and the tourist resort area often becomes a meeting place of different sets of values and concepts. In consequence, the tourist resort area is a catalyst of change, a physical reminder of questions about what a society wishes to achieve. The place where tourists play out their fantasies, relax, seek to satisfy their cultural curiosity about another land or travel to museums, is thus not simply a statement about the tourist, but is also a statement about the area, region or country that has permitted the tourist resort area to take place. In practice, therefore, the tourist destination is a place of power structures and political processes. Consequently it is also a place of unequal sets of power nodes, where, for example, business interests are often better able, through access to finance if not political decision takers, to better present their side of the argument. Because tourism is a consumer activity that takes place within the social environment that produces the product, it is more highly visible than are many other economic processes. The development of the resort or destination therefore implies a need for political structures that legitimise and give voice to different stakeholders if development is to proceed in a manner that is acceptable to the competing interests that exist within a destination. It is these questions that will form the content of the next three chapters.

It has become a cliché that the impacts of tourism can be categorised as economic gain versus social and environmental loss. It will be argued that the issues are not as clear cut as this; and that it is possible to regenerate natural environments and social communities, but that there is a need for careful planning if this to occur. However, such planning is difficult to obtain, is accompanied by political processes, and requires continued monitoring to better reflect changing realities. Indeed, as will be noted, it is these very requirements that led some to argue that market mechanisms are the best means by which optimal solutions might be gained.

Chapter 7

The Economic Impacts of Tourism

Introduction

It has become a cliché to state that tourism is the world's largest industry. Many writers make this claim and support the contention by citing World Tourism Organisation and/or World Travel and Tourism Council data on shares of Gross Domestic Product or the numbers of passengers flown. To be honest, this author does not know the veracity of this claim, for much depends on the definitions and the methods of counting used. There are few alternatives or comparisons offered when this contention is made. Perhaps information technology, food production or entertainment are really the world's largest industries, because they are just as pervasive in the daily lives of most people, perhaps even more than tourism. Does the claim really matter? Perhaps it was a claim made simply to attract the attention of politicians and those who fund research, many of whom, or so it is said, have difficulties in treating seriously the claims of importance from an industry or field of study that is concerned with pleasure and fun. To study tourism seems to offend the traces of puritanical thought that remain in Western culture (Hall & Page, 1999)! In many senses the claim of being 'the biggest' is inconsequential. What can be stated beyond any doubt is that tourism is a major economic force in the world economy and therefore one purpose of a chapter such as this is to reiterate, albeit briefly, the importance of tourism as an economic activity. However, economic importance goes beyond the parading of numbers that quickly date, for the issues are often ones of who is being employed, where and who are they, what levels of remuneration are being gained, what costs are being sustained, and what are the consequences of these patterns of income and employment? In turn such issues generate a subsidiary set of questions – how are these flows and impacts to be measured, what data exist, and how might such data be used? The generation of data, however, does more than simply permit measurement, for a series of other questions comes to the fore. These questions include: what are the associations between tourist expenditure and income in the form of wages and profits, are there interactions between investment flows and job creation, what is the nature of such relationships, and is it possible to conceptualise and predict from the proposed models? Such questions form the content of this chapter.

The chapter will therefore commence with an overview of the economic benefits of tourism and the nature of the benefits. It will describe the theories behind the multiplier process on the premise that this model adequately describes the ways in which benefits are distributed through the economic system. Adopting this approach also acknowledges the pioneering work undertaken by people such as Brian Archer in the 1970s (Archer, 1980). The chapter then undertakes a review of the findings derived from this approach, followed by a discussion of the related technique of input–output approaches, expenditure modelling and tourism satellite accounts. Within this discussion a number of *leit motifs* are identified, and these include issues pertaining to income and employment generation. Because multiplier effects partly depend on structural factors, a discussion on the nature of employment and its productivity is also included. Additionally a description of the problems involved in estimating economic impacts is offered. Some of these are common to different methodologies, and hence some points are repeated, but this is done to specifically emphasise the advantages and disadvantages of the various methods that are used to estimate economic impacts of tourism.

The Economic Benefits of Tourism

The economic benefits of tourism can be classified as being primarily eight-fold.

(1) First there is the earning of foreign exchange that results from the spending of overseas visitors and contributions to exports. Equally, of course, the spending of a country's citizens overseas represents a loss to the economy. and is thus entered as an import.
(2) Visitor spending represents a source of taxation revenue for the government of the tourist-receiving country. This may be quite direct, as a specific tax on visitors, or through the normal mechanisms of indirect taxation such as a sales tax or value-added taxation.
(3) Visitor spending generates profit for those businesses in tourism and those organisations that in turn provide services and capital to the tourism industry.
(4) Employment is created.
(5) Various economic benefits are derived from what Dwyer and Forsyth (1998) termed 'externalities'. These are defined as above-normal profits through transport operations such as airports, port expenditure (including crew expenditure) – in short operations that would not occur if it were not for travel and tourism.
(6) There are the impacts on the terms of trade that can be beneficial as demand for a currency arising from tourist movement alters the cost of that currency against other currencies.

(7) Of particular importance to small economies, tourism permits the gain of economies of scale. For some countries this can be quite significant. For example, in the case of New Zealand, which has a population of about 4 million people, the 2 million overseas visitors each year represent substantial increments to demand that permit economies of scale in some operations. Indeed, arguably this effect is not restricted to countries that have small populations. Thus the UK, with a population of about 58 million, still derives economies of scale in various industries associated with travel by receiving about 20 million overseas visitors each year.

(8) Finally tourism offers the opportunity for a redistribution of income and employment to regions that are traditionally peripheral to the mainstream of economic life. This is because many of tourism's assets (such as historical heritage and scenery) may be found in zones now marginal to the urban, First-World countries that dominate the twenty-first century.

It should be noted that each of these categories is not only a potential gain, but also a possible cost. Tourist-receiving countries are also tourist-generating countries, and so both positive and negative financial transactions can occur. In some instances it is the flow of tourist numbers that generates the economic benefits, and the direction of the flow may be immaterial. This is at its most evident in people handling and transport systems. From the perspective of airport operations, other than in the case of migration, most travel requires both an outward and a return trip, and thus the revenue gained by an airport is dependent on numbers of clients. Whether these are residents flying out and then returning, or overseas visitors arriving and then departing is, in a the narrow sense of revenue generation for an airport, immaterial. Again, it can be argued that marginal zones sustain values and environments that possess values not caught by economic values measured by market transactions, and that to develop them as part of mainstream economic activity implies losses as well as gains. The nature of some of these losses is examined in Chapters 8 and 9.

Finally, it should be noted that, while there is a presumption that tourism tends to generate specific economic benefits, it should be remembered that this is not automatically the case. Indeed one of the implications of the destination lifecycle considered in Chapter 6 is that economic success may turn to failure with significant longer-term costs. Indeed Arell (2000) provides a longitudinal study of the Swedish resort zone of the Tärna Mountains from the 1920s to the early 2000s and concludes his study in a period when construction has stopped and property prices have fallen to half of their value in the 1990s. In short, there is no guarantee that tourism will sustain economic success.

The Economic Value of Tourism

In both developed and developing countries government authorities have identified tourism as a means of generating employment and income in vulnerable economies. For example it was noted that, among the 49 least-developed countries surveyed by the World Tourism Organisation (WTO) in 2001, in 7 cases tourism was the leading source of foreign exchange earnings, while in 10 others, tourism earnings were among the top three sources of foreign exchange income (WTO, 2001a). Nonetheless, such countries account for only 0.59% of total international air passenger kilometres (WTO, 2001a). But it is argued that, from one perspective, such small market shares indicate the levels of progress that can be made with carefully planned small tourism flows. Thus countries such as Ethiopia launched development plans for 2000–2005 in an attempt not simply to attract more visitors but to develop an infrastructure appropriate to their own needs as well as those of the tourism industry. In the First World it can be claimed that one of the environmental successes of tourism has been the revitalisation of nineteenth-century decaying waterfronts and associated urban renewal. Different cities, including Baltimore, Sydney, Birmingham, Liverpool and Boston, have been able to reclaim former decaying ports or canals in phased developments. Here the attractions created for tourism have been an important part of a retail and restaurant mix that is also attractive in creating an ambience for the offices of the service sector industries such as finance, insurance, consultancy and legal services. Consequently such zones bring employment, and in many cases they also contain residential areas. In some cases sporting success has been a catalyst for urban and waterfront renewal, but tourism has sustained demand once the initial event has taken place. Fremantle and Auckland offer two such examples based on the defence of yachting's America's Cup (Barker *et al.*, 2002).

In short, major initiatives have been and continue to be generated. In Eire the government's plan for National Recovery of 1987 targeted a number of key industries to generate prosperity. One of these was tourism. In the UK the English Tourist Board (ETB) in 1987 published its planning document 'Vision for England' (HMSO, 1987). Under these plans a public sector investment of £570 million was planned to develop a total investment of $4 billion by 1992, with the creation of an additional 250,000 jobs. Just over a decade later, in the report *Tomorrow's Tourism*, the Department for Culture, Media and Sport (UK) noted that tourism, with 1.75 million jobs in 125,000 businesses, accounted for about 13% of all new jobs created in the previous decade, was worth £53 billion annually, and attracted about 25 million overseas visitors to Britain (DCMS, 1999). The document than proceeded to list 15 action points to create a tourism strategy; these ranged from a better use of information technology, better marketing and more staff training to policies designed to ensure sustainability.

In the 1970s the French government partly financed developments in the Languedoc-Rousillion region of the south not only to relieve tourism congestion on the Cote d'Azure, but also to generate employment and income in an area perceived as having a marginal economy. Policy consideration and implementation for this region has continued over the intervening decades, and a summary of these was provided by the 1999 conference hosted by the German–French planning seminar of the Institute of Regional Planning and Regional Sciences (1999).

Such pressures for tourism development come from many different sources. For example, local government seeks to attract funding to support tourism development as a means of revitalising waste land and so converting it into a prosperous area that becomes, not a drain on local authority resources, but an actual contributor to the tax revenues through higher property taxes and other forms of tax revenues. Hoteliers and other commercial interests are also an important pressure group for tourism. Thus, for example, in the 1960s, the British Hotel industry continued to press government for grants similar to those given to manufacturing industry in areas where unemployment was higher than the national average. Indeed, partly as a result of this pressure, the government responded with the Hotel Incentive Development Scheme in 1969, which offered grants to all hotels regardless of area (HMSO, 1969). However, when the industry sought to obtain better recognition of tourism and to obtain tax, grant and administrative concessions prior to the UK government's 2000 budget announcement, it was less successful.

There is little doubt that in many cases the economic importance and consequences of tourism have brought it into the political arena, as is discussed in Chapter 9. If, however, the tourism industry is going to seek specific concessions from both central and local government, it is then necessary to understand the nature of the determinants of economic impacts, and how they might react to policies designed to promote the interests of the tourism industry.

The Determinants of Economic Impacts

The determinants of the economic impacts of tourism and the modelling of those impacts depend on the unit of analysis that has been selected. For example, if one is seeking to examine the impact of tourism on a national economy, then, as noted in Chapter 2, a range of macro-economic variables need to be discussed. For example, just as exchange rate movements were identified as a determinant of international tourism demand, so too any contribution made by tourism earnings to the balance of payments may well in turn impact on the value of the currency of the tourist-receiving country as its balance of payments records either a deficit or surplus. Therefore one unit of measurement to be defined is the time period to which a study applies. Again, when assessing the economic impacts of an event, or the flows of tourist movements through a local government administrative region, issues specific to that event or region might arise. However, for success in tourism at national, regional or local levels, some basic factors in calculating economic impacts would seem to apply. Places and events must be attractive to people who do not ordinarily live there. Transport systems must make the host region accessible, and that region must possess an infrastructure that is able to derive revenue from those visitors. For example it must maintain an appropriate accommodation stock, as the duration of stay and the nature of accommodation used are key determinants of the generation of income from tourism.

Hence, even this simple description of process indicates a number of key variables that must be considered when assessing the economic impacts of tourism. Therefore, it might be useful to list the variables that might be important in order to develop a context for more detailed discussion. The first of these is the structure of tourism and the infrastructure of the tourism industry itself within the designated zone. As Dwyer (2000) comments:

> It is the net visitor expenditure that determines the economic contribution of tourism to a destination. In general the magnitude of leakages will depend on such things as the structure of ownership and control (of) the tourism industry, the type of accommodation and other tourism facilities offered, and the extent of linkages between tourism and other sectors such as agriculture, food processing and manufacturing. (Dwyer, 2000: 93)

Several variables need to be considered.

The level of economic development of the destination area

The size of the economic unit being considered is important. If a hotel is built and attracts visitors, there is a significant difference between whether that hotel is built in a town or a village. Within a town the spending of hotel guests will represent but a small proportion of total spending. But in a village it will be a significant addition to the total income of the village, subject to the important proviso that the expenditure of the guests and the hotel actually does take place in the village.

The nature of the tourist facilities and their attractiveness

The nature of the tourist facility helps to determine the total expenditure that takes place. As will be discussed below, generally a higher proportion of any one pound, euro or dollar spent in farmhouse accommodation will remain in the local area than is the case if the money is spent in a hotel. This reflects the fact that the farmer (or spouse) has a greater propensity to buy goods and services locally. However, against that fact, visitors staying in a hotel are more likely to be paying more for their accommodation. Although a smaller proportion of tourist expenditure in hotels finds its way into the local economy, it is nonetheless a smaller proportion of a much larger sum of money. Therefore, in strict terms of additional revenues the local economy may gain more from the hotel than from the farmhouse. This argument is, however, totally negated if the visitors do not find the hotel to their liking, and tourists are in fact demanding the experiences associated with staying with local farmers.

The degree of foreign or out-of-region ownership of hotels and tourism infrastructure

Although the hotel may be successful in attracting guests, the leakage of revenue away from the area in which it is located may be increased by factors other than simply where the hotel management buys its resources. One factor that has attracted attention in the literature is the ownership of the assets. If, for example, a hotel is in foreign ownership, then the profits may be remitted back to the parent company, and thus again leave the local economy. This phenomenon is not simply restricted to hotels or retail businesses that are owned by foreign nationals, but is repeated wherever tourist businesses are not owned by local proprietors. For example in many of the Greek islands the ownership of the restaurants or shops may be in the hands of Athenians who, at the end of the season, close their business and return to their other businesses in Athens. That such leakage occurs reflects direct ownership patterns. But one implication of the arguments of Buhalis (2000, 2001) in his analysis of the policies of European package-holiday companies is that leakage can result from patterns of market power, and not simply from ownership. For example, suppose Greek accommodation owners are faced with higher costs, but are unable to pass those higher costs on to many tourists because the package companies are threatening to reduce demand for Greek destinations by more heavily promoting Turkey, which is offering lower-cost accommodation. In this scenaro, any one of a number of leakages of revenue can occur. First, of course, Greece might lose revenue to Turkey. Second, if Greek hotel owners maintain their lower prices to attract the revenue, then lower profits are being made, which in turn might mean lower entrepreneurial income and/or investment. In practice, Buhalis's arguments simply point to the implications of any competitive situation where, if there are no distinguishing features between products, then lower prices can become the drivers of demand and subsequent income distribution.

The employment of non-indigenous labour

The impact of tourist expenditure in terms of generating local revenues may also be partly diminished by the employment of labour from outside of the area. A number of reasons can dictate such a practice. First, there might be insufficient local labour to meet the demands of the peak season. Local people might be reluctant to be involved because their own economic base is sufficiently developed to provide employment alternative to the tourist industry, or there may be social factors that prevent them from seeking jobs in tourism. If the businesses are owned by large international companies, they might require practices or skills not found in the host community, which may lack the experience of management in large-scale organisations. On the other hand, if the small businesses are owned by entrepreneurs of the same nationality, but from outside the local area, they may employ family members in preference to local labour. Finally, of course, a significant reason for the use of non-indigenous labour may be the fact that such labour is cheaper. As will be discussed, there are significant numbers of examples of tourist areas attracting labour from rural economies that are characterised as low-income areas with high levels of unemployment or hidden unemployment. Thus tourism copies other industries that attract migrant labour from marginal economies. An example of both phenomena is found in Spain, where migration has occurred from the hinterland to the coastal tourist strip. Yet this must be placed within a context of Spain's tradition in the 1950s of being a source of emigrant labour to the industrialised northern European countries, whilst within Spain itself from the 1950s to the present day there had been migration from the poorer southern areas such as Andalucia to the industrial areas of Barcelona and Bilbao.

Whatever the reasons for the use of non-local labour, the consequence is that a payment of wages is made to non-local people, and again it is customary that a proportion of such wages is sent home. This is shown by Alison Lever (1987) in her study of Spanish migrant workers to Lloret del Mar and by Milligan (1989) in her study of Portuguese workers in Guernsey.

In addition to the loss of revenue to the host community, there is also a cost associated with this practice. Local workers require accommodation, medical services, transport and other services. Whilst it can be argued that the provision of such services in themselves generates flows of income, the practicalities of the situation may mean that the additions to local income may be marginal and may be associated with a number of social disbenefits. This point is further discussed in Chapter 9, on the social impacts of tourism.

Government provision of infrastructure

Whilst an area may have initially attracted those types of tourists designated by Cohen (1979a) as 'explorers', if it seeks to attract more tourists and move into mass tourism, then additional investment will have to be made by both private and public sectors. While the private sector will provide the hotels, bars, restaurants, discos and many other forms of entertainment facilities, the government will have to provide a range of infrastructure support. Accessibility will be improved by the provision of roads and car parking spaces; services relating to hygiene including sewage disposal and treatment, the provision of public toilets and water treatment plants will be needed; medical facilities might be needed to treat not only the tourists but also the influx of labour that may be created; and plans relating to property development will be needed, and implemented. The provision of such services generates a complex pattern of revenues and costs. The building of these services is obviously a means of generating employment, and in an area of high unemployment, if local labour is utilised, the very building programme itself will be viewed as a positive economic impact. Indeed, the provision of these services will help to attract private sector investment not only for the tourism industry, but for other economic sectors such as retailing and other service industries through the provision of office accommodation, and possibly light manufacturing industry. In fact this is the very sort of process that has characterised waterfront developments in North America, Europe and Australia. But the provision of such services requires funding, and thus a series of costs are initiated. Where central government is involved, the costs of these investments are shared amongst the wider community, and not simply amongst the host community in the tourist destination. The host nation considers that it will gain from increased foreign currency earnings and additional revenues on its balance of payments, and thus such investment is justified on these grounds. However, where investment is financed or implemented by local government, the host community bears the costs as well as the rewards. Taxes may be raised either to meet the expenditure directly, or to service the loans borrowed to finance the building. The final balance sheet of costs and revenues will thus depend on the success of the venture. For there is no guarantee of success, particularly in the case of marginal economies (marginal in either national or world terms), for tourism is subjected to whims as to which location or type of holiday or leisure day-trip activity is in fashion. The initial euphoria of success may, after a brief period, turn sour as tastes and the market move on. Examples of such changes in fashion include the success of UK safari parks in the 1960s, the changing fortunes of Turkish tourism in the period from the mid-1980s, and the transient success of countries such as Kenya and South Africa that have struggled to hold on to past tourism gains because of fears of violence and reports of muggings and killings of tourists.

The type of tourist

All of the factors listed above have tended to be 'supply led' in nature, that is, they indicate the economic flows that arise from the provision of services to tourists. But what of tourists themselves? The economic impacts are obviously greater the higher the number of tourists and the higher the average expenditure per tourist. But the nature of their demand is also important. If mass tourists require items that the local community is unable to provide, the result is that a significant proportion of the revenue gained from tourism is immediately lost because of a need to import those items from outside the region or country. In this sense there may be a series of trade-offs for any tourist planning authority. Greater numbers of high-spending tourists may, perversely, have less beneficial impact than a smaller number of lower spending tourists if the latter creates a lower need to import. Equally, it can also be argued that larger numbers of tourists generate higher social costs in terms of their impingement upon the life styles of the host community. This is particularly true if wide disparities exist between the life styles of the tourist and that of the local population. It is now a cliché to say that an American tourist visiting Canada has very little impact, but that same American tourist in, say, Bangledesh, will have a much greater economic influence.

Links with other parts of the economy

In part, the economic activities associated with tourism become important when considering the purpose of tourism within a general economic framework. In the case of marginal economies, whether regional or national, it can be argued that the import requirements to service the tourists are themselves an important part of the overall economic objective of bringing the area back into the mainstream of economic life. Importing means dealing with those located in the economic mainstream, and thus the lack of trade that initially created peripherality is itself corrected even if (at least initially), the cost is one of a deficit trading account. Second, there is a need to consider the interactions between tourism and other industry sectors within a destination zone. Many of these issues are illustrated by Dwyer's (2000) study of the potential that tourism possesses for the economy of Andhra Pradesh in India. The means of strengthening links between tourism and the local economy listed by Dwyer include increasing the duration of stay to increase visitor expenditure by establishing tour circuits that offer shopping opportunities for the local industries (handicrafts, pearls and jewellery, garment, and leatherware), and to reducing leakages by making better use of the local agricultural, construction and furniture-making industries. He also identifies as being important the role of the tourism industry as a source of employment for women, noting their low participation rates in the formal economy in this part of India.

The Measurement of Economic Impacts

The question of how to measure the economic impact of tourism is both important to ask and difficult to answer. In practice four related techniques are commonly used to calculate these impacts:

(1) the use of multiplier studies taken from macro-economics;
(2) the use of input–output measures, again taken from macro-economics;
(3) the development of satellite accounts; and
(4) local impact studies utilising a number of ad hoc measures of varying degrees of sophistication.

The Multiplier Process

From the 1960s various studies have been undertaken throughout the world to assess the economic benefits of tourism to the host community. Many of these studies took place throughout the 1970s, but increasingly researchers became aware of just how difficult it was in practice to measure the flows of income and the numbers of jobs that were being created, and to some extent multiplier studies became less frequent in the 1980s. However, with the emergence of tourism as a means of helping to regenerate inner city areas in both Europe and North America, there has been some renewed interest in the use of such techniques. Essentially the reasons for this are pragmatic. Local authorities have had to justify the spending of public money to their own elected councillors and rate payers, especially where the local authority is one of the major sources of revenue for local and regional tourism organisations (as in countries such as the United Kingdom, Australia and New Zealand). Additionally, at least in the United Kingdom, many public sector expenditures on tourism ventures have been justified as 'pump-priming' exercises where local and national government fund projects that in turn attract money from the private sector. Such schemes have had mixed patterns of success. In the late 1980s and early 1990s the then Conservative Government attempted to use a series of Garden Festivals to promote areas of economic decay. Some were more successful than others. For example, Liverpool did arguably obtain some longer-term benefit, whereas the unkind might say that all that Ebbw Vale obtained was a supermarket and a car park! Some such schemes were highly controversial, with the Millennium Dome having a chequered history including the successful foiling of a jewellery robbery by the police.

The Dome's critics point to the millions of pounds lost, its defenders argue that without the Dome the much-needed improvements to roads infrastructure in Greenwich would not have taken place, and that there is still hope that longer-term gains can result. In short, the effectiveness of such expenditure is often assessed, albeit with perhaps varying degrees of care, as will be discussed below. This new spirit of pragmatism had two further effects. The first was in the methods used to assess the economic impacts, because simpler methods of measurement came to be used, particularly at sub-regional level. Second, tourism became increasingly perceived as part of a total package of economic regeneration that included retailing, property development and general leisure provision. The presence of these facilities is subsequently used to attract other forms of industry.

One of the controversial aspects of these studies is the use of the multiplier. Initially the concept of the multiplier is taken from the ideas of Kahn (1972) and Keynes (1936), as developed in their seminal works of the 1930s. Keynes argued that economic growth was dictated by two broad groups of flows of activity: 'leakages' from the economic systems, and 'injections' into that system. The 'injections' consisted of investment, exports and government expenditure. Investment was important for at least two reasons. The very act of creating the investment was in itself a means of creating jobs and income, while the investment also became a means of perpetuating employment and income for the future because it added to productive capacity by creating new equipment. Exports meant selling goods overseas, and thus earning money from overseas residents. Government expenditure was a means of financing investment and also a means of transferring income to individuals who could then purchase items and generate a demand for goods and services. Such redistribution of income was often to individuals with high propensities to spend (for example low-income groups on benefit) and so consumer spending was higher than it would have been in the absence of such payments. In short, the injections added to economic growth. From the viewpoint of tourism, the building of the tourist attraction is thus an investment; its existence helps to attract overseas visitors and so it is a form of export, whilst simultaneously the enhancement of tourist facilities within a country may be an import-saving investment for it means that its citizens will holiday within their own country rather than spend their money overseas.

The 'leakages' in the system are savings, taxation and imports. The act of saving withdraws money from the economy, and diminishes overall levels of demand for goods and hence employment. Savings only become 'useful' when used by financial intermediaries to fund investment. The same is true of taxation. By raising taxation, the government withdraws money from the economic system, and so again diminishes levels of demand. It is only by government expenditure that that money is released back into the economy. Imports are a leakage in the sense that by purchasing from overseas, the jobs associated with the production of those goods are also to be found overseas, funded by the expenditure of the importing country.

Keynes (1936) argued that when both the 'injections' and 'leakages' are in equilibrium, then the economy is also in equilibrium. Economic growth is generated by the 'injections' being greater than the 'leakages'.

There is another important economic flow, which is consumer expenditure, and this Keynes placed on both sides of the equation. Consumer spending is an injection because it is the spending that fuels the demand for goods and services and so creates employment and income. On the other hand, if the recipient of the consumer expenditure does nothing with the revenue, it is money taken out of the economic system. Accordingly, the timing and sequence of flows of consumer spending are of importance. Both Keynesians and Monetarists also recognise that money is a commodity like others in that it has a cost, namely interest rates. Consumer spending can therefore be affected not only by taxation (which removes money from or adds it to the consumer's budget), but also, in advanced economies where credit is often used, by alterations in interest rates. In addition, in societies with high levels of home ownership, and where much of that home ownership is financed by mortgages, interest rates can act like taxes. Increases in interest rates raise the value of monthly repayments by mortgage holders, and thus reduce their ability to spend on other items. Evidence of this at work was arguably present in Britain in 1989. Increases in mortgage rates to over 13%, following an explosion in house prices in 1988, meant that subsequent spending in retail sales grew more slowly, and the demand for overseas package holidays fell from some 13 million holidays to approximately 11 million. The relationship was, however, far from clear as the British summer of 1989 was one of the sunniest and warmest for decades, and holidays in Britain experienced a boom. Additionally, as noted in Chapter 2, holidaymakers had bitter memories of aircraft controllers' strikes and long delays at airports in the previous summer of 1988.

The above discussion can be summarised in Keynesian terms as economic growth occurring where:

$$I+X+G+C > S+M+T+C$$

where I = investment
X = exports
G = government spending
C = consumer spending
S = savings
M = imports
T = taxation.

Equally, the national or regional income can be said to be in equilibrium where:

$$I+X+G+C = S+M+T+C$$

Tourism therefore has economic impacts by:

(1) *Contributing to the balance of payments.* Holidays taken overseas are imports, overseas visitors coming to the host country are counted as exports, and every time citizens takes their major holiday in their own country it might be said that import substitution has taken place.
(2) *Creating employment and income by generating:*
(a) initial investment in tourist facilities;
(b) creating consumer expenditure in a given location;
(c) in many cases releases flows of savings into the economic system.

The actual employment and income generated will depend on the nature of the 'leakages' in the system, and the size of the original 'injection'.

Consider a simple example where trade into and out of an area is (conveniently) not taken into account, and where government action can also be discounted. Under these circumstances economic growth will be generated by consumer spending, savings, and investment. Initially consumers' income is disposed of by savings and spending, hence:

$$Y=C+S$$

Now consider Figure 7.1. On the vertical axis are 'consumption' and 'savings'. As the total of both equals 'income' (measured on the horizontal axis), a 45° line indicates the points where $Y = C+S$. Let us suppose that earners spend 75% of any addition to their income, and save 25%. Therefore, if their income increases by £100 they will spend £75 of that increase and save £25. This permits a 'consumption line' to be drawn, indicating the levels of consumption associated with any given level of income. Where the consumption line (C) crosses the 45° line, 'consumption' equals 'income', and hence savings are equal to zero. To the left of this point, expenditure exceeds income, and hence savings are negative. To the right of this point, income exceeds consumption, and savings are positive. The savings line (S) shows this relationship. The slope of the consumption line is calculated from the relationship of the changes in expenditure divided by the changes in income, i.e. the slope equals what Keynes (1936) called the marginal propensity to consume (MPC). MPC is that part of additions to income that are spent, and is calculated by dividing the change in consumption spending by the value of the change in income. In the example, if income increases by £100 and as a result spending increases by an additional £75, then the MPC = £75/£100 = 0.75.

Suppose the initial equilibrium level of income be £100,000, is shown in Figure 7.1; that is the level where consumption equals income and savings is zero. Now suppose that there is a £20,000 investment in tourism. The total demand in the economy now rises by £20,000, but the new, higher level of

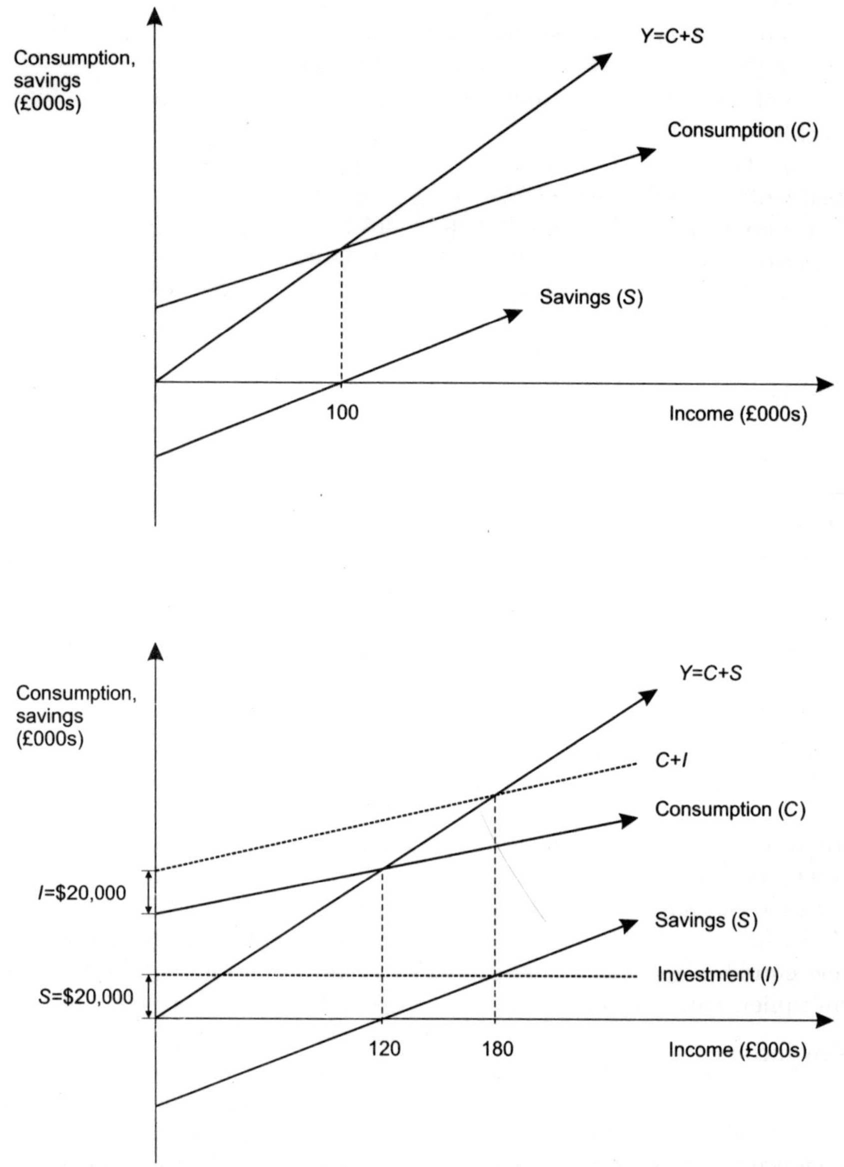

Figure 7.1 The multiplier effect

equilibrium income is shown as being not £120,000, but £180,000. Total income has risen by £80,000, and this increase consists of two components: the initial £20,000 investment and an increase in consumer spending of £60,000. In short a multiplier process has taken place. Note that in Figure 7.1, at the new, higher level of income, the difference between the consumption plus investment line (C+I) and the original consumption line (C) is of course £20,000, and at the point where the C+I line cuts the 45° line, the value of savings is also equal to £20,000. A new equilibrium income has established itself.

How has this come about? The answer lies in the process whereby the recipients of additional income spend part of that income, which in turn therefore becomes income for others. The investment forms an initial impetus into the economy. The recipients now spend 75% of this £20,000 (i.e. £15,000) and save the remaining £5,000. This, of course, assumes that the MPC is a constant. The recipients of the £15,000 spending in turn save 25%, and spend 75% (i.e. £11,250). In turn, the receivers of this £11,250 spend 75% of it, and save 25%. Table 7.1 shows the process continuing into subsequent rounds of expenditure and saving.

In the first 5 'rounds' the total additions to income are not only the initial £20,000 investment but also £15,000 + £11,250 + £8,437.5 + £6,328.1: i.e. £41,015.6 of consumer spending can be added to the initial £20,000 investment. How is this reconciled with the diagram? Figure 7.1 represented the final equilibrium position of a new, higher level of income of £180,000. The flows of Table 7.1 represent the process of arriving at that final position of equilibrium. It can be noticed that, with the passing of time, the successive additions to income are becoming weaker. Keynes argued that the final position can be deduced from the formula:

$$\text{Value of the multiplier} = \frac{1}{\text{MPS}}$$

where MPS = marginal propensity to save, i.e. that proportion of any addition to income that is saved.

In the example, the value of MPS is 1/4 (25%). (In a closed economy MPS + MPC = 1, and hence if MPC = 0.75, MPS = 0.25.) Therefore, to find the new equilibrium level of income we multiply the initial injection by the multiplier. Thus:

$$\begin{aligned}\text{New income generated} &= £20{,}000 \times 1/0.25 \\ &= £20{,}000 \times 4 \\ &= £80{,}000\end{aligned}$$

Hence, the value of the multiplier is determined by the value of the leakages. The higher the value of the leakages in the economic system, the lower

Table 7.1 The flows of the multiplier process: Initial injection £20,000

	Periods of time				
	1	2	3	4	5
Saved (25%)	£5000	£3750	£2812.5	£2109.4	£1582.0
Spent (75%)	£15000	£11250	£8437.5	£6328.1	£4746.1
	£20000	£15000	£11250	£8437.5	£6328.1

is the value of the multiplier, and the lower the resultant flows of additions to income. For example if the marginal propensity to save was 0.50 (i.e. out of every additional £1 earned, 50p was saved), the £20,000 injection in our example would have produced an addition to income of:

New income generated = £20,000 x 1/0.5
= £20,000 x 2
= £40,000

From the example it can be seen that any injection into a local economy produces these flows of income. Thus the investment referred to might not just be the building of industrial investment, but can equally well refer to the building of hotels, or the expenditure of tourists visiting an area. Economists therefore, in the 1960s, began to apply Keynes's concept of the national income multiplier to the calculation of regional or local economic systems in order to assess the economic impacts of tourism at subnational level. Foremost among these in the English speaking world was Archer, who with Owen, published the results of an application of the multiplier to the island of Anglesey in 1971 (Archer & Owen, 1971). In order to illustrate the types of calculation undertaken, some of their formulae are reproduced in an appendix to this chapter.

In assessing these impacts, three categories may be calculated, namely:

(1) *The output multiplier*. This measures the total output (or sales) induced in the economy, per unit of extra spending, and is expressed in the form of a multiplier coefficient.

(2) *The income multiplier*. This shows the relationship between extra spending and changes in income.

(3) *The employment multiplier*. This indicates the relationship between the extra spending and the number of additional jobs that are created through primary and secondary employment. Primary employment would include the actual number of jobs directly generated by the tourist spending or investment (e.g. jobs in restaurants), whilst the secondary effects would include, for example, those jobs created by the spending of restaurant employees.

In the case of tourism, the value of the leakages will be determined by the proportion of tourist spending that remains in the area, the proportion of tourist spending that is received by local people, and the propensity of local people to spend in their local area. The basic formulation of the tourism multiplier is thus:

$$\text{Tourism multiplier} = A\left[\frac{1}{1-BC}\right]$$

where A = the proportion of tourist expenditure remaining in the area after first round leakages,
B = the proportion of income that local people spend on local goods, and services – the propensity to spend locally
C = the proportion of expenditure of local people that accrues as local income.

The logic of the formulation is in the fact that, as most tourist regions/ destinations are comparatively small, the highest element of leakages occurs in the first round when imports are undertaken, and in consequence the additions to income in the local area are felt from the second round on. However, an important determinant of the value of the tourist multiplier continues to be – who are the recipients of the income, and what are their spending patterns? If, in the second round, the recipients of tourist-initiated expenditure spend money outside the area, the value of the multiplier is undermined. Hence the importance of values B and C in the equation.

However, in practice this simple formulation is insufficient. In the initial discussion of the concept of the multiplier, some obvious questions arise. How can we be sure that recipients of income maintain the same consistent propensities to save and consume? How long are the time periods or rounds, and as money trickles through the system over time, can we again be sure of consistency of behaviour by those who receive the additions to income? For example, if the farmer's wife takes in bed-and-breakfast guests, is this addition to the farm's revenue perceived by the family as additions to their savings, or as money for the wife to spend on herself, or as a means of paying the farm's bills? Is the attitude to these sums the same at the end of the season as at the beginning of the season? In short, researchers have had to disaggregate the data, often by the type of accommodation used by the tourists. As Archer (Archer & Owen, 1971) showed in his studies of Anglesey, there are distinct differences in the types of expenditure patterns of those who use hotels, bed and breakfast accommodation or caravan sites for their overnight stays. Equally there are differences in spending by the recipients of the first round of tourist expenditure. It can be hypothesised, for example, that proprietors of bed-and-breakfast accommodation may be more prepared than hotel chains to use local suppliers. As already noted, the appendix to this chapter indicates some of Archer's work in this respect.

It should also be noted that, within any economic system expenditures, incomes and employment are closely related. Tourist expenditure should equate to income for those who receive that expenditure, while the business recipients of tourist spending will employ people, thereby establishing a ratio between tourist expenditures and employment generation.

Murphy (1985) provides a summary of some of the findings undertaken by researchers for the period 1966–1977, and clearly shows that the smaller the area, the smaller is the multiplier. At national level Murray records multipliers from 0.78–2.7, at a state or provincial level the multiplier values range from 0.35–1.7, and at regional/local areas the multipliers range from 0.32 to an exceptionally high value of 1.67 in one case. With that one exception, all the other multipliers he cites are below 0.73.

To some extent, studies of multiplier values based on the Keynesian multiplier are no longer in such vogue as they were in the period from the 1960s to the 1980s. A number of factors explain this. First, economists have been making distinctions between the calculation of tourism as an industry, and its impacts on the economy, and the economic impacts that arise from tourism associated with specific events. In the former case, one of the more important techniques that has emerged in the period since about 1995 has been the use of tourism satellite accounts. These are discussed in more detail below. Second, there has been a greater recognition of the sheer complexity of the data required. Third, has been a sense of distrust of such calculations caused by what Getz (1997) has termed 'boosterism' as event promoters seek to secure public funding for events by over-promising economic gains. Fourth, as Burgan and Mules (1992: 703) comment, 'There is no general agreement among economists on how best to model an economy'. Nonetheless, references to the multiplier concept continue to be found. For example, a consultant's report on the economic impacts of tourism on the economy of Northland, New Zealand, states that a multiplier of 2.1 can be used, and undertakes the calculation, but provides no justification for the use of this multiplier value (Price Waterhouse Cooper, 2000). In an estimation of multiplier impacts of seven events in Palmerston North Ryan (1996b) quite specifically excludes the use of the multiplier on the grounds of complexity and high leakage rates at a local level. But Ritchie (1996) applies a value of 0.9 to an event in Dunedin, again simply importing a value from other studies.

To a large extent, many consultancy reports have been suspect and, according to Crompton and McKay (1994) double counting is one of the major problems. Lea (1988) also provides examples of how faulty calculations of multipliers in the Caribbean gave rise to poor policy decisions. Indeed, in his studies of the economic impacts of events, Ryan (1996b) specifically distinguishes between four categories of tourist expenditure in any calculation of economic impacts. These are:

(1) *Displaced expenditure:* residents from a city or zone who attend an event only because the event was in home area. The expenditure of this group can be regarded as *displaced* expenditure and not *additional* expenditure, i.e. it is expenditure that would probably have occurred in the city on other items. Thus it should not be included in any estimate of the economic impact of an event.
(2) *Retained expenditure:* residents for whom the event was important. In this case their expenditure can be regarded as *'retained expenditure'*, i.e. their expenditure would have taken place because of the event, but the fact that the event took place in their home area meant that the zone concerned did not lose the economic effects of such spending. In other words it is expenditure by those who would have travelled to the event if it was held elsewhere.
(3) *Partial retained expenditure:* visitors from outside the event zone for whom the event was of relative importance only, but was a primary catalyst for the timing and duration of a visit to friends and relatives living in the event zone. In this case the destination would have derived some spending from this group in any case, but it might be that the event elicited some additional spending because it made the trip more expensive than might otherwise have been the case. This might be termed *partial incremental* spending.
(4) *Wholly incremental expenditure:* finally, there are visitors whose spending in the destination area is solely due to the event. Their expenditure was *'wholly incremental'*, that is, it would not have taken place in the destination region if it had not been for the event. This group represents a true economic gain.

For their part, in the context of event tourism, Burgan and Mules (1992) very specifically point to a need to distinguish between the economic impacts of an event, and the financial outcome. Indeed, the same authors in 2001 produce evidence from studies of a number of events in Australia that showed a financial loss for the event management, but which nonetheless produced significant positive economic impacts for local or regional economies (Burgan & Mules, 2001). Examples include the Brisbane Masters' Games of 1994, which produced a loss of $A2.8 million for the organisers, but which injected $A50.6 million into the local economy. Again, the 1996 Adelaide Wine Festival cost the organisers $A3.5 million, but produced an overall benefit of $A11.6 million. Of course such findings do not in themselves provide solutions for what are essentially political decisions. Among the issues discussed are to what extent should the public sector sponsor events at a loss that generally generate private sector gain and profit? To what extent do the calculations of economic gain take into account all of the costs? For example, while the Wellington V8 Super Saloon motor races generated economic gain, their demise was due to local resident antipathy to the closure of roads and the noise and disruption that was caused. The same arguments surrounded the Birmingham Formula 3000 Halford Grand Prix races in the UK in the 1980s. Another argument has emerged in the case of the Canberra V8 Super Saloon races, and that is whether the image of such races and their appeal to 'petrol heads' is consistent with the image of Canberra as a centre of government and culture. While it is possible to allocate costs to such issues through the use of cost benefit analysis, it is the experience of this author that those with strong views are resistant to the use of such calculations where the results do not support the entrenched position. In the long run non-economic arguments can outweigh the economic, and the reasons for this are discussed in Chapter 9.

Data Requirements for the Calculation of Economic Impacts

What needs to be appreciated is the complexity of data required for the calculation of such multipliers. While, to again cite Burgan and Mules (1992: 704) 'it is generally accepted that the economic impacts are expenditure driven', to correctly identify that expenditure is problematical. To give a simple example, when undertaking an economic impact of a bowls championship that included singles, doubles and foursomes, it was found necessary to carefully check the accommodation expenditure being reported by respondents because of the amount of room sharing that was taking place. In some instances it might be easier to identify activities and then calculate expenditure from prices charged by suppliers, than to depend on the recall of respondents, particularly if accommodation bookings were made well in advance and by other than the respondents. Indeed, to undertake even simple calculations, a number of parameters must be defined. One of the more fundamental of these is the definition of the region under consideration. As discussed in Chapter 6, the concept of the tourist destination area is fixed neither spatially nor temporally, for different aspects of a region will appeal to different types of tourists, and attractions change over time. It may be possible to define the tourist area by an analysis of tourist trips within the region, so identifying perhaps a 'core' tourist area. However, there is no guarantee that such an area corresponds to the administrative area used for the collection of other data. For example the tourist area might span more than one local authority, or travel-to-work area, and these areas might be the basis of statistics relating to public sector expenditure or employment. Reference has also been made to the different types of tourists. Day visitors will obviously not be spending on accommodation, whilst short-break holidaytakers may have a higher spend per day, but a lower total spend per holiday visit when compared with longer-stay visitors. Users of hotel accommodation tend to have higher expenditure than users of caravans.

One interesting fact that has emerged from more recent studies is that VFR (visiting friends and relatives) tourists may have as high an expenditure as tourists staying in hotels, if the area is a well-established tourist area. The evidence for this is mixed, but is supported by Vaughan's (1986) comparison of the expenditure patterns of tourists in Cumbria, Merseyside and Bournemouth in tthe UK. It has also been clear from studies undertaken in New Zealand that expenditure figures by VFR tourists on activities other than serviced accommodation are just as high as those using the serviced accommodation sector (Ryan, 1996b; Ryan & Lockyer, 2001). Indeed, there might be comparatively little difference as, in the case of sports events Ryan and Lockyer found that many sports people used comparatively cheap forms of accommodation (e.g. camping grounds and caravan sites). However, there is, it is suggested, a caveat and this relates to the maturity of the event. In the case of the South Pacific Masters' Games, there were differences between the 2002 and the 2000 event. In 2002 the ratio began to change in favour of more out-of-region visitors, with more visitors also using the higher-priced serviced accommodation sector, thereby increasing the economic impact of the event.

What Vaughan (1986), Ryan and Wheeller (1982), Hobson and Christensen (2001), Young and Littrell (2001) and many other studies also indicate is just how important shopping is to the tourist. Shopping for other than food and drink can easily account for 25% of tourist expenditure. In consequence the economic impacts of tourism in an area can be affected by the nature of the retail provision to be found in the host community, the ownership of the shops, and the propensity of the shops to purchase locally. It is self evident that souvenir shops in local ownership using local craftsmen to supply the souvenirs will have a higher economic impact on the native population in the tourist area than will nationally- or foreign-owned chains who import souvenirs. In essence this last point illustrates another problem in the calculation of multiplier effects, and that is the need to identify not only the average daily expenditure of tourists, but also its breakdown between different types of business and the ownership of those businesses.

The Economic Impacts of Tourism: Multipliers and Employment

The impact of ownership on businesses has been demonstrated by Sinclair in her studies of Malaga hotels (Sinclair, 1981; Sinclair & Sutcliffe,

1982). The highest multiplier effects were associated with tourist miscellaneous purchases (i.e. expenditure on items other than food, drink, entertainment and accommodation), and thus relate to those items most likely to be supplied by local suppliers. The multiplier was estimated at 0.99. The second highest multiplier values were associated with accommodation (0.66), partly because of the employment of labour living in the area. However, there were notable differences in the levels of employment between Spanish-owned and foreign-owned hotels. Whilst foreign-owned hotels tended to employ more staff (52.2 per hotel) than Spanish-owned hotels (42.3 per hotel), this was a reflection of the fact that foreign-owned hotels tended to be larger. In terms of numbers of employees per bed space, the average employment (for coastal areas) was marginally less in foreign-owned than in Spanish-owned hotels, (0.29 as against 0.30). But in the case of hotels located in cities, the difference was far more pronounced, being 0.49 for the foreign multiple and 0.68 for the Spanish hotel. As a general conclusion it can be hypothesised that access to economies of scale and more cost-effective modes of management may produce lower multiplier effects through the process of fewer employees per bed space. In the case of foreign-owned hotels, the position may be further exacerbated by a tendency to remit profits. Sinclair and Sutcliffe (1982) estimated a value of first round propensity to remit profits (for the Malaga area) as being equal to 39% of the long-run GNP multiplier. Does this necessarily mean that non-local and foreign ownership of assets is to be discouraged? The position is not as simple as first appears. The levels of payment to staff must be taken into account. If the large multiple takes advantage of economies of scale and management techniques to not simply save on labour per bed space, but also to pay a higher wage per employee than their less efficient local supplier, then the initial negative multiplier effects are offset by the higher wages. But the final calculation of multiplier effects will then require an analysis of expenditure by the employees.

Differences might exist between the tourism impacts at a destination based on holidaying, and impacts resulting from tourism based on a specific event. In assessing the economic impacts of an event on employment, it is necessary to consider the actual infrastructure of the tourism industry. For example, Burns, Hatch and Mules (1986), while estimating that the Adelaide Grand Prix contributed an extra $A20 million to the local Adelaide economy, found that no additional employment could be discerned as a result of the event. Similarly Ryan and Lockyer (2001) noted that the South Pacific Masters' Games produced no extra employment in the accommodation sector. In both cases any additional demand for services was met by existing staff working longer hours and overtime. This implies that much of the extra revenue in the accommodation sector was ploughed into profits rather than wages, and thus the expenditure patterns of profit receivers rather than wage earners become a major determinant of the multiplier effect. In a Brazilian study Wagner (1997) was able to calculate the employment multipliers and found that $US1515 of tourist expenditure created 0.4 full-time employment jobs. Wagner comments that it takes 233 tourists to create 1 full-time tourism job.

Nonetheless, if tourism is to be promoted by public authorities, there is an obvious need to assess the possible outcome of developments and to ensure that appropriate methods are used to calculate those impacts. In 1986 the English Tourist Board commissioned a study to see whether or not it would be possible to devise a means of calculating not income but employment multipliers in a way that was both meaningful and comparatively straightforward. It was finally concluded that whilst there were two methods (either utilising Census of Employment data or transferring multiplier values from past studies into the area under study), neither method was ideal. Vaughan (1986) writes:

> The conclusion presented in this report is that both methods can provide broad indications of the likely size of the tourism related work force. Both methods are subject to a number of important limitations and assumptions, so neither is obviously superior to the other. The qualifications of each approach should be respected in using the estimates produced as it could defeat the object of advocacy to publish estimates which are too open to question. Neither method can fully replace a local study if qualitative information on types of jobs and types of workers is required or to provide assurances that job estimates actually reflect the particular circumstances of the local tourist industry. (Vaughan, 1986: 1)

Vaughan's warning is particularly apposite in a situation where governmental authorities at both local and national level seek to promote tourism development in the belief that economic benefits will emerge. Traditionally tourism multipliers have been found to be weak, and a number of reasons can account for this:

(1) the comparatively low levels of pay in the industry;
(2) costs as well as income are generated; and
(3) the nature of the tourist regions.

Tourism, even in advanced economies, has been associated with low levels of pay. The Low Pay Unit in the United Kingdom reported in 1986 that nearly 40% of hotel and restaurant employers visited by the Government Wage Inspectorate were found to be illegally underpaying their workers (Low Pay Unit, 1986). Bland (1987) commenting on the position in Cornwall, noted:

> In Cornwall, and doubtless in other counties, no effort is made to check that hotels and restaurants who are receiving grants, publicity and facilities paid for by tax and ratepayers are paying their workers legal wages. Public funds are in effect going to support and encourage criminal employers. (Bland, 1987: 14)

If the situation is thus in advanced economies, then it is worse in developing countries. Cater (1988) argues that, in the least developed countries, tourism imposes a high cost on infrastructure. The energy requirements of luxury hotels are high and place a stress on the hosts' electricity-generating capacity, and in turn load shedding, blackouts and poor water pressure pose problems in attracting western guests. Imported managerial labour also increases leakages. In consequence, in developing economies, tourism may not only have positive multiplier effects from the 'injections' of tourist spending, but also costs, and, indeed may not generate as much additional income as is hoped. Farver (1984), in his study of Gambian tourism, concluded that the tourist industry employed fewer Gambians than hoped for, and also paid wages that, whilst higher than possible earnings in alternative forms of employment, were not high enough to improve workers' standard of living to any great extent. It would seem from many studies that local ownership and control of tourist enterprise is important in ensuring that the host community derives the highest possible tourism multipliers. However, a contrary viewpoint is that, whilst this is true, there is still nonetheless an important need to obtain access to the markets that exist beyond the tourist area, and locally-based businesses may not be able to do this. There is, therefore, inevitably a need to utilise businesses located in the tourist-generating areas. Only rarely, and generally only in the cases of mature tourist regions receiving governmental backing, can businesses located in the tourist-receiving areas reach directly to consumers in the tourist-generating regions.

The problem of low wages in the industry might be, arguably, a reflection of more generally low levels of productivity and added value. There is ample evidence that in advanced economies the hotel industry is characterised by high levels of staff turnover, and small units. In a survey of the tourist and leisure industry, which included not only hotels but also nightclubs, leisure facilities and museums, the Institute of Manpower Studies (1988) found that 63% of the 170 businesses examined had fewer than 20 employees. Only 8% had more than 50. Because of the small size of business units, it was found that, whilst the industry does have a reputation for employing part-time, seasonal labour, this was not in fact borne out by the sample, for 68% of all jobs were counted as being permanent ones. However, the permanent jobs included of course those of the entrepreneurs involved, and hence the picture is one of several small businesses, capable of supporting the founders of the business, or the management staff of multiples, but generally being unable to support larger number of workers. But the position is varied, and the report concludes that it was evident that the extent, and pattern, of use of seasonal and casual workers varied greatly within the sector as a whole, as did the employment of permanents and temporaries.

One of the important implications of the IMS findings is that for many employed in the industry the actual career path is short, with limited opportunity for career enhancement as the industry is currently structured.

> The overall picture is of extensive movement between companies but usually without promotion. Managers and Professionals are the only group for whom careers could be common, as promotion was reported by many establishments for recruits and leavers. This was the only group for whom internal careers appeared to be a well established feature of the employment structure. For all other occupational groups, not only was promotion reported as common by a minority of establishments only but movement out of employment entirely was not uncommon. (IMS, 1988, cited by Ryan, 1991a: 83)

Of importance in establishing a high-paid, high-multiplier industry is the establishment of corporate career structures. In most countries, however, the major part of the total accommodation stock is proprietor-managed and small in size. While representing an important part of small- to medium-size enterprise, such employment is not notably associated with high levels of remuneration. Based on a biographical study of 284 hotel managers, Riley, Ladkin and Szivas (2002) report that 50% attained the position of general manager by the age of 30, which represents a significantly early career advancement. However, what is also evident is that the main route to career advancement in the hotel industry lay through food and beverage management rather than through housekeeping, marketing, accounting or finance, while 5.5% reached the post of general manager from outside of the industry without any prior experience of hospitality. It is suggested that such early promotion through comparatively restricted routes represents an industry that is both relatively immature and conservative in its approach. Rapid advancement is in part possible because of a tradition of labour turnover and advancement by movement between rather than within organisations. One implication of the importance of the food and beverage route is that, as this is male dominated compared to a number of the other functions, female management career paths are more restricted than those of their male counterparts. It also represents a paradox in that for many hotels the more profitable sector is accommodation rather than food sales. Thus issues pertaining to accommodation pricing, conference and banquet business generation and yield management might be thought to be more important to profitability than restaurant and bar sales are. Riley, Ladkin and Szivas (2002) several times hint that work in the hotel industry implies acceptance of a specific culture. Part of this culture is that tourism and hospitality is perceived as interesting work representing opportunities for travel. In consequence it might be argued that employees have several different perspectives of what constitutes a career within the industry, of which movement across destinations might be as important to some as movement along a more conventional corporate career path. Whatever the reasons, a combination of transience, forms of employment that include payments in kind such as food and accommodation, seasonality and a lack of strong unionisation help explain why wage levels are comparatively low.

There is little doubt that in the past the value of multipliers in the industry was undermined by comparatively low levels of pay and the associated problem of seasonality. In one sense these imply costs additional to those being considered by Hanna (1976). It might be objected that many of the above studies relate solely to the United Kingdom and are representative of a position that might no longer exist. However, studies of employment in the industry continue to show that, compared with other industries, tourism and hospitality retains its position as a relatively low pay industry because of the issues of seasonality. For example Thomas and Townsend (2001: 299) note that: 'hourly earnings for males were 75% of the average for all sectors, and that for females the figure was 83%. Throughout Europe turnover is notoriously high: the average employee tenure is shortest in hotels and restaurants, at 4.1 years compared with 7.8 years in all sectors'. The House of Commons Employment and Education Committee Report (1999) also comments on the problem that part-time working has negative implications for staff training, pay and discrimination.

However, the hitherto conventional viewpoint that tourism is characterised by low productivity has been challenged. Medlik (1985, 1988), in particular, argued that comparisons between industries are distorted if no allowance is made for the differing proportions of full-time and part-time labour. Secondly, he argued that, in many parts of the tourism industry, increasing use of information technology meant that the conventional arguments are no longer supported by the evidence. Utilising UK data between 1979 and 1985 Medlik argued that 'the tourism sector' increased its productivity (as measured by value-added per full-time equivalent employee) from £7,200 to £7,900 compared with £8,800 to £10,000 for the whole economy. From the viewpoint of the British tourist industry, these dates are not particularly conducive to such comparisons as 1979 represented the peak of a business cycle, and 1985 was not higher than 1979, so arguably the potential productivity per employee is understated, and Medlik's forecasts for the period 1985–1990 were for stronger growth. However, Medlik's work again illustrates the difficulties involved in assessing productivity and consequent economic impacts. The period of the 1980s was one of a retailing revolution with a greater use of EPoS (electronic point of sales) systems, more efficient stock control and a reinforcement of trends towards more economic retail operations using edge-of-town and purpose-built shopping centres. Thus, the retail sector is included within Medlik's definition of the tourism sector to take into account the proposition that tourist expenditure involves shopping. In calculating the productivity of tourism labour the use of national retailing data poses problems. The shopping experience of the tourist will vary considerably according to destination and, whilst the retail revolution is fuelled by the multiples, for many tourists part of the holiday experience is shopping in smaller, locally-owned outlets. Secondly, it may be argued that increases of productivity in retailing have little to do with tourism expenditure, but more to do with the adoption of EPoS and other factors, and thus to allocate such increases in retail productivity to tourism is slightly misleading. On the other hand, there is a movement towards a combination of retail and leisure activities, as evidenced by West Edmonton Mall and the Metro Centre, and there is no doubt that some types of tourism and tourists will actively seek out the newer, more productive forms of retailing.

Nonetheless, subsequent to Medlik's pioneering work, there is evidence of a growing level of labour productivity. Thomas and Townsend (2001) point to the situation in London where, over a period from 1991 to 1996, a 6.7% increase in employment was associated with a 67% increase in visitor numbers. Yet, at the same time, London hotels and restaurants increased their dependency on part-time labour, which grew from 31.8% to 37.5% of the London labour force. It would appear that significant regional variation occurs in the United Kingdom. But one sign of a possible improvement in labour practice is that seasonality is beginning to decline and that, at least in some parts of the industry outside of London, there is a substitution of full-time for part-time workers. For his part, Choy (1995) also challenges the preconceptions of the industry as lacking career paths and being one of low pay. In an analysis of Hawaiian employment patterns he finds that, while the industry did offer below-average levels of pay, it nonetheless ranked fifth overall in the service sector. Second, some occupations in travel and tourism are among the highest paid (e.g. airline pilots). Third, the proportion of staff engaged in managerial positions compared well with other sectors of the Hawaiian economy. Choy concludes by stating that the level of job satisfaction is high and that the quality of employment being offered is 'much better than is usually recognised by those outside the industry' (Choy, 1995: 137).

It must also be recognised that the measurement of productivity in the tourism industry is itself a difficult task. Medlik (1988) uses financial measures, and hence the value of turnover is a key measure. Amongst the measures that might be used are:

(1) the ratio between the turnover of the unit and the total payroll (i.e. wages plus pension, insurance costs, etc.);
(2) the value added (i.e. sales minus purchases of goods and services) divided by payroll;
(3) total turnover divided by number employed; and
(4) total value added divided by number employed.

Under such circumstances the value added per employee might therefore be no more than a reflection of increases in prices, and not of volume of output. Hence such measures must attempt to take into account inflation – not simply a weighting by the average retail or consumers prices index, but the actual rate of inflation in tourist-related industries (as shown by, hotel tariffs, for example). Equally 'productivity' may seem to suffer, but this may be due to an increase in the cost of the hotelier's raw resources. From the viewpoint of the host community, whilst productivity may appear to suffer because wages increase, thus reducing the ratio between turnover and payroll, the additional wages being spent in the host community might in fact be beneficial. Consequently the issues of productivity within tourism are, to put it mildly, somewhat complex. However, even utilising the methods indicated above, it would seem that in spite of evidence of increases in tourism productivity within the UK, the productivity of labour in the tourism sector is marginally below that of other service industries and the economy in general. Indeed, for the period 1979–85 it appeared to be significantly below the average by a factor of about 20% (Medlik, 1988).

The economic-impact implications are thus relatively clear. Not only are the income multipliers reduced because of comparatively low levels of pay, but the position is reinforced by most of that labour force being comparatively unqualified, and hence not able to command higher levels of wages in the labour market generally. Add to this the fact that high levels of casual and temporary employment make it more difficult for trade unions to organise themselves, so again wage levels (and hence multipliers) are not as high as they might otherwise be. But there are caveats even to this statement. In circumstances where the tourist industry is a major employer, and a significant contributor to overall economic growth, it escapes from being marginal and becomes part of the main economic processes. Under these circumstances, it becomes possible for labour to command higher wage levels, given perhaps exceptional circumstances. An example of this occurred in Spain in the period after the death of Franco and the democratisation of the Spanish Constitution. The recognition of trade unions and the popularity and enthusiasm for democratic action led to the Spanish Unions being able to increase wage levels in the hotels that were trading on the

Spanish Costas. Also, given the prevailing demographic trends described previously, it can be anticipated that earnings will need to increase in order to attract labour.

To argue that wage levels are low, that labour is comparatively unskilled, and that employment may be at best seasonal may partly explain low multiplier values. But it is not in itself an argument that attempts to improve local economies might be better undertaken by means other than encouraging tourism. In many cases, whether in the Third World or in areas within advanced economies where unemployment is higher than the national averages, the support structures for any industry tend to be weak. Consequently weak multipliers from tourism may be no more than a reflection of deficiencies in such economic systems. If labour is comparatively unskilled, if there are shortages of assets and infrastructure, then almost by definition *any* economic activity will suffer, not just tourism. Evidence for this comes from work undertaken by the Tourism and Recreation Research Unit at Edinburgh University. In 1976 Brownrigg and Greig were arguing the then conventional wisdom that the benefits from tourism expenditure are more apparent than real – it involves a lot of noise and activity but, at the end of the day, locals have surprisingly little to show for it (Brownrigg & Greig, 1976). By 1981, on the basis of work undertaken in the Exmoor National Park, the Unit was reporting that, whilst the multiplier from hotels was but 0.22, this actually compared well with the norm of 0.26 for mixed farming and livestock activities. Moreover, it was actually higher than the 0.13 found in manufacturing processes taking place in the region. The highest multiplier of 0.70 related to bed-and-breakfast accommodation. Certainly in the case of rural economies, tourism is actually attracted to those regions by the very fact that they are underdeveloped. From this viewpoint, tourism does generate flows of income that would not otherwise be forthcoming, although the social and environmental impacts of mass tourism in such areas might arguably create urban-style problems (and costs) in areas still without the infrastructure of cities and towns.

In the above discussion, the assumption has been made that multiplier processes are positive in nature, that they create additional incomes. But they may also create additional costs. Hanna (1976) makes this point:

> For many practical purposes, it is crucial to appreciate that the local multiplier studies of economic gains are just that, and no more. They leave three questions unanswered. First, what are the costs? ... But a more important question arises from the intensely narrow viewpoint of local economic analyses, whether for tourism or any other activity. The local multipliers measure the gains locally; so what will be the gains nationally? ... Rational planning must take account of the whole benefit, not just the local benefit. The third question arises as the

> obverse of the second; what about the gains to an area through the secondary economic effects of tourism in other areas? Just as tourism in a small area 'leaks' benefits to other areas outside, so each small area gains the indirect benefit of 'leaks' from other areas. (Hanna, 1976: 9)

In any assessment of the economic impact of tourism, it must be recognised that the resources allocated to tourism are thus denied to other means of development, and so the opportunity cost of tourism should be taken into account. For example, in a study on the possible extension of a runway for Rotorua's airport, Ryan and Rippey (2000) ask whether the opportunity cost involved for the Rotorua Council had been considered, and what alternative investments had been appraised.

One might say that such considerations 'should' be considered because it is valid to ask whether or not finances ploughed into a tourism development might not have generated a higher economic return if invested into other commercial or social enterprises. However, calculating such a process might be even more complex in terms of data requirements than attempting to calculate the multiplier! Certainly there is evidence that tourism may have unlooked-for costs. Many of these are social and environmental in nature, as discussed in Chapters 8 and 9, but it is possible to provide a few examples here. In July 1987 the Dutch company, Sports Huis opened its leisure centre in Sherwood Forest in the UK with, as it central feature, a dome containing water amenities facilities in a constant temperature of about 80°F set in parkland with other sports facilities. In 1988 Councillor Carol Turner, Chair of Central Nottinghamshire Community Health Council, speaking about her Health Authority's report that in the 12 months since Center Parcs opened nearly 400 people from the complex attended Mansfield General Hospital's Accident and Emergency Department, stated:

> The County and the Districts are all pushing for tourism and Central Notts is one of the main areas because of Sherwood Forest. But they ought to be considering the likely impact. If you bring more people in, even if it is only on a daily basis, it's going to create extra demand on health services. (Carol Turner, 1988, cited in Ryan, 1991a)

Murphy (1985) quotes the circumstances surrounding the building of Florida's Disney World where unskilled construction workers were attracted to the site. The result was that the local Salvation Army was forced into an appeal for $400,000 to build a new shelter, and the City had to employ 150 more police and build a new $6 million police station to deal with the problems of prostitution, drugs, hippies and migrants attracted to the site. On the other hand, it should be noted that such apparent blindness to the nature of economic accounting based on market transactions and failure to account of the social costs is not unique to tourism. For example,

Waring (1988) criticises the composition of National Income Accounting as totally underestimating the contribution that women make to the economy simply because there is no estimate of the value of their labour in the home.

Tourism Expenditure Modelling

Because of the problems of estimating multipliers at regional and subregional levels, and the need for detailed inter-sector economic data, some studies have simply sought to better understand tourist expenditure and to estimate economic impacts from these calculations alone. For example, Ryan (1996b) argues that, when assessing the economic impact of events, the key variables are simple to identify, and include the numbers of out-of-region visitors that are attracted to the event, the duration of their stay, the main types of accommodation used and the spending on such accommodation. To these can be added expenditure on food and drink. An estimate of these main variables will account for much of the first-round impact of tourist spending. Given that, in the short term, the determinants of the multiplier will be fixed, then the first-round expenditure flows will be the major determinants of economic impact. Aguiló Perez and Juaneda Sampol (2000) adopt a similar argument with reference to mass package holiday destinations such as the Balearic Islands. They note that in such cases much of the tourist expenditure is initially paid in the tourist-generating country and as a result only 'pocket money expenditures' occur outside of the accommodation in the tourist-receiving country. In their view it thus becomes important to disaggregate tourist spending to estimate tourist income at a destination. Accordingly, having surveyed 5,500 tourists at Balearic Island airports, they propose a regression model within which the key variables are the duration of stay and the numbers of people in declared expenditures that comprise two components, expenditure in the country of origin and spending at the destination. These data are associated with other data derived from the survey, including nationality, age, profession, type of accommodation used, type of booking and some attitudinal measures. From these figures Aguiló Perez and Juaneda Sampol (2000) were able to derive spending per type of tourist. One implication of this approach is that, by applying these expenditure figures to the total profile of Balearic island visitors, it is easy to assess total economic impact.

One of the implications of the growing use of expenditure-based modelling of tourism impacts is the growth in the number of studies that are very location- and time-specific. While arguably these studies are primarily of interest to those responsible for tourism promotion and planning in those areas, on occasion such studies make an additional contribution to conceptual or methodological thinking. In some instances the researchers might do little more than identify problems that might be of note to others undertaking similar work. For example Ryan and Evans (2002) note the problems of estimating economic impacts in regions of secondary importance in tourism, but which straddle transport routes that connect two or more primary tourism regions. In their study of the Rangitikei region in New Zealand, in one estimate of economic impacts they exclude much of the out-of-region visitor spending in cafes, restaurants and petrol stations in the region as not being attributable to the tourist attractions in the Rangitikei region. Instead they argue that the impacts are due to the tourist flow on State Highway One that arises from movements to the ski-fields of Tongariro, or from the flow of tourists to and from the tourist regions of Taupo and Wellington. In short, in this instance visitor expenditure is derived from other regions and their attractiveness and so might be categorised as 'indirect economic impact'. For their part Walpole and Goodwin (2000) indicate the nature of leakages when studying the impacts of tourism on Komodo National Park, Indonesia. It is evident that the main economic benefits are unequally distributed over the communities near the park, with Labuan Bajo receiving almost all the visitor spending on accommodation owing to its near monopoly of hotel provision during the study period. Walpole and Goodwin note that only about 1% of visitor spending accrues to those actually resident in the park, while 50–60% of tourist expenditure leaks out of the region owing to the import of goods and services and non-local ownership of businesses in the region. Additional factors that reduced the level of economic impact were again a lack of local capital and the low levels of wages being paid.

Input–Output analysis

One of the means of assessing the impact of tourist expenditure on other areas of the economic system is the use of input–output analysis. Essentially this technique attempts to show the flow of economic transactions through the economy within a given time span, usually a year. It is a further refinement of the basic multiplier processes in that it seeks to show the inter-relationship between defined sectors of the economic system. Traditionally undertaken with industrial sectors, its transference to service sectors (and in particular to tourism sectors) is partly handicapped by the lack of definition of what exactly is the tourism industry. Whilst it may be defined as a series of consumer experiences relating to leisure and recreation requiring trips away from home, in terms of a supply-led definition there is a problem from the statistical viewpoint in that formally there is no standard industrial classification. S.L.J. Smith (1989) highlights the problem thus:

> Tourism often lacks credibility in the eyes of policy analysts and decision-makers because the field is poorly defined and because the data

> used to substantiate many of the claims concerning the size and importance of the industry are inadequate ... A data-collection problem even more frustrating than double-counting is the omission of data. (Smith, 1989: 9)

Within many countries there is no Standard Industrial Classification (SIC) code for the 'tourism industry'. Thus attempts to show the pattern of flows of expenditure between economic sectors often require the researcher to utilise subcategories, to estimate proportions of a sector or subsector that tourism might account for, or even to ignore some activities. For example, for a restaurant located in a city, how much of its lunchtime trade might be trade to local office workers, and how much to tourists who are visiting the city?

In spite of the difficulties, some attempts have been made to undertake such an analysis. One of the first was that of Richards (1972), who constructed a matrix covering 27 UK industrial sectors. This type of approach was adopted in early work on economic impacts and multipliers in the 1970s for Anglesey and other parts of Wales and was developed by a team initially based at Bangor University. This pioneering work is reported by Archer and Owen (1971) and Archer (1977, 1980, 1984). The approach permits estimates of the impact of tourism on other sectors of the economy, for example the employment that tourism generates. For example Richards (1972) calculated that tourism accounted for 12.61% of employment in the rail transport industry, and for 1.13% in the chemicals industry. It cannot, however, be emphasised too much just how difficult it is to undertake such estimates. Archer (1976), Murphy (1983a), Mathieson and Wall (1982), and S.L.J. Smith (1989) all indicate the difficulties associated with such techniques. Yet there are many instances where, in spite of these difficulties, researchers have utilised findings from one area and applied them to another. Vaughan (1986) indicates the types of assumptions that researchers are thus making as:

> This method, therefore, assumes that the pattern of spending, and in some cases the total amount, in the area in which the original study was conducted is the same as in the area for which the estimates are being made. It also assumes that the combinations of business types are the same. (Vaughan, 1986: 3)

Another factor relating to such studies is the size of the region being considered. It is becoming more common for input–output analysis to be conducted at regional as well as national levels because of the improvement of statistical series at regional level owing to the greater use of computers to extract regional statistics from national data. However, it should be noted that such regions are generally based on administrative zones rather than on tourist flows – in short it is the availability of the data that drives the calculation rather than the actual patterns of tourist trips. One such example is the work of Wagner (1997) in Guaraqueçaba, Brazil. However, Wagner departs from a conventional input–output matrix by developing what is termed a 'social accounting matrix' (SAM). It is suggested that three advantages accrue from the matrix. First, it describes the economic links between production, income distribution and demand. Second, the presentation of the data is a synthesis of different forms of data collected for differing administrative purposes. Third, it permits the calculation of regional multipliers. Indeed Wagner (1997: 593) goes so far as to suggest that 'While an I/O model can do similar analyses as a SAM, the latter is a more thorough methodology. In fact, an I/O model is a subset of a SAM'. Consequently the matrix consists of the datasets shown in Table 7.2, which represents but a summary for in the original some of the cells were further sub-divided (for example the Households sector is divided into different income groups). The blank cells are in fact completed with the appropriate values derived from the statistics of inter-related economic flows based on expenditures (listed in the columns) and receipts (listed in the rows). The matrix 'works' on the assumptions that expenditures equal receipts; therefore, as an example, household incomes would be the receipts resulting from expenditures by institutions. (For a fuller description and description of input–output analysis, see Sohn, 1986). Although this is not stated by Wagner, it is evident that some of the data can only be best estimates as, for example, the detail provided in the notes explain that food manufacturing 'describes the process of legally and illegally *palmito*' (Wagner, 1997: 595). This implies a further problem with such approaches that are based on formal statistical series, and that is the degree to which a black economy exists. There is little doubt that, particularly in marginal economies where tourism is often being promoted, the black or informal economy can be very important. In consequence it will be difficult to assess the true importance of tourism as an economic activity.

Wagner (1997) then calculates the output and employment multipliers, which are found to possess values between 1.0 and 2.0. From the description it is obvious that a number of problems exist with this approach, as with others. For example, it is assumed that the coefficients between the different industry sectors remain a constant. For example, it might be stated that within a regional economy tourism accounts continually for 0.6 (or 60%) of the expenditure on road construction and maintenance, or that the ratio between hotel expenditures and wage costs is continually 0.4 (or, to express it another way, wage costs account for 40% of hotel costs). It has been questioned whether such assumptions are valid even in the short term, much less over a longer term. For example if, as a response to a major event, hotel employers respond either by employing more people, or by

Table 7.2 A social-accounting matrix

Receipts	*Activity*	*Factor*	*Institutions*	*Exports*	*Totals*
Activities					
Rural farms					
Rural business					
Construction					
Manufacturing					
Commerce					
Services					
Transportation					
Government enterprise					
Factors					
Indirect business taxes					
Capital rent					
Labour income					
Institutions					
Households					
Capital investment					
Enterprises					
Government					
Imports					
Totals					

After Wagner (1997)

paying overtime rates, then the ratio between labour cost and hotel revenue changes. Again, over the longer run, more competition for labour might occur, thereby increasing labour costs. One implication of this is that the application of any method of calculating economic impacts requires a process of continuous monitoring, otherwise one is simply left with 'snapshots' that might be less applicable over time. It can also be observed that concentration on economic transactions is only a partial view, as the increase in visitor numbers may be having longer-term environmental or social costs that are slow to become apparent in market transactions. For example, the government–household sector might be subject to 'ratchet' effects where, after a growing social problem, a government might respond by significantly increasing expenditure on, say, law enforcement, thereby affecting both employment and tax flows. In short, market transactions become reactive to 'real' changes and have failed to measure the actual process of those changes.

Nonetheless, before concluding that input–output analysis may be fundamentally flawed for these reasons, it is still possible to argue that the technique possesses many advantages. For example an interesting attempt to combine input–output analysis with a study of the impacts of tourism at a regional level is provided by Freeman and Sultan (1997). In a study of the impact of tourism on the Israeli economy, they identified not only different economic sectors, but also six districts within Israel in order to identify the inter- and intra-regional effects of tourism. They also estimated the multiplier effects from domestic and international tourism in each of these six regions. As might be expected, a range of multiplier values emanated that depended on the type of tourism and the economic structure of each of the regions, with a key component being the visitor/employee ratio. While this study possesses interest, it also reveals some of the weaknesses involved in such studies. First, it assumes that the inter-sector coefficients remain constant and do not change in response to changing prices, although the authors argue that this is justifiable on the premise of short-term rigidities in the system. Second, the data requirements are large and are inevitably derived from a number of different sources, some of which were collected over different periods. For example the data include: a survey of 1000 respondents about domestic tourism collected over a period from 1991 to 1994, a 1993 survey of various service providers including restaurants and car rental companies, input–output coefficients for 1988, and other different sources. The study therefore reveals, in part, issues about the nature of tourism statistical series and their relationships with other sets of statistics.

In another study of inter-regional movements, Smale and Nykiforuk (2001) utilised data based on the 25 Canadian major census areas to develop a series of location quotients of tourist movements, noting the dynamic nature of changes in the creation of these location quotients. But, as S.L.J. Smith (1989) pointed out in his use of spatial modelling of Canadian tourism flows, such techniques may be pertinent to a country like Canada, where much of the movement of visitors is tied to VFR and hence metropolitan zones dominate tourist flows because of their population densities. Nonetheless, this study provides further illustration of the means by which economic data can be related to spatial distribution and movement.

Satellite Tourism Accounts

It was partly this issue of statistical series that accounted for the development of satellite accounts. Satellite tourism accounts are fairly well known in principle, but comparatively new in implementation. The purposes of satellite accounts are:

(1) To make tourism definitions and classifications compatible and consistent with those of other industries within the purview of national income accounting.
(2) To integrate tourism into the framework of the national accounts. (WTO, 2001b)

The term, 'satellite' therefore implies a derivation of statistics from national accounting procedures. The French were among the first to establish and calculate statistics based on these premises (Soisson, 1979), and in 1982 the General Assembly of the World Tourism Organisation considered a report by its Secretary General on the use of such accounting methods (WTO, 1982). The adoption of satellite accounting by the WTO led to renewed interest, and in 1991 Canada proposed a methodology and calculations (Wells, 1991) that were to become the model for many of the initiatives that occurred in the last decade of the twentieth century. Indeed it is a policy among WTO members and other countries such as New Zealand to produce such accounts, and by 2002 satellite accounts had been produced by countries such as Canada, the Scandinavian countries, Australia and New Zealand.

The calculation of satellite accounts depends on three categories of economic activity, these being:

(1) characteristic tourism commodities;
(2) tourism-related commodities;
(3) non-tourism commodities.

Soisson (1979) indicated the nature of the relationship, as shown in Figure 7.2. The application of this methodology is shown in Figure 7.3, which is derived from the New Zealand Satellite Accounts for the year 2000 (Statistics New Zealand, 2001) although the data are derived from 1996.

Satellite accounts are gaining acceptance because of their relationships to national accounting and their ability to incorporate generally-accepted source's of statistics. One of the problems associated with other methods of data are that, particularly in tourism expenditure modelling, the sample sets may be comparatively small and subject to unknown degrees of error. Even when discussing such basic data sets as the numbers of overseas visitors, the data may not be based on an examination of every landing card completed by arrivals, but on a sample of such cards. Consequently while

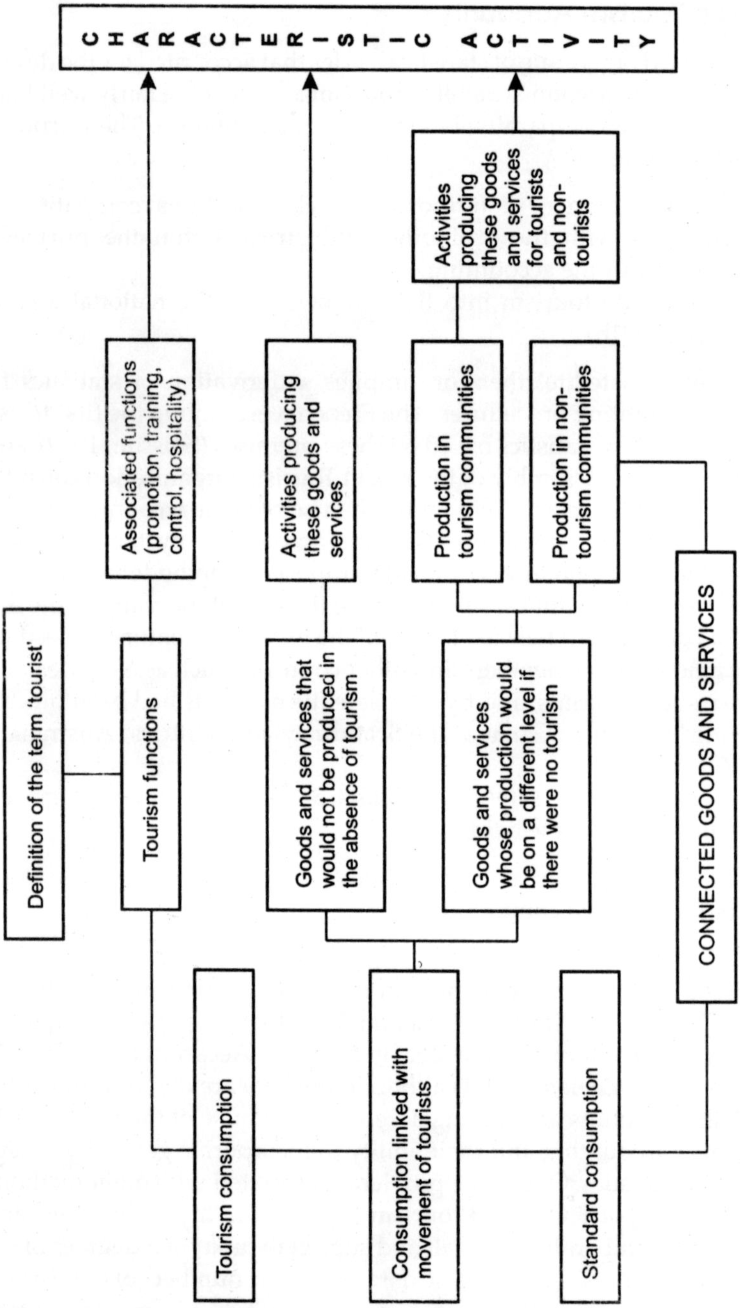

Figure 7.2 Tourism account: Methodologies

the total number of arrivals is known, the countries from which they arrive, data on the purpose of the trip and the possible duration of the stay will be derived from sampling the total numbers of cards. Immigration authorities around the world are increasingly setting up computer systems that will directly record each arrival and indeed, for security reasons, are examining methods based on techniques such as retina examination that will both speed up arrival immigration clearance times and present higher levels of

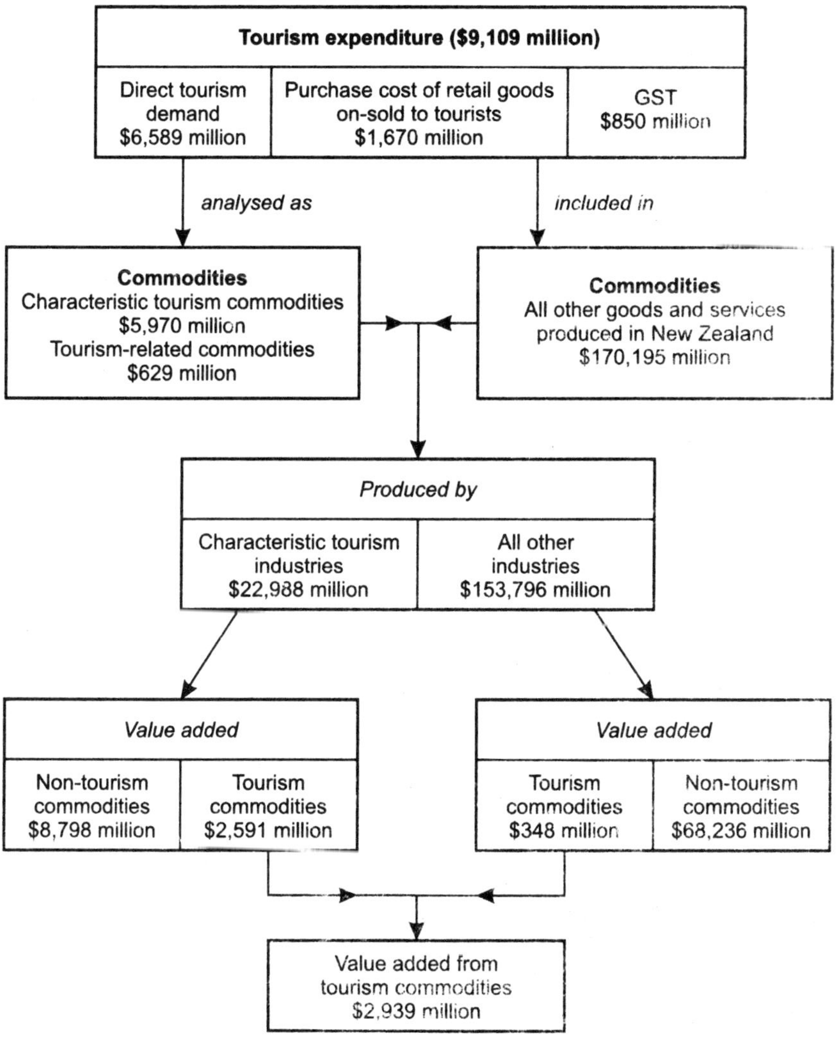

Figure 7.3 The 2000 New Zealand satellite accounts
Based on 1996 data (Tourism Research Council, 2001)

security. Again, estimates of visitor expenditure based on surveys are still subject to the problem of respondent recall of that expenditure. On the other hand satellite accounts are derived from such sources as taxation records and census data and thus possess higher degrees of stability and probably accuracy.

This is not to say that there have not been critics of the methods. Smith and Wilton (1997), for example, queried the accounting procedures being suggested by the World Travel and Tourism Council (WTTC) and indicated discrepancies between those methods and the guidelines issued by the World Tourism Organisation (WTO). Of concern to Smith and Wilton is that the WTTC methodology seems to have over-estimated the impact of tourism in Canada by perhaps as much as three times. The WTTC (1997) also acknowledged that its own estimates for the Danish economy were much larger than those calculated by Hansen and Jensen (1996) in a report commissioned by the Danish Tourist Board. Examination of the debate reveals a dispute over definitions and the arbitrary nature of some of those definitions. Indeed, the very definition of a 'tourist trip' is in dispute as definitions of domestic tourism trips vary. For example (Smith, 1995), is a shopping trip by car in North America that extends over a distance of 58.5 miles or more a tourist trip? For their part the WTTC would allocate jobs involved in the manufacture of caravans. not to the manufacturing sector, but to the tourism-related sector. Another problem is that sometimes the data did not permit the fine distinctions required by the methodology. For example, in the first set of satellite accounts for New Zealand, day-trip expenditure estimates were based on surveys of Australian in-state trips (this was subsequently corrected when the findings of the New Zealand domestic visitors' survey became available). In both the 2000 and 2001 accounts, airline freight revenues were attributed to tourism but, in capital expenditures, while hotel construction was attributed to tourism, airport construction was not. In short, there remain practical decisions as to what is, and what is not, a tourism-characteristic activity or service even before finding out what data actually exist.

Do such problems invalidate the attempt? In the early 2000s the state of satellite accounting is still embryonic and there is no better way of understanding the nature of the problems than by attempting the calculations and comparing results and methodologies across different countries. Recognising this, in September, 1999, the WTO-OECD-Eurostat Inter-Secretariat Working Group was established to develop a series of technical documents. Throughout 2001 the WTO published a series of such papers dealing specifically with definitions and practices, and some of this material is available through the Internet. At the end of the day, it can be argued that no mode of calculation will be entirely beyond criticism because to some extent there will be an arbitrary component in the definition of any activity; but a commonality in definitions is emerging. One advantage of such commonality is that the definition drives the nature of the data collection. However, from the author's own experience of being involved in New Zealand's consideration of its own tourism statistics, an important relationship exists between data collection, statistical generation and the uses to which the statistics can be put. One aspect that emerged very clearly from the discussions of the New Zealand Tourism Research Council Working Group on tourism statistics in 2002 is that what might be sufficient for national bodies (including government) is not always sufficient for those responsible for tourism planning at regional level. This is particularly true when it comes to advising entrepreneurs on capital investment or advising local authorities on the implications of local taxation policies. Consequently, progress on the development of satellite accounts is seemingly being accompanied by a resurgence of interest in regional and local economic impact studies as those concerned with site specific and local tourism flows and investments seek to better understand their relationship with the national economy. Accompanying this movement are advances in computing that permit much better analysis of such issues at subregional level, although in some administrations the costs of such information derivation still impede some advances. Some of these issues are again referred to in Chapter 9.

Tourism and the Balance of Payments

There is at least one further impact of tourism that requires some consideration, and that is its impact on the balance of payments. In the case of developing countries, one rationale for tourism is that it is a means of earning foreign (hard) currencies, and indeed it may be one of the only few means for such economies to earn export revenue. This becomes especially important at times when world prices for raw commodities such as sugar, rubber and minerals may not be high. In the case of developing countries, however, the expected earnings from tourism may not be as high as initially hoped for, especially if they depend on tour operators and airlines that are based in the tourist-generating countries. In the case of package holidays, approximately 37–40% of the cost paid by the tourist will relate to travel to the tourist-receiving country, and that is usually paid to the airline within the tourist-generating country – an airline that may itself be a subsidiary of the tour operator (Flook, 2001). An approximation of the tour operator's cost structure indicates how little of the tourist's expenditure actually reaches the tourist-receiving country. Indeed, it may be as little as one-third of the package holiday price paid by the tourist. Consequently, the expenditure by the tourist at the holiday destination on souvenirs and other elements of the holiday can be seen as being important in terms of generating income for the host society.

In terms of payment to the hotelier, much of this is in turn used by the hotelier for the purchase of imports. Evidence for this comes from studies undertaken by the Caribbean Tourism Research and Development Centre (1984) in its study of the links between tourism and local agriculture. In the case of St Lucia in 1983, an estimated 58% of the food consumed by tourists was imported. In particular 82% of the meat eaten by tourists was imported. Henshall-Momsen (1986) notes that in many cases hotels in the initial stages of tourism attempt to provide tourists with the diet that reflects the eating patterns of the tourist-generating country, and only later introduce more local foods cooked in the local manner. (To the imports of food, must also be added the imports of furniture, equipment and perhaps even significant parts of the very hotel itself.) However, increasingly tourists will adopt the cuisine of the host country, and indeed some types of tourists will actively seek an 'authentic' experience. The Caribbean again provides an example of this with the development, since 1978, of the 'SuperClub' hotels, which are owned by Jamaican businessmen. One of their hotels, 'Jamaica Jamaica' specifically seeks to reproduce a Jamaican 'experience' rather than an 'international' one.

The developing country, in its attempts to build up tourism, generally needs to import many other commodities. In his study of the role played by the establishment of National Parks in Africa as a tourist-generating asset, Marsh (1986) notes that Park Lodges are often constructed with imported materials and have foreign staff; park agency vehicles such as Land Rovers are imported, and National Park tours are organised by foreign companies that repatriate the profits. The host country is further disadvantaged by the fact that it may not have well-established banking facilities in the tourist-generating country. Tourists buy their travellers' cheques in the country of trip origin, and it is their banks that obtain the first round of commission. It is the banks in the tourist-receiving country that sustain the costs of remitting the cheques back to the original issuer. If tourists use their credit cards, it is the retailer in the tourist-receiving area who pays the fee to the card issuer, whilst the bank in the issuing country receives the interest on any loan that is made.

The great propensities to import, and the high percentage of the tourists' expenditure that actually never leaves the shores of the tourist-generating country, thus means that the net gains to the tourist-receiving country are less than might otherwise be expected. In the case of the Caribbean area, the Caribbean Tourism Research and Development Centre estimated that in 1979 out of total earnings of $US3.3 billion just over one-third was retained. Lea (1988) quotes the example of Fiji where approximately only 20% of tourist earnings are retained.

Whilst the developing tourist-receiving countries may not gain as much as might at first sight seem possible, it is nonetheless important to retain the fact that such countries do actually receive a surplus on their tourism balance of payments. This is not the case for many developed countries, which as the tourist generators actually sustain deficits on their balance of payments from the tourism account. As such these deficits can be regarded as not simply 'leakages' within their own economies, but, possibly optimistically, a means by which monies are transferred from the richer nations to the poorer. Whether the social costs associated with such earnings are worth the revenue is, however, a question that needs to be considered. Nor must it be seen as axiomatic that richer nations sustain deficits on their tourism balance of payments. For example Britain has often sustained a surplus on its tourism invisibles.

Determinants of the Local Impact of Tourism

The economic impacts of tourism are thus complex to assess. From the above it is, however, possible to begin to identify some of the variables that will determine the value of the impact. These can be summarised as being:

(1) *The nature of the tourist facilities and their attractions.* The size of the tourist destination and its context is important. Can the tourist destination absorb large numbers of tourists and does it have the necessary infrastructure, both physically and economic not only to support any given number of tourists but to also retain tourist expenditures within its own area?

(2) *The volume, and nature of the tourists and their spending patterns.* Can the area sustain tourists who require overnight stays, or is it simply meeting a need for day visits? What are the forms of accommodation that are available? Are the tourists visiting all the year round, or simply at certain times of the year? Do they tend to patronise local businesses? Do they require resources from outside the host community?

(3) *The skills of the host community and the levels of, and numbers of jobs held by them.* Do tourist organisations import labour of all types, or can the local labour force meet the requirement of the tourist enterprises? What impact does tourism have on wage levels, and is tourism competing with other occupations for labour? Does tourism attract labour that might otherwise enter other professions that might not pay so well but which have social significance (e.g. teaching, nursing)?

(4) *The facilities themselves.* Are local tourist facilities owned by members of the host community? What are the sizes of these businesses? To what extent are they locally financed?

Mules (2000) notes that economic impacts have to be interpreted far more widely than in the past. First, he argues that economic impacts were traditionally restricted to the positive, and not to the negative. Secondly, not all positive impact are measured, and Mules cites the business deals done in hospitality tents at events as being potentially important, but not being measured. However, the traditional methods of economic impact assessment have, at times, been driven by data availability, or by the nature of the economic model being adopted, and to some extent therefore, the estimate contains somewhat arbitrary. Fourth, economists have been slow to adopt feedback mechanisms within their models. For example, in the short term the demand generated by tourists might increase land values. But if these increased land values subsequently make it difficult for a local labour force to purchase homes, or if increased land prices deter some investments, then the consequences of short-term gain will not have been incorporated into the economic modelling process. In part, this argument is a subset of those arguments that note the problems of assuming fixed coefficients between the factors of production. Consequently Mules (2000) notes the advantages of more general equilibrium models that incorporate the effects of things such as changing exchange rates, changing government responses to changed revenue sources (such as tourist spending on non-refundable goods and services or value added taxes), and wage and employment levels. Unfortunately, it has been a common refrain in this chapter that the economic modelling of tourism requires considerable volumes of data, and computable general equilibrium models probably require even more than those needed by multiplier or input–output analysis.

Theoretically general equilibrium models effectively incorporate opportunity costs, and thereby can generate surprising results. A controversial finding in Australia was that tourism was effectively reducing the Gross State Product of Queensland, where tourism is one of the major drivers of the economy. Adams and Parmenter (1995) concluded, however, that the growth of tourism was creating an overall negative impact on the Queensland economy as compared with Victoria. One of the reasons for their finding was the less productive use that the tourism sector was making of assets when compared to other industries, plus the fact that many of the head offices of the hotels and airlines operating in Queensland were actually located elsewhere. There are, however, significant problems with this approach, and much of it relates to the basis of comparison and the nature of the assumptions being made. For example, could it be argued that slower growth rates in tourism would have released economic resources for use by other industry sectors? And would those industry sectors have been run by Queensland-based business organisations?

In 2001 the World Travel and Tourism Council (WTTC) commissioned a study to examine more carefully the use of general equilibrium modelling and its links to tourism satellite accounts in order to better understand the real-time implications of tourism and its impacts. Richard Miller, Vice President of the WTTC justified this interest on the premise that:

> CGE (computable general equilibrium) models have advantages over a pure TSA/input–output analysis in guiding government policy and can be very useful for addressing particular questions. So, for example, economists working in the UK Treasury use CGE modelling techniques on the economic implications of changes in indirect taxes...
>
> WTTC believes that recent events in the UK (foot-and-mouth) and the USA (the terrorist attacks on New York and Washington, DC) have highlighted the vital importance of real-time economic information on travel and tourism and raised the value and urgency of this new research. (Miller, 2002: 5)

Consequently Cooper and Wilson (2002) used satellite accounting and input–output data relating to the UK to estimate the impact of shocks to travel and tourism in the UK. These shocks were assumed to be a permanent change, and included changes such as a 10% increase in travel and tourism demand, and a 10% increase in travel and tourism prices relative to all other prices. This latter might occur because of increases in fuel costs, taxation changes aimed at conservation of energy, or other similar policies. Cooper and Wilson concluded that a short run 0.5% decline in UK GDP would result and GDP would continue to be lower than would otherwise be the case. Among the rationalisations provided for this type of modelling is the observation that, as travel and tourism become increasingly important in GDP formation, so too the importance of shocks to tourism are translated into significant implications for the wider economy. Finally, it is of interest to note the concluding comments of Dwyer *et al.* (in press), who argue that CGE models emphasise the importance of the structure of tourism industries and that a state of market share maintenance might well actually hide losses of GDP in that part of the economy relating to tourism. These losses are not being revealed in GDP data because of growth in other sectors. Dwyer *et al.* also conclude that the whole area of tourism economic forecasting and impact assessment is about to enter an interesting phase. Certainly it can be concluded that there is a significantly better understanding of the nature of tourism impacts than existed only a decade ago, but equally it appears that the same problems surface with recurring frequency. To some extent any modelling process is going to be constrained by the nature of the parameters thought to be important, the available data and the time and destination zones being analysed. Much of the progress of the last decade is based on computerisation making various datasets more available to economists, and on the ability of desktops to utilise new computer-based econometric and statistical modelling programs. In one sense there remains one other persistent problem not discussed in the chapter, and that is whether there is a growing gap between those producing the forecasts and assessments, and those who are supposed to use them. Do the latter appreciate the nature of the work undertaken by the former? To what extent do the assessments appear as if by magic from a computerised box? In short, is there a further power differential based on knowledge and understanding that has yet to be considered within the political processes that surround tourism policies and their implementation?

Appendix

Archer's Tourist Expenditure Model for estimating the multiplier effects for tourist expenditure is as follows.

$$1+\sum_{j=1}^{N}\sum_{i=1}^{n} Q_j K_{ij} V_i \left[\frac{1}{1-L\sum_{i=1}^{n} X_i Z_i V_i}\right]$$

where j = types of tourist accommodation, 1 ... N
I = types of consumer outlet, 1 ... n
Q = the proportions spent on each type of accommodation
K = the proportions spent on each type of consumer outlet
V = the income generation in each category of expenditure
Z = the proportion of income spent within the region by the inhabitants.

The above gives an aggregated model for tourist expenditure, but what is important is to disaggregate data in order to assess the multiplier values associated with different types of accommodation and tourist activity. Archer and Owen (1971) suggest the following form.

The multiplier for a given category of accommodation is:

$$1+\sum_{i=1}^{n} K_i V_i \left[\frac{1}{1-L\sum_{i=1}^{n} X_i Z_i V_i}\right]$$

where K_i = the proportion spent on each type of consumer outlet
V_i = the income generation in each category of accommodation
L = the propensity to consume
X_i = the pattern of consumer spending
Z = the proportion of income spent within the region by the inhabitants.

Wheeller in his study undertaken for the Wales Tourist Board (cited in Ryan, 1991a) comments that the estimation procedure thereby falls into two parts: first, the income generation associated with each item of tourist expenditure (the direct effect), and second, the multiplier effect of the spending of this income within the local area by residents. To assess the income each activity needs to be separately identified, and Archer and Owen (1971) identified separate values for:

(1) tourist expenditure on hotel and guest house accommodation;
(2) income generated by tourist expenditure in hiring stationary caravans;
(3) income generated by tourist expenditure in farmhouses and bed-and-breakfast houses;
(4) income generated by of tourist expenditure on camping;
(5) income generated by tourist expenditure in shops;
(6) income generated by tourist expenditure in garages;
(7) income generation from money circulating into rates and building.

In seeking to calculate the value of the multiplier, technically the calculations need to take into account the proportion of expenditure that arises from additions to income that results from tourism. In practice it is simpler to use the average propensity to consume, rather than the marginal propensity to consume. Arguably, within the short term, if spending patterns by the recipients of tourism expenditure are consistent, then by definition the average propensity to consume (APC) is equal to the marginal propensity to consume (MPC). Practically the APC is a much easier figure to collect from respondents.

One of the major problems is evident, and that is the information requirements. Without surveys, there is usually little regional data that can be used. Thus for example, in the original study undertaken on Anglesey, Archer and Owen (1971) had to use an estimated APC drawn from national data of 0.9. This was itself an estimate where the Family Expenditure Survey indicated a value of 0.84 for Rural Households, whilst National Income Tables gave a value of 0.93. Another practical problem that Ryan and Connor (1981) came across was in estimating proportions of retail expenditure in areas where tourism is still developing, as retailers have difficulty in assessing the proportion of sales that are accounted for by visitors, whilst the nature of the retail mix is also important. In practice many multiplier studies do not go beyond the first couple of rounds of the process. It is also difficult to check the results that are obtained, although one method is to utilise input–output analysis, but again the feasibility of this will be constrained by the availability of the required data. If a multiplier study is being considered, it is also important to be able to identify the nature of the activities undertaken by tourists, and their comparative

Table 7.3 Employment directly and indirectly due to tourism in the UK economy

Industry Group	*% of Employment due to Tourism*
Agriculture	0.22
Extractive	1.86
Food, drink, and tobacco	0.48
Chemicals and allied industries	1.13
Metals, engineering and vehicles	1.26
Textiles, Leather and clothing	0.26
Other manufacturing	2.53
Construction	0.36
Gas, electricity and water	1.41
Road transport	6.89
Rail transport	12.61
Other transport	9.46
Communications	8.13
Distributive trades	2.47
Other services	9.58

Source: Richards (1972)

importance. Thus, for example within a Canadian context, the role of the outfitters will be of importance; within the UK, day-trip activity will be important; within an Australian context, beach use is important. The nature of the tourist destination zone is a significant variable, and is thus another reason why the non-survey techniques described by Vaughan (1986) are of limited usefulness.

Chapter 8

Tourism Impacts on the Environment

The tourism literature is rich in examples of tourism impacts on the natural environment and the various species that depend on those environments. The concern of this chapter is to examine, by giving examples, the types of conflicts that have arisen and then to argue that even while tourism may, in places, threaten the environment, equally, those factors that cause adverse changes in our biosystems also adversely affect the quality of the tourist experience. Finally, the chapter looks at some of the ways in which the negative impacts of tourism might be minimised.

Tourism as a Threat to the Environment

It is not difficult to make the case that tourism is damaging to the environment. One example of significant impact can be found in the Alps. Approximately 40–50 million people visit the Alps every year, and these tourists are supported by an infrastructure of more than 40,000 ski runs and 12,000 ski lifts and cable railways. Mader (1988) notes that previously-unvisited areas are continually being made accessible. Bulldozers reshape the mountains, and trees are felled. The result is that the drainage patterns are continually being altered. Trees no longer halt the rush of melting waters; the roads, trails and hardened soil become ducts by which waters are carried further than before. In 1983, the area around Axamer Lizum in Austria, which had been developed for the 1964 and 1976 Winter Olympics, suffered from mudslides caused, according to environmental conservationists, by the bulldozing of the area to create 68 hectares of ski runs. It would appear that landslides are becoming more common, and, in 1987, 23 people were killed in a landslide at the camping site near Annecy in the French Alps, while 3 villages were buried in a landslide at Valtellina in the Italian Alps. Mader (1988) further comments that, on any Sunday when the weather is fine, 6,000 cars drive to Grindelwald, and in doing so consume 80,000 litres of petrol to produce 9 tons of carbon monoxide, 1.3 tons of hydrocarbon, 1.7 litres of nitrogen and 24 pounds of lead. Such emissions are also accumulatively damaging to the environment.

In the Himalayas, the trek to Everest is now so well established as a tourist path that, in 1989, a special expedition was mounted to clean up the litter that lay around base camp. It was estimated that, between 1953 and the early 1990s, more than 50 tons of plastic, glass and metal had been dumped in what was termed 'the world's highest junkyard'. Subsequent expeditions have been necessary to clean up the area and other parts of the mountain chain. For example, clean-up operations were launched in 2001 and 2002 under the auspices of Dhauli Guéri to undertake further cleaning on the world's seventh highest peak, that of Mount Dhaulagiri (http://www.dhaulagueri.com, 2002). In the month of May, 2001, alone, 40 people reached the peak of Everest. This number, repeated subsequently, is due to the advent of guided tours to the Himalayas. In August, 2001, the BBC ran, on its web pages, a debate about over use of Everest and the dumping of rubbish. A wide range of international opinions was elicited, and opposing views discussed. However, there appeared to be considerable support for imposing extra fees for removing rubbish from this highest of all tourist locations. Elsewhere in the Himalayas, where trekking holiday companies operate, a continuing history of other tourism impacts has been recorded since the 1960s. Tuting (1989), for example, noted the use of wood to heat water to meet the needs of tourists for a wash and shower after their day's trek. It has been estimated that the trekking tourist burns about 14 pounds of wood per day, leading to further deforestation (Mader 1988), resulting in damage to the water drainage patterns. The Nepalese government has had to develop schemes of afforestation, whilst stopping local people from using wood for heating, a practice carried out from time immemorial. The costs of tourism thus include afforestation, and the starting of hydroelectric and other electrification schemes (Cullen, 1986).

Just as the physical environment is threatened, so too is the flora and fauna of different tourist locations. Renton (1989) describes the impact of tourism on the breeding habits of the loggerhead turtle on the Greek island of Zakynthos thus:

> A female, on average, lays five nests a summer, and can hope that two or three of her hatchlings will survive natural predators at sea and hope to make it to adulthood. But these statistics are thrown awry on beaches where man plays. The first hazard the mother turtle faces is from motor boats and jet-skis as she approaches her ancestral breeding ground; the noise can send her back to sea ... Then, on the beach, plastic bags get mistaken for jellyfish, and are eaten with fatal mistakes. Should she manage to lay her eggs undisturbed, they are then at the mercy of sand-castle diggers, cars and motorbikes or even people planting beach umbrellas. But the most dangerous time is at hatching. As the young turtles scuttle to the surf, any light or noise can disorientate them. Then they can wander off to eventually die of dehydration and heat exhaustion. (Renton, 1989: 39)

The example of Zakynthos represents, in a small way, the nature of the conflict between tourism and the environment. Until 1977 the beach at

Laganas was comparatively under-developed, but in 1982 it was necessary for the Greek authorities to impose a ban on building. Even so, it has been estimated that about 50% of all Zakynthos tourist facilities are to be found in the Bay of Laganas (Katselidis & Dimopoulos, 2000). Consequently the use of the beach by holidaymakers clashed with the nesting needs of the turtles. In 1983 the Sea Turtle Protection Society was formed, and in 1986 an EC-funded monitoring project was commenced with support from the World Wildlife fund. By 1987 it became necessary to impose bans on beach use between dawn and dusk and bans were also imposed on the use of speed boats. For those local people attracted to the tourism industry from the rural hinterland, and who invested family savings in the paraphernalia of the modern beach tourism industry, the turtles became a threat to their livelihood. Initially occupancy rates in the hotels fell as the foreign tour operators moved their business elsewhere in response to the growing tension between local people and conservation groups. The landowners at Yerakas, who hoped to take advantage of the tourist, were afraid that their hopes to cash in on tourism would be thwarted even while tourism development was permitted elsewhere on the island and, in short, local people expressed fears that their own economic development would be frustrated. Early in 1991 proposals were mooted for the development of a marine reserve and the creation of a new form of tourism, where no motor boats would be permitted. There was considerable local opposition to this with, among other things, expressions of considerable concern about a loss of fishing rights as well as a loss of income from tourism. The environmental lobby found that it had to address these issues; that it was not enough to simply appeal to altruistic concerns about animal welfare, and long negotiations were commenced in order to arrive at a satisfactory solution. It was not until 1999 that the marine reserve was finally declared by the Greek Government. The promise, of course, was that tourism based on eco-tourism and conservation values was more than possible, and that the turtles possessed economic value beyond the food that might be derived from their eggs. In short, an attempt has been made to modify tourism, create an attraction from the turtles that both generates economic value and complements existing tourism, and thereby sustain both the wellbeing of the turtles and local people.

Yet, in spite of the perspective that animals left in the natural state are assets and should be protected, evidence persists that tourism might still threaten the wildlife that tourists come to see (Myers, 1972; Reusberger, 1977; Rivers, 1974a). For example, the lions of the National Parks of Africa may have their feeding and breeding activities interrupted as tourist-laden Land Rovers surround them so that tourists can take photographs (Shackley, 1996). Predator/prey and migratory behaviour may be disrupted (Carbyn, 1974; WTO, 1983). West, a gorilla expert based at Bristol

Zoo, in 1988, expressed concern that tourism, whilst offering opportunities to save the gorillas of Rwanda, might also threaten them. He stated:

> Too many visits from tourists could prevent gorillas from breeding. They live in a fragile habitat, and the damaging of footpaths and the lighting of camp fires, will stop them from living their normal lives. We have to regard the gorilla population in Rwanda as one that is going extinct. [As gorillas are closely linked to humans] they can pick up human ailments such as colds, flu, pneumonia and measles – a disease like measles can kill a gorilla. Before tourists get close to gorillas they ought to be screened for infection. (West, 1988, cited by Ryan, 1991a: 98)

There exists evidence that these worst fears were fulfilled. Butynski and Kalina (1998) record how, in the Kahuzi-Beiga National Park in the Democratic Republic of the Congo, 6 gorillas died of respiratory diseases, and 27 needed to be treated with antibiotics. In 1990, a bronchopneumonia outbreak in a group of 35 gorillas visited by tourists affected 26 animals, two of which died. Vaccination programmes now have to be carried out among the gorilla groups, although, in the light of the violence that subsequently occurred in Rwanda, such concerns might now seem comparatively minor (Shackley, 2001a). Nonetheless concerns about human–animal interaction continue to be identified in new locations. Lunn (2001) describes the advent from the 1970s of polar bear tourism within the Canadian Arctic, based at Churchill. Specialised forms of transport (including helicopters) are used to view the bears, and other forms of intrusion duly resulted. By the mid-1980s there was a fear that unregulated polar bear viewing would threaten the species, and in 1996 the Wapusk National Park was created to help regulate visits through a permit system. Elsewhere some of the fears about the overloading of natural environments by tourist actions seem to have been been well founded. In New Zealand, in 2001, a period of several weeks went by without Whale Watch Kaikoura spotting a sperm whale. A report in 2002 (NZPA, 2002) noted that at least 11 dead whales had been washed up in the area since 1993. This was in excess of those found in earlier periods, although Coventry (2002) notes that in the period 1993 to 2002 a total of 11 dead sperm whales had been found on the New Zealand coast. Combined with evidence of changes to the movements of whales and their feeding grounds, there is some concern that the intrusion effects from boats, helicopters and fixed-wing aircraft are having an adverse effect on the whales' behaviour, and the Department of Conservation has declined to offer more permits for whale-watching tourism operations. Concerns have been expressed about the impacts of commercial dolphin watch companies on pods of dolphins, and a growing number of studies are raising both concerns and ethical questions about the use of wildlife for commercial gain (e.g. see Dunn & Goldsworthy, 1997, 1998, 2000).

One of the emergent themes of ecotourism operations based on wildlife is that the commercialisation of wildlife requires management of the sites and increasing human intervention in the care of the species that are the attraction. The example of vaccination of gorillas has been noted. Higham (2001), in the case of the albatross colony near Dunedin in New Zealand, commented that one impact of the movement of birds' nesting sites away from the viewing spot to less-optimal nesting sites has been that a quarter of the birds are now dependent on assistance with hatching and supplementary feeding. There is some concern that practices relating to the feeding of animals, whether by tourists or by operators to attract species so that they are more easily observable, might have longer-term impacts on mating, hunting and territory sizes (see, for example, Ryan, 2001b; Morgan, 2001; Newsome *et al.*, 2001).

Nor are the examples of tourism damage restricted to 'exotic' locations. Within Britain, the National Parks are under considerable stress. In 1979 there were approximately 90 million visits a year to the National Parks. A decade later there were 100 million, and the Brecon Beacons, Dartmoor, the Lake District, North York Moors, the Peak District, Snowdonia and the Yorkshire Dales were all reporting problems of footpath erosion. The upland environments, with their slow plant growth, are vulnerable to damage, and the usual problem is that people tread the top surface away. The grass becomes worn, is unable to grow, and the result is a muddy path. The trail then becomes wider as people make a detour from the muddy morass (or, in dry weather, the rutted uneven path) and use the grass borders of the path. This in turn becomes eroded, and thus the path becomes wider over time. In 1987 a survey of National Trust coast line sought to record the patterns of use and the ecological damage arising from recreational and tourism activities. Edwards (1987) then analysed the sensitivity of land types to recreational usage, and found that, in effect, the damage depended on the nature and intensity of the activity and the nature of the soil. In addition, however, the environmental impacts of tourism were both direct and indirect. Thus, for example, there would be direct damage from wheeled traffic on grassy areas, whilst there would be indirect damage resulting from disturbance effects. Further, this is damage that relates solely to normal patterns of use, and does not take into account the problems that can arise from litter, vandalism or other irresponsible behaviour. Edwards's results are summarised in Table 8.1.

On other occasions the threat posed is primarily an aesthetic one. In 1989, as part of its campaign for stronger controls on new housing in the unspoilt areas of the highlands and islands, the Scottish Scenic Trust prepared a list of housing developments, which included a group of chalets on the island of Mull. In many such locations, housing development is for holiday homes or the building of timeshare complexes, as has happened in the Lake

Table 8.1 The sensitivity of, and ecological damage due to, recreation and tourism

	Cliff tops	*Quarries*	*Rocky shores*	*Shingle*	*Sand dune*	*Salt marshes*	*Mud*	*Reed beds*	*Woodland*
Off-road vehicles	++ $	– $	–	+++	+++ $	+	+	+	++ $
Camping cravans	+++ $	– $	–	++ $	+++ $	+	+	+	+++ $
Trampling	++ $	+ $	– $	++ $	+++ $	+ $	–	– $	– $
Path erosion	+++ $	+	+	++ $	+++ $	+ $	–	–	– $
Horse riding	+ $	+ $	–	++	+++ $	+	–	–	+ $
Diving	–	–	++ $	–	–	–	–	–	–
Canoeing	–	–	–	–	+	+	+*	+*	–
Powerboating	–	–	–	–	+	+	+*	+*	–
Sailing	–	–	–	+	+	+	+*	+*	–
Windsurfing	–	–	–	–	–	+*	++*	++* $	–
Rockclimbing	+ $	+	–	–	–	–	–	–	–
Wildfowling	–	–	–	–	–	++*	++*	–	–
Fishing and bait digging	–	–	–	–	–	++	++ $	–	–
National history interest	–	+	+ $	+* $	+ $	+ $	–	+* $	–

Key
– little or no sensitivity
\+ slightly sensitive
++ moderately sensitive
+++ highly sensitive
* effect due to disturbance
$ recorded damage within heritage coasts

Source: Edwards (1987)

District. The Lake District, Britain's largest National Park, in spite of its undoubted beauty and literary connotations with Wordsworth and the other Lake District poets, failed to achieve the status of a World Heritage Site. This was in part due to the stresses caused on the road systems and the levels of congestion. In other cases the sheer volume of tourism development causes a total change in landscape. Barrett (1989) compares the development of the Algarve with the onslaught of the Industrial Revolution in the valleys of South Wales in these terms:

> This frenzied activity is how it must have been in the South Wales valleys at the start of the Industrial Revolution: endless digging, building and labouring. In those days the commodities were coal, iron and steel. In the Algarve today they labour for tourism. But the results are similar. Cliff top by cliff top, beach by beach, valley by valley – the natural beauty of the countryside is being eroded. No dark satanic mills or slag heaps, perhaps, but the landscape here is being disfigured just as badly by tower blocks of hotels and apartments. (Barrett, 1989)

The quality of development in such resort areas is often questionable. There may be a concern with quantity rather than quality in the rush to ensure that the new crop of the post-industrial world, the tourist, is housed and fed. The result of such developments is often a tourist complex that could be located on any part of the Mediterranean coastline, so indistinguishable is it from its counterparts. Even the signposts, in a mixture of Northern European languages, are the same.

Nor must it be thought that the damaging effects of tourism are restricted to the large scale. Small-scale examples can be found in almost any location where visitors come to stare. At the site of Gabriel Dumont's grave at Batoche National Historic Park, the site of the 1885 rebellion in Canada, the effects of trampling on the grass before the grave can be observed, for the grass is worn away. Areas with comparatively little tourism might also feel the effects of tourism, albeit perhaps as just one more component of environmental change which threatens the status quo of the existing habitat. For example, in the lakes of northern Canada increasingly strict limits are being imposed on the amount of fish that can be caught, or game that can be shot, as the tourist hunter adds to the problems being caused by wider environmental change. In 1989, the limits on fishing in the Prince Albert National Park had once again to be reduced because of a diminishing stock of fish. In 2002 the draft plan for the Park recognised that there was a need to designate specific recreational fishing lakes and to monitor impacts as a means of limiting damage to fish stocks.

This apparently sorry story of negative impacts has perhaps two underlying themes. The first is that tourism brings not only clients to the unspoilt area, but currently also brings much of the support structure that the clients are used to in their home environment. The beauty of the unspoilt area is to be enjoyed along with all the comforts of home, modern sanitation, and hot and cold running water, as well as the luxury of being on holiday. The problem then becomes intensified by the very numbers of visitors. Sax (1980) describes this process thus:

> Tourism in parks today ... is often little more than an extension of the city and its lifestyle transposed onto a scenic background. At its extreme in Yosemite Valley or at the south rim of the Grand Canyon, for example, one finds all the artefacts of urban life: traffic jams, long lines waiting in restaurants, supermarkets, taverns, fashionable shops, night life, prepared entertainments, and the unending drone of motors. (cited by Ryan, 1991a: 101)

Sessa (1988) refers to this process as the development of urban tourist poles, and perceives it to be an important part in the development of the 'econo-tourism system'. But there is yet a further added twist to this process, and that is that the imported lifestyle is not necessarily that of the host community. English owned and managed bars dominate the southern Spanish coastline, and Japanese signs and businesses are abundant in Banff National Park in Canada. Searle (1989: 9) traces the growth of the 'Cineplex with 40,000 square feet of retail space soon to open, the 16 luxury condominiums available soon' at Banff, and the expansion of the township to over 10,000 permanent residents within the National Park. Today the Lux Cinema Centre can be accessed on the net by the enquiring tourist looking for an alternative to skiing.

Tourism as the Ally of the Environment

But there is a second important issue. Tourism is not the sole cause of environmental change. Nor is it simply an agent of negative or detrimental change to the environment. It, too, is adversely affected by the threats to the environment caused by pollution. Again the evidence is easy to find in reports that come from around the world. It is, for example, well known that Bondi Beach is not the paradise that it has been painted to be. In January 1989 a clean-up operation, in which 20,000 Sydneysiders participated, produced 3000 tons of rubbish, amongst which there were 5 cars, 3000 hypodermic needles, 1000 used condoms, tyres, shopping trolleys, mattresses and the body of a dead man, believed to be that of a missing Sydney fisherman (Milliken, 1989). Even in 2002, a report of the annual Clean Up Australia Day noted that below Bondi's sand lurked 700,000 cigarette butts with an estimated 110 butts in each 10 square metre of sand (Jamal, 2002). However, a growing consciousness of the need both to generally protect the environment and to safeguard the health of visitors and beach users has produced some improvements. For many years Bondi was known not only for its beach, but for the pollution of its waters caused by three sewage outfalls. Often surfers were advised not to enter the waters after heavy rainfall because of the leakage from both the sewage and stormwater pipes. Perhaps because of the use of Sydney Harbour and Bondi Beach during the Sydney Olympics, various improvements began to be put in place. Stormwater control devices were installed at Bondi, and slowly the waters are beginning to improve, even though there are still deepwater discharges of sewage (Waverley Council, 1999).

A combination of environmental and user pressure groups has slowly been effective in improving water quality in many parts of the world. In 1988 Jackman (1988) described the north beach of Scarborough, where the resident population of 52,000 doubles in the summer, as one where:

> Bacteria lie in wait – capable of causing diarrhoea, vomiting, salmonella, enteritis, hepatitis, cystitis, skin rashes, infections of the nose, ear and throat and, for unvaccinated swimmers, even typhoid and polio. (Jackman, 1988)

Consequently, in 1989, a £12 million scheme, which included a sewage treatment plant, was commenced by the resort in an attempt to overcome the possible impacts of such sewage on its tourism trade. Surfers Against Sewage, a UK-based environmental lobby group, has waged a long campaign for the improvement of water quality and a tightening of legislation that permitted sewage discharge during the winter months in South West England. The group's web page (www.sas.org.uk) lists summaries of research papers relating to the issues of polluted waters and the various responses by water bodies and the UK government. Among the papers it is noted that some authorities have recognised that claims to clean beaches and water can help generate additional revenue only from tourists who are sensitive to such claims. For example the Island of Jersey has installed disinfection systems in its sewage treatment plant, so complying with the tightest standards on water discharge into the sea. Such a policy helps to sustain the island's claims to having the cleanest water in Europe. Welsh Water, Wessex Water and Yorkshire Water have all followed suit. In March 2002 the UK Department for Environment, Food and Rural Affairs announced that 180 additional coastal areas were declared as sensitive areas (bathing waters) under the Urban Waste Treatment Directive, which meant that such areas will receive tertiary UV treatment to reduce pathogens in sewage discharges.

The improvement in bathing water quality has been one of the success stories of environmental improvement. In 1988 only 60.5% of English and Welsh beaches complied with the EC Bathing Waters Directive, but by 2000 95% of 480 sampled sites met the requirements. However, for various pressure groups there still exist concerns that the standards being adhered to are not as rigorous as they would wish. First, as the European Union admits in the document, *Developing a New Bathing Water Policy* (European Commission, 2000a), the current guidelines were drawn up in 1975, and since then technology has substantially changed. The UK's Environment Agency (UKEA, 2001: O'Connell, 2002), while pleased to record the continuing improvement in Britain's bathing water quality, also noted that compliance was against two standards. The mandatory standard is the more lax of the two and, as might be expected, environmental groups would prefer the higher guideline standard to be achieved. Briefly the two standards are:

- The *mandatory standard*, which should not be exceeded. It requires that 95% of the samples should contain not more than 10,000 total coliforms per 100 ml of water, or 2000 faecal coliforms per 100 ml of water.
- The *guideline standard*, which should be achieved wherever possible. This standard requires 80% of the samples to have no more than 500 total coliforms per 100 ml of water, or 100 faecal coliforms per 100 ml of water. In addition to this, 90% of samples should have no more than 100 faecal streptococci per 100 ml of water. The EC derivation does not necessitate the monitoring of faecal streptococci.

These issues are further discussed later in the chapter.

As tourists increasingly access the previously inaccessible, so too the expectation that there exists a pristine environment as yet unspoilt by human activities proves to be unfounded. The debris of the modern world is found in the most inaccessible spots of the world. In 1988 it was reported that even on the uninhabited island of Amchitka in the Aleutians off Alaska, the US National Marine Fisheries Service found 1375 pounds of plastic litter on a beach just a mile long (Smith, 1988). In a world of linked ecological chains the potential cause for disaster may be found many miles away from the tourist resort area. Because of such findings, concern is being expressed over the growth of tourism to Antarctica. Thus far this is among the least affected areas of the world. Today scientists working at the various sites take far more care than their predecessors over minimising their impacts. For example the Australian Antarctica Division requires an environmental impact assessment to be completed before any activity occurs within its territory. These requirements are also enforceable in the case of touristic activities, so operators offering tours to Antarctica formed the International Association of Antarctica Tour Operators (IAATO). IAATO's 46 member companies (in 2002) agreed to a set of objectives, the purpose of which is to sustain appropriate, safe and environmentally-sound private-sector travel to the continent. In May 2001 IAATO reported on research relating to the possible transmission of pathogens by visitors. Although the evidence was not conclusive, some evidence was found that there was some substance to concerns (McFeters *et al.*, 1993; IUCN, 1998).

Accordingly, in 2002, there was the adoption of procedures that require passengers landing on Antarctica to have to pass through troughs containing disinfectant on both disembarkation and embarkation.

One of the threats to tourist locations comes from modern agricultural practices and the heavy use of herbicides and pesticides. In 1989 the tourist trade of the Italian Adriatic was adversely affected by a mysterious alga that bloomed in the sun on the waters of the Mediterranean. Following television pictures around the world of deserted beaches edged by an unsightly scum, hotel occupancies fell as British and German holidaymakers switched to alternative destinations. The toxicity of the algae was such that it was thought to be harmless, but sun, sea and beach holidaymakers are not ones to take risks, and hence the Italian tourism industry suffered. The cause was unknown, but one theory was that it was related to the fertilisers and pesticides being used by the farmers of the North Italian plains; others blamed industrial pollution, and yet others blamed a mild winter (Hallenstein, 1989; Sheridan, 1989). Tourism thus also suffers from the pollution of the environment that is caused by patterns of modern life and production methods. The acid rain that kills the forests of Germany, or those of Scandinavia, also indirectly threatens the tourism interests of those areas. In theory therefore, the tourism industry can become an ally of environmental conservationist groups, as there is a common cause in preserving the quality of the landscape. Examples exist where tourist business organisations have appreciated the need to enhance landscapes so as to simultaneously enhance the quality of the tourist experience. Perhaps the most successful of these partnerships have been within the urban landscape, as property developers, local government authorities, hotel groups and others respond to a growth both of interest in industrial heritage and of recreational time. This has led to the re-development of previously derelict waterfronts, old areas of warehousing and factory plant, and also to attempts to enhance central business districts in towns to combat the move to the suburbs. An example of this type of process is provided by Salford docks on the Manchester Ship Canal, in England. In 1980 Salford Council began a long process of renewal of the 150 acres of land and water that was characterised by rusting wrecks of old machinery and desolate waste land inhabited by a large population of rats. The council's initial attempts came to naught, but in 1982 it allocated 30 acres to a local businessman, Ted Hagan, with the mandate that he could retain the freehold on the 30 acres if in turn he could generate £9 million of investment within three years. With council cooperation, this target was achieved, and within five years a complex of residential homes, hotels, retail outlets and offices and workshops had replaced the devastated area. Similar examples can be found the world over. Harbourplace in Baltimore attracts 20 million visitors each year and has become a model for other developments. Toronto has changed 100 acres of under-used, derelict waterfront into an urban park. Sydney has created for itself a new asset in the Darling Harbour, which has not only transformed what was formerly known as the 'City Sink' into attractive surroundings, but has also generated 10,000 permanent jobs (Collinge, 1988). Ghirardelli Square in San Francisco today plays host to street theatre both for its residents and for 14 million tourists, whilst Faneuil Hall has become an inherent part of Boston.

In addition, examples can be found where tourist organisations have sought to develop tourist complexes in harmony with their surroundings, and indeed to improve on the existing scenery. Center Parcs, in Nottinghamshire, developed a site within Sherwood Forest that featured the planting of several thousands of trees, the creation of a 15-acre lake, a nature reserve, a deer sanctuary and improvements to existing drainage patterns. In addition they planned not only an existing pattern of footpaths through the forest, but also future routes, so as to avoid the problems associated with over-trampling. All this was done in what was previously 400 monotonous acres of commercial Corsican Pine (Phillips, 1988). There are many schemes that attempt to develop networks of paths that permit exploration of an area without threatening wildlife, and the use of cork chips, wooden boardwalks and other techniques can minimise path erosion problems. But all too often such schemes are restricted to public-funded bodies or their like or, if in the commercial sector, relate to the immediate environment of the commercial organisation concerned. In the case of the package holiday, the tour operator and the travel agent usually undertake little direct investment in the areas where they take tourists. Often it is argued that they will comply with local laws and regulations, and will use only those institutions and organisations that concur with legal requirements. Until comparatively recently there was little evidence that tour operators questioned the validity of local laws, whether they related to aspects such as the fire regulations of hotels, or to the fact that tourist complexes are being built in areas of ecological value. Pfäfflin (1987) quoted one speaker from the tour operator industry at the Third World Ecumenical European Conference (ECTWT, 1986) as stating 'Development aid is not our task. Our aim is profit.' Today, however, some companies, particularly smaller tour operators but also including some of the bigger 'names', warn their clients about fragile ecosystems, and are seeking to improve matters, either by direct action or by financial support of conservationist and scientific groups. For example several tour operators pay a premium to bodies such as Worldwide Fund for Nature. There is a much higher level of awareness about the need to develop 'sustainable tourism' and this is evidenced by the industry adoption of the 'Green Globe 21' initiative and certification, which is discussed below.

The Measurement of Impacts

Thus far the chapter has described, with reference to various studies, the possible impacts that tourism might have on natural and built environments. Is it possible to discern any trends, identify any indices that might help measure the nature of these impacts, identify what needs to be measured, and indicate any management policies that might help to mitigate the worst of these impacts? Among the variables thought to be of importance in determining the impacts of tourism are:

(1) the numbers of tourists;
(2) the nature of the activities in which tourists partake;
(3) the infrastructure provided by tourist planners at the site;
(4) the nature of the information provided to tourists – for example are guidelines for appropriate behaviours issued to tourists;
(5) what have tourists been told to expect – what promotional promises have been made in any site advertising?
(6) what levels of fragility exist within the natural or built environments that host the tourists?

This list suggests the types of measures required. First, records need to be kept about tourist numbers and the behaviours of animal species, rates of erosion or other measures of environment in order to assess the correlation between visitation rates and impacts. The intervening variables are those of management policies and infrastructure of place. Therefore the remainder of this chapter will concentrate on these issues.

It is not uncommon for researchers to develop various categorisations within which to define the problem and thereby determine the modes of measurement that can be applied. For example the Batelle Environmental Evaluation System identifies four components of the natural environment: ecology, pollution, aesthetics and human interest. It allocates a points system to each of these classifications, and to subsystems within the categories. For example, it attributes a weighting to impacts on water fowl, fisheries, air quality, visual quality and the like. While it has the advantage of adopting a holistic approach, one problem is that it is very much a case of 'one model fits all circumstances'; and therefore, arguably, it ignores the issues of those things that have specific importance in given contexts. In practice, most research has applied similar and well-proven methodologies to specific locations in a pragmatic manner. This section will examine some of the practical ways in which researchers have sought to examine the impacts of tourists with reference to flora, fauna, water quality and air pollution. Some of the impacts are listed in Table 8.2

Table 8.2 Possible impacts on the environment arising from tourist behaviours

Activity	*Nature of impact*
Transport and travel	Pollution from burning of fossil fuels. Disturbance of species, displacement from nesting, feeding sites, hunting sites, migration flows, movement to sub-optimal locations.
Recreational nature based pursuits	Trail erosion, trampling effects, soil compaction, insect dispersal, disturbance of nesting sites, biodiversity adversely affected. Introduction of new species, viruses and bacteria to sites.
Souvenir purchases	Threat to wildlife numbers, disruption of natural processes.
Infrastructure changes	Alter natural environments, create different micro-climates – change balance of species, remove nesting/breeding/hunting sites. Can enhance built environments, create more profitable and productive use of land in areas of urban decay.
Feeding wildlife	Behaviour changes, change in diet and nutrition, increase densities of population beyond normal, change territorial patterns
Litter and noise	Disturb breeding patterns, aesthetically not acceptable, hazard to animals
Untreated waste	Lowers water quality, increases turbidity, nitrates in water,.etc.
Improper dumping of waste	Possible sites for animal feeding, injurious to health, spillovers into water supplies and degradation of downstream waters.
Use of firewood, harvesting timber	Changing ratios of naturally dying debris – ill effects on insect life, ever-widening trampling effects in wood collection for fires, reduction of tree cover, habitat modification, erosion, ecological change.
Snorkeling and diving	Impacts on coral, removal of organisms, ill effect on fish scales, sea mammal skins

Trampling

Trampling effects are often a major concern. The scarring of hillsides, the widening of tracks and erosion of marginal vegetation from tramping, or from other activities such as skiing, are very evident in many parts of the world. In the case of informal and formal tracks used for walking, rambling or tramping, path widening occurs when walkers begin to avoid the original beaten or marked path and walk at its edges, often because of poor weather and its effects on unprotected soils. Paths become muddy and possibly slippery underfoot, and so tourists will want to avoid such areas. As wet and muddy footpaths sometimes freeze over, the path becomes rutted and uneven, and thus even when it dries out walkers will tend to avoid such areas. Therefore, informal tracks, given usage over time, will become wider to the detriment of the natural environment. This occurs in many sorts of terrain, as is demonstrated by the photographs taken by Ward *et al.* (2000) in a study of geothermal active areas around Rotorua in New Zealand (see Figure 8.1).

The impact of tramping has been well established in the literature, even to the extent of measuring the pressure imposed by a walking boot. For example, to measure the pressure asserted by walking boots with Vibram soles in park areas, Holmes and Dobson (1976) derived the formula:

$$\frac{(M_{\%})(M_w) + (F_{\%})(F_w) + (BC_w)}{(M_{\%})(Boot_m) + (F_{\%})(Boot_f)} = \frac{\text{average weight}}{\text{average boot area}} = \begin{array}{c}\text{weighted}\\ \text{average}\\ \text{pressure}\end{array}$$

where $M_{\%}$ = percentage of males in group
M_w = average male weight
$F_{\%}$ = percentage of females in group
F_w = average female weight
Bc_w = weight of boots and clothes
$Boot_m$ = male boot area in cm^2
$Boot_w$ = female boot area in cm^2.

Liddle (1997: 10–11) presents a table that lists total weights, ground contact area pressure and calculated ground pressure associated with various outdoor activities, vehicles and animals. Table 8.3 shows just a small proportion of this table.For comparison Liddle (1997) also includes similar results for animals, and his work shows that a sheep has an average total weight of 80,000g resulting in pressure of 941g/cm^2.

The consequences of trampling are quite well known, and Liddle (1997) provides many examples of the impacts and the sensitivity of different terrains and flora to trampling by recreationists and tourists walking through the countryside, the outback or other landscapes. One summary of the impacts is provided by Landals and Scotter (1974), and is shown in Figure 8.1. This diagram indicates how, with increased trampling effects, the vegetation cover is reduced, and areas of bare ground and dead vegetation increasee. The evidence is that for some types of flora negative impacts can occur very quickly. For example, alpine meadows are very susceptible to trampling effects, and as few as 5–10 people per week can reduce species

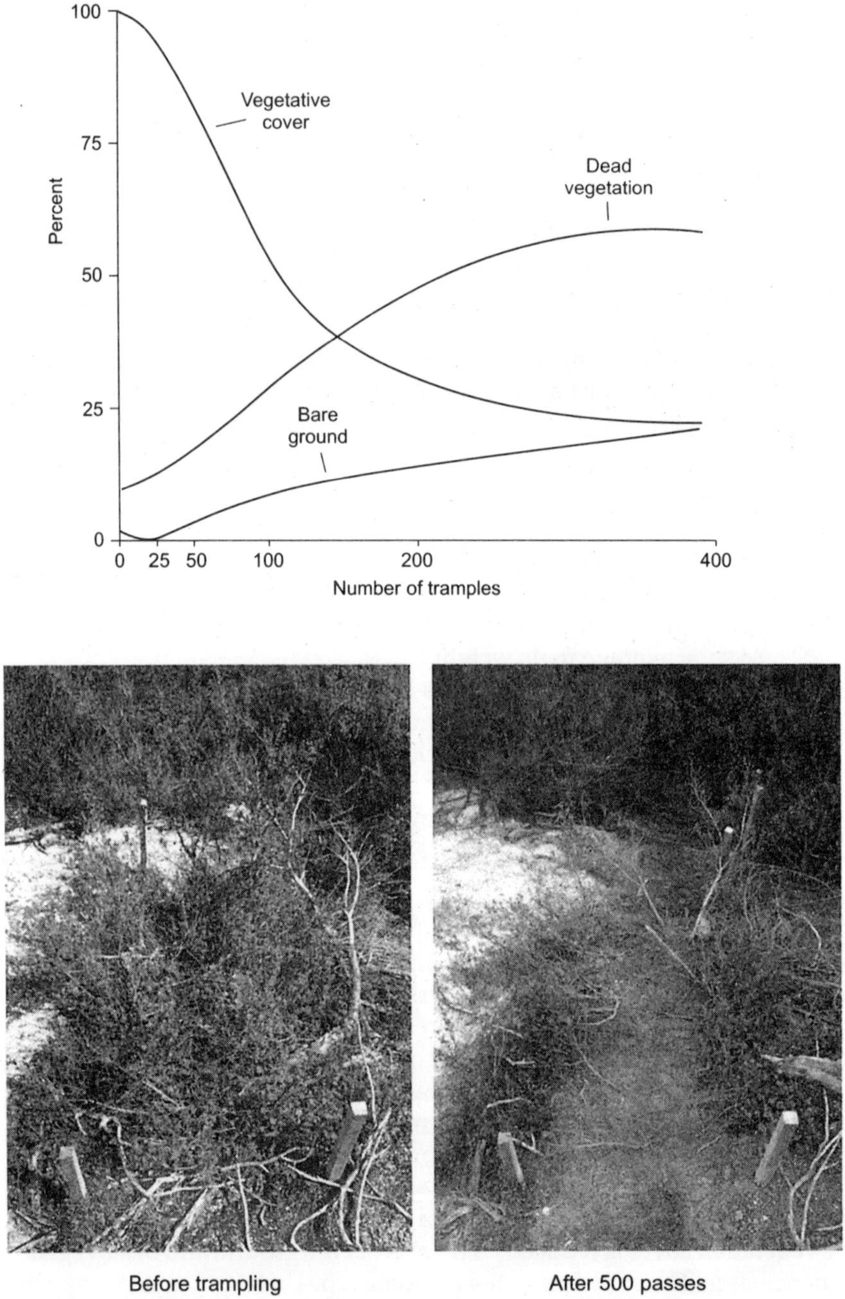

Figure 8.1 Patterns of trampling
Diagram: Landals & Scotter (1974); Photographs: Ward *et al.* (2000)

Table 8.3 Impacts on ground of touristic/recreational activities

Static ground pressure	*Average of total weight (g)*	*Ground contact area (cm²)*	*Pressure (g/cm²)*	*Source*
Human – bare foot on hard ground	73,000	262	297	Liddle, 1997
Human – on snow skies	75,000	2,660	28	Liddle, 1997
Trail bike	229,000	114	2,008	Eckert *et al.*, 1979
Four wheel Drive Toyota – loaded with 4 people and gear on hard ground	2,500,000	1,483	1,686	Liddle, 1979
Hovercraft SK5 air-cushion vehicle	7,264,000	484,266	15	Rickard & Brown, 1974

diversity by up to 10%, increase the amount of bare ground by 10–20%, and increase the density of the soil by anything from 10 to 40% (Hartley, 1976).

The reasons for this type of negative environmental impact are generally well understood. The increased pressure on the soil means that the soil becomes more compacted and more dense, and the macro pore cavities are consequently squeezed. All of this increases the resistance of soil to root penetration, thereby making it more difficult for plants to grow. Root structures take longer to become established and are smaller than might otherwise be the case, and so the plant is less able to derive nutrients from the soil. Other related issues occur. The greater density of the soil makes it more difficult for water to penetrate, and indeed over small areas of heavily compacted soil local and micro drainage patterns can be changed. During late summer, when plants might be trying to seed, a series of results can occur, all of which reduce biodiversity and plant cover. Seeds may land on dense, compacted soils where they are unable to establish themselves. They may become desiccated in the higher temperatures associated with hard ground. They may be washed away by rainfall. They become more susceptible to frost damage. Trampling certainly affects soil porosity and hence the moisture–root relationships. The relative lack of water percolating through the soil can result in nutrient-deficient soil. Thus a combined result of wear and tear on plants and these other effects leads to a reduction in biodiversity of species and, if bare ground is averted, it is because more hardy, durable plants (often grasses) succeed where other plants fail to establish themselves. Hence trampling also changes the natural balance between different plant species. These factors are taken into account by

Leung and Marion (1996), who construct a model of trail degradation. Their model adds factors such as climate, user types and intensity of use, as well as soil and plant types. The same authors (Leung & Marion, 1999a) subsequently concluded that these problems are a growing world problem, and trail erosion as a result of increasing numbers of trampers has become one of the major problems facing park authorities. Additionally, the problems are not restricted to trampers, but are caused by mountain bikers, horseriding, sand dune buggies, cross-country bikes and other forms of transport (Newsome *et al.*, 2001). Studies of horse riding have also been undertaken. For example, Beeton (1999) examined the social interaction between horseback riders and other users of trails. From an environmental perspective, Lull (1959) reported that a horse can exert pressures of up to 2.8 kg/cm^2 compared to 0.8 kg/cm^2 for hikers. It has also been observed that horses effectively spread weeds that germinate in the faeces of horses, which are rich in nutrients (Newsome *et al.*, 2001).

While the principles of trampling are easy to describe, specific location predictions are less easy, for a number of reasons. Seasonal and temporal factors have a role. Trampling during early spring may have more deleterious results than at other times of the year because this is a time of early growth. On the other hand, hiking later in the year during periods of seed dispersal can be just as harmful. Therefore, as noted, site management becomes very important. Without management of paths and walkways, trampling can quickly have a negative impact on an otherwise-pristine environment, or at least change its composition of plants and biodiversity. This can have subsequent effects because changes in plant composition can lead to changes in insect populations, and possibly, over time, changes to bird and native mammals.

The method of trampling measurement is well established, and basically quite simple. It requires the identification of formal and informal paths and the pegging out of the sample path area. Measurements of soil density, numbers and distribution of species within the zone are taken at a number of points within the zone, to the side of the zone and generally at about 1 and 5 metres away from the path. A number of 'tramples' are then recorded over specific periods of time, with continuous measurements being taken of not only soil density and species, but also plant recovery rate (e.g. how quickly trodden-down stems resume erect positions). To take account of changes in rainfall, temperature, etc. the path data are compared with those of the points away from the path. Generally such studies initially show a change in biodiversity as the more resistant plants take over the soil space from the more fragile ones. But with increasing time and more 'tramples,' the amount of bare ground and dead vegetation increases (see Figure 8.1).

Fauna

This section will consider only non-consumptive wildlife tourism – in which wildlife is sought for purposes of spectating, photography, perhaps painting or study, but the animals or birds are not captured or killed. One implication of this, discussed by Ryan, Hughes and Chirgwin (2000), is the elevation of 'the spectacle' above other aspects of nature tourism, including study. In an analysis of an area in the Northern Territory of Australia, they discuss how the abundant bird life dominates the tourist gaze to the almost total exclusion of other natural attributes of the study area, Fogg Dam. The fact that Fogg Dam has a very dense, rich biomass that includes not only flora but dusky rats, snakes and other reptiles and mammals, is almost wholly ignored as the tourists are directed to the birds from specially constructed platforms. These platforms not only provide better views of key waterholes, but also provide shelter from the sun, catch the breeze, and to some extent provide a limited protection from mosquitoes and other insects. Hence, while the tourists tended to term themselves as 'eco-tourists', and spoke of enjoying and feeling at one with 'nature', the nature with which they identified was a manipulated nature – the climate of that area being hot, humid and associated with a rich insect life. Indeed, walks in the nearby freshwater mangrove zones (mangroves themselves are a significant and threatened species) had signs warning visitors to carry water and to use insect spray. On the other hand, it can be argued that such site management is actually achieving its purpose of generating highly satisfactory experiences. It permits visitors to enjoy and value natural land-scapes, while at the same time it reduces potential damage to the areas of greater ecological value, namely the mangrove swamps.

In consequence, it has been suggested that nature tourism is orientated toward some species and away from others. Shackley (1996) presents evidence that in the African game parks some species account for a significantly higher proportion of animal–human interactions than others. It appears that almost all visitors wish to see lions, few wish to see warthogs. Ryan and Harvey (2000) suggest a possible classification of animals based on perceived levels of likeness to certain human traits (dolphins, for example, are seen as intelligent, fun and caring of their young, while crocodiles are reptilian but can evoke respect, perhaps fear) and thus some species tend to attract more visitors than others. Whatever the reason, visitors wish to see animals in natural habitats. However, even in those instances where the main objective of travelling through natural environments is not to gaze at animal or bird life, the very presence and movement of humans can have a disturbance effect on wildlife. Liddle (1997) identifies three types of disturbance of wildlife, these being:

Disturbance type 1: awareness of human presence, but there is no contact;

Disturbance type 2: changes in habitat due to clearance, building, food provision etc;

Disturbance type 3: extreme disturbance where there is direct and damaging contact with the animal.

It can be argued that disturbance type 1 can be extended into situations where there is contact or at least potential contact. Indeed a series of situations can be identified, which may be listed as:

Situation 1: awareness of human presence, but no immediate change in behaviour;

Situation 2: awareness evokes withdrawal of the animal or bird. If the human presence is passing, the wildlife may return to the original site and continue past behaviour, and thus it might be said the impact is minimal;

Situation 3: awareness may lead to warning – the animal or bird begins to display warning behaviours;

Situation 4: attack behaviour;

Situation 5: retreat behaviour – the wildlife may eventually move to a new site;

Situation 6: habituation behaviour – the wildlife may come to accept the intrusion of humans as part of its normal context, and continue its past behaviours;

Situation 7: habituation and behaviour modification – wildlife 'accepts' human intrusion, but has now its modified behaviour in some way, such as through new modes of feeding.

This listing begins to indicate the actual measures that might be adopted by researchers to gauge the impact that humans might be having. These measures include:

- measuring approach distance, i.e. just how near can humans approach before animals or birds begin to display any form of behaviour modification. Examples of such behaviours might be animals stopping activities to view humans;
- identifying these types of wildlife behaviour and measuring its duration;
- measuring the distance the species move from their original spot;
- timing how quickly re-grouping and the re-adoption of former behaviour occurs.

Table 8.4 Measurement of seal behaviours resulting from human contact

Responses	*Identifying behaviours*
Contact response	Fur seal aware – has eyes open
Tracking response	Fur seal tracks response – follows by turning head.
Alert response	Seal prepares to take action – shows signs of being alert.
Threat response	Seal defends territory – ritual threat posture, vocal open mouth threat, mock lunge.
Attack response	Seal defends territory – makes physical movement and attacks.
Moving away from stimulus	Seal escape response – orientates body towards the sea and moves away.

Longer-term measures that are significant include whether there is any change in hunting, mating or, in the case of birds, nesting behaviours (e.g. Higham, 1998, 2001). Other longer-term criteria of adverse changes to be watched for include whether animals are straying from established territories.

In a number of cases of wildlife tourism, guidelines are established as to just how close tourists may approach wildlife. For example, whale-watching operations often have restrictions imposed on them as to how close boats can approach a whale on the surface of the water, and at what point they must cut or reduce their engines and engine speed. The concern is that the observers must avoid forcing the whale to dive early, before it has taken sufficient air. If it has taken in insufficient air, its hunting, feeding and nurturing activities might be adversely affected. In describing issues pertaining to manatees and sting rays, Shackley (1992, 2001b) also identifies a number of more direct effects on sea-based life. These include injuries from outboard motors, and skin diseases from handling by tourists apart from any possible change in feeding habits and the effects of a more homogeneous diet.

One example of the type of measures used is provided by the study undertaken by Barton *et al.* (2001) into fur seal behaviour at Kaikoura in New Zealand. A centre for watching whales and other sea mammals, the area has faced increasing numbers of tourists. The study identified the criteria listed in Table 8.4.

In this particular study it was found that seal cows tended to be much more sensitive to approaches by visitors than bulls were; the cows showed tracking responses at greater distances from humans than did the bulls.

Many other studies of impacts on mammals, reptiles and other species exist. For example Walther (1969) found that male Thompson's gazelle in the Serengeti National Park had lesser flight distances than females. Jacobsen and Kushcan (1986) found examples of aggressive behaviour by Florida alligators because of an habituation effect – they had come to expect food from tourists. Work undertaken in the Northern Territory of Australia with saltwater crocodiles revealed that older crocodiles tended to be more cautious of approaches by humans than younger crocodiles were. This was thought possibly to be due to older crocodiles surviving from a time when they were being hunted (Lyon, 1998). There have been numerous studies undertaken with reference to birds, and Liddle (1997: 394) summarises a number of these. Birds tend to show fairly high habituation effects, although Higham (2001) found that albatrosses on the Tairua peninsular near Dunedin in New Zealand had, because of noise intrusion from the visitor centre, over time moved nesting sites away from a visitor centre to what was thought to be a less optimal site. On the other hand, for example, van der Zande, van der Ter Keurs and van der Weijden (1980) found that the distribution of oystercatcher nests was unaffected by more than 54,000 cars per day passing on a nearby road. In yet another study, that of American flamingos in the Celeston Estuary in Mexico, boat visits increased the alert time, but reduced feeding times by 24–30% (an average of about 30 minutes per day). Also boat movements caused movements away from optimal feeding grounds (Galicia & Baldassarre, 1997). In some instances birds quickly adapt to human presence, for example by scavenging for food in rubbish bins – as demonstrated by Figure 8.2, which was taken by the author by the side of the Gold Coast Highway at Broadbeach, a major conurbation of holiday apartments and flats.

Figure 8.2 Ibis foraging by the side of the Pacific Coast Highway in Queensland, Australia

Several factors have been found to account for the sensitivity of species to tourist and other human intrusion. One obvious factor is the presence of newly-born young. Nearly all species become protective of their young, and are more likely to engage in threat behaviours if disturbed. Human actions can trigger different animal or bird behaviours depending on the speed of approach by humans, the number in the group, levels of noise and similar factors. Equally, whether animals are isolated or part of a larger herd can also influence situations.

In spite of the many studies of intrusion effects, the longer-enduring impacts on wildlife environments are much more likely to arise from infrastructure encroachments on habitats than from any impact arising from the behaviours of tourists in natural settings. The building of car parks, hotels, roads, railways, even visitor centres (as noted in the case of the albatross colony in New Zealand), can all cause significant changes to species diversity, density, distribution and subsequent behaviours. It might be observed that not all of this is necessarily detrimental to all species. Indeed some species, such as rats, seem to thrive on being in close human contact. However, there exists a tension between what tourists wish to see, and the conditions under which tourists might want to see it. Ryan and Saward (2003), in a study of Hamilton Zoo, observe that many visitors recognise the conservation values of zoos and, given enclosures that resemble closely the natural habitat of the observed species, this might well meet a number of declared intentions of ecotourists. But are ecotourists really environmentally friendly? Some evidence that this is not the case is discussed below. Given that technology today is capable of reproducing natural environments far away from their original location (as evidenced by Disney's Zoo in Disneyland, Florida), the issue arises as to whether there is any need for tourists to intrude upon the original habitats in order to satisfy what may be little more than a whim.

Water quality

One of the most popular of all tourist pastimes is spending time in or by water. Tourists also like to spend time in accommodation by water. Whether it is messing around in boats, swimming in the sea or, more prosaically, flushing the toilet, there is a potential for changing the marine or freshwater environment. Water environments are much more complex than those of land for a number of reasons, including:

- Waterborne life may be dependent on what is happening on a sea or lake bed several metres away from the levels at which any one species actually exists.
- Water quality may depend on inflows and outflows that can be affected by events at some distance away from the main body of

water. These might, for example, affect temperatures in the water, and change inversion effects. Indeed, even changes in the riparian edge can change water temperatures, reduce vegetation in the water and increase turbidity (Hammitt & Cole, 1998).

Turbidity might also impact on water quality because of the amount of daylight that is now able to penetrate the water. Shallow water growing macrophytes (i.e. higher plants such as water lilies that grow at the edge or float on freshwater) might have their spread constricted by more opaque waters. Again, this directly affects not only the plants, but also waterborne insects and larvae and, in turn, possibly fish populations. The water quality might also be affected by lead from petrol-driven two-stroke engines, and certainly many people may be aware of seeing a thin film of petroleum vapour that settles on the surface of water by jetties. Although vapour associated with the starting of two-stroke engines contains a mix of carbons, oil and phenols that fall back into the water, and such combinations can be toxic in high concentrations, there is little if any evidence to suggest problems under normal conditions of use. Nonetheless, one can only be concerned at the findings of studies like those of Mosisch and Arthington (1998), who estimated that for the lakes and reservoirs they studied, a total of some 380–600 million litres of outboard motor oil were discharged into waters each year. They also provide evidence of hydrocarbons being found in fish.

Boating may have little or significant impacts depending in part on the number of boats involved. Liddle and Scorgie (1980) indicate the possible impacts using the diagram shown in Figure 8.3. In a study of 105 New Zealand lakes, Johnstone *et al.* (1985) were able to trace the dispersal of five aquatic weeds because of recreational boating. Similarly, with reference to waterborne plant life, there have been reports that water lilies found in waters with significant boat traffic are smaller than average, reports of damage to reed beds, of the disruption of shallow-rooted and floating plants and of the redistribution of silt from the centre of river beds leaving sand and gravel in the centre – all possibly caused by boat action (Liddle, 1997).

The wash from the propellers of fast and powerful motor boats can create significant water turbulence, which has an impact on the sediment of river, lake or sea bottoms, and on the banks of estuaries or inland waters. The result is a possible increase in the turbidity of the water, although Liddle (1997) comments that there is little actual quantitative evidence for this. Other factors might be important – for example the amount of clay in the soils, the depth of the water, and the power of the craft involved. Any increase in the cloudiness of the water, if long lasting, will have an impact on the growth of waterborne plants, and hence on the feeding and breeding of fish and other aquatic life such as frogs and oysters. Shackley (1992) has reported another boating issue with reference to the manatee of Florida. A threatened species, manatee have become a tourist attraction, meaning that more boats are now to be found in the waters which they inhabit. Shackley reports increases in the number of manatee being found with wounds that probably have been caused by boat propellers, although whether these wounds are due to tourist boats or others is not known. She also shows a correlation between an increase in boat registration and the number of perinatal deaths and of manatees killed by collision with boats (more than 40 in 1988). In New Zealand the introduction of fast ferries across the Cook Straits created considerable controversy because of the alleged consequences of a powerful wash on the banks of the Queen Charlotte Sounds and the negative impacts on mussel beds. Subsequently speed restrictions were imposed on the ferries, and this, argued the operators, began to reduce the advantages of such ferries while negatively impacting on

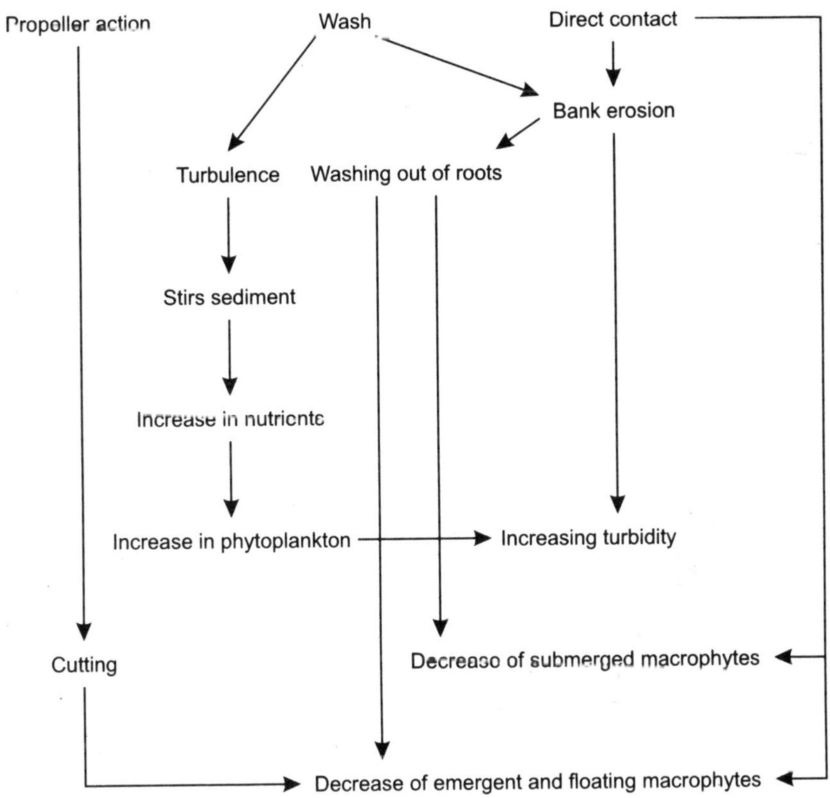

Figure 8.3 The impacts of boating on water environments
Source: Liddle & Scorgie (1980)

operating costs. One solution being explored was the construction of alternative ports; this solution in itself would have significant economic implications because of the impacts of changed traffic flows on accommodation and other businesses based on existing ferry infrastructures.

Another associated negative impact that has attracted attention in the tourism literature has been the taking of tourists to coral reefs. A number of problems have been identified, and include the dragging of anchors and anchor chains through live coral (thereby knocking coral away from the remainder of the reef), the touching of coral and associated coral-supported life forms by tourists and, finally, the very volume of visitors throughout the year, which magnifies substantially the damage that a single tourist might inadvertently cause. Higher levels of coral breakage have been found in areas of recreational snorkelling than in other areas, (e.g. see Hawkins & Roberts study of the Red Sea, 1993 and Allison's study of the Maldives, 1996).

One problem that has attracted a lot of attention has been that of sewage disposal. Sewage may be discharged from boats, or released from shore-based hotels and other accommodation units, although usually after some form of treatment. The main issue associated with the discharge of sewage, treated or untreated, is that it potentially contains large amounts of nutrients such as phosphorus and nitrogen. Organic pollution can cause algae bloom, but severe pollution will eliminate algae. However, the complexity of the issues is shown by Mason (1991), who found that the filamentous alga *cladophora* became more dominant in less polluted waters, and provided some cover and food for invertebrates. However at night *cladophora* could de-oxygenate the water, thereby suffocating small fish. Additionally sewage may contain bacteria that could be harmful to humans swimming in the waters. While the bacteria might not be present in very high amounts, there is always the danger that a swimmer could unknowingly swim through a localised concentration and swallow the water or let it through his or her nasal passages. Waterborne bacteria can cause typhoid, cholera, Weil's disease, intestinal infections, tuberculosis, gastroenteritis and dysentery to mention just some illnesses. Waterborne viruses can cause meningitis, poliomyelitis, hepatitis and diarrhoea. As previously noted, one group of recreational water users in the United Kingdom that is very aware of the dangers inherent in the discharge of sewage into the sea is Surfers against Sewage. As a group of committed surfers who surf all year round, for over a decade they have engaged in active debate, action and data collection relating to the quality of waters around the British coast, especially with reference to south-west England and the Cornish coastline. Evidence cited on their website (http://www.sas.org.uk) indicates greater incidences of minor illnesses such as rashes, upset stomachs and similar problems among those holidaymakers who engage in full immersion in waters than among those who are content to paddle in the shallows.

One of the consequences of such concerns is not only environmental legislation around much of the world that, amongst other environmental controls, has sought to control sewage disposal, but also the adoption of enforceable criteria for bathing water quality. At the time of writing, the European Union is still debating changes to existing standards of bathing water quality, but the Blue Flag scheme has become an established part of the Western European holiday scene. In 2000 the European Commission issued a communication notifying member states that new criteria were to be established (European Commission, 2000b). Up to 2002 there were 27 criteria for beaches and 16 for marina, and these were classified under four main headings: water quality, environmental education and information, environmental management, and safety and services. A key concern has been the quality of bathing water and the two main sets of parameters, the microbiological and physiochemical. One issue relates to coliform content, as it is possible (but increasingly unlikely) that a beach where coliform content is not counted may gain a Blue Flag if such counts are not part of a national policy. However, a member country must provide evidence as to why such a policy is thought proper. Also if a beach is affected by any sewage-related or land-waste run off, then remedial action must be undertaken as soon as is possible. The regulations also state that a beach must have at least one sampling site but, more importantly, the number and location of sampling sites must reflect the concentration of bathers along the beach as well as sources that potentially affect the water quality at the beach. The sampling must be done, first of all, where the concentration of bathers is highest. Quoting directly from the website (http://www.blueflag.org/frameset/criteria.htm as at June, 2001), the regulations go on to state that the location of sampling sites must also reflect the location of potential sources of pollution. Samples must be taken near the sites where streams, rivers or other inlets enter the beach in order to provide documentation that such inflows do not affect bathing water quality. Alternatively, the inflowing water must have been analysed at source, confirming that it meets the Blue Flag criteria for bathing water quality. Similarly, in the case of inland waters, where the water is supplemented by outside sources during dry periods, the water quality of that outside source must meet the Blue Flag criteria. In addition, samples should be taken 30 cm below the water surface, except for the mineral oil samples, which should be taken at surface level. An independent person officially authorised and trained for the task must collect samples, and an independent laboratory must carry out an analysis of bathing water quality. The laboratory must be nationally or internationally accredited to carry out microbiological and physico-chemical analyses. The laboratory must also be authorised to collect and analyse the bathing water by the authority responsible for the implementation of the national regulation on bathing water quality and monitoring. The first sampling has to be undertaken within the fortnight before the beginning of the official bathing season and, during the bathing season, sampling must be carried out at least fortnightly. The last sampling of the season must be taken within one fortnight of the last date of the bathing season. Additional regulations relate to the levels of treatment that ali waste water should be subject to before it is discharged into the sea.

There is little doubt that this approach has benefited water quality and, with newer regulations to come into effect, there is hope that cleaner waters yet will result. There are encouraging signs with, for example, fish stock assessments showing improvements in the surveys undertaken by the Environment Agency Southern Region since 1995. On the other hand, in 2000, the UK Environment Agency released reports that oestrogenic (feminising) changes in fish in rivers had been found as a result of endocrine-changing substances in sewage effluence, so it is obvious that there is still a need for a tightening of regulations (UKEA, 2001; O'Connell, 2002). It is equally obvious that on the whole the tourism industry would welcome the long-term effects of such moves.

Air pollution

Air pollution is more often associated with city lifestyles, although localised pollution might be caused by the burning of wood fires by campers on still evenings. However, the major problem associated with campfires is not the immediate risk of pollution but the dangers of forest fires that are associated with campfire not properly doused. Another environmental issue associated with the lighting of campfires is the danger of denuding trees in the immediate vicinity of the campsites. To avert these types of problems many parks authorities around the world place embargoes on campfires at certain times of the year or in certain locales. For example, Ryan and Sterling (2001) mention how the Northern Territory Parks and Wildlife Authority provides specific barbecue points and makes available cut logs to those camping at Litchfield National Park.

However, one of the main causes of urban pollution is the internal combustion engine, and cars and coaches are also to be found in tourist regions. Becken (2001) has estimated power usage by tourist accommodation and attraction providers, and has found that the per capita (tourist) energy use in New Zealand was 9.4 megajoules at an entertainment complex, while hotels are major energy users (the energy used by a hotel guest is estimated as being the equivalent of the energy used for a 45 km car journey). Not surprisingly the car-borne tourist is amongst the heaviest users of fossil fuels, and hence is a source of pollution.

Another issue that is important in some parts of the world is whether or not air transport makes a significant contribution to pollution. It has been claimed that aircraft movement into and out of Los Angeles International Airport is one of the major contributing factors to the 'smog' that can often be seen hanging over the city. Modern jet aircraft are at their most efficient when at cruising speed and height; it is then that they obtain the most efficient fuel consumption and the cleanest burn from their engines. But airport movements are periods of less-than-efficient fuel burn. The take-off procedures for an aircraft can be broken down into the periods of engine start up and idling during periods of passenger boarding, a sequence of approach to runway, waiting for clearance and then actual take-off from the runway, followed by a period of a few minutes during which the aircraft climbs to operational height and speed. It has been estimated that during these stages a modern jet such as the Boeing 767–200 will emit a total of over 30,000 kg of hydrocarbons and over 130,000 kg of carbon monoxide. Given the total number of carrier movements at Los Angeles International Airport (about 2.7 million in a year , June, 2002) this represents a significant amount of pollution emission. As the geographical position of Los Angeles between the sea and the mountains lends itself to inversion effects (where currents of air are caught and remain static), then such levels of pollution are not always immediately dispersed. One possible consequence of this would be an increase in respiratory illnesses around the airport and on approach and take-off paths over residential zones. To this might be added the problem of noise pollution.

These issues are important, and to some extent help to explain the delay in the approval of London Heathrow Airport's fifth terminal. The public enquiry into the possible construction of this fifth terminal began in 1995 and the report was duly handed to the UK government in December 2000. Eleven months later, on November 20, the government announced its decision and approved the construction of the terminal (DTLR, 2002). Newspaper reports of the decision presented the decision in terms of economic vs. environmental impact, the decision being described by Webster and Hurst (2001: 7) in these terms; 'Business groups and trade unions welcomed the approval of a fifth terminal at Heathrow but residents and environmentalists remained bitterly opposed'. In practice, of course, the issue is not that black and white. For example, businesses at London's other airports or in the regional airports may well have preferred an expansion of services at their terminals, while environmentalists and residents associated with other airports may prefer increased traffic to be handled in London rather than impinging on as-yet-unaffected locations. Indeed, it is anticipated that the noise levels by 2016 will not exceed those of 1989 thanks to new generations of quieter aircraft, while the number of aircraft movements will not necessarily increase in direct proportion to the increased numbers of passengers because of the larger size of aircraft that are currently envisaged.

Ecotourism and Certification: Is This an Answer?

Tourism has a potential for both good and ill and, in assessing the problems that tourism creates, such problems must be placed within the context that many other industries have far more direct impacts on water quality, and on fauna and flora distribution. Can the potential situations of harm be identified? The World Tourism Organisation (WTO, 1983) identifies five situations where tourism might harm the environment, these being:

(1) alteration of the ecological situation of regions where the environment was previously in good condition from the natural, cultural and human viewpoints;
(2) speculative pressures leading to the destruction of landscape and natural habitat;
(3) the occupation of space and the creation of activities producing irreconcilable land-use conflicts;
(4) damage to traditional values in the zones concerned, and a lowering of standards on the human scale in existing developments;
(5) progressive over-capacity, which drains the environmental quality of the area concerned.

In recognition of the problems posed by tourism developments, some writers have sought to promote the concept of 'Green Tourism'. Amongst the foremost of these writers is Jost Krippendorf, who, in his book *The Holidaymakers* (Krippendorf, 1987), argues that tourism should be consistent with its environment, and arise naturally from the activities that are natural to the area. To that end, he quotes examples from the Swiss Cantons where the host communities have sought to impose regulations that limit tourism to within what might be termed the carrying capacities of the area. This viewpoint is endorsed by Phillips (1988) who, in relation to rural tourism, propounds six principles, these, briefly being:

(1) The promotion of tourist enjoyment of the countryside should be primarily aimed at those activities that draw on the character of the countryside itself, its beauty, culture, history and wildlife.
(2) Tourism development in the countryside should assist conservation and recreation, by bringing new uses to historic buildings, supplementing the income of farmers, and aiding the reclamation of derelict land.
(3) The planning, design, siting and management of new tourist developments should be in keeping with the landscape and. wherever possible, seek to enhance it.
(4) Investment in tourism should support the rural economy whilst encouraging a wider geographical and temporal spread so as to avoid problems of congestion and damage through over-use.

(5) Those who benefit from rural tourism should contribute to the conservation and enhancement of the countryside.
(6) The tourist industry itself should seek to develop the public's understanding and concern for the countryside and for environmental issues generally.

As will be discussed in Chapter 9, concerns about the threat posed to the ecological environment are paralleled by similar concerns about social impacts. In both cases, the proponents of a more ecologically or socially responsible tourism are to a large degree dependent on normative arguments that seek a change of behaviour by tourists based on changes of values. The argument is, however, quite logical, given Krippendorf's model of tourism as an extension of a social pattern that is itself of such a form that it denies opportunities for creativity. Krippendorf argues that man is not born a tourist, but becomes one because of 'escape' needs, but 'sick societies create sick tourists'. Equally, as has been discussed in Chapter 5, this argument is but an extension of the viewpoint of Boorstin, Rivers and others who claim that tourism creates nothing more than a series of pseudo-events. To argue that tourism must change in order to preserve ecologically fragile areas that are nonetheless attractive to tourists, and to place hope in educative forces, as Krippendorf (1987) and O'Grady (1981) do, is of little immediate help to planners and those responsible for the management of tourism areas. What needs to be done is to translate the concerns into management plans and practice. Phillips (1988) at least provides a series of possible objectives, and so the question becomes one of how to achieve those objectives.

It is true that for some time there has been a growing recognition by the tourism industry of its responsibilities. For example, the 1987–1989 South Australian Strategic Tourism Plan refers to strategy 14, which is to 'Manage tourism to minimise adverse impacts' (South Australia Tourist Commission, 1986). It outlines specific actions, such as the requirement that major proposals must specify environmental safeguards, whilst the appendices to the plan listing 'key issues' indicated that to 'develop at any cost pressures' would, in fact, be contrary to the State's interests. It might be argued that the slow acceptance of a need for such exercises is due to the educative processes desired by Krippendorf (1987), O'Grady (1981) and Wheeller (1987), as they represent a response to public concern about environmental issues, and increased interest in forms of tourism that emphasise nature. However, between 1988 and 2000 the cynic might have observed that ecotourism was being proposed as *the* answer to every ill associated with both the environment and tourism. In May 2002, more than 1100 delegates attended the World Ecotourism Summit in Quebec to endorse the Quebec Declaration on Ecotourism, described by leisuretourism.com (June 12,

2002) as 'an aspirational new tool for the development of this type of tourism'. Equally, for its part, in 2002 the United Nations Environment Programme called for governments and businesses to achieve sustainable tourism practices (UNEP, 2002). Meeting in Bali, the Fourth Preparatory Committee meeting for the World Summit on Sustainable Development noted in its papers a growing gap between the efforts of business and industry to reduce their impact on the environment, and the worsening state of the planet (see http://www.unep.org).

Certainly, at the beginning of the twenty-first century, after perhaps several decades of rhetoric, some practical responses to the environmental pressures being created by tourism are emerging. It would also appear that the nature of the debate about ecotourism has also significantly changed. Among the much-cited original definitions of ecotourism was that of Ceballos-Lascurain:

> Travelling to relatively undisturbed or uncontaminated natural areas with the specific objective of studying, admiring and enjoying the scenery and its wild plants and animals, as well as any existing cultural manifestations (both past and present) found in these areas. (Ceballos-Lascurain, 1987: 14)

It has been queried to what degree ecotourism has achieved the aims of re-education. In a keynote speech to the Conference of the Council of Australian Universities in Tourism and Hospitality Education in February 2002, this author commented that one of the consequences of television programmes such as those of David Attenborough or David Bellamy, or those shown on the *Discovery* Channel is that of increased pressure on natural environments as viewers seek to see the species concerned before they became extinct. To use Wheeller's (1993) much-cited expression, it is a case of ego- and not ecotourism. Where is the evidence for such scepticism? As has already been noted, in a study of visitors to Fogg Dam in the Northern Territory of Australia, Ryan, Hughes and Chirgwin (2000) found that most tourists (97%) defined themselves as 'ecotourists'. However, it has already been argued that their experience of nature was manipulated in terms of what they experienced and in terms of what was drawn to their attention. It might be argued that that is an issue for the Parks Authority. However, if ecotourism is about education it was found that, in spite of the Parks Authority's attempts to inform, these ecotourists had learnt comparatively little – as evidenced by poor recall of quite basic information about the site. It can be objected that this may have been because the information giving was comparatively rudimentary, being provided primarily by the written word. On the other hand, as will be discussed in Chapter 9, if other forms of information provision are required, then it may mean that tourists seek information through entertainment, and that it is the latter that is more important than the former. Further evidence was provided by a study that applied the New Environmental Paradigm. Ryan (2000b) reports that those tourists who recorded the highest levels of environmental sensitivity on the scale showed no discernible differences in attitudes towards wildlife-viewing experiences from those of the general body of tourists. These tourists still tended to prefer to join small groups to view animals, even when told that such small groups increased the likelihood of intrusion impacts on wildlife owing to the greater number of trips required to provide any given number of tourists with a viewing opportunity. It might appear that *all* tourists feel it is all right for them to observe the threatened species, it is for others to have obstacles imposed on their access.

It can be objected that there is a fault in this line of argument. The surveys relate to actual tourists. Those who are sensitive to these issues and do not wish to impose strains on natural environments will stay at home, and thus will not be surveyed. However, from a management perspective, the Parks Authority or the tourism-attraction owner must cope with those who actually visit. Also, in the private sector, it is unlikely that operators will turn down business. There are examples of operators who do refuse entry to visitors thought to have an inappropriate attitude. For example Rod Rae of 'Swimming with Dolphins' in Whitianga in New Zealand, to reduce impacts on dolphin pods, specifically restricts the number of trips he takes. He also instructs the sales office to refuse ticket sales to those who ask for a guarantee that they will swim with dolphins (Ryan, 1998b). However such an entrepreneur represents a minority. Indeed, even the most well meaning of tourists, when faced with that once-in-a-lifetime opportunity can find it difficult to resist the temptation to engage in actions that he or she knows might have deleterious consequences. Markwell (1998) in his study of a group of students on an ecostudy tour of Sumutra recounts how some respondents found it impossible to resist touching and holding hands with a baby orang-utan, in spite of being knowing the risks of communicating diseases and smells.

If, therefore, it is not possible to fully entrust tourists to engage in self-denying behaviours, then arguably there is a greater imposition of duty on the operator to take care that is imposed. Some writers have expressed the belief that codes of conduct are one way forward. However, if these are to be effective, then it seems that there must be some means of enforcing compliance with the codes.

Clarke (1997) discerns a shift in the understanding of ecotourism. She argues that there has been a paradigm shift from the original understanding of ecotourism as being small scale, educative and a minority interest towards an understanding of sustainable tourism that requires best practice by tourism operations of all sizes in terms of minimising their impacts on the environment. Evidence for this can be found in various initiatives like that of the PATA Green Leaf programme aimed at hotels. This programme encouraged hotels to engage in environmentally-friendly practices such as using long life light bulbs, encouraging guests not to require clean towels and sheets each day (thereby requiring less laundry and less disposal of detergents), where possible using alternative sources of energy such as solar power, and using best practices in terms of water usage, sewage and refuse disposal. Further examples include the sorting of rubbish into recyclable categories and the disposal of food scraps into bins so that earthworms can help generate natural compost.

Praiseworthy though such schemes might be, they still founder on criticisms that they only marginally offset the environmental demands made by the very existence of the hotel in terms of power generation, the pollution created by tourists in burning fossil fuels in travelling to the hotel, the additional demands that might be imposed on local agriculture and so on. Second, while it might be nice for tourists to stay in such a hotel as it engenders a feeling that management practices provide guests with comfort, and reduce their negative impacts on the environment, there remained little evidence that such schemes were proactively attracting visitors. For these reasons the industry, under promptings from bodies such as the World Tourism Organisation, PATA and other international organisations, has sought to consolidate the myriad schemes that emerged in the 1980s and the 1990s to produce an internationally-recognisable scheme and symbol that could be branded and sold to tourists. The concept was that, by creating a brand awareness of good practice, the industry would both persuade and inform tourists of means by which negative environmental impacts could be minimised, if not totally averted. The unkind might remark that the premise is that it is possible to both have one's cake and eat it!

For these reasons the Green Globe 21 initiative has been much praised and promoted. The International Ecotourism Standard for Certification was developed by the Ecotourism Association of Australia and the Cooperative Research Centre for Sustainable Tourism, Australia, to form the basis of the Green Globe 21 Ecotourism Certification Program that has now been adopted by PATA in lieu of its former Green Leaf programme. It has thus been accepted as the standard for certification of sustainable tourism practices in the Pacific Asia region, and is being adopted elsewhere. The promoters of the scheme hope that not only will it encourage companies to become 'sustainable' but that tourists will prefer to patronise companies that display its symbol. Thus adherence to its structures will be of commercial benefit to participating organisations. Evidence of its adoption is provided by a list of its adherents. In early 2002 participants included the Foping National Nature Reserve in North-West China, the Turtle Island Resort in Fiji, Malla Treks in Nepal, and the Inter-Continental Hotel in

Singapore, to mention but a handful. Yet even this example shows that certification is open to all, from the largest to the smallest of tourism operators. Crabtree, O'Reilly and Worboys (2002) described the purpose of the scheme as:

(1) providing a means of identification of genuine ecotourism product;
(2) giving visitors and other stakeholders (e.g. local communities) an assurance that the ecotourism product will be supplied in accordance with, and a commitment to, best ecotourism practices and provision of quality experience;
(3) encouraging and rewarding product that continually improves best practice or develops innovations that increase ecological sustainability;
(4) providing a blueprint for new and developing ecotourism product.

The process of certification revolves around eight core principles that permit measurement. These principles are that ecotourism should:

(1) have a natural area focus that ensures that visitors have an opportunity to directly and individually experience nature;
(2) provide interpretation and educational services that give visitors an opportunity to experience nature in ways that lead to greater understanding, appreciation and enjoyment;
(3) represent best practices in ecologically sustainable practices;
(4) contribute to the conservation of natural areas and cultural heritage;
(5) provide ongoing contributions to the local community;
(6) respect and be sensitive to cultures existing in the area;
(7) consistently meet consumer expectations; and
(8) be marketed and promoted honestly and accurately so that realistic expectations are formed.

Certification thus involves a three-stage process. The first is to develop an environmental plan that is registered with Green Globe 21. The plan must cover items such as key performance area, identification of impacts and an action plan to address those issues. The second stage is, put simply, the implementation of the plan. Finally there is a process of accreditation where the operator is externally appraised as to the effectiveness of the plan and its implementation. At this point the operator becomes an accredited operator and is permitted to display the Green Globe logo with a 'tick'.

While this is commendable in many ways, the fact remains that there are still myriad certification schemes. For example, in November 2001 a new initiative was announced involving the Rainforest Alliance with support from the JP Morgan Charitable Foundation and the Ford Foundation. In some instances the same personnel remain linked with the different schemes. For example, Graeme Worboys is CEO of Green Globe Asia-

Pacific, and a member of the advisory group working for the Rainforest Alliance certification scheme. For his part, Geoffrey Lipman, Chair of Green Globe 21 (Global), has argued that other certification brands should be supported and not marginalised (Green Globe 21, 2001). Some question the principles on which some statements are based, and this refers to a wider debate between those who perceive sustainability permitting restriction and the WTO interpretation whereby green tourism is contextualised within free trade and open access. For example, in 1995 the Earth Council, The World Travel and Tourism Council and the World Tourism Organisation released a joint document as to how tourism should implement the Rio Earth Summit's *Agenda 21* (WTTC *et al.*, 1996). However *Agenda 21 for the Travel and Tourism Industry* makes clear that the industry identifies sustainable development with free trade, privatisation and government deregulation. Two of the twelve guiding principles specifically state that protectionism in trade in Travel and Tourism services should be halted or reversed, and that open economic systems should be fostered. As described above, the Green Globe certification process seeks both sustainable practice and quality experiences for visitors. While recognising that this is indeed possible, a context that might regard restrictions on access as inimicable to open economic systems is open to criticism that the economic system might have precedence over the preservation of an environment. Nonetheless, initiatives like Green Globe represent some advantages over schemes like the ISO 14001 certification. Established by the International Organisation for Standardisation, ISO 14001 is an environmental management system. It has been criticised as being more concerned with process rather than with what is being done. Krut and Gleckman (1998: 8) in particular have been critical of ISO 14001, arguing that 'following this logic a company making weapons for biological warfare can be certified to ISO 14001'. At least Green Globe is explicit as to its function and purpose.

In some instances of certification there is a high degree of specificity. In 1999, funded by the European Commission, a series of workshops were held relating to the establishment of an eco-rating for accommodation. Strong industry support for a single European-wide system was founded on the premise of tourist confusion, ignorance and suspicion of credibility about eco-labelling (see www.europa.ei.int/ecolabel). But it might be argued that the very plethora of certification systems impedes understanding by both industry and tourists.

However, the actual process of undertaking the environmental assessments that are required for certification is not cheap. For example, the president of the US-based Environmental Training and Consulting International, Inc., which has conducted various ISO14001 appraisals for hotel companies, estimates that developing an EMS (environmental management system) can cost as much as $US30,000–60,000 for a medium-sized hotel (e.g. see www.envirotrain.com). There is a relationship between credibility, payment for apposite appraisal by credible neutral third parties, and being able to claim rigour for any certification process. This triumvirate of concerns might mean that the very small ecotourism operators who appear to be the epitome of ecotourism as originally defined by Ceballos-Lascurain (1987) might be dissuaded from seeking certification on the basis of cost. This is not to say that examples of low-cost, credible eco-labelling do not exist, but unfortunately their history is chequered. For example, the much-cited ecotourism policies of Costa Rica – see for example, Weaver's (2001: 90) description of Costa Rica 'as one of the world's model ecotourism destinations – included a 'green-rating' in the guide book *The New Key to Costa Rica*, which first appeared in 1992 (Blake & Beecher, 1992). The model subsequently developed into eight pages that focused on three areas: (1) the environmental impact of the lodge, including use of natural and energy sources, (2) how much revenue remained in the local community, and (3) how knowledgeable owners were about local culture, and in what ways did they seek to reinforce it. Initially seen as a low-cost, but labour-intensive method of measurement, over time the assessment became unsustainable in the face of commercial pressures and changing individual priorities. Other guidebooks, notably The *Lonely Planet* series, became more popular, while the initiators of the method, Beatrice Blake and Anne Becher moved away from Costa Rica. Unfortunately, while Costa Rica subsequently created its Certificate for Sustainable Tourism (CST) for hotels, it has not, thus far, been overly successful. By the end of 2000 only 51 of about 400 hotels had been certified, and the need for financial sustainability tends to reinforce processes where those with money are able to fund certification. As already noted, with certification schemes the potential irony arises that the need to produce rigorous assessment combined with financial sustainability (and it should not be forgotten that bodies like those of Green Globe have to financially sustain themselves) might conspire to set costs above those that small lifestyle ecotourism organisations can afford. Therefore they do not become certified as being 'green', while the larger accommodation units and attractions are able to afford such certification as an investment in attracting visitors. The continuing danger is that the question of whether such an operation should be present is not asked – the focus is on a process of minimising negative impacts, rather than asking whether a natural environment should suffer any impact at all. It can be questioned whether processes of open economic systems, inhibitions on restrictions under World Trade Organisation rules and the costs of certification do not combine to ensure the long-term financial viability of larger enterprise with a green face. To some extent the answer to such questions depends on the ability to sustain natural resource management policies within any country's individual legal framework. This is discussed in a little detail below.

Managing the Environmental Impacts of Tourism

General issues

Arguably the first stage in planning tourism is the development of an audit of resources, markets, activities and competition. It can be maintained that there is a symbiotic relationship between tourist resources within the destination zone and the market for, as has already been examined, certain tourist types will be attracted towards certain tourism areas. Equally, however, it is known that the tourist zone is not stable, but can change, as was described by Young (1983) in his description of the 'touristisation' of a Maltese fishing/farming village. The implication of the concept of the tourist area lifecycle is that planning needs to be undertaken from the initial period of development, particularly if the development is taking place within an ecologically fragile area. Unfortunately, the first stages of tourism may occur almost unnoticed. At first there may be only a trickle of tourists who are not only non-threatening in numbers or in type, but are indeed careful and appreciative of what it is they see. At this stage it may seem that there is little need for planning, but both the concept of the lifecycle and the past history of many destinations indicates that such an attitude cannot be maintained. From the practical viewpoint, this poses severe problems for planning authorities. It may be difficult to persuade communities that restrictions need to be determined at an early stage when currently there appears to be little need for such restrictions. Charges of elitism may well be made, and perhaps not without foundation. The host community will be asked to make difficult decisions that might imply a restriction on economic returns from tourism when the costs and implications of future tourism flows are difficult to assess, and can be nothing more than speculative. In the case of ecological considerations, the reasons for such restrictions may seem intangible. The problem may be further exacerbated if the self-same authorities are also responsible for the economic well-being of a community that might be marginal to the mainstream of economic activity within its country, and is thus looking to tourism to generate income and employment. Initially, indeed, tourism can be seen as the "lesser of two evils". Thus, in parts of Colorado in the USA, tourism, based on skiing and mountain resorts, provided a means of revenue that compensated rural communities that had chosen this path rather than permit the mining of molybdenum deposits from the surrounding hills, arguing that such mining would have detrimental environmental effects. However, these communities have subsequently found that tourism too has its costs in terms of stresses on water quality, impacts of tourist numbers and the other well-documented ills (Nova, 1990). Perhaps what is required is a recognition that natural resources are finite and, like other resources, are subject to disrepair. In this respect the concept of assessing the environment using techniques such as cost–benefit analysis, in order to help not only tourism planning, but also any other form of physical development, would seem not only logical, but necessary. Without any requirement for an environmental impact analysis, the environmental cost is in danger of simply being disregarded. Unfortunately, as appears to be the case in New Zealand, such a requirement may be seen as unnecessary, costly and an impediment to economic development. In 1991 New Zealand introduced its Resource Management Act both as a rationalisation of existing planning legislation, and as a means of ensuring environmental sustainability. It created a process whereby those initiatives thought to have an environmental impact would need to be subject to processes of review and, effectively, an environmental impact analysis. However, in many rural local authorities, because of little population pressure, the process has come to be perceived as not only unnecessary but also as inconsistent in application between different local territorial authorities. In fact there are growing demands from rural and business organisations (including some tourism entities), for not simply a review but indeed a watering down of the legislation (see, for example, Page & Thorn, 1997; James, 2002).

Therefore, there are very real problems in beginning the planning processes relating to tourism development, for the very process of planning in itself requires a recognition that the market forces of demand and supply are going to be subjected to restrictions. However once such a review is commenced it can be argued that a first requirement is an audit of the area. Mill and Morrison (1985) quote the methodology used by the Marshall Macklin Monoghan Consulting Group (1980) in their study of a tourism development strategy for southern Ontario. Natural resources need to be identified, as do resources that are man-developed and man-controlled. They developed a basic grid, which is shown in Table 8.5. The markets to be examined in more detail may be further subdivided into local, regional, national and international markets. It then becomes possible to develop a coding that indicates the level of investment that may be needed to support the infrastructure development required to reach the desired market. So, in this example, the lighter the shading, the more is the required additional investment. In the Ontario study, a simple three-fold visual symbolisation was used that indicated 'high', 'medium' and 'low' investment need, development or density depending on the measure being used. As such, the market may be defined in terms of numbers or even types of tourists. The opportunities that exist may have to be further analysed by their duration throughout the year; some may be possible only during winter or summer months. Climatic conditions may also have to be part of the audit, as perhaps might be tourism policies, labour policies and other socio-legal aspects. The location and distribution of resources may have to be examined, and in short the audit might well utilise the descriptive techniques

Table 8.5 The matrix used in the Collingwood impact assessment: A partial example

	Existing market				*Markets desired*				*Potential markets*			
Natural resources	*Local*	*Regional*	*National*	*International*	*Local*	*Regional*	*National*	*International*	*Local*	*Regional*	*National*	*International*
Water-based recreational opportunities		☺					☺				☺	
Land-based recreational opportunities			☺					☺				☺
Air-based recreational opportunities		☺						☺				☺
Man-developed and man-controlled resources												
Natural resource opportunities			☺					☺			☺	
Historical resource opportunities		☺					☺				☺	
Cultural resource opportunities		☺					☺				☺	
Leisure opportunities			☺				☺				☺	

examined in Chapter 6. Indeed, as was noted in that chapter, the advent of GIS (geographical information systems) has aided the process of environmental audits. It is now possible to develop alternative scenarios that can not only be quantitatively modelled on a computer, but can also be associated with alternative graphics, including film and photographs, that clearly show how different developments might appear. This eases processes for local stakeholder consultation because it becomes more possible for people to comprehend the implications of alternative proposals and the magnitude of proposed changes. Theoretically at least, the infamous 'architect's drawing' can be replaced by more realistic photographs and other images.

It can also be noted that in some instances there are no planning controls, in other cases planning controls are simply being ignored. Murphy (1985), Barkham (1973) and many others require that communities play a role in a rational planning process, but this assumes that the community is a homogeneous unit that is capable of making decisions not only in its own self-interest, but also for the interest of others. It is perhaps a questionable assumption. In addition, it is perhaps worth noting that both Murphy (1985) and Krippendorf (1987) write from the background of political systems in Canada and Switzerland, which permit plebiscites to be held on issues where a comparatively small proportion of the population (in some instances as little as 5%) can sign a petition to the effect that a plebiscite ought to be put before the electorate. This method of community control is lacking in many other countries, including the UK and France to name but two.

Functional measures

What remains? Possibly what might be achieved is at least some degree of consensus over potential measures of carrying capacity. It might appear this reduces the process to a mechanistic one rather than the dynamic process required by Getz (1983), but at least it is a starting point and might serve the required process. The WTO (1982b) noted a number of measures when it considered the problem in its report *Risks of saturation, or tourist carrying capacity overload in holiday destinations* which considered practices in twelve of its member countries.

One of the problems facing tourism destinations is the seasonality of the business, and hence measures of the temporal dispersion of business may be useful. Measures relating to the question of peakedness of demand can include:

(1) A measure of the maximum numbers of people that can be carried at any one time. The WTO recommends a measure of two-thirds of the maximum number of recorded visitors in order to conservatively establish the maximum carrying capacity (1983).
(2) Weekly/daily maxima can then be calculated on the basis of the peak capacity measured by the time period concerned. In the case of annual figures, the figure will be based on the number of days the attraction remains open.
(3) A measure of the level of crowding can be simply assessed by taking the number of arrivals in a given time and dividing by the total number of arrivals over a longer time period.
(4) A better statistic that measures the peakedness of the distribution of visitors is the kurtosis. This is calculated according to the formula:

$$K = \sum_{i=1}^{n} \frac{(X_i - X)^4}{n(\text{SD})^4}$$

where K = the value of kurtosis
X_i = the number of users at the time
X = the arithmetic mean of all X_I
n = the number of time periods
SD = the standard deviation of X_i

If K has a value of 1 then the curve has a normal distribution. If it has a value of less than 3, it is relatively flat in shape and is said to be platykurtic. If it has a value of greater than 3 then it is said to be leptokurtic, and is relatively peaked. In such a case it might be said that the tourist area is heavily congested for at least some small period of the total time.

The level of crowdedness can also be calculated with reference to space. It might, for example, be said that the number of people should not exceed a given number per hectare of space. Perhaps a beach should not have more than 1000 people per hectare. However, it has to be noted that such a measure of crowdedness fails to take into account the psychological components of the concept of a crowd. For popular beaches part of the fun of the situation, and a generator of the beach atmosphere, is indeed the fact that it is crowded. People go to see people. In other situations, if what is being sought is peace and quiet, ten people on a beach may be a crowd.

Carrying capacity is sometimes related to the expected numbers of people. This is the case with the calculation of car park spaces, the number of restaurants or the number of shops that are required. Thus, one might say that 1 restaurant place is required per 2000 tourists, or 0.2 square metres of shop floor space is required per tourist, or 1.2 car parking space per available bedspace, or 250 car parking spaces per hectare. Another approach is to assess thresholds. If a factor such as water supply is limited, then the number of tourists that can be catered for may be estimated along the lines of available water supply divided by the consumption per tourist per day. If car parking space is limited, then the number of visitors that may be catered for is the number of car parking spaces divided by the average length of stay per tourist per time period, multiplied by the average number of tourists per car. For example, if there are 100 car parking places, and each tourist stays approximately 30 minutes, then within 10 hours, 2000 tourists can be catered for if each tourist arrives separately by car. If each car carries 3 tourists, then the limit is 6000 tourists. If it costs a given amount to develop a tourist attraction, say an interpretation centre, then the number of tourists required to cover the costs, the break-even point, is the total cost of the development divided by the expected average expenditure per visitor.

A popular measure is the host–visitor ratio, and Defert's tourist function is one such measure. This states that:

$$Df = \frac{\text{number of bed-spaces in a region}}{\text{population of the region}} \times 100$$

With specific reference to ecology and rural activities, the number of visitors depends on the definition of the area. For a forest park, the daily allowable visitor rate per hectare may be 0–15, whereas for a surburban natural park it may be 15–70, and for a recreation sports facility, 80–200. Campsite standards vary around the world, again depending on the nature of the zone in which the sites are found. In France, many sites operate at 300 persons per hectare, whereas in the USA in wildlife zones, the figure only be 2.5 people per hectare (WTO, 1983).

Types of zones and permitted usages

So complex is the measurement of carrying capacity that an alternative approach might be adopted, which is to undertake an impact study – although it might be said that from many perspectives such studies are complementary to, and not alternative to, the concept of carrying capacity. The idea behind impact studies is to examine development projects with the purpose of identifying the potential environmental impact. Having identified such impacts, the initial proposals may then be modified to minimise the negative impacts. Often associated with the concept of permitted impact is an identification of levels of allowable development. In short, planners identify zones of different usage patterns. In practice, from the viewpoint of tourism, many of these zones relate to rural areas, but of course such zoning also occurs within urban areas. Thus, some urban areas will permit only low-density residential development, whilst other zones may have higher-density housing and some retail development, whilst yet others may be characterised by industrial activities. One aspect of urban zoning that relates to tourism is the protection of historical heritage and buildings of historical value within a town. Such buildings may be subject to preservation orders, and in addition any adjacent development that is permitted will have to be of a nature that is sympathetic to the original ambience of the area.

One of the best examples of a hierarchical classification of rural landscapes that indicates levels of potential development is that of Parks Canada. Parks Canada has adopted a five-fold classification, as indicated in Table 8.6. It is illustrative of one of the common techniques of tourism management in that it indicates permitted levels of recreational use, with the type and intensity of use being determined by the nature of the ecology of the area. It also highlights the importance of the role of accessibility as a

Table 8.6 Zoning: An example from Parks Canada

Zone I: Special Preservation Specific areas or features that deserve special preservation because they contain or support unique, threatened or endangered natural or cultural features, or are among the best examples of the features that represent a natural region. Preservation is the key consideration. Motorised access and circulation will not be permitted. In cases where the fragility of the area precludes any public access, every effort will be made to provide park visitors with appropriate off-site programs and exhibits interpreting the special characteristics of the zone. About 3.25% of the parks system is zone I.
Zone II: Wilderness Extensive areas that are good representations of a natural region and which will be conserved in a wilderness state. The perpetuation of ecosystems with minimal human interference is the key consideration. Zones I and II will together constitute the majority of the area of all but the smallest national parks, and will make the greatest contribution towards the conservation of ecosystem integrity. Zone II areas offer opportunities for visitors to experience, first hand, a park's natural and cultural heritage values through outdoor recreation activities that depend on and are within the capacity of the park's ecosystems, and that require few, if any, rudimentary services and facilities. Where the areas are large enough, visitors will also have the opportunity to experience remoteness and solitude. Opportunities for outdoor recreation activities will be encouraged only when they do not conflict with maintaining the wilderness itself. For this reason, motorised access and circulation will not be permitted, with the possible exception of strictly controlled air access in remote northern parks. About 94.01% of the parks system is zone II.
Zone III: Natural Environment Areas that are managed as natural environments, and that provide opportunities for visitors to experience a park's natural and cultural heritage values through outdoor recreation activities requiring minimal services and facilities of a rustic nature. While motorised access may be allowed, it will be controlled. Public transit that facilitates heritage appreciation will be preferred. Park management plans may define provisions for terminating or limiting private motorised access. About 2.16% of the parks system is zone III.

Table 8.6 *(continued)*

Zone IV: Outdoor Recreation   Limited areas that are capable of accommodating a broad range of opportunities for understanding, appreciation and enjoyment of the park's heritage values and related essential services and facilities, in ways that impact on the ecological integrity of the park to the smallest extent possible, and whose defining feature is direct access by motorised vehicles. Park management plans may define provisions for limiting private motorised access and circulation.   About 0.48% of the parks system is zone IV.
Zone V: Park Services   Communities in existing national parks that contain a concentration of visitor services and support facilities. Specific activities, services and facilities in this zone will be defined and directed by the community planning process. Major park operation and administrative functions may also beaccommodated in this zone. Wherever possible, Parks Canada will locate these functions to maintain regional ecological integrity.   About 0.09% of the parks system is zone V.

Parks Canada (1988)

means of protecting the natural environment. Numbers of tourists expand once access is made available. Supply of an area appears to create its own demand and, with a growth of demand, there appears to be a process of further improving access. Distance is no longer the barrier it once was, and even the furthest flung parts of the globe are susceptible to the visit of the tourist, as is witnessed by the growing numbers that visit Antarctica. Creating roads generates traffic that may far exceed the calculations of the road planner, and this phenomenon is not restricted to tourist areas. The M25 orbital motorway around London is such an example. Within a year of its opening it became evident that the traffic flows far exceeded forecast demand, and schemes to widen the six-lane motorway to eight lanes were subsequently announced in 1989. Equally, the very existence of the motorway has helped to generate submissions by property developers for new retail/leisure centres around London's perimeter. So, too, with tourist destinations. One such example is the Greek island of Lefkas, which in the early 1980s had some tourism based in Lefkas Town and the village of Nidri. To a large degree this was local Greek tourism, attracted to the island not only by its natural beauty, but also partly by its proximity to Scorpios, an island made glamorous by its connections with the Onassis family. By the mid-1980s Nidri was being used by a few, small, specialist holiday companies; at the same time the village of Vassiliki in the south of the island was becoming known amongst the windsurfing fraternity for its strong winds on summer afternoons. However, until 1987 the village of Vassiliki was accessible from Nidri only by a rough road, but in that year the road was made permanent with a tarmac surface. Consequently, the larger holiday companies that had followed the smaller, specialist companies to Nidri began to offer Vassiliki in their brochures for 1988, partly because the travel time to Vassiliki had been reduced by the improved communications. Other factors were also important. A similar aspect of accessibility was the increased frequency of flights to the airport of Prevaza, which serviced the island of Lefkas. In consequence, the villages of Nidri and Vassiliki began to change their character in the way described by Young (1985). Thus, accessibility becomes a determinant of change that initiates not only a change of land use from a strictly environmental viewpoint but also a social change.

It must also be noted that classifications of areas are an important step towards zoning, and hence care must be taken over the categorisation of land, for such categorisations determine the level of development that will be permitted. For example, within the USA the Wilderness Act defines wilderness in the following terms:

> A wilderness, in contrast to those areas where man and his own works dominate the landscape, is hereby recognised as an area where the Earth and its community of life are untrammelled by man, where man himself is a visitor who does not remain. (Wilderness Act, 1964: section 2c)

Searle (1989) argues that, if this definition is applied to areas such as Banff National Park, then the true wilderness of Banff is reduced to only about 60% of the park. This is because the Canada Parks Service subcategories of wilderness include 'semi-primitive wilderness', which permits commercial lodges, large group camps and site hardening. Within the United Kingdom, National Parks policy has always had to recognise that much of the land is in private ownership, much of it being worked by farmers. Indeed, much of the area covered by UK National Parks would fail the US definition of wilderness. Consequently, the English authorities have had to set up systems of permitted land use, which contain within them the potential for conflict between the right of individuals to develop their own land as they see fit, and the right of a wider society to open spaces.

If the type of tourism that exists is indeed a reflection of the needs and aspirations of a society, then the relationship between tourism and the physical environment mirrors the values of that society. Arguably, the literature of holidays, with its promises of an unspoilt destination, contains two implicit premises. The first is the recognition of the desire for escape into a 'paradise', a notion of nature as a means of renewing the spirit – an attitude that arguably may be seen as both unnecessarily romantic and mistaken (Walter, 1982). Secondly, holiday brochures imply that the 'unspoilt destination' is a tourist resource for mankind; and it is perhaps with this premise that environmental pressure groups would most argue. Dearden (1989) and Dearden and Rollins (1990) have argued, within a Canadian context, that, historically, the environment has been viewed as a storehouse of raw materials, and that the wilderness has value or worth only in relation to its usefulness to humans. In consequence, National Parks, beautiful scenery and the unspoilt areas, have value only if perceived as a resource for tourism and economic benefit. Such a viewpoint, Dearden argues, fails to recognise the integrity of the areas for their own sake, and instead places on them a value that has everything to do with economic rates of return and nothing to do with intrinsic values. And therein lies the crux of the matter. On the one hand there exists a valid longing for escape, for the pleasure to be found in skiing down the slopes, or sailing in blue seas, or communing with nature within isolated areas, or simply sharing beauty with family and friends and so reinforcing the feelings of togetherness of any given social group. On the other hand, such desires, when translated into the wishes of thousands if not millions wishing to share the same experiences, become a threat not only to the sought-after experience, but also to the flora and fauna and, as waters become poisoned and air polluted, to the host communities themselves. Nor, as will be discussed in the next chapter, are the changes posed by tourism limited to the physical environment alone.

Management Techniques

The above discussion begins to indicate ways in which the planning authorities can start to minimise the negative impacts of tourism, whilst simultaneously, at least under certain conditions, perhaps even enhancing the degree of visitor satisfaction. A number of policies might be identified. Essentially, these techniques can be divided into two broad groupings: macro-techniques and micro-techniques. Macro-techniques relate to planning sites within a zone, and the relationship between them, whilst micro-techniques relate to the management of flows of people within a specific destination and place in the zone itself. Both are orientated towards maintaining sustainable levels of usage.

Macro-techniques

The setting up of 'honeypots'

This involves the development, or the permission for development, of popular resort areas in an attempt to relieve pressure on more sensitive areas elsewhere. One example of such a policy would be the development of recreational parkland near centres of population in the hope that such areas would attract users, so protecting the more distant fragile zones. Another example would be to permit the development of major tourist resorts. It might be expected that such resorts would help protect their hinterland in two ways. The very gaudiness of the resort would deter the allocentric, explorer type of tourist, whilst the psychocentric, mass-organised tourists would remain content within their touristic bubble experiencing its fun-packed delights. But such a policy may not work. As any visitor to the Costa del Sol would testify, the hinterland of Andalucia is indeed visited by tourists. In areas such as Ojen, foreign ownership of property is not uncommon; whilst by the 1980s the town of Ronda boasted souvenir and antique shops that it did not possess a decade earlier. Incidentally, both of these developments have, in part, been encouraged by the improvement of roads that lead from the coast through the mountains, again illustrating the importance of accessibility. However, the policy of 'honeypots' might not work because the types of tourists described here are partly a caricature of reality. As indicated in Chapter 1, the modern tourist is capable of playing more than one role, of seeking one type of holiday on one occasion and another at other times. Even within the one holiday, whilst adopting predominantly one mode of behaviour, alternative patterns will be taken up at other times. So the mass-organised tourist will take some days out to explore the hinterland, and thus visit the less popular areas. The 'honeypot' thus becomes a nodal point for a series of day-trip activities. Equally, the 'honeypot' tourist area may well be capable of meeting the needs of more than one type of tourist simultaneously, or at least temporally. The types of tourists that visit a popular area in the off-peak season may differ from those who visit during the main season. Consequently, in the off-peak season, visits to the hinterland may not decline in proportion to the decline in visitor numbers to the 'honeypot'. This implies that the policy of adopting 'honeypots' requires careful planning in relation to their location to the more fragile environments. Certainly such fragile areas must be more than a day-trip's distance away. Yet, what is a day-trip's distance away? There is no such set distance, in terms either of miles or of hours spent in travel time. The question of accessibility is important. The policy of the 'honeypot' must go hand in hand with other policies, such as zoning and route planning.

The policy of dispersion

The problem of the 'honeypot' is that the natural and man-made resources within the area may become stressed. Even if this is not the case, and the policy is successful, then, by implication, the economic benefits that accrue from tourism are being denied to other areas. In consequence, to help maintain a higher quality of natural environment within the main tourist resort area, a policy of tourist dispersion may be adopted. The objective of this policy is to avoid overloading the capacity at the main resort and to spread the benefits of tourism. Again, this may also help to enhance the level of visitor satisfaction. Such a policy may be illustrated with reference to South Wales and the Gower Peninsula. The Gower, with its beautiful sandy beaches and coves, has long been a tourist area for the centres of population of the South Wales valleys, and with the completion of motorways and railway links, it has succeeded in attracting tourists from a much wider area. During the 1970s, however, problems became apparent. With increased car ownership, and the improvements in roads as part of the industrial reinvestment in South Wales, on a fine summer's day the bays became packed with people, and the car parks were full to overflowing. The installation of a noticeboard on the Gower road leading out of Swansea that gave information on the car parks, and thus warned motorists that there was no parking available, seemed to have little effect. Arguably, therefore, there was reason to develop other tourist destinations that could help to relieve the stress. Equally, it could be argued that, as a tourist area, the Gower was over-dependent on its beaches. When the weather was poor, there was little alternative activity to which tourists could turn, and thus a potential existed for disappointment. Therefore, in the period from the late 1970s to the late 1980s, a series of alternative tourist attractions was developed in the Vale of Glamorgan and the area north of Swansea, and subsequently in Swansea itself. Tourists may now visit Aberdulais Basin where redevelopment of the old canal basin has taken place. Margam Park has opened, mining museums exist within an easy car journey from Swansea and other developments have occurred.

Has this policy been successful? On fine summer days tourists still prefer to be by the beach, and the car parks are still full to capacity. The entrance to Caswell Valley has long since become a tarmac area, and only older people can remember its original beauty. The village of Mumbles still suffers from a surfeit of cars, and the sand dunes of Oxwich and Port Eynon are protected only by areas being fenced off and access to the beach being controlled by other forms of resort management. To some extent, the problems arise not only from tourism, but also from increased building in the area from the 1970s as South Wales recovered from recession and its past over-dependence on coal mining and agriculture. Its very success in diversifying its economy led to some of the strains briefly described. Yet, as a case study it illustrates some of the problems of diversification policies. The alternatives may not be powerful enough to divert people from the major touristic activities that caused the initial stress. If the alternatives are strong enough to attract visitors away from the original magnet during peak periods of activity, then the new combination of tourist assets will probably engender more visitors in total. This general principle is illustrated in Figure 8.4. Here it can be seen that at the 'old carrying capacity' excess demand exists between months of a and b (generally the summer months). However, increasing the number of attractions creates a new, higher carrying capacity that would permit the numbers of visitors associated with demand P^1 to be easily catered for. However, the problem is not solved and the increased attractions result in a higher demand (P^2). The effect is that, while the season is extended, excess demand now exists between months x and y. One implication of this analysis is that excess 'removal' of demand requires not only the addition of visitor attractions to cater for visitors, but also the addition of roads and accommodation infrastructures that again impose demands on land use and stress on natural environments. Hence, it is argued, there is a need for planning controls and restrictions on private sector use that results from adopting 'market led' policies. The 'user pays' scenario of the market-led approach to tourism results in a distribution of costs that involves stake holders other than the commercial bodies that attract revenue from direct market transactions.

In consequence, the policy succeeds in attracting more visitors and in potentially generating land use pressures over a greater area. Some forms of relief have come to the Gower Peninsular, but this is because, like many other coastal regions of the United Kingdom, demand has ceased to grow at the previous rates because overseas destinations have become both more affordable and more attractive to British holidaymakers.

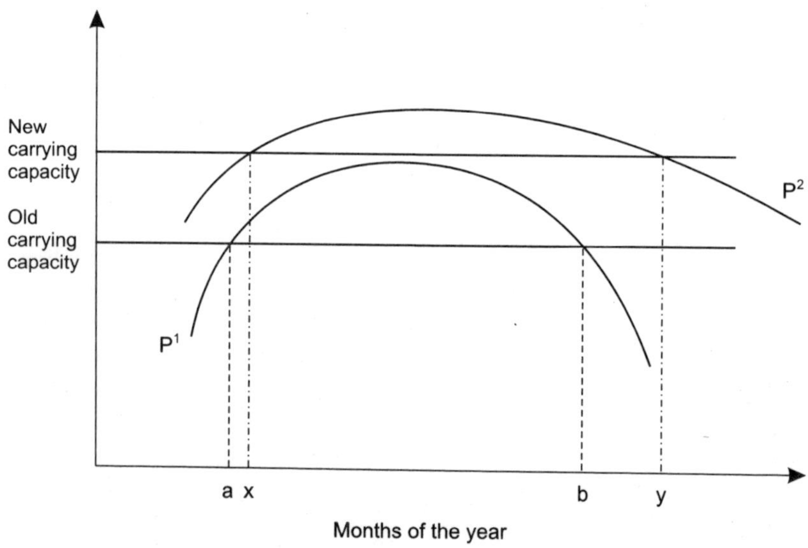

Figure 8.4 The possible effects of adding visitor capacity

Zoning

Zoning involves the identification of areas of land, those uses that will be permitted there, and those that will not be allowed. Within Britain, a major example of zoning is the categorisation of land near cities as Green Belt, where neither residential nor industrial development is permitted. Initially these controls were implemented by various Town and Country Planning Acts (notably that of 1971), but in the 1980s a series of orders and circulars was issued that had the effect of making land development by property developers that much easier. For example, the Department of the Environment circular 22/80, *Development Control Policy and Practice*, stated that when there is a decision to be made there must be a 'presumption in favour of development'; in other words, permission will be granted unless there is a strong counter-argument (DOE, 1980). Circular 2/87, *Awards of Costs and Planning Procedures*, indicated that costs could be awarded against planning authorities for 'unreasonable' delay in granting planning permission (DOE, 1987). The consequences, particularly in urban locations where listed buildings might be found within conservation areas, were the exercise of significant pressure on planning authorities for development, and a potential danger that out-of-character development might be permitted. However, the market-led, 'user pays' approaches of the Thatcherite years in turn gave way to the new political processes of Labour Party government. The changes that took place resulted in the Green Paper, *Planning: Delivering a Fundamental Change*, which was subject of consultative processes until December 2001 (Office of the Deputy Prime Minister, 2001). At the time of writing it is not possible to say with certainty what outcomes will take place, but the changes being proposed include several that are important. As noted in debates about planning and environmental impacts elsewhere, a middle path is sought between the market-led policies of the past and the over-fussy regulations of other periods. The Green Paper seeks to 'reduce uncertainty by identifying realistic and definitive time-scales', to provide efficient and friendly service through a well skilled and supported staff and a greater use of new technologies to speed processes. Development plans are contextualised within local development frameworks, and to a large extent it can be argued that the Green Paper is about processes rather than about macro-concerns. To some extent these concerns are already to be found in legislation about environmental impacts and the work of the UK Environment Agency among other bodies. However, process is important. The conceived checklists for seeking approval require clear statements about environmental impacts (Office of the Deputy Prime Minister, 2001: section 5.9), and this would be consistent with European Union legislation and overseas practices. This clearly imposes a need for territorial authorities to maintain consistency of overall land-use patterns, while the test might be: what amount of detail will suffice to meet the impact assessments required by the local authority? New Zealand's experience of the Resource Management Act and its consultative processes has been one of an unequal relationship between stakeholders: community groups have sometimes felt disappointed by their inability to match the resources available to commercial enterprise who produce environmental consultants reports that indicate minimal negative environments. For their part, entrepreneurs have expressed dissatisfaction about the increase in start up-costs that such consultancies and time delays impose on their plans. Consequently proposals exist that some form of public sector support should be made available for local pressure groups. On the other hand, businesses have expressed concerns about 'frivolous' objections and in New Zealand there has been recognition of the need to recompense business for extra costs resulting from appeal procedures where the original application has been approved. It might be concluded that apparently rational processes simply give rise to unlooked-for consequences.

From a tourism perspective, one of the common problems associated with tourism development is that, in order to protect the important or fragile area, tourism development may be restricted at the location itself. Nonetheless, visitors may continue to arrive, and hence there is a need for a tourist complex of hotels, swimming pools, restaurants, campsites and souvenir shops at some distance from the tourist attraction. One such example is the creation and subsequent expansion of the resort complex at Yulara near Uluru-Kata Tjuṯa National Park (Ayers Rock) in Central Australia. In the longer term one problem that might emerge is that of poor access to the attraction from the support tourist complex, and some have argued that the construction of an airport at Yulara had significant impacts on visitation patterns to Uluru.

The encouragement of 'soft tourism'

The purpose behind this policy is that tourist activity should be dovetailed into existing facilities, and that tourist developments that are extraneous to the nature of the area are forbidden. As previously indicated, it commonly proposes a form of tourism that is consistent with rural and agricultural pursuits. It is argued that tourism should serve a purpose of supplementing the major economic activities that exist, rather than supplanting them. Attractive as this idea is, and consistent as it may appear with environmental concerns and the changing patterns of tourism demand previously discussed, this policy is also not without its difficulties. Logically, it would restrict large-scale tourist development, such as theme parks, to only one of two types of areas, namely the already urbanised, developed area, and the area of derelict or desolate wasteland that has little economic or ecological value. In the case of already-developed areas, such proposals might perhaps create the problems of stress that are associated with the 'honeypot' policy. It also denies to those living in rural areas the chance of significant economic investments that may serve as a catalyst of change. Some such developments may be held to be consistent with the inherent nature of the area (for example, major attractions based on rural technologies such as dairy production), yet actually have significant income, employment, social and environmental implications because of the very scale of any proposed development. The objective of soft tourism is one of slow evolution rather than revolution, and one problem might be that host communities might not willingly accept these restrictions. Much depends on how the host community values the quality and form of the landscape that external bodies feel has value and is deserving of protection. The proponents of 'soft tourism' argue that only this form of tourism offers any form of practical solution to the economic needs of the community and the requirements of conservation.

Sometimes, however, the proposals that are accepted do not always have the desired outcomes. For example, it is often suggested that farm-stay holidays generate additional income, particularly for women, and permit them to develop entrepreneurial skills. For her part, V.L. Smith (1994) reports research from Belize that showed that small-scale, family-based tourism produced little return for female workers, and that in fact chambermaids in hotel complexes enjoyed more free time and higher levels of retained income. Also, organised patterns of work as an employee were actually far less intrusive on home life.

The encouragement of 'green policies'

The encouragement of 'soft tourism' is closely related to the establishment of 'green policies' that seek not only to protect but also to restore the environment and offset problems generated by acid rain and other threats, even whilst improving recreational resources. The proposals of the Countryside Commission to develop urban forests provide such an example. The plan called for the commencement of tree planting in the Black Country and Tyneside in 1989, with, within five years, further planting in the London Green Belt, and on the perimeters of Manchester and Sheffield. A second phase subsequently took place around Nottingham, Leeds, Cardiff, Swansea and Middlesbrough. In Scotland, the Scottish Office announced a £50 million woodland planting programme for Glasgow and Edinburgh. The Countryside Commission proposed that the woodland should consist of a 50:50 mix of broad-leaved and coniferous trees, thereby achieving objectives of a quick-growing green landscape that possesses economic value while also permitting a re-establishment of oak, beech and other broad-leaved trees that provide animal shelter. At the same time, the policy would help restore the loss of such broad-leaved trees – the

Nature Conservancy Council having estimated that 40% of ancient woodlands had disappeared in Britain in the period 1945–1990. Predecessors of this type of initiative are not unknown in Europe, and the Countryside Commission cited as examples the Bos Park near Amsterdam (2200 acres of recreational forest) and the Stadtwiilder (town forests) of Germany (Countryside Commission, 1989). Granger (1990) describes ways in which parks in Ontario are being 'naturalised' as part of a process of the 'greening of cities'. Berg (1990) indicates ways in which the 'greening' of US cities such as San Francisco not only generates a greater ecological awareness but also supports a 'profound shift in the fundamental premises and activities of city living'.

Community Forests have become a reality in the United Kingdom. Twelve such forests now exist, the largest being The Mersey Forest, which covers an area of 92,500 acres. They serve as a major recreational resource while incidental by-products exist because of the trees' ability to act as carbon sinks. Since the programme began more than 6,220 hectares have been planted, and more than 5,000 kilometres of woodland trails have been created. The planted hedgerow was estimated to be 783 kilometres in length (http//www.communityforest.org.uk, June 2002).

From a touristic and recreational viewpoint, urban forests present an opportunity for becoming settings for art galleries, concert venues, dry ski slopes, cycle trails and science parks. At the same time their very existence might help to relieve tourist pressures on existing woodland. Other aspects of green policies might have implications for tourism. The growing demand for organic foodstuffs means that farmers are reducing their use of herbicides and pesticides, and thus in the longer term the quality of water may improve. Currently there are examples where recreational use of water has been stopped because of fears of water pollution from these and other sources. For example, in the late summer of 1989 the use of Rutland Water, a 3000-acre lake in Leicestershire, by windsurfers and others was stopped because of health fears. Since that time there have been other reports of environmental problems adversely affecting recreational and leisure use of natural resources. For example, in June 2002, the State of Vermont had 126 streams, lakes or other stretches of water officially designated as polluted, with Lake Champlain suffering from an excess of phosphorus run off that can cause toxic algae blooms as occurred at Rutland Water.

Unfortunately, as forested areas are so attractive to tourism operators, some come under threat of 'development'. For example, in the UK in 1998 the Rank Organisation sought to develop a resort complex, 'Oasis Village' with 350 waterside villas, 400 forest lodges, 90 studio apartments, golf courses and staff accommodation for the provision of short-break holidays for up to 4000 guests at any one time. The site for this development was to be Lyminge Forest in East Kent. The artificially constructed lake would have required 17.5 million gallons of water with maintenance needs, or so it was claimed, of over 100,000 gallons per day. The result, in spite of planning permission being granted, was a noisy and effective opposition of sit-ins and demonstrations. Environmental pressure groups led the campaign against the proposed development and adverse comparisons were made with Rank's competitor, Center Parcs Limited. At the end of the day, Rank Organisation sold its one northern Oasis Village to Center Parcs and withdrew from the resort complex market.

A development that has gathered strength in the first years of the twenty-first century has been the concept of 'inland islands'. Conventionally many conservation efforts have been concentrated on islands because of the ease of controlling access to them. For example, once introduced predator species such as stoats, possum, rats and others than prey on birds nests are cleared from an island by a policy of hunting, trapping and killing, distinct improvements in the native bird population have been found to occur. Native species are able to reassert themselves once the natural environment is freed from predators that are present because of past human intervention, although in some instances special breeding programmes may be required. Examples of these policies would include the New Zealand Department of Conservation breeding programmes for places such as Kapiti Island, Poor Knights and Great Barrier Island. In some instances these might be combined with marine reserves. The same policy is now being adopted for inland sites, and one of the first of these was in the city of Wellington, New Zealand. The old Karori water reservoir catchment area had been closed to the public for 120 years. In the early 1990s James Lynch, then Chairman of the Wellington branch of the Royal Forest and Bird Society, led a movement to repossess the area as an inland sanctuary wherein fauna, flora, habitats and processes representative of an indigenous lowland forest could be restored to a managed area. The total area was fenced off with a specially constructed fence that went underground to defeat invasion by burrowing pests. Vegetation was cut back from the fence for a distance of at least a metre, and trees in particular were cut back so that tree-based predator mammals could not jump across the gap. The fence was also specially shaped to defeat such attempts. A campaign of hunting introduced predator species (particularly rats, stoats, weasels and possum) was mounted and then native New Zealand birds were introduced. These included, in June 2002, the first saddleback bird to be re-introduced to the New Zealand mainland for 100 years, thereby improving the long-term breeding programme and chances of survival for this once almost-extinct species. Within a few years it has been noticeable just how rich in bird life the area has become, while native tree and shrub species that have little protection against the voracious appetite of the possum have begun to thrive. The area is becoming a notable tourist attraction. Five themes are presented to visitors who are taken on guided tours, these being heritage, restoration, education, the kiwi trail and wilderness. Figure 8.5 shows the entry point for visitors and the nature of the fencing. The metre-wide path around the sanctuary has also had an un-looked for benefit, as it has become a popular resource for mountain bikers, and of course in this instance the trampling effect is generally beneficial. Plans for other such inland sanctuaries are being advanced both in New Zealand and in other parts of the world to help restore environments to their natural condition.

However, 'green policies' and green tourism do not provide instant solutions to the environmental problems created by recreation and tourism. They often take time to develop, and long-term horizons need to be considered. Long-term commitments are required. The UK Community Forest scheme and the Karori Sanctuary are but two examples of this, and further evidence is provided by two Canadian examples: the Weyerhaeuser Forest and the Meewasin Valley Authority plans (Weyerhaeuser Canada, 1989: MVA, 1987). The Weyerhaeuser 20-year Forest Management Plan is primarily concerned with the creation of forests that can sustain timber processing, but the plan also considers, based on forest simulation models, other activities including recreational use of forest areas. Indeed, it can even project forest growth over a 220-year period to evaluate the impact of various forest management systems and usage patterns. This plan was also subjected to a resource management approval process in Saskatchewan and was approved in 2001. In 1979 the Meewasin Valley Authority began a 100-year plan to consider the use of the valley for both tourist and recreational use within a context of environmental conservation. The initiative was not without controversy, and at one stage, in 1981, one of the Saskatoon city parks was removed from the jurisdiction of the Authority. However, work has continued in the period since that time and in 2002 the third phase of the Meewasin Riverworks Weir redevelopment commenced. As in many such instances the objectives are those of land reclamation, an improvement in recreational facilities, and an improvement in the overall ambience of the area.

Figure 8.5 Entry to the Karori inland sanctuary

The provision of tourist/recreation facilities near urban centres

Such developments as the Meewasin Valley Developments or the UK urban and community forests are just a few examples of creating a recreational resource near the home of the tourist. If tourism does indeed pose a potential threat to ecologically-fragile areas and if people's working patterns are indeed changing to permit an increased demand for leisure near to the home location, the implication is that tourist authorities can respond to the increased demand for day-trip activity near to home by establishing a number of recreational facilities. Such facilities include not simply urban forests, but also urban farms, the use of water splash parks, the greater use of rivers and riversides within towns, and the use of canals. Weekly, as well as occasional events can be organised within urban settings that attract tourists and local people, and can enhance the local economy. For example, Portland, Oregon, like many North American cities, features special Saturday markets. Farmers markets and regular bric-à-brac markets have become very popular the world round. In some instances they incorporate local heritage themes and involve local museums. They provide an outlet for historical societies to re-enact events or display aspects of their activities (as shown in Figure 8.6, which shows a scene from a Sealed Knot muster or battle re-enactment in the UK). The resulting economic impact is a form of import-saving in the sense that the home area retains spending that would otherwise have taken place elsewhere. At the same time, pressures on other areas are diminished, whilst costs of travel are likewise reduced. It might also be argued that the escape motivations for holidays are equally mitigated in some form or other, and indeed perhaps the very need for holidays is diminished. If it is thought in the final analysis the potential harm that tourism can cause can be met only by reducing the demand for travel, then such policies are at least part of the answer in that they lessen the distance travelled.

Figure 8.6 A Sealed Knot muster, or battle re-enactment

Create environmental-awareness holidays and tourists

A further policy that might be adopted is to ensure that tourists are aware of the stresses that large numbers of tourists can cause, so that they might mitigate the pressures by behavioural change. For example, the Centre for Development Education in Stuttgart has worked with tour operator representatives and charter flight companies to provide literature for their clients that makes them aware of cultural differences and the scarcity of natural resources. In Australia the Co-operative Research Centre for Sustainable Tourism seeks to engage with the tourism industry in finding ways in which impacts can be minimised. One such project related to the minimisation of waste from in-flight catering services, and other programmes exist elsewhere. In 1976, in Lower Casamance in Senegal, a programme commenced whereby tourists stay, not in large hotel complexes, but in huts and as part of the village community. These initiatives have been sustained with, today, for example, eco-cycle tours being offered in the same region and using much of the same accommodation. Whilst one may question the degree of authenticity this actually creates for the tourist in terms of the social experience, it does have the benefit of helping to reduce the negative ecological impacts of tourism. It also brings income to regions while still adhering to principles of small groups of tourists that do not overwhelm local cultures.

Micro-techniques

All of the above policies might be said to be planning policies on a 'macro' scale, i.e. they are concerned with allocating tourists between destination areas. What about the means of mitigating the tourist impact on the environment when they actually arrive at the destination? At the 'micro' level there again exists a number of policies that managers might use.

Structured visitor management and monitoring

Park managements have become practised at developing structured visitor management and monitoring procedures, and the literature is rich in acronyms. These include:

ROS Recreation Opportunity Spectrum
LAC Limits of Acceptable Change
VIM Visitor Impact Management
TOMM Tourism Optimisation Management Model
VAMP Visitor Activity Management Process

There are high degrees of similarity between these different approaches, and all are predicated on rational, logical and scientific management procedures based on goal setting, measurement and monitoring. This section of the chapter will briefly describe these methods and then highlight at site level some of the specifics that relate to management of natural areas.

ROS: Recreation Opportunity Spectrum

Associated with work undertaken in the United States Forest Service in the 1970s, this method is based on a categorisation of zones –from those that have no facilities and accessible only by foot to those that are highly developed with resorts and lodges. Associated with each class or zone is a range of possible recreational activities. The approach is often summarised in the form of a grid with zones forming the columns and activities forming the rows, and degrees of development being allocated to each cell. Clark and Stankey (1979) effectively laid down the ground rules for this approach.

LAC: Limits of Acceptable Change

This approach derives from combining the concept of carrying capacity with the classifications of the Recreational Opportunity Spectrum. It too was compiled by George Stankey and colleagues (Stankey *et al.*, 1985) in the United States Forest Service and tries to provide an answer to how many people should visit a site by asking what is the acceptable number before change due to impacts becomes unacceptable. It reinforces the importance of selecting appropriate measures and continuous monitoring. Stankey *et al.* (1985) argued that indicators should possess four attributes. They should:

- be capable of being measured in a cost-effective way at an acceptable level of accuracy;
- have as direct a relationship as possible to the amount and type of use of space that was occurring;
- be related to the concerns of the users;
- be responsive to changes created by management policies.

The technique therefore includes measures of the type already discussed (i.e. water quality measures, trampling effect measurement), but is associated with usage patterns. In practice, however, the weakness of the methodology has been the obtaining of agreement about the meanings of such measures. In short, interpretation of results and the actual implementation process may be more due to political processes than to 'scientific objectivity' (McCool & Cole, 1997).

VIM: Visitor Impact Management

VIM sought to carry forward the LAC methodologies but also to incorporate the components of subjectivity that are associated with the management of open and natural spaces. As before, it describes a process of logical review, proceeding from a statement of objectives to the selection of criteria, and then the implementation of those criteria at sites and a comparison of what is occurring with what is thought permissible. From this point, however, the management then seeks to identify what are the probable causes of the impacts, management strategies are aimed at causes, and their success is measured by continuous monitoring using the agreed criteria. These criteria include social as well as environmental objectives. A problem is the allocation of weighting between social and environmental criteria. A second problem is that, while the measurement of natural phenomena is generally recognised and well understood, the measurement of social perspectives as they apply to natural places is more complex. However, in a report for the New Zealand Department of Conservation, Cessford (2002) reported that a simple Likert-type question seeking degrees of satisfaction with a site had high degrees of validity as a measure of satisfaction. Their work looked at differing constructions of scale and correlations with attributes that are thought to be important, including measures of perceived crowding.

TOMM: Tourism Optimisation Management Model

Developed by the Sydney-based consulting firm, Mandis Roberts, this model is described as a community-based monitoring initiative. It was developed for assessing the long-term sustainability of tourism on Kangaroo Island and collects information on the general health of the local economy, the numbers and types of visitors arriving, the health of the environment, the types of experiences that visitors are having, and the social well-being of the host community. It differs from the other measures by seeking not to limit tourism but to optimise it, by which is meant the creation of optimal income from careful marketing aimed at specific market segments consistent with the host community and environment. So, in the case of Kangaroo island, at Seal Bay, it considered options ranging from closure of the beach to marketing messages about the declining opportunity to view seals, while this was contextualised within a framework that considered the effects of any policy on other parts of the island.

While holistic in approach, and trying to be based on easily-obtained datasets and criteria, the possible weakness of the method lies in the very quantity of data that is required, and the weightings allocated to various parts of it. A key objective is the creation of attitudinal change and awareness of environmental issues by differing stakeholders, and the web pages associated with TOMM claim that such change has been occurring (http://kitomm.webmedia.com.au/publications/files/AnnualReport2000v2.pdf).

VAMP: Visitor Activity Management Process

VAMP was developed primarily within the Canadian Parks Service and seeks to identify visitor activities and the service plans required to meet thir needs. This is contextualised within two frameworks: a National Park Management Process that seeks to include community involvement in planning for particular areas, and a natural Resources Management

Process based on resource planning and conservation issues. Newsome, Moore and Dowling (2001) comment that the plan has received little attention outside Canada, although the New Zealand Department of Conservation has expressed some interest. Like TOMM it places the visitor activity more to the fore and requires a more market-oriented approach in the sense that visitor activity modification can be undertaken only with reference to visitor motivation and understanding of environments.

Visitor management

No matter which of these approaches is adopted, in practice managers of natural and many man-built tourist attractions have to make a series of decisions about site infrastructure, which includes reception areas, footpaths, numbers to be catered for and so on. The following section of the chapter identifies some of the more specific components of structure and offers comments on each of them.

Restrictive entry

The first of these techniques is to control numbers simply by permitting only a few to enter. The levels of control can vary from exhortation (as illustrated by the car-parking signs in the Gower Peninsula mentioned earlier in the chapter), to the maintenance of quotas by restricting entry to only those with permits, to, at the final extreme, permitting no entry at all. In the tourism of the wilderness areas of North America, the impacts of hunting are controlled by the issue of licences, and by anti-poaching campaigns. Entry may also be permitted to national parks at certain points only, and in this respect the location of roads is important. Parks may permit only a limited number of roads, which enter the park at specific points and, beyond any given point, no wheeled traffic may be allowed. In consequence, distance from the access point becomes a means of reducing usage rates, as tourists may gain access to some areas only on foot. In addition, restrictions might be imposed on the type of camping that is permitted, and the actual number of camping points also becomes a means of control. The Himalayan Kingdom of Bhutan maintains a policy of restricting numbers of tourists, and such tourists are permitted only to travel in groups with qualified guides. Entry to the Kingdom is permitted through only two access points: by road through Phuentsholing or by air through Paro Airport. Booking can be made through only 80 approved tour operators, and visitors can stay only at certain approved accommodation. In 2000 the limit was set at 6000 visitors. The purpose of the restriction is at least twofold. First, it reduces the social as well as the economic impacts of tourism to levels that the country can easily absorb. Second, it permits a greater direction of the economic flows that tourism creates, without causing negative economic impacts such as too high an inflation rate in certain geographical areas, or the sucking in of imports at too high a level.

Price

One simple way of reducing numbers of tourists is simply to charge high prices and create 'exclusivity'. This sense of 'exclusiveness' in turn helps to justify the high price. Obviously, therefore, the higher the price the fewer the number of people who are able to take advantage of the area. However, this conflicts with policies of open access in some spheres of activity. National Parks may be part of the tourist package that is offered to visitors, but equally the concept of a National Park is that it is open to its own nationals and is for educational as well as recreational purposes. Restrictions on access are thus not always constitutionally possible, nor is the use of pricing mechanisms. The problem becomes more apparent when National Parks are designated, but include within them private property, as is common in Britain. Thus, water authorities and other private landowners can indeed charge admission, and will often use such admission charges to raise revenue to maintain the quality of the recreational provision. Van Sickle and Eagles (1998) trace the experience of Canadian Parks over the period 1975–1995 and show the result of declining financial support from central government. This has not been unique to Canada, and has been experienced elsewhere in the English-speaking world. One consequence is an increased dependency on revenues derived from fees and services, and Van Sickle and Eagles note four possible ways in which park fees can be used. First, fees are a means of creating value for the visit. Second, they can be used to offset costs. Third, they can be used as a management tool to deter visits at certain times by using differential pricing. Finally, they might be used to generate profit. However, Van Sickle and Eagles (1998) also note that, in 7 of the 13 cases they studied, the agencies had to remit revenues to other organisations. One major implication across all of the Park's managements was the implication for management, with financial objectives becoming much more important than in the past.

Site management sign posting

One aspect of site management is the use of wardens with various duties including conservation work and the provision of information to visitors. Working from interpretation centres, the aim is to inform visitors so as to make them appreciate the natural environment, and so modify their behaviour. One means of behaviour modification is to create signposted walks. The visitor will tend to keep to the 'approved' trail, and this behaviour is reinforced by the provision of information points along the route. Given a leaflet, the visitor is drawn from one point to another, and attention is directed to various features. Not only, therefore, are visitors taught how to observe and appreciate nature, but they are also kept to those areas that can

Figure 8.7 Examples of signposting

sustain high pedestrian flow, and so are kept away from the more fragile areas, so permitting flora and fauna to sustain themselves. Underlying this policy is also a belief that elitist attitudes towards nature are eventually self-defeating. Minorities may serve to act as catalysts within societies. But only if the majority are at least sympathetic to the minority viewpoint can desired policies be put into practice. Thus, whilst studies may illustrate that few visitors will move far from their cars, and the clichéd picture of the family sitting in the lay-by viewing the countryside from the car is not without truth, arguably people will not be moved to protect areas or appreciate the need for protection unless they have greater knowledge. It has been found that behaviour is changed by the provision of information. If, on arriving at a park, people are told that a number of walks exist, that these walks are of a certain distance and duration, that the terrain is easy or otherwise, then the distance travelled from the car park tends to increase. People hence enjoy the visit and obtain more from it. Equally, just as the provision of information influences behaviour, so too does the withholding of information. Nonetheless, the desired result is a greater use of areas, the acquisition of knowledge and an appreciation by the public of the importance of things natural, and in the end, hopefully, an increased readiness to support policies of conservation. Figure 8.7 illustrates two forms of signposting used at Litchfield Park in Australia by the Northern Territory Wildlife and Parks Authority. The first is a simple directional sign and the second is a more complex sign providing some information as well as a map of the immediate area.

Footpaths and car parks

No policy is without associated costs. The paradox is that increased usage may often be needed to obtain public support for parks authorities that are increasingly constrained financially, but the routes chosen must retain a state of 'naturalness'. The selected routes must thus be capable of supporting high levels of pedestrian flow. Care must be shown in the planning of the paths. Where possible it is preferable to use natural rocks and hard surfaces that can sustain higher traffic than grass or soil can. Within woodland settings, cork and tree chips may be used for the paths. In using such wood-based products there is a need to take care that, wherever possible, non-treated wood product is used, as the chemical leakage from treated wood might have unlooked-for consequences. Boardwalks may be used near streams and rivers to protect the banks. Car parks may indeed be parks, but there is a need to protect grass from the wear produced by tyres. One solution is to use small hollow concrete squares. The soil sits within these squares and is seeded. The grass grows, but the concrete protects the roots of the grass, which is therefore not worn away by the tyres. Aesthetically, the area retains its greenness and freshness. Other advantages also accrue. The soil is not beaten down and denuded to become a hardened area off which water flows. The drainage patterns are less adversely affected, the rainwater can still percolate through the soil, and hence trees continue to be nourished.

On open areas of moorland it may be necessary to use even more expensive techniques. Whilst paths may be created from tarmac to overcome the problem of path erosion and of path-widening due to trampling effects, there is a resistance to the concept of wild open areas being criss-crossed by black tarmac paths that stand out against the natural terrain. Such paths are man-made and man-imposed on an area that is supposedly being protected as far as possible against encroachment by man. Rebuilding footpaths with natural material might appear to be an answer, but the problem is that the very transport of rocks and stones can make the problem worse. In fact in Snowdonia, helicopters have been used to transport stone material to help restore footpaths with natural rock. On moorland a number of 'high-tech' solutions are being used to create footpaths that can sustain high pedestrian flow whilst at the same time blending into the natural terrain. The Peak District National Park in the UK in 1989 experimented with a footpath comprising three different levels (Cohen, 1989). At the base is laid a nylon membrane that allows water to drain through, but stops mud from coming up when pressure is laid on the path by the walker. Over this is placed a synthetic net that helps to distribute the impact of the walker over a greater area, thus lessening the pressure on any given surface. Finally, over this is laid a combination of basalt and grit stone that is consistent with the terrain of the Peak District. However, such footpath building is very expensive. In other areas grass is sown on top of various layers of material such as fibretex so as to be consistent with the terrain, and indeed in some cases grass and other plants are being 'forced' by the use of carefully planned applications of fertiliser. Alternatively it is possible to use 'sacking' made of natural materials that decay over time, but which help to stabilise new grass growth from seed in the initial stages. Figure 8.8 illustrates such an example from Hamilton, New Zealand.

Figure 8.8 Stabilising new grass growth on a bank

Opinions about the use of fertilisers are divided, but the reasons that prompt their use are easily understood. In some areas users may be asked to voluntarily adhere to certain practices, for example, to walk in small groups and in single file. Across sand dunes walkers may have to keep to board-walks to avoid the wear on the grasses that help maintain the sand dune's formation. As the boards become bleached and are covered by drifting sand, they do not appear to be out of place, but there is a continuing need for maintenance.

In establishing paths there is also a need to assess the likely routes that people will take. The temptation to take a short cut seems to be too much for many people to resist. Observation of any park in an urban area, or any open piece of grass where paths are provided, will often reveal worn areas of grass where people take short cuts. This provides a problem for parks departments. The same sort of path erosion problems that might be found in the open areas of the country can be found in a city's local parks. For example in England, in the deer park at Woollaton, Nottingham, the circumference of the park now has worn paths created by joggers who use the park for training. Cars had worn away the grass to such an extent that it was replaced by a shale-type surface, and car parking is now restricted to specific areas in order to protect other parts of the park.

Footpaths in areas of heavy usage have to also be protected. A common method is to install wire mesh over wooden paths or bridges as this serves two purposes: it both protects the wood and makes the surface less slippery in damp conditions.

Control of access points

Whilst there may be a reluctance to directly control access to what are deemed to be national heritage areas or wilderness areas that belong to the nation, or to areas featured in tourism-promotion programmes, indirect controls are often used. Controlling the number of access points is possible, as has already been noted. Thus, within park areas, the location and size of car parks, and the spatial relationship of roads to zones of activity within the park are important. For example, in 1988 the car park at Dove Dale in the English Peak District was made smaller in order to reduce the numbers who parked there and then walked through the dale. This was to ease the pedestrian flow through the dale in order to permit recovery of paths and to begin to offset trampling effects. Alternative means of access may be made possible. Again within the Peak District, schemes that reduce car traffic and offer instead a bus service or cycle hire have proved successful. This was done in the Goyt Valley, and an interesting side effect has been that the social composition of the visitors changed, with higher socio-economic groupings becoming a larger proportion of visitors (Murphy, 1985). In the Snowdonia National Park in Wales, the Mountain Goat bus service was established to relieve stress on car parks around Snowdon where walkers parked before taking one of the routes up the mountain. Naturally, people were somewhat reluctant to forgo the use of their cars, but the bus service offered real benefits to walkers in that they could now take two routes in the same trip. There was no longer a need to go up and return by the same route, when they could take a different path down and be picked up by the bus. So, a marginal dispersal effect has been created.

An important aspect of accessibility is the location of accommodation facilities. These have to be sufficiently near to allow time for visits into the vulnerable areas, but far enough away to protect the area from the support infrastructure that accommodation requires. Sometimes the trip into the protected zone becomes part of the visit experience. Thus, within the Maldive Islands, tourists may visit certain islands but not stay on them. The boat trip under blue skies on blue waters is obviously an inherent part of the whole experience, and generates visitor satisfaction. Management of zones must therefore look into means of replicating this type of satisfaction under less-promising circumstances.

Changing usage patterns

One of the great problems in tourism site management is the protection of sites where tourists have already established behaviour patterns that may be inimical to the long-term integrity of the area. Through custom and usage, interests have been generated that some would wish to protect. This perhaps represents one of the major challenges to planning authorities, and one of the most difficult to cope with. The degree of difficulty associated with this is illustrated by Waiser (1989), who describes the difficulties that the Prince Albert National Park authorities had in reversing the development of summer homes erected by local residents within the park in the 1960s. Based on the town of Waskesiu, development had spread into the park, and after the Second World War visitor numbers increased from 50,000 in 1949 to 136,529 in 1958. By the summer of 1950 there were 412 'shack tents' (wooden shacks) in the Waskesiu campsite, and an association was formed that petitioned for them to be recognised and kept for the duration of the whole year rather than having to be dismantled at the end of every season. However, in 1959 a planning report commented that:

> The present spectacle which confronts the visitor is not a pleasant one, where the key areas in the developed portion of the park are dominated by semi-permanent occupancies. It can be expected as the proportion of touring recreationists grows so will the indignation against the present type of development grow. For it is most obvious this is a misuse of a national park. (Parks Canada, 1959)

Equally, by the mid-1960s new demands were emerging, and in 1966 the park appointed its first warden for the development of park interpretative services. The result was that in 1967 a plan was announced that only existing shack tenters could apply for permits for a lot in a relocated area. However, faced with opposition, a series of 'temporary' arrangements were made so that by the early 1970s the shack tents had become all-year-round structures plugged into the electricity mains supply. In 1971, after further review of the role of National Parks, Prince Albert was designated as a 'national wildland park'. The public hearings revealed a conflict of perception and use between those who perceived the role of National Parks as a means of preserving wilderness areas and the flora and fauna they contain and, within Prince Albert, the majority who saw the park as an area of recreation – as a family park. The latter group saw the whole attempt as a means by which distant central government ignored local custom and sought to impose its will on those who had developed the park. The conflict is described by Waiser as one where 'the townsite serves the park, not vice versa, and that the natural heritage values of the park should govern Waskesiu management and development' (cited by Ryan, 1991a: 128). By contrast, local townspeople argue that the town constitutes but a small part of the total area and, from the viewpoint of visitors, the park primarily serves local people.

The same type of issues have arisen in New Zealand relating to 'baches' located on that country's conservation estate. They date from more relaxed times of less pressure, and what emerges from these type of debates is that the owners of such summer homes have established close identities with the places where these simple homes are located. Often the homes have been in the possession of a family for generations, and with the sense of ownership comes a sense of responsibility for the immediate area, with many families voluntarily undertaking refuse collection and cleaning of the natural environment within which their homes are located. In many senses they possess a potential to be allies in any conservation movement, and consequently parks authorities have tended to be sympathetic in their treatment of such owners. In a sense it is often unborn generations that will bear the loss of such family assets, as arrangements are usually based on reclamation of property at some future time.

Encouraging natural processes

By seeking to meet recreational requirements, many of the natural processes of a wilderness area are interfered with. For example, dams may be built, or woodland fires fought. The Yellowstone National Park provides a graphic example of conflict between permitting areas to be 'true' wilderness areas, and meeting preconceived notions of beauty. In 1972 the park authorities decided to permit predators to re-establish themselves within the parklands. Then, in the 1980s, the authorities decided that they would reverse their earlier policies on fire fighting. It was argued that forest fires should be left to burn out, for this creates opportunities for shrubs and grasses to flourish where they would normally be suppressed by the shade of the trees. The policy generated many new findings. For example, it was found that 80% of fires burnt themselves out quite quickly, particularly if started by natural causes such as lightning strikes. Secondly, it was found that elk, deer and bison manage better with recently-burnt ground. However, in the summer of 1988 the park authorities permitted, as had become normal practice, the fires to rage in June in the expectation of rain in July. But the rain failed to materialise, and the American media showed pictures of fires apparently destroying the park. It did not matter that the park authorities spent $120 million in fire-fighting; the impression was conveyed that crazed environmentalists were letting the park burn down (McKenzie, 1989). The problem was one where, although park managers have moved on to sophisticated theories about biosphere management and ecological preserves, people tend to seek the same things from parks that they have always sought (McKenzie, 1989). A year after the fire, as North (1989: 11) commented, the park was a 'wilderness enriched by fire', as it bloomed yet again.

However, there is no doubt that the public reaction to the fire policies being pursued at Yellowstone affected the park management. It was also obvious that there had to be a careful monitoring of fire and at least a basic division between those fires thought to be part of the natural process and those caused by human intervention, such as out-of-control camp fires. In 2002 Yellowstone maintained several fire crews, helitrack (a helicopter based tracking patrol) and several land-based tracking and fire-fighting teams. A detailed fire-fighting plan has been created and different techniques and scenarios have been identified. For those interested these plans are available for inspection on the web (e.g. www.nps.gov/yell/technical/

fire/hazard.pdf). Associated with this is a careful monitoring programming on the effects of fire. This programme was partly established in response to demands after the 1988 fire so the park's authority was able to cite specific evidence of the benefits of fire on vegetation growth. At the same time such data collection becomes part of the fire-fighting programme by highlighting the collection of litter and depth of duff (fine material), the dryness of areas and so on – in short, areas of potentially easy burn are established.

Such concerns are mirrored in other parts of the world. Fire is also part of the natural cycle in the Northern Territory of Australia and again policies of letting a fire burn itself out are enforced. However, unlike Yellowstone, much of this area is also prone to flooding when it is wet, and the environment has created a specific flora and fauna for which such extremes are indeed the norm. New Zealand faces a slightly different problem, with many unique species of flora and fauna and, while natural fire can occur, it is generally less frequent than in other parts of the world. One of the problems that New Zealand faces is that in cases of extreme emergency large monsoon buckets suspended from aircraft or helicopters will be used. Unfortunately the nearest expanse of water may be the sea, and thus fire-fighting has the added detrimental effect of salinisation of natural vegetation, and heavy dousing of areas ablaze might thus mean very slow recovery rates of the natural vegetation. Consequently an emphasis is laid on fire prevention, and a common sign in New Zealand is a fire sign showing the sensitivity of areas to fire, and warnings to the public not to start fires.

Summary

The controversies over both the Prince Albert National Park and the Yellowstone National Park indicate that park management and, in a wider sense, the management of tourist and recreational areas, is not simply a technical one of assessing visitor numbers, planning footpaths, calculating the number of car park spaces, ensuring the quality of water supply, and all the other aspects mentioned above. Tourist areas carry with them a heritage and a received perception of roles and functions. It is this aspect of the tourist resort lifecycle that perhaps needs examination. Butler (1980), Young (1983) and others generally relate the cycle to built-up tourist zones, but there is also a need to establish a lifecycle of perceptions of use of 'wild' and natural areas. Many tourists, as Walter (1982) argues, derive their notions of the countryside from the romantic literature of the late nineteenth century, and thus have perceptions of countryside as both unspoilt and serving purposes of renewal of the human spirit. These notions are projected on to the National Parks of many nations, and foster sets of expectations and perceptions. The case of Prince Albert also shows the conflict that arises between local users of a park and the viewpoint of distant government, which sees a park as part of a national asset that plays a role on a larger stage. The management of tourist zones is thus no mere matter of mechanics, but rather a complex balancing act between past heritage and changing perceptions of the future needs of many participants – not only human, but also drawn from the natural world of mammals, fish and plant life, as is indicated in Figure 8.9. The techniques of tourist zone management require a recognition of problems, and a willingness to accept and impose constraints on use – a willingness that is easy to preach in the abstract but difficult to practice in the reality of any given situation. Whilst difficulty is no reason for aborting the effort to develop tourism that is consistent with the needs of ecological systems, such developments possibly require different motivations for tourism than those that have characterised much of tourism's growth in the last three decades. So, whilst, as argued in Chapter 6, tourist zones become statements about the hosts as well as the tourists, so too, the tourist zone becomes a commentary about the wider issue of man's relationship with nature.

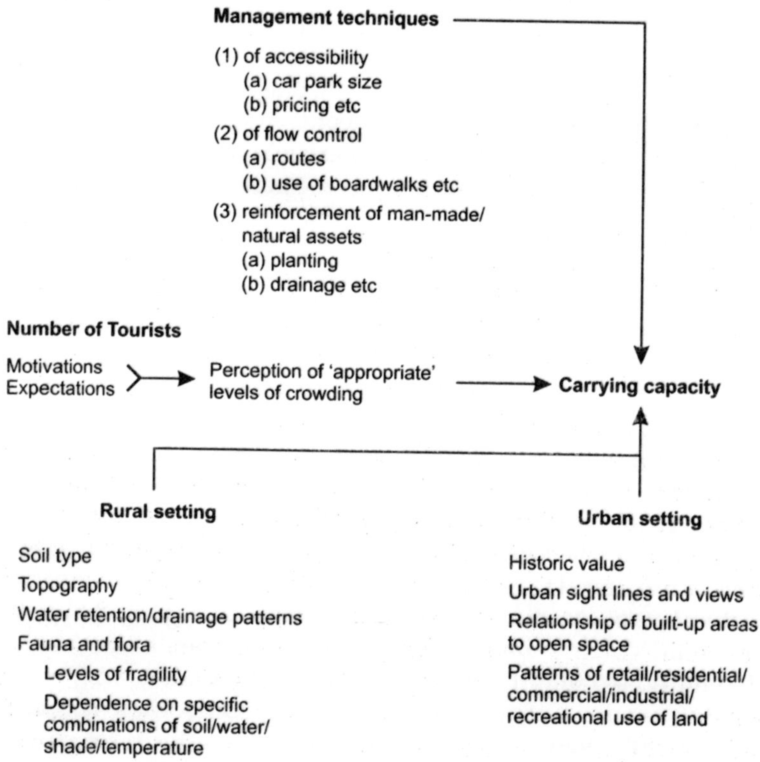

Figure 8.9 Indicative schema for factors determining the ecological aspects of tourism

Chapter 9

The Social Impacts of Tourism

The Nature of the Problem

In 1989 the author and naturalist Gerald Durrell wrote in relation to his beloved Corfu:

> Tourism is a curious modern disease. It attacks the shoeless man, the man of meagre wealth and the bloated man of affluence, whereupon it becomes an epidemic like the Black Death that stalked through Europe in the Middle Ages. It now ranges all over the world. The people of Corfu were blessed with a magnificent, magical inheritance, an island of staggering beauty, probably one of the most beautiful islands in the whole of the Mediterranean. What they have done with it is vandalism beyond belief. (Durrell, 1989)

Two years earlier the travel writer Jan Morris wrote with great intensity about what she felt tourism had done to her home area of the Llyn Peninsula in North Wales. She stated that:

> For years I have tried to defend it [tourism] as a valuable asset to a poor region ... I stood up for the vast caravan parks which disfigure so much of our coast on the grounds that the caravan was the poor man's holiday cottage ... No longer, something has cracked in me. I have come to detest all aspects of mass tourism ... It has gone too far, has got out of control – not just in Llyn outside my window, but wherever in the world affluence, big business and officialdom have made it possible ... too many of the entrepreneurs who are developing tourism in our part of Wales are not local people at all. They are English people who have come to Wales to develop tourism! Their oblivion to the local history and culture is generally absolute – few of them have the courtesy to put up their shop signs in Welsh – and their contribution to the national well-being, vociferously though they claim to represent Welsh progress at planning enquiries or in Letters to the Editor, is virtually nil. (Morris, 1987)

The complaint of Durrell and Morris (both of whom are significant travel writers) is not simply one of tourism damaging the landscape, but of more insidious damage to a way of life, to a culture and to sets of values. Pfäfflin (1987) quotes one Hawaiian delegate at the 1986 Third World People and

Tourism Conference as stating, 'We don't want tourism. We don't want you. We don't want to be degraded as servants and dancers. That is cultural prostitution ... There are no innocent tourists.' MacNaught (1982) lists the negative themes that are stated about the cultural impacts of tourism as being six in total. These are:

(1) tourists do nothing to promote international understanding;
(2) the strains of hospitality eventually become intolerable;
(3) employment in the tourist industry is often dehumanising;
(4) tourists have undesirable 'demonstration effects' on residents;
(5) tourism debases local forms of cultural expression;
(6) the tourist industry adversely affects community life.

Nor should it be thought that tourism brings these ills only in situations where the tourist is a foreigner in a foreign land. Ragan (1989) reported on the tourist influx into the Yorkshire village of Malham in these terms:

> Malham is finding it increasingly difficult to cope with the ever-growing numbers. More leisure time and easier access have made a day out in the Dales a popular outing. But although residents are growing disillusioned with the situation, they accept there is no easy solution. The numbers taking to the hills and walkways are taking their toll on the landscape. Footpaths are being eroded; dry stone walls damaged and meadows ruined. While locals say they do not want to deny people the right to enjoy the countryside, they say unless something can be done to preserve it, the village will no longer be worth visiting. (Ragan, 1989)

Why is it then that tourism, which brings so much enjoyment to people, and which contains the potential to indeed broaden the mind and enable people not only to relax, but also to marvel at the world they occupy, and possibly reinforce concerns over environmental issues – why is it that tourism attracts these criticisms? In Chapter 6 it was noted that the tourist area is not fixed either spatially or temporally. The change that was described in Young's model of spatial change (Young, 1983), implied a process of social change as the former fishing/farming village became an international tourist centre complete with marina and casino. This process of social change has long been recognised, and various authors allocate to the resort lifecycle different social implications at each of the stages concerned. This chapter will describe some of the changes with reference to the work of Butler (1980), and will subsequently amplify specific aspects of the relationships between tourists and guests that have emerged as being of importance in the studies that followed the publication of Butler's description of destination change.

The Changing Attitudes of Host Communities

Butler identifies a six-stage cycle in the evolution of a tourism area, and as such it relates to the product lifecycle of marketing theory. The stages are:

(1) exploration;
(2) involvement;
(3) development;
(4) consolidation;
(5) stagnation;
(6) decline or rejuvenation.

The following descriptions of the Destination Lifecycle are intended to supplement the description provided in Chapter 6 by relating business change to social impacts on the resident community that result from changing resident/visitor ratios. It should be noted that the descriptions are based on resort destinations that evolve from the 'discovery' of undeveloped or marginal regions and, as has been previously discussed, not all destinations fit this pattern. For example, reference will be made to the resort of Cancun in Mexico. This is an example of a resort complex that was primarily purpose-built and thus the early stages in this and other similar cases are simply highly concentrated or avoided.

The exploration stage

This first stage is characterised as the exploration stage during which there are only a small number of visitors. They may be identified as akin to Plog's (1977) 'allocentrics' or Cohen's (1979c) 'explorers' in that they make their own travel arrangements and seek to merge with the local host community. Often they will speak the language of the hosts and identify with their culture. The hosts themselves will welcome their 'guests', for they bring novelty and open a window to the outside world. They may not realise that these tourists are part of what Turner and Ash (1975) called the 'pleasure periphery'. That is to say, these are the tourists seeking new destinations away from those areas that were once 'unspoilt' but which now have grown in popularity and thus are of no further interest to the 'explorer'. These tourists return home, and might enthusiastically tell friends about the 'great, unspoilt places' and the 'friendliness of the locals'; thereby 'selling the place' to yet more tourists. Therefore these 'explorers' may be precursors of what is to come.

Within the exploration stage, the social impact is small. Any commercial activity that occurs is small scale, is individualistically or family based, and there is effectively no adoption of formal marketing strategies by members of the host community.

The involvement stage

Should the numbers of tourists increase, the second stage is entered – the involvement stage. Local residents now begin to respond to the increasing numbers of visitors by providing some additional facilities specifically for tourists. In the early part of this stage, such entrepreneurial activities still tend to be family based. Some members of the host community might set aside part of their home and take in visitors. Levels of tourist/resident contact remain high, and the marketing of the area remains subdued. Owners of accommodation may simply display signs indicating rooms to let, and possibly a few might later print some leaflets to give to their guests, who will subsequently pass them on to friends. At this stage the relationship between host and tourist is still harmonious, and the tourists still possess high levels of interest and sympathy with the local way of life. Indeed, the term 'paying guest' rather than 'tourist' might still be appropriate at this point.

In the later stages of the involvement stage some of the resident community might recognise that tourism will continue to grow, and that in order to earn more from it they will have to expand the facilities being provided. Accordingly, they may have recourse to borrowed funding, and may not simply involve family members but also refer to commercial sources of finance. At some stage, if there has not previously been a branch of a bank in the village, one will become established as local entrepreneurs seek safety for their money, a means of earning interest, and, of course, a source of capital borrowing. At the same time the 'entrepreneurs' within the village will become more professional in their marketing efforts. Unable to reach directly into the tourist-generating areas they will have recourse to those organisations that can. In many instances the first such body is the country's own tourist organisation, which generally would be keen to promote a new area because it adds to the nation's portfolio of attractions, and allows it to offer something new to overseas tour operators. Either directly, or through the tourist board, members of the village might also approach other intermediaries, such as inbound tour operators. They may form a local tourism organisation that will help to achieve some economies of scale in printing brochures, and will represent the entrepreneurs in the region.

The processes of commercialisation can be traced to such roots. The levels of income emanating from tourists begin to rise and become more important to the entrepreneurs, who become increasingly 'professional' in the service they render. The relationship between host/resident and guest/visitor changes slowly to that of service provider and client, albeit still within a framework of cordiality and good relations.

The development stage

Butler then assumes that the process continues, and the numbers of tourists arriving now begin to grow quite significantly, as illustrated in Figure 9.1. The third stage, that of development, is now reached. Butler describes this stage as being the one where the community becomes a tourist resort. Plog's (1977) 'mid-centrics' or Cohen's (1979) 'institutionalised tourists' now appear. In the period of late involvement and the early development stages, the community begins to attract the interest of outside bodies. New retail businesses appear. Some of these are owned by local people and some by nationals, drawn from the centres of population, who have retail or catering experience. As described by Tsartas (1992) in his case study of the Greek islands, some of these people may have family connections with residents, and thus the developing resort permits opportunities for the employment of returning family members. In the early stages of development the first of the package holidaymakers appear. However, these are holidaymakers who are using the services of 'niche' companies who serve that part of the market and have much in common with the attitude of 'allocentrics', but who are not 'full-time' travellers and are operating within constrained time periods. As the development stage progresses, the spatial dimensions of the village begin to change rapidly, as described by Young (1983).

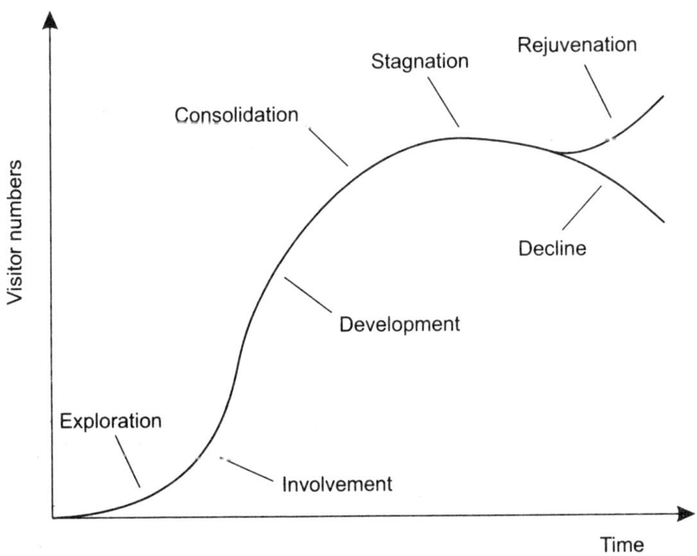

Figure 9.1 Butler's destination lifecycle theory

After the 'niche' tour operators come the larger tour operators who deal with a mass market within the tourist-generating regions. In terms of the total activity that is now being generated, the locally-owned businesses are becoming marginalised. The hosts have now delegated the main marketing efforts to organisations that are not only outside of their area, but are also, perhaps, outside of their country. The relationships between tourist and host have changed, and tourism is now a business, and no longer enjoys the novelty and excitement that it once possessed. Indeed, in the well-developed tourist enclave, the host community may increasingly have less contact with tourists as the tourist area attracts migrant workers into the hotels and restaurants. In time the growth of the industry slows down. The 'pleasure periphery' has long moved on, the niche tour operators have either left the area, or now market the destination in another way, or have had their operations taken over by the larger, mainstream companies.

With the combination of the commodification of the tourist product and the changing nature of the tourists, it is inevitable that the host/guest relationship will change. From the perspective of those in the industry, the service provider/client relationship may still be characterised by friendly commercial interaction, but the increasing professionalism of the industry also creates a possible division between those local residents involved in the industry, and those who are not. This implies that the relationships between those visiting an area and those residents not directly involved in tourism have to be considered. The issue is whether the residents not employed in tourism are still well-disposed towards tourists as individuals and towards the industry as a whole.

The consolidation and stagnation stages

The consolidation phase begins. As the expansion ceases, attention is paid to the control of costs as hoteliers and tour operators find that this is the only possible way of increasing profits. Revenue earned per tourist tends to fall, as the resort loses its 'exclusivity' tag. 'Resort loyalty' is low, as the resort has come to resemble many other locations. Take-overs and mergers occur within the industry as the transport-leisure-accommodation company buyouts occur and industry structures are 'rationalised' on the basis of cost reduction and profit absorption. The tourists now being attracted are the 'organised mass market' and the 'psychocentrics'. Company strategies turn to maintaining the visitor numbers, and hence the stagnation phase is reached. The resort has reached full capacity, perhaps even exceeding it at certain times of the year. The resort has an image abroad of its own – it is distinguishable from the surrounding hinterland. Unfortunately it is not a 'fashionable' area. In order to sustain visitor numbers, the tour operators may have to resort to low prices to attract the volume of tourists that they consider necessary to sustain their investment.

Falling profit margins mean that maintenance programmes are put off, and the resort begins to look dowdy. The attendant environmental, social and economic problems associated with areas past their prime begin to emerge. The host community is faced with a resort where local tourist companies are a minority in their own home area. Associated with the decline, there is the possible withdrawal of foreign-owned businesses. The host community is left to 'pick up the pieces'. The locale can never regain its original standing as a fishing/farming village, but it might be able to regain its status as a place in which local people can have pride. The local authorities, mindful of the economic implications of decline, might seek to develop a process of renewal with those organisations that remain in the area, and rejuvenation might then become possible. Thus, new forms of tourism might be sought. Alternatively, the facilities are switched to other uses. The hotels become nursing homes, and the once-thriving seaside resort becomes noted for its numbers of retired people. Failure either to rejuvenate or to find alternative uses for tourism assets means that the area will continue to decline. The resort sees brief bursts of activity in the height of the season but, with a continuing erosion of its assets it becomes characterised by peeling paint, rusting rails, and memories of days when the place had glamour and excitement.

On the face of it would appear that relationships between visitors and local residents can only become strained. The scenario appears to be one where residents/tourist ratios are high, and where the retail developments are dominated by the needs of visitors. However, the very size and changing land use patterns might effectively create buffer zones. Tourists will tend to adhere to those parts of the locality that cater for tourists, and so contact between residents not employed in the tourism industry and tourists might actually be quite low. Much may depend on the actual spatial arrangements, nature and size of the tourist zone. At beach resorts the beach can become a shared terrain between locals and visitors, as might other community assets such as theatres, swimming pools and the like. But if hotel resort complexes have been established, they may become 'tourist ghettos' and thus contact with local people not employed in tourism may be effectively minimised.

Social Impact implications of the Butler Destination Lifecycle Theory

Butler's Destination Lifecycle (Butler, 1980) permits a series of models of resident/visitor relationships to be considered. These relationships can be categorised as being:

Micro-individual interchanges. This relates to social exchanges at the level of individual experience. The measures that apply here include the number of interactions a resident has with out-of-region arrivals, the duration and nature of those meetings, and the ways in which those meetings are characterised and evaluated.

Macro-social impacts. This relates to the way in which a social and physical environment begins to change in response to growing levels of tourism. It will be argued that change in the physical ambience is not value free. Changes in physical environments dedicated to tourists engaged upon generally hedonistic pursuits freed from normal constraints might be said to potentially represent a specific set of values that may or may not be congruent with those of a resident community. Consequently sets of cultural change arising from demonstration and affiliation effects can occur that impact on the social cohesion of the resident community and the ways in which this is expressed. Therefore macro-social impacts refer to broad patterns of cultural and social patterns of behaviour.

That these processes exist has long been evidenced by various studies, but the conceptualisations arising from findings and their interpretations have changed over time. One of the first studies, and certainly an influential one, was that of Doxey in 1975. In the Irridex model, Doxey suggests that, as the destination cycle unfolds, specific changes in attitude occur within the host community towards tourism. As indicated above, initially there is what Doxey terms 'euphoria'. The host community is pleased to see the tourists for reasons relating, at the very least, to hospitality; and if that community is economically poor, then the economic promise of tourism is welcomed as a source of income that, at least in the initial stages, supplements the region's low wages. As the cycle moves into its involvement stage, Doxey observes that it is generally only a minority of the host community that is involved. As the numbers grow, the tourist is no longer a rare sight. A process of habituation occurs. The later arrivals may not speak the language of the host community, and are perhaps less interested in the daily life of that community. Apathy sets in on the part of the resident community, and the second stage of Doxey's model begins. By the time development is well under way, the tourist/host ratio has so changed that the host community increasingly feels marginalised in its own home area. The resident faces queues in the shops. Many shops change their role, and souvenir shops are of little use to the local person. The roads are full of traffic. and it becomes difficult for local people to park in areas that are convenient to them. They may well feel that they live in a car park for, while each individual tourist is present for but a short time, the local person lives in the area throughout the whole tourist season. Apathy turns to annoyance. In turn, faced with the problems of over capacity that can occur at the stagnation phase of the lifecycle, annoyance turns into antagonism, as was perhaps

Table 9.1 Doxey's Irridex and Milligan's modification model

Doxey's Irridex		*Milligan's modified version*	
Euphoria ↓	– visitors are welcome and there is little planning	Curiosity ↓	– that people should accept jobs that the hosts consider beneath them in status, pay and career prospects
Apathy ↓	– visitors are taken for granted and contact becomes more formal	Acceptance ↓	– of immigrants on the island, tourism is no longer a concern of the local people
Annoyance ↓	– saturation is approached and the local people have misgivings. Planners attempt to control via increasing infra-structure rather than by limiting growth	Annoyance ↓	– coupled with an annoyance with tourists is apathy towards immigrant workers who are seen as contributing to deteriorating standards
Antagonism	– open expression of irritation, and planning is remedial yet promotion is increased to offset the deteriorating reputation of the resort	Antagonism	– both sides are aware of resentment and the situation amongst young people is volatile, Immigrant workers are blamed for all that for which tourists cannot be held directly responsible

demonstrated by the quotations at the start of this chapter. As a highly visible industry characterised by the fact that the consumer comes to the provider of the service, tourism is blamed for changes that have taken place in an area.

Nor is the antipathy reserved for the tourists alone. Milligan (1989) parallels Doxey's earlier work in her study of Portuguese workers in Guernsey. As indicated in Table 9.1, Milligan argues that, just as the local people become annoyed with the tourists because of the problems of crowding that they cause, so, too, that anger can be directed at those who serve the tourists, particularly if they are also 'outsiders'. Milligan's study was within a somewhat different context than those usually associated with applications of Doxey's Irridex as Guernsey is not a developing area, but enjoys all the advantages of being a tax haven – with all that that implies for employment in the financial sector. Nonetheless, tourism has for many years been a significant part of Guernsey's economy. However, with local people having full employment, they were not dependent on jobs in the hotel and associated sectors. Consequently Doxey found that many of the hotel workers were 'imported'; particularly from the island of Madeira. As Portuguese speakers, often living in not-overly-spacious accommodation that was offered by the employers, they nonetheless often stayed for long periods of time in Guernsey because they worked through the whole of the tourist season. Many of these workers were young adults. Milligan reports that they had to use many of the same shops, bars, cinemas, discos and places of entertainment as local residents, and many felt a sense of being treated as 'inferior' because they were temporary, not local people, and yet they might be competing for space in the same places patronised by local young residents. In short, a tension of difference was observed.

The Social Impact of Tourism at the Individual Level

Traditionally, academics have tended to follow the early work of Valene Smith (1977), who wrote of *Hosts and Guests* when examining the relationships that occur between tourists and local people. However, to the mind of this author, these are value-laden words that are inappropriate to the realities of the experiences of many people. Simply because a tourist may visit the area in which a person lives does not, in itself, require the latter to meet the responsibilities associated with the word 'host'. Equally, given that in most cases a tourist interacts with other tourists, or with tourism industry employees, the role of 'guest' seems secondary to the role of 'client'. Therefore, for this author the preferred term is that of resident/visitor when describing these exchanges and the impacts that might result, but from time to time 'host/guest' might be used to avoid tiresome repetition of a phrase.

To state the obvious, there is a link between the social impacts of tourism at the level of the individual resident and those at the macro level of culture expressed through architecture and social movements associated with gender roles, artistic expression and the myriad factors that come to form 'culture'. With immediate reference to the theories of Butler and Doxey, at least two questions immediately come to mind. The first is, what are the causes of the process that is envisaged? Second, is the process inevitable? Certainly there is much to indicate that annoyance with tourists is not restricted to situations where the host country is a developing country and there are large gaps in cultural and social norms. Murphy (1985) notes that there are three determinants of community attitudes towards tourists. The first is the type of contact that is made with the tourist. Krippendorf (1987) makes the point that there is a specific truth about the tourist/host relationship. One is on holiday and seeking relaxation, the other is at work. Krippendorf describes the relationship thus:

> Tourist and native are in diametrically opposite positions. The one is at leisure, the other at work. Natives distinguish between tourist and guests, and tourists are merchandise. Spontaneity is difficult for the umpteenth group of tourists. Meetings are meaningful when there is common ground, but there is little of that. The tourists are visiting a phantom of a place – an illusion of clichés – they are drawn by the unusual – not the minutiae of everyday reality – the very thing they seek escape from. Natives also view tourists through stereotypes – they are rich, they come from cold countries. Neither knows the world of the other. (Krippendorf, 1987: 87)

Does this matter? There are a number of reasons why the views of residents about the nature of tourism that exists in their locale are important. From the perspective of the tourism industry itself, the reasons include:

(1) Residents may have contact with tourists. How tourists are treated might impact on their levels of holiday satisfaction, and thus have an effect on any evaluation of the services being provided by the formal structures of the tourism industry.
(2) Residents are potential employees for the industry.
(3) Residents pay local taxes, including property taxes that provide revenue for local government. In turn local government often supports the tourism industry both directly and indirectly: directly by often being a part funder of tourism organisations and maintaining structure such as tourist information centres, and indirectly by providing infrastructure such as roads, sewage and refuse disposal. If residents are not well disposed towards tourism they may resent such expenditures. That leads to:
(4) Residents vote! If residents are distrustful of tourism, they will seek candidates that reflect those opinions. As, in many cases, local authorities may be the territorial authority involved in planning procedures and permits, policies that inhibit tourism might result.
(5) Residents are a permanent pressure group in planning procedures and appeals, and can participate in various ways in local politics.
(6) Residents are potential customers. If tourism is characterised by high degrees of seasonality, then local tourism businesses may require local, resident demand to help sustain it during the off-peak period.

From the perspective of local people, the relationship a community has with tourism is important because:

(1) Tourism structures offer many recreational and cultural structures beyond what the community itself may be able to sustain.
(2) Tourism offers employment, and in particular hospitality enterprises can offer travel opportunities and career enhancement;

(3) It has been argued that tourism potentially offers more employment and income to females than is the case in many other industries, particularly in marginal economies based on traditional enterprises.
(4) Tourism brings people from outside the region, and their requirements can impact on daily life in a number of ways, including extra traffic, changed retail structures, competition for land that drives up land prices (and values), and therefore can create series of costs even for those not involved in tourism.
(5) Visitors exhibit behaviour patterns that might differ from those of the local community, and that serve as a model for some within the community. This is the basis of the 'demonstration effect'. To the extent that some modes of thinking and behaviour are adopted as a result of these interactions, a degree of acculturation takes place.

For these and other reasons, the nature of the resident/visitor exchanges needs to be considered. However, it must be stressed from the outset that, while conventional analysis has focused on these relationships when social impacts are considered (see for example Pearce *et al.*, 1996); tourists and residents are simply two of the stakeholders involved in the system of social interactions. Of necessity, any analysis of social impacts must recognise that pressure groups exist and that political processes are part of the equation. Therefore the resident/visitor exchanges are mediated through structures created largely by industry and prevailing political structures. As Aramberri (2001) argues, much of the literature on host/guest relationships seems to ignore the basic facts of many touristic destinations. These facts are: that the relationship is between clients and employees of multinational organisations; that these organisations may be present because of the actions of political hierarchies; that most tourists primarily interact with other tourists and industry employees rather than with residents; and that most tourists have little interest in seeking contact with residents for the sake of such exchanges, but rather such meetings are coincidental. The meetings that tourists have with residents are not, as Ryan and Huyton (2000) point out, because holidaymakers are 'lay anthropologists' but because they are tourists seeking amusement, and thus residents may be stereotyped through performance in order to earn a dollar, yen, pound or euro for both locals and intermediaries. Therefore, following academic tradition, the initial discussion will follow in the footsteps of researchers who have examined local resident attitudes, but the discussion will be broadened to take account of these other issues.

With reference to resident/visitor exchanges, De Kadt (1979) noted that there are three contact situations. The first is when the tourist buys goods or a service. The second is when tourist and host find themselves side by side at an attraction that both are using, for example, a beach, golf course or nightclub. Finally, the third situation is when the two come together for an exchange of information and ideas. As the first two situations are by far the most common, the great majority of tourist/host relationships are marked by their transitory nature. In addition, it might be argued that the third type of situation can have differing degrees of informality. If, therefore, the nature of the relationship tends to be so fleeting, how is it that tourists present the challenge that they do to the social and ethical norms of the host society?

The answer to this question, Murphy (1985) believes, lies in two other domains: the relative importance of the tourist industry to the individual and the community, and whether or not a host group can handle the amount of traffic that tourism generates. Tolerance of the tourist is thus a function of the returns and compensations that tourism creates, and the amount of 'nuisance' that it brings. It can, therefore, be easily envisaged that, if tourists are large in numbers but bring little economic or other benefit, and intrude on the local patterns of activity, then the stage is indeed set for Doxey's annoyance and possibly antagonistic stages. In a sense, therefore, Murphy pre-shadows Ap's use of social exchange theory. Ap (1995) proposes a social exchange model that comprises four key components: (1) initiation of exchange, (2) exchange formation, (3) exchange transaction evaluation, and (4) reinforcement of behaviour. Ap argues that residents will accept tourism if their needs are being satisfied, but the model stands and falls on a number of factors. First, it assumes rationality and high degrees of (if not perfect) knowledge of, potential outcomes. However, Ap does discuss the importance of power within the relationships, and the possibility of unequal power relations. Second, the issue of degrees of homogeneity is not really discussed in detail within Ap's model, and there seems to be an implication that high degrees of homogeneity exist within the resident community. There appear to be a number of issues that influence this mutually beneficial exchange between resident and visitor, for clearly most communities are at some point between the continuum of welcoming or hating tourists. In short, degrees of tolerance exist for the costs associated with the gains. Indeed, from the evidence that is reviewed below, it can be concluded that there is no simple linear or sequential set of relationships that determines the degree of social change that tourism might create. It is, for example, difficult to relate social change to tourism alone. While tourism may bring economic wealth, how that wealth is spent is determined by the recipients of the income, and it is not inevitable that they spend it in ways that simply ape the lifestyles of the tourist. Local individuals or for that matter, communities, are not passive sponges that soak up foreign ideas, and any resulting social change is a reflection not only of tourists, but also of the underlying strength of the host culture. Furthermore, it might be argued that, in well-established tourist areas, what emerges is not a culture that reflects fully the culture of either the visitor or the native, but some hybrid that reflects the non-permanent relationships that occur within tourism. In short, a 'tourist culture' emerges, that is recognisable to all participants as being something outside the norm. The characteristics of such a culture might be said to include the following:

(1) large numbers of visitors staying for a short duration;
(2) large numbers of seasonal workers;
(3) transient relationships between visitor and visitor, and between visitor and temporary worker;
(4) tourists are freed from the constraints of their normal life style;
(5) leisure is the main motivation;
(6) spending is comparatively unrestrained;
(7) neither worker nor tourist fully conforms to the habits or norms of his or her usual peer groups, i.e. the groups from which they come, but are selective as to those norms they wish to adopt;
(8) usual patterns of daily activity are different, even the normal patterns of sleeping and waking times;
(9) businesses reflect the importance of tourism, e.g. retail outlets have a different merchandise mix compared with shopping centres in non-tourist areas;
(10) the cultural expressive symbols are based on stereotypes and caricatures;
(11) superior/inferior relationships exist in varying degrees between guest and host;
(12) lack of long-term commitment to the area by tourists and possibly many of the workers;
(13) communication may be through intermediaries and partly-spoken languages. If it is argued that language is the medium of conveying complex ideas full of nuances and subtleties, the fact that the parties concerned may have an incomplete knowledge of one another's language means that communication lacks those facets that are of importance in conveying culture. The communications within the tourist area may thus be dominated by 'crude' concepts related to only a few (leisure) aspects of human behaviour.

Additionally it must be noted that the channels of cultural change are many, diverse and complex. In the emergence of the 'global village', where American 'soaps' are beamed by satellite into villages with a communal television set, or where instant access to news is available through the Internet, it is difficult to disentangle the separate processes of change mechanisms. Tourism may be a catalyst of change, but the direction of change is uncertain. Or tourism may simply be a reinforcement of trends set in motion by other social forces operating within a resident community. Nor must it be thought that the participants within the process are tourist and host alone. Some tourists come to stay, while immigrant workers are attracted to the jobs that tourism brings. Thus, the social changes that tourism brings are not restricted to the tourist zone itself, but are felt in the hinterland from which the workers come. Nor must it be thought that the quality of change is always 'bad'. Travis (1982) noted at that time just how 'grossly inadequate has been the consideration given to the dis-benefits of tourism' in the previously mainstream writings of authors such as Burkhart and Medlik (1974), and even today similar criticisms can still be made (Middleton, 1988; Pearce *et al.*, 1996). However, there is equally a danger that all tourist activity is perceived as negative; in his review of the then-prevailing literature, Travis (1982) indicated that studies considering the sociocultural and political impacts of tourism are overwhelmingly of the opinion that tourism generates negative impacts by a ratio of almost 3.8 : 1 (an admittedly crude calculation, it must be emphasised). What then are the processes and issues that need to be examined?

The process of social change induced by tourism is illustrated in Figure 9.2. Within the tourist zone, the nature of the interaction between resident and visitor is determined by the nature of the tourists, the belief and cultural systems of the host, and the physical carrying capacities of the area, which determine the degree of stress that is being generated. Physical carrying capacity possesses psychological implications. Not only is it a question of the perception and tolerance of physical crowding by the tourist, but also by the resident – a set of perceptions and expectations that are shaped by their own culture. Within this process of interaction, sets of behaviour have demonstration effects. Again, this can be on both tourist and host. Generally, the literature describes the demonstration effects on the host community, particularly on the young within that community (Cohen, 1982a, 1982b; Loukissas, 1982; Jafari, 1981, 1982; Krippendorf, 1987). But theoretically, and especially when the tourist/host ratio is low, residents can influence the behaviour of tourists, at least within the setting of the host community. Thus, the tourist complies with the norms of the host. Such demonstration effects feed back into the nature of interaction. However, in the more developed tourist areas, the host community also has two other groups to cope with: those who are drawn to the area seeking work, and those visitors who come to stay. Both groups also have their norms. Indeed, those visitors who come to stay in the area might be the very people who exhibit most alarm over physical changes in the zone.

It can be argued that the impact that tourism will have on a society is the result of an interaction between the nature of the change agent and the inherent strength and ability of the resident culture to withstand, and absorb, the change generators whilst retaining its own integrity. From the viewpoint of the host culture there may, therefore, be mechanisms of

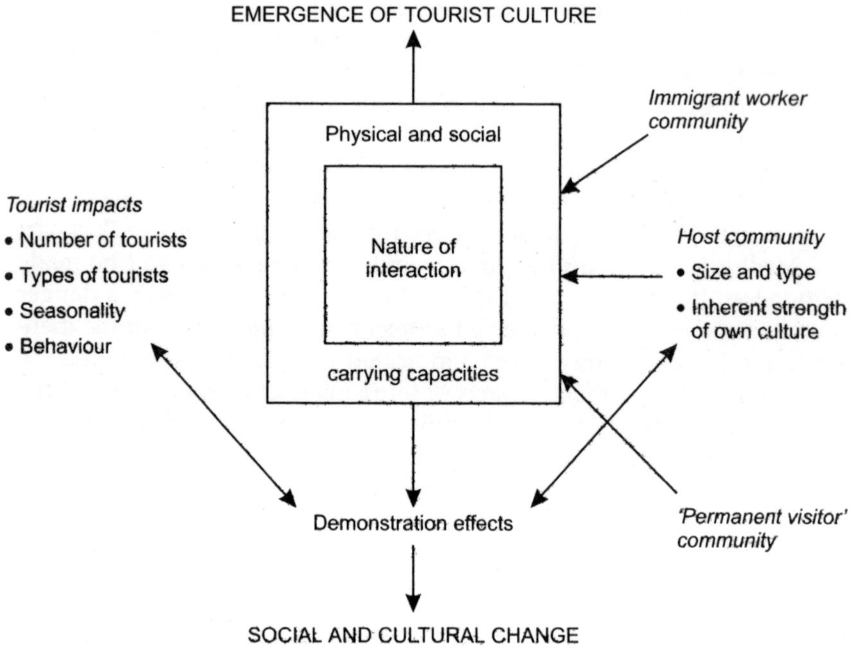

Figure 9.2 The process of social change

protection such as withdrawal from tourist activity, or the confinement of tourism. The 'pseudo-event' and the 'tourist bubble' become protective mechanisms in that they limit touristic impacts; and there are 'erosion' factors, such as the type of tourists, the number and background of immigrant workers, and the 'permanent visitor'. An important component of the protective mechanism of the host culture is the role and views of 'opinion leaders' within their own community (Long & Nuckolls, 1994; Victurine, 2000). Ryan (2002b) has argued that commodification can be a protective mechanism and is not simply a description of the commercialisation of culture. This is premised on the specification of a particular role for the tourist product that is a copy of the original and which separates its meaning from the performance originally undertaken. Therefore two sets of meanings may co-exist, or intermingle, as required by the resident community and culture.

Communities are not necessarily homogeneous, and the Doxey Irridex can be criticised for implying both a process of inevitability and a homogeneity of opinion. Bjorklund and Philbrick (1972) present a matrix whereby the hosts may be active or passive in terms of their behaviour towards tourism, and negative or positive in terms of their attitude. This gives rise to

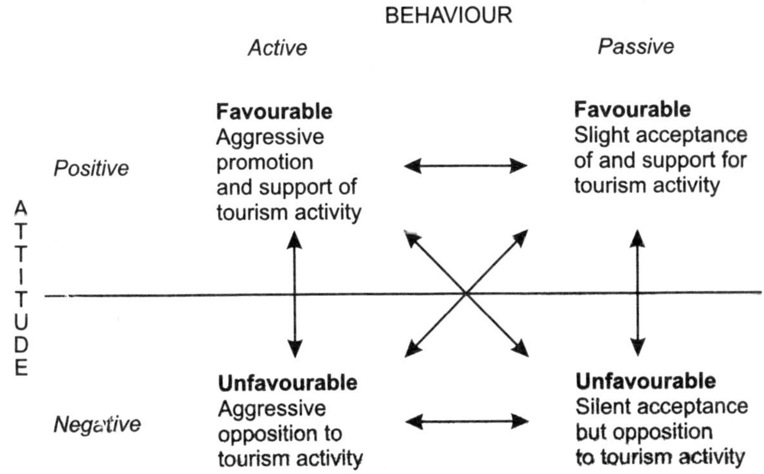

Figure 9.3 Resident–visitor behavioural responses to tourist activity

a four-cell matrix, as indicated in Figure 9.3. The difference between this and Doxey's framework is that the matrix recognises that a variety of opinions may be found within the host community, and that opinions can indeed change in any one of the four directions. It may be that Doxey's Irridex represents the general tone of opinion, whilst the Bjorklund and Philbrick model represents the attitude disaggregated into its various components. Each of the various sectors within the host society – the entrepreneurs, public planning authorities, general public, and conservation groups – will have their own paradigms of behaviour and attitude. Murphy (1983b), in a survey of residents, the business sector and local government, found that the entrepreneurs generally had the most positive attitudes towards tourism. If they and the local authorities are the change agents and opinion leaders within their own communities, then tourist development is more likely to occur.

Moreover, it should not be thought that residents have a simplistic attitude towards tourism, for it has been shown that they are more than capable of distinguishing between different impacts. Liu, Sheldon and Var (1986), in a comparison of Wales, Turkey and Hawaii, found that, whilst the economic benefits of tourism are recognised, residents tend to rate the intangible dis-benefits of tourism as more important to them, particularly in the more developed tourist areas. For both Hawaii and North Wales, notions such as environmental protection ranked higher than certain expected costs and benefits. The rank order was as follows:

Environmental protection > economic benefits > social costs > cultural benefits

However, there were differences between aspects of the different dimensions. For example, residents of Hawaii were concerned with the ability of tourists to create higher standards of living, whilst 'Residents of North Wales' appeared to be more altruistic and willing to undergo personal sacrifice for environmental protection (Liu *et al.*, 1986). Similarly, Milman and Pizam (1988) interviewed residents of Florida and found that whilst residents recognised the economic benefits of tourism, tourism was perceived as a factor that would contribute to worsening traffic conditions and crime. Ryan (1989) used the same questions as Milman and Pizam for the town of Nottingham in England, and found that the results were comparable, in that the economic benefits were recognised but, if anything, there was greater doubt about the social implications.

The measurement of resident perceptions of tourism has now a particularly rich literature and, unlike many other areas of research in the field, possesses a reasonably high degree of commonality in terms of the questionnaires being applied. Many studies have contained within their questionnaires items derived from the work of Allen *et al.* (1988) and Long *et al.* (1990). For example, various workers (Evans, 1993; Hernandez *et al.*, 1996; Lindberg & Johnson, 1997, Ryan *et al.*, 1998; Lawson *et al.*, 1998; Williams & Lawson, 2001) have used scales that possess high degrees of similarity using dimensions identified by Long *et al.* (1990). Among such dimensions are items that relate to the economic impacts of tourism, traffic conditions, retail mix, crime, revitalisation of local crafts, recreational facility provision and attitudes towards local authority and community tourism policies.

The relationship between attitudes and behavioural change is not a simple one. Attitudes may be said to comprise three components:

(1) *the cognitive component:* what is, or is thought to be, true about a situation. A process of belief as much as perceived objective truth;
(2) *the affective component:* the emotional aspect of attitude;
(3) *the conative component*: the predisposition to act on the cognitive and affective components.

In the case of tourism, the cognitive component may be based on a series of, at best, partial truths – the tourist may have a stereotyped image of the place, whilst the resident of a developing country might perceive the tourist as a rich, leisured person and have no concept of the work that that person usually does. A series of emotional (affective) feelings might result from these cognitions; and the predisposition to behave in a particular manner consistent with the feelings of being a tourist emerges. However, given any set of cognitive, affective and conative aspects, the link between attitude and behaviour is still complex because a series of inhibiting, external factors may dampen the behaviour consistent with any given attitude. Thus, tourists who are unhappy about aspects of their holiday may be reluctant to express an opinion if their peers are seen as 'having a good time'. In this respect, as Fishbein (1967) observes, it is not only the content of belief, but the importance attached to that belief, that is important. The reluctant tourists may, in spite of inhibiting pressures, act in accordance with their beliefs if these are deemed important enough. Equally, in Fishbein's extended model, they may take into account the perceived outcomes of their actions. In such a case, whilst attitude may motivate change, equally, the expected outcome can also determine behaviour. Thus, the attitude of, and towards, tourists depends on a complex pattern not simply of belief, but also the importance of norms and the values attached to potential outcomes of behaviour. Host societies may not like some aspects of tourist behaviour, but they tolerate it on the basis of expected economic benefits. What might be said is that the attitude of hosts towards tourists is not always revealed by their behaviour towards tourists – their behaviour is simply the result of a series of compromises between conflicts of objectives of varying importance to them.

Ryan, Scotland and Montgomery (1998) utilise such arguments in trying to reconcile different findings relating to resident perceptions of tourism. Many studies of resident groups reveal a range of attitudes to tourism from support to opposition and, as might be expected from Butler's (1980) theory of the lifecycle, the stage of development of the resort is one determining factor. The issue that they consider is possible movement from membership of one cluster to another cluster – that is, does opinion change over time from support to modified support to opposition? One very common finding from many studies of resident attitudes is that tourism is recognised as a source of income and employment, and this is generally rated positively, even where the respondent receives no direct benefit from such economic advantage. In Ap's (1995) terminology, there is no social exchange contract, yet the resident is supportive of tourism. Ryan, Scotland and Montgomery (1998) therefore ascribe to the resident an altruistic motive of support for tourism because it is thought to aid others at no cost to the respondent. This support of tourism is even evidenced where there is no knowledge of the policies being adopted towards tourism by planning authorities. The process might be described in Figure 9.4.

The argument is that, at the early stages of tourism development, residents will not be overly concerned with tourism or its impacts. If they feel that benefits might accrue to others, they will voice support for the development of tourism, even if they receive no direct benefit. However, as visitors grow in number and spatial change occurs, then that view might

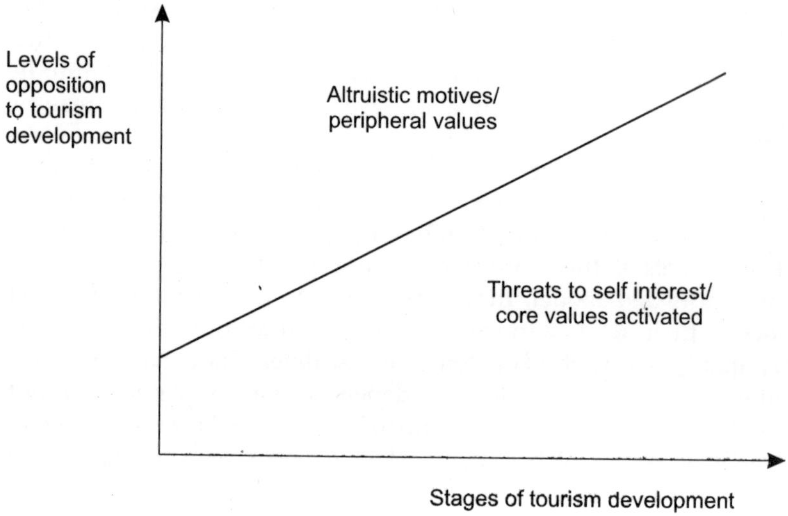

Figure 9.4 Changing attitudes towards tourism development

change. The altruism felt towards changes, the resident's own core values or perceived threats to aesthetics or way of life, or indeed the nuisance value of tourism as it affects the respondent's own lifestyle, means that the early altruism is weakened and less strong support for tourism development is evidenced. This theory, however, is really applicable only to those not directly employed by tourism. For those so employed, an opposite process might occur. Originally they will be supportive of tourism, but that support may subsequently be reinforced further by the income and career opportunities that the industry provides. Lindberg and Johnson (1997) found that residents tended to sustain support for the economic values of tourism, but that issues pertaining to congestion, litter and crime were reported as being of concern to residents. However, when they tried to assess the influence of these latter factors by modelling based on the technique of structural equation modelling, they found poor levels of fit, and suggest that their results 'must remain tentative' (Lindberg & Johnson, 1997: 418). Nonetheless they suggest that the cognitive and affective components of attitude might be susceptible to messages about tourism, but such messages need to be congruent with both experience and corresponding attitudes, otherwise they will be rejected as being inappropriate and incorrect.

The issue of messages about tourism ties closely to the nature of ownership and control of processes that direct peoples' lives. Accordingly, many commentators have espoused a community approach to tourism in the belief that, by adopting such processes, tourism will be supported and not threaten patterns of lives in varying communities. This is thought to be particularly important in the case of rural communities where the need for supplementary income might be high, yet equally the negative impacts of tourism may be at their most apparent. An area that has received attention from this perspective has been the Bow Valley and surrounding areas in Alberta, Canada. Draper (1997) and Getz and Jamal (1997) are among those that describe the processes that have taken place there. The latter describe the Alberta government-funded processes that led to the formulation of *Social Planning Goals* and *Economic Development Strategy* for Canmore and the Bow Valley, the area lying south of Banff and just north of Calgary (Town of Canmore, 1995). These procedures were undertaken under the Community Tourism Action Plan initiated by Alberta Tourism in 1987. About 231 communities in Alberta were involved, with some 3200 local residents serving on committees, 5000 attending public meetings, and $CN30 million of expenditure. Getz and Jamal (1997) describe the different twists and turns of the controversies that ensued at Canmore, and the high costs in time and finances that such community approaches involve. For her part, Draper (1997) considers one aspect of the tourism planning there, water resource management. Both sets of authors point out the resulting high levels of awareness of issues that emanated from the consultative procedures, but also the need for continuous monitoring and consultation between all stakeholders. Were the plans any the better for these processes of consultation? For Getz and Jamal (1997), the issue is far from clear. They note that what emerged was a plan oriented towards conservation, but wonder whether a sustainable plan for tourism had been produced. Indeed in a number of articles Getz and Jamal have examined the whole issue of collaboration in tourism planning. In 1995, they examined collaboration theory with reference to five key components: the independence of stakeholders, constructive dealing with difference, joint ownership of decisions, collective responsibility for ongoing direction, and collaboration as a collective process. They suggest six propositions for success in tourism planning, and essentially argue that the fragmented nature of the tourism industry leads to complexities and a high need for management for any community-based planning (Jamal & Getz, 1995). Later Jamal and Getz (1999) revisited the planning processes of Canmore and again noted the immense effort that was required in such participative planning. For example, more than 25,000 hours of volunteer time were recorded, as were tensions and feelings of winning and losing. They noted that collaborative planning is not a warm, fuzzy feeling and that, for constructive progress to be made, it is important that 'space for change, resistance and dialogue are enabled in the mediation between structures and participation' (Jamal & Getz, 1999: 305).

Another interesting study of the socioeconomic impacts of tourism is that of Tsartas (1992), who studied the general impact of tourism on the Cyclades islands of Greece with more specific detail relating to Serifos and Ios. Tsartas identified three categories of island, the first being those islands that responded positively to the challenge of tourism development in that they created the necessary infrastructure of small hotels and tavernas. He particularly notes the role played by islanders who had previously left the islands in search of work in Athens and Piraeus, and who were often instrumental in creating businesses on the islands. But he notes that, within the comparatively short time of 5–10 years, compliance with the wishes of the external package tour operators very quickly changed the social and economic framework of these islands to the point where their dependence on tourism was absolute.

A second group comprised smaller and poorer islands, and in their case the development of infrastructure was delayed. They thence became a satellite group of tourist destinations and their target market became 'good tourists'; 'that is, big spending and socially acceptable tourists' (Tsartas, 1992: 522).

The third group was the most traditional group of islands, characterised by strong religious traditions, who opposed tourism development as being a 'destructive force'. However, Tsartas notes the presence of alternative sources of important economic activity, notably ship building. It is in this group that the problems associated with tourism are least evident. He identifies five factors that helped to explain the different rates of tourism development, these being:

(1) returning migrants, seaman and Athenian investors as change agents;
(2) local social groups, their value structures and processes of lobbying at local government level;
(3) foreign tour operators;
(4) national tourism policy;
(5) the 'poor past and rich present' factor – and the demonstration effect of those nearby islands that gain from tourism.

Many of the instances noted in the literature about stakeholder approaches to community responsive planning seem to omit one significant stakeholder from the discussions, and that is the tourist his or herself. The reason for this is obvious. How might visitors from outside a region become consistently involved in long, drawn-out processes of consultation? And it can be objected that they are indirectly represented through the presence of entrepreneurs who wish to provide product for the visitor, while indeed those within the community will often be tourists visiting other locations. Nonetheless, it can be argued that planning processes that seek to mediate resident/visitor exchanges within the local social and environmental frameworks that create a tourism product will always be deficient if they do not refer to the ways in which visitors can use both space and product. As already discussed, tourists are proactive, imaginative users of place, and future behaviours may not accord with those expected by planners, no matter how much consultation with residents occurs. Thus, almost inevitably, as described by Jamal and Getz (1995), planning will give priority to the needs of residents as it is they who either directly or indirectly fund the planning process and provide the major part of the input. Therefore concerns about local environment will almost inevitably take precedence over touristic experience, and thus, as noted, it might be that any plans that emerge are plans of conservation rather than of tourism.

If this is to be avoided, then, of necessity, the role of the entrepreneur as a stakeholder is important. For Hall (2000) this raises an important issue, and that is the one of realpolitik. What is the nature of the relationship between the tourism industry and government agencies? It might be argued that in the case of Alberta's rural communities the Provincial Government was prepared to permit long, drawn-out consultative processes that stretched out over many years because it had no core interest that was being threatened. It might be asked, where were the long, drawn-out discussions over the hosting of the Calgary Olympic Games? For Hall (2000), tourism is about client politics – that is specific groups benefit, but the costs are distributed amongst all. Hall and Jenkins (1995) analyse the roles of pressure groups and policy-making decisions within government in so far as they relate to tourism, and conclude that by its nature tourism 'is a fractured and ill-defined policy area' (Hall & Jenkins, 1995: 96), but throughout their text there is an implicit assumption that tourism is important. But is this, in fact, the case when national policies are being debated? There is no doubt that tourism policies and plans abound in many countries, but it is also true that in many countries, for all its economic importance, tourism is not well represented at the central points of political power. How often are tourism ministers members of cabinet as of right? For Sharpley and Crave (2001) the experience of British tourism during the 2001 Foot-and-Mouth Crisis is educative. They point out that the potential value of lost livestock exports was no more than £315 million, whereas rural tourism generates almost twice as much revenue as livestock farming. In total, they suggest that they UK may have lost over £1 billion in tourism earnings from overseas visitors. Yet they characterise the responses made to the tourism sector as late, confusing and inadequate. The answer to why this happened is, they argue, a lack of recognition of fundamental changes that have occurred in the English countryside, the influence of the National Farmers Union as representing farming and not countryside issues, the fragmentation of tourism as undermining its political 'clout', and a failure by national government to fully appreciate the importance of tourism. Or, to put it simply, tourism had less political presence in the policy decision-making processes than farming. Foot-and-mouth was, understandably, initially seen as a farming issue, and the case for a wider appreciation of countryside and rural tourism issues was seen as of secondary importance; thereby pointing to a political failure by the decision makers.

One interesting implication of the fragmented business and political nature of tourism is that the individual can still attain an importance as a catalyst for change. Reference has been made to the concept of 'shakers and movers' postulated by Russell and Faulkner (1999) in their application of chaos theory to tourism and their description of tourism development on the Gold Coast of Australia. Reed (1997) analyses the politics of tourism development at Squamish in Canada and relates how the advisory committee was divided over the development of a ski hill. In this instance it was the failure of clear alternatives to the conventional power elites that produced slow processes of decision taking, as, according to Reed, the conventional power elites had resort to both modified co-optation and marginalisation of proposed tourism plans. In short, not being able to get its way, the power elite sought to incorporate proposed plans within a context that included its own preferences and, while approving alternative projects, did little to effectively implement plans. Reed comments that collaborative planning and community involvement is, by its nature, pluralistic; but pluralism does not equate to equality of power.

Finally, McGibbon (2000) provides an interesting example of how power elites sustain some tourism stories but continue a silence about others. In her analysis of the development of Tyrolean ski tourism at St Anton am Arlberg, McGibbon notes that the local museum, which records the growth of local ski tourism, is generally silent about the period from 1933 to the immediate post war period. This was an important time in Tyrolean tourism, because it was in this period that skiing emerged from being the pastime of a few into mass tourism; in 1939, a million arrivals were recorded. The selective history that is represented records the earlier contribution of pioneers such as Schneider and Gomperz, but not the reason for their departures from St Anton, which was due to their anti-Nazi sentiments and, in the case of the Gomperz, his death in a concentration camp.

Tourism and Social and Cultural Values

In the reported research about social implications of literature, there has been a considerable emphasis on the impact of tourism on marginal or economically developing regions or areas. This is because it can be envisaged that the greatest impacts will be made where there is the greatest gap between the culture and/or income of both resident and tourist. It is a cliché of the literature that the American tourist in Canada will have little impact, but the same American tourist in a developing country will have a far greater influence. Adapting the arguments of Heron (1989, 1990), it may be argued that cultures are characterised by differential use of three types of time dimension. These are:

(1) *sacred time* is time used for communal participation, not simply for worship, but in any type of rite that establishes the relationship of that community with its environment. Its characteristic is that it is a time shared with others where common beliefs are expressed and reinforced.
(2) *profane time* is functional and mechanistic in nature. It is time that is measured, time where appointments and meetings are made, where timetables are established by man and are adhered to.
(3) *personal time* is time that is used for personal reflection and re-creation in the sense of determining the individual's relationship with environment, community, family and self.

Heron argues that developed nations tend to emphasise profane time, whilst a characteristic of developing nations is the more central importance of sacred time. Hence, the impact of the industry of tourism (with its time schedules of events, arrivals and departures) includes a fundamental cultural change whereby the host community shifts from using sacred time to profane time. Therefore a common criticism of tourism is the manner in which it has created commercial packages of culture based on performance arts timed in one hour or half-hour slots to meet the requirements of coach schedules and other pragmatic requirements of tour operators. It has been argued that such performances stereotype: they create performances that meet the preconceptions of tourists rather than challenge or inform. In short the cultural performance of the residents is down graded and commodified for profit. Moreover, it is argued that these performances are decontextualised from their original setting: dances used in religious or community-based functions such as weddings are taken and transposed into the hotel saloon or restaurant to provide photo opportunities for tourists. Therefore, such performances become stripped of their meaning, secularised, commodified and in short, debased. Moreover, it is argued, such performances come to emphasise the spectacular and the exotic, and in consequence another's culture is represented to the tourist shorn of its nuances, presented only as theatre, and deprived of meaning.

Such criticisms of tourism were much heard in the period from the 1970s following critiques such as Turner and Ash's book, *The Golden Hordes* in 1975, and echoes of these critiques can still be found in books such as those by Frances Brown (1998) and Martha Honey (1999). Academics continue to support, at least in part, this form of analysis. For example, Taylor (2001), writing of representations of Maori in tourist brochures in New Zealand, states:

> Within brochures and on postcards, almost without exception, Maori appear in the standardised, contemporary version of ceremonial costume and are posed in acordance with the gender constructs of Maori maiden/Maori warrior made fashionable at the turn of the century. (Taylor, 2001: 20)

Taylor argues that, by emphasising an apparently timeless culture, the actual history of Maori is made silent, and the people become staged. While there is much to support such criticisms, an alternative perspective is emerging that, while recognising the possibilities of such things, also questions the simplicity of the interpretation. Even Taylor notes that such (mis)representations of Maori are not those of non-Maori alone, and he suggests that Maori seek to portray a sincerity if not authenticity about their culture. For her part, Daniel (1996) argues that by its very nature dance incorporates creativity, even when performed for tourists. From the dancer's perspective, the act of dancing creates an existential authenticity – it is their movement, their own physicality, that imbues the performance with movement and hence meaning. Equally, tourists get caught up with the dance and 'for many tourists, the dance becomes their entire world at that particular moment' (Daniel, 1996: 789). Daniel asks for a re-examination of the processes of dance performed for tourists. Indeed it can be observed that touristic dance and classical ballet share similar constraints of repetition of movement, time constraints, an evolution of creativity through experimentation and the effort of performance. Tahana and Oppermann (1998), through Tahana's tribal affiliation and status, were able to obtain the views of Maori performers about the nature of their participation in tourist performances. It is clear from their account that performers have considerable control over the content of the shows, and that performances are changed because 'People like challenges, they are all fired up and once this challenge is lost they start to *tutu* (fiddle) around' (Tahana & Oppermann, 1998: 29). Indeed Maori, especially the *Te Arawa* people, have a long history of performing for tourists, and this history is part of their own culture (Ryan, 1997).

The social and cultural impact of tourism is not always restricted to the immediate tourist zone. In her study of Spanish immigrant workers in Lloret de Mar, Lever (1987) traced, over a five-year period, the effect of working in the tourism industry on young people from the village of San Santiago, a village in the hinterland of the Costa Brava. The majority of such workers were females, and from the poorer sections of village society. The demonstration effects of tourist behaviour, as well as the changes of life involved in working in a bar or as a chambermaid, created a number of social impacts. The young women were freed from the conservative lifestyles of male-dominated homes, and could go to discos and have relaxed friendships with males. They lived in flats with their peers with no parental presence, and they became important sources of family income, perhaps earning more than their fathers did from the soil. They might have played a role in the burgeoning trade union action of the immediate post-Franco period. In short, the traditional, conservative lifestyles with clearly-defined gender roles were being both challenged and changed. Further, the changes were recognised by the village, if only because a person who was financially independent and who contributed to the family income had to be treated very differently from someone who effectively worked as a subordinate on the family farm. Overall, because tourism created a new role for women, it might be said to have been beneficial. Further, the income that tourism generated helped to sustain the farms, for without such an income the area might have followed what had long been a traditional pattern of Spain, and that was the emigration from the land to the city. In various other studies of tourist souvenir production, the same impacts have been identified of an outworking of production beyond the point of retail sale, as is the case of the production of Australian Aboriginal paintings and carvings, or South American weaving and fabrics.

The relationship between tourist city and rural area is a complex one. In some areas of the Mediterranean, for example in Cyprus in the 1980s, it was the males who tended to go into the tourist zones, (such as Ayai Napa in Cyprus), in order to start up tourist-related businesses such as snack bars and restaurants. While the younger women worked in the hotels, it was the older women who took over some of the work on the farms such as picking fruit and vegetables. Thus, the women were displaced from a purely domestic role into more of an income-earning role, but still in a subsidiary function. The development of tourism in developing, peripheral economies undoubtedly changes female roles, and potentially male/female relationships within the host society. McGibbon (2000), when describing Alpine tourism, also notes the strains on females. Much of that tourism is still within the hands of family-owned businesses, but for those seeking to start a business, business development and the mothering of young children often coincide. McGibbon also notes the ambivalence that some children show towards inheriting a family business. Some note the financial gain, but also the wear on family life, the unequal experiences of both men and women as the men play the 'glamorous' role of ski instructors and women play the role of caterers and housekeepers. Yet even this is not without advantage for many women, and McGibbon notes the financial independence of many of them, although she still concludes that, partly because of legislative frameworks relating to social benefits, females still tend to be valued for manual labour and not for entrepreneurial skills.

Certainly the monies created by tourism are important. For rural societies that are little mechanised, the burdens of hard work are well ingrained. The work in hotels and bars, whilst hard and exhausting, might be seen as being easier than agricultural work, particularly if the tourist season is well defined and restricted to approximately the four or five months from spring until autumn. If locally-owned businesses are able to flourish, then the tourist area will attract workers from other industries. It might also attract the better qualified and educated into supervisory management roles and away from other jobs that might be more needed by the local community, but which are also low paid. Such alternative jobs might include teaching, nursing, social work of various forms, and local authority administration. For the balance to be rectified, it becomes important to know how much of the economic benefits generated by tourism are retained by the host community, and the means by which these benefits are distributed.

Reference has been made to tourism not only influencing the host community, but also having a wider impact on immigrant workers. In Lever's (1987) example there was homogeneity in the culture of the immigrant and the host, but that is not always the case. In his study of the islands of southern Thailand, Cohen (1982a) traces the development of two beach resorts. In the second resort, that on the island of Phuket, he observed that much of the property ownership was not in the hands of the Thais, but in Chinese ownership. He commented that 'The marked difference in the ownership structure of the tourist facilities on the two beaches is of crucial importance for their differential developmental dynamics' (Cohen, 1982: 226). In the case of Phuket, the beach sites evolved with little outside interference. On the other hand, on Sawadee, the islanders had no comprehension of the motives that brought the tourists, and there were diametrically opposed sets of opinions as to the value of sunshine. The tourists perceived the beach as an island paradise, and swam naked in the blue seas. For the natives, naked bathing was indecent and sunshine was damaging to the skin. In Phuket, the landowners were in negotiation with multinational hotels. Cohen's study of the 'marginal paradise' raises a whole range of issues about tourist/host interactions, but is also of interest in terms of the role of the outsider as landowner and intermediary between tourist and host.

If host communities are to retain the integrity of their own culture, they have to develop means by which they can restrict the influence of the tourist. Paradoxically, the 'tourist bubble' and the 'pseudo-event' that is so much criticised by Boorstin (1961, 1962) is just such a means. If tourists stay within the walls of the holiday village, then it is true that their appreciation of the host culture is small. But equally, it is true that the demonstration effects of topless bathing, of affluence, of drinking alcohol and other practices that might give offence are not on display for the mainstream of life within the host community. The 'pseudo-event' satisfies the tourist's wish to see the culture of the area, and it does so in a package that is of meaning to the tourist. It avoids the situation whereby the host community finds that its own events become a 'theatre experience' for the tourist. The host community is able to retain the meanings of its own events. MacNaught (1982) argues that host societies are quite able to distinguish between the tourist show and the real event, and thus it is simplistic to argue that tourism undermines the integrity of the host culture. The danger, however, is that the host community is unable to maintain its own social events without them becoming a 'sight' for the tourists, and thus the very presence of the tourist begins to change the ambience and, in time, the meaning of the event for the host community. Equally, it must be recognised that social events are not fixed in format. Increasing affluence generates change. People reach gatherings by car and not by foot; food is cooked in ovens and not over fires; the externals of the social meeting are changed. The question is whether or not tourism changes the internal meanings of the event for the host community. Certainly there is evidence that tourism creates stress. Smith (1977) relates how the Eskimo women of Kotzebue in Alaska, had to build fences and barricades to stop tourists photographing and viewing the process of butchering carcasses. Finally, they had to take the carcasses into the privacy of their own home, and thus the social aspects of the process were being destroyed. To complain that tourism changes a society in terms of the female/male roles, that it leads to the emigration of young workers from the rural areas to tourist complexes, that it changes traditional patterns of extended family networks, that it even changes the frequency of use of minority languages (White, 1974) is, in many cases, no more than to state that the areas so changed were areas that were economically vulnerable to change. But the argument can be taken further. The charge against tourism may not be that it has induced change, but that the nature of the tourism permitted has generated a change that is potentially inimical to the culture of the host society, and not one that is supportive. Tourism developments do not have to take the form of a wide dispersal of large numbers of people that create a tourist/host ratio in which the hosts are unable to escape from the tourists. As previously indicated, soft tourism policies are possible. Yet the case against tourism is far from proven. It may be argued that, in the case illustrated by Lever (1987), the position of young females was improved, that the conventional male-orientated society of rural Spain needed to be changed. It can be argued that no culture is either 'sacrosanct', to be preserved from change, or indeed necessarily contains within its norms and values ethics that are beyond challenge. In the final analysis, it may be that those cultures that have modes of life that have meaning for their citizens will prove to have the tenacity to meet any challenge that tourism poses.

Tourism and Expressions of Culture

Ritchie and Zins (1978) identified eight areas in which tourism might have an impact. These are listed below with a short commentary about each.

Handicrafts

As has been noted, in the 1970s and 1980s criticisms were made of 'airport art' and the decontextualisation of style from original meaning. On the other hand, tourism was often credited with a revival of interest in traditional arts as the commodification of the art form created a market and hence an income for the producing communities. Ryan and Crotts (1997) provide examples of long relationships between tourism and carving, weaving and metalwork with reference to Maori and Navajo cultures. Essentially they argue that in both cases the original work has benefited from contact with tourists; not only do tourists provide a market but, by producing work for the tourist market, the artists themselves have incorporated new colours and themes into their work. Whereas in the past this may have been seen as a form of bastardisation of traditional art forms, Ryan and Crotts tend to perceive this process as an enrichment of such art forms and a means by which artists are better able to exercise creative judgement. Certainly from the Maori perspective, as published in documentation by the Aotearoa Maori Tourism Federation (1995, 1996), the issue is not one of compliance with a deemed 'authenticity' but of control and recognition of the value of Maori art forms. Such documentation defines Maori art forms not wholly by design, but by whether the work is conceived and executed by Maori. The concerns of the Aotearoa Maori Tourism Federation were met in 2001 with the establishment of the *toi iho* label by Creative New Zealand, and in 2002 37 artists were credited with the right to use the mark. Two classifications exist *Toi iho maori made* and *Toi iho maori co-production* – the latter applying to work co-produced by Maori and non-Maori. The criteria for the former work is that the artist must prove that he or she is of Maori descent, must produce work that is distinctly Maori and be a person of standing in the Maori community. However, in spite of the good intentions behind the branding, it has not been uniformly adopted or accepted even within the Maori community. Certainly in 2002 it would be fair to state that many of the artists approved would not see themselves as meeting primarily a demand from tourists, especially from those paying only small sums of money.

In some cases the industry has been quick to identify local design as a means of making statements that have marketing value. For example, various national airlines now have aircraft painted in varying traditional designs that are unique to their part of the world. For example Qantas worked with Aboriginal Dr John Moriarty's Balarinji design studio to paint two Boeing 747 aircraft. In 1994 Qantas unveiled a Boeing 747-400, *Wunala Dreaming*, painted in an Aboriginal design depicting the story of journeys by spirit ancestors, in the form of kangaroos, across the Australian landscape. In November 1995, the airline 'launched' *Nalanji Dreaming*, a Boeing 747-300 painted in an Aboriginal theme, this time depicting the rainforest and reef. The airline company feels that it has enabled Balarinji's team of Aboriginal and non-Aboriginal artists to develop distinctive contemporary imagery using Northern and Central Australian style motifs in order to create two of the world's largest – and most mobile – pieces of modern art.

Indeed, in this particular instance the airline goes further in its support of Aboriginal culture. For example, Qantas is the Official Airline for the Bangarra Dance Theatre, and a sponsor of the National Aboriginal Sports Council. The airline also, in 2002, sponsored Bungabura productions (the production company of singer, director and actor, Leah Purcell) as well as the production of Purcell's book and documentary, *Black Chicks Talking* (Purcell, 2002). Qantas is also major sponsor of the Tjapukai Dance Theatre in Cairns. Other airlines can cite similar examples of corporate sponsorship aimed at activities that are consistent with the uniqueness of the main destinations they serve.

Traditional clothing and textiles

There is little doubt that, in a world increasingly subject to fads of fashion, what were once perceived as traditional forms of dress have influenced designers from the major fashion studios. In the summer of 2002, for example, influenced in part by Andrew Lloyd Webber's support for 'Bollywood' music, Indian design percolated the British High Street – although fashion and art critics maintained that this was once again simply a case of 'high fashion' catching up with what had been a trend among the young on the streets for at least two years. More traditionally, from a perspective of tourism studies, there have been several studies of the South American textile industry and its linkages with tourism (e.g. Cohen, 2001). These studies often trace a pattern. Opportunity for home-based production is frustrated by merchant and distribution chain intermediaries coming to the fore as traditional clothing is sold through recognised tourism retail outlets, and then a subsequent countervailing market reaction occurs as producers try to directly access the tourism market by various means. Examples include the promotion of areas as the 'authentic' places of production in order to redraw the tourism routes to them, and the formation of co-operatives or the use of textile and arts fairs to sell direct to tourists. In some places attempts might be made to establish 'authentication' labelling schemes, as in New Mexico with Navajo Indian art.

Certainly there is significant interest by tourists in the purchase of souvenir clothing. Healy (1994) points out that, although the value of individual transactions may be small, in aggregate they can account for significant proportions of the total tourist retail expenditure. Asplet and Cooper (2000) are among those who have surveyed tourists about this issue, in this instance about the level of interest in purchasing 'authentic' Maori designs on t-shirts. In their work they found that about 40% of tourists attached some importance to local *motifs* on souvenir clothing and, if supported by labelling, would be persuaded to buy such clothing in preference to other designs.

Languages

Language has an important role, for it is not only a means of communication but also a way in which perceptions of the world are shaped. For example, the Inuit are said to have about 40 words for the descriptions of snow. Is it a coincidence that in English one speaks of the buying and selling of 'goods' and not 'bads'? Language thus beomes an important component in sustaining a culture, and it is for this reason that minority groups seek to maintain the health of their language. For example Welsh speakers sought long to obtain the Welsh television channel SC4, and the success of that station has become a model for others including, for example, speakers of Maori in New Zealand. Again, for example, in the United States of America, the proliferation of Hispanic television channels over cable television is a testimony to the Spanish-speaking cultures and has proven to be a boost for entertainers who have gained experience prior to achieving success in the more mainstream culture. The erosion of a language thereby carries the implication of changing norms of expression, and thus thought. The issue is whether tourism is important in the erosion of languages. From the viewpoint of this author, what evidence that does exist seems to produce two conclusions. First, the pressures on the maintenance of a language seem to come from far more influential sources than tourism, namely business and the international media of television and the Internet. Second, there are examples of where tourism, by creating a market value for a culture, has actually helped to sustain a language. One of the most-cited examples is that of the Tjapukai or Djabugay language of the Aboriginal people of Queensland, Australia. The commercial success of the Tjapukai Dance Theatre has led to a resurgence of interest in Tjapukai culture among its own people, and its language, which was once being slowly forgotten, was, in 2002, being taught again at two local primary schools (Ryan & Huyton, 2002).

Traditions

Tourism creates work opportunities, but sometimes these may be inconsistent with past patterns of work. For example, when the design was undertaken for the interpretation centre at Wanuskewin in Saskatechewan in Canada, which exists to explain the culture of North American Plains Indian peoples that occupy that area, there was a desire to have some story telling. In a primarily oral tradition, story telling is a means of passing on values and the commonalities that help identify a people. Saskatechewan Province experiences several months of snow during the winter, and historically that was a period when, after the American Indian Wars that forced some of the tribes to stay north of the border, the peoples concerned would engage in story telling. Hunting opportunities were limited in the depth of winter, and so the tradition grew up that stories were told only in the winter. However, tourist trips to Wanuskewin occur primarily in the summer. A number of the elders were opposed to a break with tradition and the original compromise reached was that some stories could be recorded and played over loudspeakers in tepees in a display within the main building. Subsequently this was relaxed when the level of interest and respect shown by visiting groups became more evident and some story telling now takes place in the specially-constructed story-telling area outside the centre.

In some instances tourism engenders interest in past traditions, especially perhaps those that are associated with both spectacle and romance. To take one example, the Maine Windjammers Association is able to maintain its fleet of sailing vessels to recreate the past by catering to the tourist trade. It has fourteen ships that operate out of Camden, Rockport and Rockland, located in mid-coast Maine. Most of these ships were built at the turn of the century when America relied on sailing ships to transport heavy cargoes from port to port, and many are registered National Historic Landmarks. Today, these vessels still rely on wind power, and tourists can choose 3-day or 6-day sailing holidays on the vessels and help sail them. The result is that a heritage is sustained in a living manner that provides an insight into the sailing skills of nineteenth century mariners.

Gastronomy

Tourism generates a demand not only for traditional foods, but also for new foods. It has been noted that Jamaican hotels began by offering what it thought its visitors wanted, which led to the import of food stuffs from primarily the USA. However, the hotels now offer a range of traditional dishes that not only provide visitors with new experiences, but also provide employment opportunities for those in the local food industries (Belisle, 1984; Henshall-Momsen, 1986). In Hokitika, Westland, South Island, New

Zealand the annual Wild Foods Festival held in March has created a national and international reputation for wild and wacky foods. In addition to the conventional venison, sheeps balls and oysters can be found a range of insects, fried, boiled and marinated! More conventionally, Getz (2000) has traced the growth of popularity of wine tourism. Not only are there wine and food festivals, but winery tours have become one of the 'hot' tourism products of the early twenty-first century.

Architecture

A conventional criticism of tourism was that, based on observation of the tourism-resort complexes that surrounded the Mediterranean, tourism property development comprised box-like structures with external walls scarred with balconies that promised views to the guests. Certainly it was not hard to find such examples, but over time architects have offered more to corporate clients who now realise that imaginative design is one means by which tourists can be attracted. Simultaneously there has been a movement to reinforce local architectural styles for reasons that include marketing, but with a growing concern to support local craftsmen and traditional industries. It is also a convenient means by which the hospitality industry in particular can fulfil the role of being a 'responsible citizen'.

This is not, of course, new, nor is it without some value. One of the loved eccentricities of North Wales is Portmeirion; the Italianate village set in beautiful surroundings and started in 1926. One difference between a location such as Portmeirion, and the various marinas and hotels that exist, lies in the motivation behind the buildings. Sir Clough Williams-Ellis, the architect for whom Portmeirion was the fulfilment of a life's dream, sought specifically to design an area that consisted of attractive buildings that harmonised with, and enhanced, their surroundings. Sight lines from the cottages and views from the wooded valley towards the village were thus carefully designed.

In Florida a similar development is the town of Seaside, a town constructed to a code that controls the shape, height, colour and materials to be used, and dictates the amount of open space, and where this is to be located. Unlike Portmeirion, Seaside has permanent inhabitants, but its popularity has brought with it increasing land values which means that only the most affluent can buy properties. The website for Seaside describes it thus:

> Seaside founders Robert and Daryl Davis drew inspiration from historical Southern towns and traditional neighborhoods of the 1920s and 30s, before the car was king. Here in Seaside people stroll, friends chat with neighbors, cars stay put, and children walk or bike to the town

> center and the beach. And, most of all, everyone shares the glorious Gulf of Mexico. (http://www.seasidefl.com, June 2002)

Whilst undoubtedly popular, Seaside has its critics. Guest (1988) refers to it as being primarily a 'rich man's holiday resort', pointing out that only about 15% of the 100 or so homes are completely occupied all the year round, the rest being rented out for holiday use. He concludes that:

> Seaside is perilously close to being a model village, a pastel coloured pastiche of classical, Victorian and Georgian versions of the old share-cropper and dogtrot houses. It either looks too good to eat or good enough to scrawl graffiti on – depending on your point of view.' (cited by Ryan, 1991a: 141)

It is also evident that Seaside is like Portmeirion in another sense, and that is that at any one time many of its inhabitants are holidaymakers renting accommodation. Yet both places inspire high degrees of loyalty and repeat visitation, implying that both have an appeal of quieter, nostalgic times.

Any discussion of the relationship between architecture and tourism must recognise that it can exist only within a wider context of the relationship between man and his surroundings. For advocates of the 'community architecture movement', such as HRH, The Prince of Wales, and Rod Hackney, former president of the International Union of Architects, it is important that architecture relates to the needs of people both as individuals and as communities. The signs are that the tower-like, 400-or-more bedroom hotels with their poor sound-proofing may be increasingly rejected by European and North American tourists who show their preference for self-catering chalets, boutique hotels and similar forms of accommodation. Yet, ironically, the search for greater individual freedom by the tourist generates greater costs. High rise is high-density housing, but low rise and low-density tourist complexes are more space demanding, with all that implies for the environment.

Some holiday destinations are very aware of these issues, and tight planning controls on construction might exist. For example, Lanzarote, inspired by the painter and architect, Caesar Manrique (who died in a car crash in 1992), has required all developments to conform to certain traditional features of its architecture. It can be argued that architecture has long been the expression of aspirations of a society; and indeed that is one reason why tourists flock to cathedrals and palaces, and to the homes of both the mighty and the humble of the past (the Welsh National Museum of St Fagans is an example of the latter). In this respect therefore, the type of architecture that is adopted for tourist complexes is, arguably, a reflection of priorities that are deemed to be important. The tower block hotel reflects priorities of cost, of seeking to achieve high rates of return on investment in the short and intermediate term. Other styles of architecture may reflect different norms. If tourism is an agent of social change, then the architecture and buildings of the tourist industry are the expressions of that process and the type of tourist activity that the host society has sought to attract.

Religion

Historically, and even today, there are strong links between tourism and religion. Pilgrimage was and remains a strong motive for travel, as is witnessed by the requirement imposed on those of the Islamic faith to travel to Medina, or by Catholics who travel to places like Lourdes or Fatima. Vukonic (1996) has also remarked on the long history of the intermixing of the profane with the religiously sentimental in souvenirs, and the ability of church authorities to reap benefit from such sales. He gives, as one such example, the minting of a special gold coin in the jubilee year of 1450 by Pope Nicholas V. Today, tourists wander through the great cathedrals of Europe with varying degrees of awe. Many churches have become, in effect, museums: the shell of a Middle Ages' culture stripped of the sense of worship that motivated their very construction all those centuries ago. Himalayan trekkers strip outside the holy places of Buddhism in order to wash after a day's climb. The bare-breasted sun worshippers regard the mullah's cry as a nuisance that breaks their reverie. While, in many countries, there may be many differences between residents and visitors, the differing attitudes towards religion may be amongst the most marked. This can be especially so when the tourist originates from an increasingly agnostic, if not atheistic, Western culture and the resident is from a world where religious belief may still be strong. Like all generalisations, neither the tourist nor the host can be so easily categorised, and the individual tourist may indeed be more religious than the individual host. The impact of tourism on religion is difficult to assess. That Western societies permit tourists to throng through the cathedrals is a reflection not simply of the impact and importance afforded to tourism, but also of the importance attached to its Christianity. It may be argued that the income from tourism is important to the maintenance of cathedrals, and indeed this is the case; but the recognition of this fact implies an acceptance that the average person is more prepared to pay to see the cathedral than to worship within it. But even this type of statement withers before the data collected by the Commons Select Committee on the Environment (in 1987, cited in Ryan 1991a), when it was found that York Minster attracted 2.5 million visitors in 1986, and raised £359,000, (an average of 14p per visitor), to help offset annual maintenance charges of £600,000. Problems may emerge when the same attitude is shown in locations where the tourist fails to appreciate the importance of religious shrines to the local resident, who views them not as curios from the past, but as an essential part of everyday life. But, as in many other aspects of the debate about the impact of tourism on components of culture, the ability of the host society to withstand the cultural changes potentially inherent in tourism depends on the strength of that culture.

Dress and leisure activities

Tourists may cause shock amongst their hosts by their dress, or lack of it. Cohen (1982a) in his paper on 'marginal paradises', the beaches of Thailand, observes how nudity gave offence to the local people; and this type of observation has been made many times. Equally, residents may view certain types of dress as inappropriate. Thus, for example, in Spain in the 1960s, female tourists had to be properly attired before entering a church, and a bare head and a mini-skirt were definitely perceived as not being appropriate. Males had to wear shirts with sleeves, and long trousers. Today, in many of the same tourist areas, the bare-headed female or the short-sleeved male may enter the church without fear of generating disapproving stares. However, to argue that this is due solely to tourism would be to underestimate the other changes within Spanish society in the last part of the twentieth century: changes that have transformed Spain from a dictatorship to a Parliamentary democracy within the European Union.

Tourism has affected dress in the sense of helping to create an interest in traditional dress. Whether it is Morris dancers in England, Highland dancers, grass-skirted 'hula' girls or North American Indian costumes and dancers – throughout the world the tourist-orientated performances help to maintain the existence of traditional dress as a means of retaining distinctive elements of a culture, and as an expressive statement of a tradition and past that are an explanation of the present. However, just as Ropponen (1976) refers to the faking of antiques for the tourist trade, so, too, it might be queried whether the occasion for the wearing of traditional dress is not also faked for the tourist. Within New Zealand the close connection between Maori performances and the dress associated with those performances has created its own rituals. Maori are able to distinguish between the wearing of cloaks for purpose of performance, and the wearing of a cloak on other occasions by people with due *mana* or authority for the occasion. However, within the performance group itself, the cloak-wearing person him or herself may possess *mana* with reference to that occasion or role. In short, the performance contains both the components of traditional authority and acting to formulate a complex set of meanings of ambiguity.

Just as it is for dress, so too with some of the traditional times of rejoicing within societies. The large processions of *Semana Santa* (Holy Week) in the major Spanish cities have become a tourist sight. Staged Indian weddings, staged African dances – throughout the world, culture is being offered as a tourist resource, a commodity to be sold to the coach parties. Initially motivated by a pride in their dance and dress, the sheer repetition means that the community event becomes a professional show performed by paid actors. As a show, the performance becomes packaged in one-hour time slots to fit the timetable of the tourist without any reference to the original purpose or duration of the event. Yet, in a changing world that moves at a different pace from that of the past, the evolving modern societies might arguably have no place for these past traditional performances were it not for tourism maintaining at least a bank of skills in dance and dress, so that the host society can call upon the traditions when it sees fit. And, as noted by Daniel and other writers, the very act of performance contains an existential authenticity for both audience and performer. The fuzziness of the margins between performance and integrity of cultural expression is perhaps exemplified by the Aotearoa Traditional Maori Performing Arts Festival. Originally created for the express purpose of improving the quality of performance for tourist production, the festival has become a major cultural event for Maori. The Festival is important for the development of dance, choreography, a sense of identity for Maori, and it also reflects the tension between that which is traditional and that which is new as both performers and choreographers wish to take advantage of new means of cultural expression. Consequently professional kapa haka (performance) groups embrace multimedia forms of presentation, just as do a number of performers at Tjapukai Dance Theatre.

It is the author's view that forms of analyses that perceive tourism as having the effect of creating little more than a stereotyped culture and of squeezing complex stories into simplified 60-minute productions, fail to appreciate the energies and creativity of those performing and the manner in which people take control over and view the performance. Performers are well able to distinguish between the forms and purpose of performance. The issue is, or perhaps was, one of control of performance, but there are many signs throughout the world that control does not lie in the hands of tour operators or hotel managers alone. Yet, as is discussed below, many tourists also conceive of such performances as lacking authenticity having adopted this form of analysis, and in doing so underestimate the complexities of process that are actually occurring.

Tourism and Heritage: Framing, Performance and Audience

There are a number of paradoxes in the relationship between tourism and culture. In the past, some critics argued that the challenge that tourism poses is not simply one whereby tourism creates change, but in fact the opposite. Tourism might calcify a culture into a 'frozen' picture of the past. For example, MacCannell (1976) argued that what takes place is a process of 'sight sacralisation.' This is characterised by a number of stages:

(1) *The naming stage:* a process of authentication whereby the site, sight or event is differentiated from its other similar events.
(2) *Framing and elevation:* putting on display and enhancement of the place.
(3) *Enshrinement*: the framing material is in place, and the first stage of the sacralisation process begins.
(4) *Mechanical*: the creation of the copy, so that the tourist becomes aware of that reproduction, and seeks the 'real' thing.
(5) *Social reproduction*: the original is a model after which others name themselves.

Whilst MacCannell's examples include the Mona Lisa, and what might be termed the expressive artefacts of a culture, it has been argued that the process applies to the very processes of culture. Nowhere perhaps is this seen more clearly than in Heritage tourism. Hewison (1989) highlights a process whereby myths of a past are created – the past is seen in the way in which we would like to see it, and not in the way that it was. Barrett (1988) comments that:

> The Rhondda Heritage Park is the latest in a series of large scale heritage parks like Ironbridge in Shropshire, the Black Country Museum in the West Midlands and Beamish in the north-east that have a 'cast' of characters in period costume. For the most part these are people recruited at Government expense from job creation schemes; the unemployed of the Eighties paid to pretend to be the employed of the Twenties. For these 'museums' the temptation is to 'sanitise' the past: trim out the nasty bits, omit the poverty, the hunger and the strikes – to see life as a newsreel film of the Thirties and Forties, where the working classes are always irrepressibly cheerful. (Barrett, 1988)

A 'culture' thereby is named and stereotyped. The visitor seeks to see the characteristics of the image of the culture, and the host society provides the expected 'treat'. Boorstin's (1961, 1962) 'pseudo-event' is born. The danger is that the myths are incorporated into the culture; succeeding generations do not know anything but the enactment of a past that may not have existed, and come to accept it. There is, indeed, a confusion of stories that are told. Ryan (2002b), in an analysis of the December 2001 Disney Holiday Parade (note, not Christmas Parade) comments on the mix of stories wherein 'Woody' from *Toy Story* is legitimised within a context that incorporated more traditional European stories of *Cinderella* and *Beauty and the Beast,* while Mickey Mouse is conveyed in an open carriage reminiscent of Dickensian images and Victorian Christmas Cards to form a whole that supports the branding of Disney. The question posed is, does this matter? To a generation that is able to distinguish between the different traditions the amalgam might be seen as creative commercialisation, but for newer generations, what message is being conveyed – that all of this is Disney?

In short, much depends on the ability of the culture to distinguish between the contrived and the real. But processes are complex and subtle because the contrived becomes its own reality for those who perform and observe. In analysing the impacts of tourism on developing countries, one concept that may help to describe the processes is suggested by Wallace (1956). According to Wallace, societies can be subjected to a revitalisation process that consists of five stages, although there is no guarantee that any society will exhibit all five stages, or indeed experience them in the order he suggests. The stages are:

(1) *The steady state:* Social and cultural forces exist in a dynamic equilibrium, whereby change does take place, but does so within the internal dynamics of the society, which thus retains its integrity and is able to handle processes that may cause stress.
(2) *The period of increased individual stress:* The society has been pushed out of equilibrium due to some external event. From our viewpoint, such an event may be the development of tourism. The previous existing cultural system can no longer satisfy the needs of all of its members. The opportunities and demonstration effects of tourism may create a process of conflict within individuals as they seek to reconcile the developing changes with a framework of values that relates to a previous social and cultural setting.
(3) *The period of cultural distortion:* This period is characterised by piecemeal attempts to restore equilibrium and so reduce stress, and the conflict between community members that is now being expressed. Special interest groups emerge, seeking either a restoration of previous ways, an establishment of a new consensus, or some other form of adaptation. Generally, however, such effects are initially ineffective.
(4) *The period of revitalisation:* This takes place with the realisation that the community's culture is maladaptive, but for the society to be successful a number of changes must occur. From the processes of cultural distortion, there must arise a 'blueprint' for a 'better' society, i.e. one that reduces stress. This new 'blueprint' acquires followers who both defend and enforce the new code. The movement must also be routinised so that the new culture can establish its own methods for handling change.
(5) *The new steady state:* This occurs when social disorganisation and personal stress return to tolerable levels and a new dynamic equilibrium is evolved.

Wallace's model relates to homogeneous native societies, but the process can be observed in relation to tourism, where resident communities develop 'coping strategies' to maintain their business alongside the tourist activity that takes place within their community. There is, however, nothing within the model that indicates the nature of the new steady state. For some societies, it may be a resurgence of old values within a new context, in that it is the traditional values that define the distinction between the residents and the guests. From the perspective of the native peoples of North America, or the Basques of Spain, it is these traditional aspects that define their being separate from the majority. Some societies may even seek to use tourism as a means of reinforcing their uniqueness both to themselves and to the tourist. Examples of this can be found in the Amish societies of Lancaster County in Pennsylvania, and the Mennonite communities of Southern Ontario. At St Jacobs, Ontario, the Mennonite community has established a small interpretative centre that portrays the history of the movement from its European Anabaptist origins. Visited by tourists, the centre fulfils many roles. It interprets the community's culture for the tourist in a manner that the Mennonites wish to portray. It seeks to establish an empathy on the part of the tourist for the community: to generate the understanding of different practices which O'Grady (1981) sees as an essential component of 'responsible tourism'. In challenging the tourist to respect the differences between the tourist's everyday life and that of the Mennonite, it also serves to reinforce the uniqueness of the Mennonite culture. In short, tourism might require sophisticated social skills from host communities if their differences are not to be submerged in some form of 'international' culture. It requires that the hosts can maintain their own homogeneity, even whilst they move from one world to another as, for example, they move from work in the hotel back to their homes. In practice, the best from both worlds will often be selected. In a sense, therefore, the hosts practise the same skills that immigrant societies practise, albeit on a different scale and within a different context.

Another important component in the analysis of the tourist/resident interaction is the position and nature of the tourist. In the emergence of ecotourism in the 1980s and 1990s, the concept of cultural tourism also emerged. Indeed the two were often linked in that ecotourism was supposed to indicate a respect not only for nature, but also for those traditional cultures and communities that co-existed with natural settings. The concept was that there was a strong demand for the culturally authentic. Certainly there were a number of statements made that a strong interest prevailed for the culture of indigenous peoples around the world. Evidence for this was supposed to exist in the numbers that, in response to questions on International Visitor Surveys such as those conducted in Canada, Australia and New Zealand, indicated that they had attended a 'cultural performance'. Little regard was paid to the nature of the performance, the frequency of such contacts, or what was in fact being sought by (or provided to) tourists. Since the late 1990s a more critical view of both 'cultural tourism' and 'ecotourism' is emerging. Duffy (2002) writes:

> Ecotourists can replicate the same problems as the mass tourists that they are expected to replace. In particular, the problems created by the meeting of very different cultures have been highlighted. New forms of tourism such as ecotourism, adventure tourism and cultural tourism have become increasingly intrusive and dependent on the destination community, and this intrusion has resulted in the development of uneven power relationships between the host and origin communities. (Duffy, 2002: 32)

Duffy's comments result from a two-year project with eco-tourists in Belize, and Duffy claims that much of the same stereotyping of people from the resident culture, and many of the hedonistic behaviours associated with 'mass tourists' were displayed by the eco-tourists. McKercher and du Cros (2002) report research into tourists visiting Hong Kong. They state that:

> Based on raw participation rates, one could assert that 33.3% of tourists to Hong Kong are cultural tourists of some description. But on closer inspection, only about 10% of all tourists surveyed indicated that cultural tourism played a significant role in their decision to visit Hong Kong, and only 4% of all tourists could be classified as purposeful cultural tourists – people highly motivated to travel for cultural tourism reasons who have a deep experience. (McKercher & du Cros, 2002: 148).

In a different context, that of visitation to place and tourist products based on Aboriginal culture in Australia's Northern Territory, Ryan and Huyton (2000, 2002) come to much the same conclusion. They state that from their research it would appear that only about 2–3% of visitors would actually want to stay in an Aboriginal community overnight. Ryan (2000b) questions just how environmentally friendly is the behaviour of ecotourists who, to his mind, justify unnecessary incursions into the natural environmental on the premise that it is alright for them to do so because they are 'ecotourists'. As McKercher (1993) propounded, a fundamental truth about tourism is that it is about polluting activities and about 'fun'. Most ecotourists and cultural tourists are motivated by the much the same thing, albeit perhaps in different settings.

On the other hand, in research undertaken in both Australia and New Zealand, the present author has encountered a reverse situation, particularly with reference to German tourists, who are strongly motivated in their search for alternative cultures. The issue here is that on occasion they meet the criteria posed by Cohen (1979a, 1979b) of tourists who are disappointed by their failure to appreciate the authentic within a performance, or who are selective in their understanding of what is pertinent about a culture. For example, a German tour guide expressed her disappointment that the Maori Arts and Crafts Institute permitted people to use flash photography and take video images of performers during the lunchtime cultural performances. She explained her view that this practice could not be 'traditional'. In return, Maori explained that a more fundamental principle was that of *Manatangita*, or hospitality, and that knowing of people's want to record the events it seemed only 'hospitable' to permit this to occur. This resulted in an attitude change on the part of the courier. In personal interviews with German tourists at the Institute it became evident that they recorded lower levels of satisfaction with their visit than other groups of visitors, often on the grounds that 'it was staged'. However, given *Te Arawa* history, the relationship of the performing groups with other forms of artistic expression, and the site as a training institution for Maori carvers and weavers, such perceptions of 'staging' are arguably being shaped by preconceived images of what is proper for a 'traditional' representation.

The Impact of Holiday Homes

Of the tourists that come, some may seek to stay. They may initially be considering a holiday home, or it might be that they are about to retire and want an escape from the winter of their home area. One of the differences between developed economic regions and the peripheral areas is not simply in the income earned during a working life, but also access to accumulating wealth. Amongst the professional groups of Northern America and Europe – areas characterised by demographic trends whereby the old are becoming a larger part of the population – part of that access to wealth lies through the possession of pension plans that offer inflation-proofed income in retirement. In addition, such social groups may also inherit wealth because their parents owned houses, whilst they too own their homes. Data drawn from HM Inland Revenue shows that in 1999 there were over 700,000 inheritances in England and Wales with a value in excess of £300,000, while the total number of properties passing at death was over 700,000 – an almost seven fold increase compared with twenty years earlier. Increasingly there is emerging a generation that possesses the means to buy holiday homes through inherited wealth. Historically, by their nature, the rural, scenic tourist areas tended to be areas of low income and low housing costs, but this is beginning to change even though the much-flaunted flight from the city that was being proposed in the 1970s has not, broadly speaking, occurred. The consequence is that this poses problems for younger people who are resident in rural areas, and many newly-married couples in such areas find it increasingly difficult to find the means of buying their own home. In the United Kingdom some local councils have sought to respond to the problem by building properties that can be let and purchased only by local people. The same problems have occurred in Whistler in British Columbia (Ritchie, 1988), where a community of approximately 3500 people has, as a result of the development of ski runs, seen tourist numbers rise to nearly a million per year in a short period, with the resulting acceleration of property prices by over 40% in just over a year in the period 1988/9. Searle (1989) gives examples of property development in Banff, Alberta, where 'prime residential' lots climbed to $CN160,000 within a few years. Fagan (1989) reports how the resort of Phuket in Thailand changed from being a haven for students and hippies in the early 1970s to a tourist-developed area where, from 1982 to 1989, seaside land increased in price from $3,500 to $350,000 per acre. In New Zealand, in 2002, the resort town of Queenstown is now one of the most expensive, if not the most expensive, areas for residential property while property prices in holiday regions such as the Coromandel peninsular have shown rates of growth that are much faster than average. It is easy to find such examples throughout the world. On the other hand, it must be recognised that property prices within communities can rise because of any influx of outside demand, and not simply because of tourism. For example, the building of the Honda Accord plant at Marysville in Ohio in the 1980s, or the Toyota plant outside Derby in the United Kingdom, led to increases in house prices in what were formally rural or dormitory areas. Thus, once again in Sessa's (1988) terminology, what may be seen as a tourism impact is in fact a facet of the process of establishing urban poles.

As well as the physical changes created by tourism, the sense of community may also change. Some villages may be characterised by an absent population; the village is 'full' only during the season. Younger local people leave to seek areas where they can buy cheaper houses. The withdrawal of such people leaves an older population. Local schools may have falling numbers of pupils, and are thus forced to close. Other village services are also threatened including general stores, post offices, medical services and the like. Slowly, the support structures of rural life may be undermined, and the businesses that may arrive cater for tourists and not for the local people. On the other hand, the purchase of holiday homes in certain areas may help to stop declining property prices that slowly undermine the wealth of families, and hence inhibit their capacity to move to other areas that do offer employment in other than a declining agricultural industry. If the homes that are being purchased become permanently occupied, then the retreat of population from the rural areas is, if not totally reversed, at least slowed. It may indeed become possible to keep schools open on the basis of existing populations and potential future births. However, the 'newcomers' may have several different social impacts. In the case of movement to different countries, as has occurred with the influx of northern Europeans to the Mediterranean, newcomers may not know the language, and hence much depends on their willingness to learn it, and the tolerance of the local community towards such efforts. Secondly, the newcomers have been drawn to the area because of its special qualities of peace and quiet; theirs is a retreat from the urban pattern of life. Newcomers might become a force for the retention of the status quo, once they have found their niche within it. Thus, they become a group that seeks to protect the environment and possibly the culture that they have entered into, but in doing so they seek possibly to hinder the evolution of a society.

In the assessment of the culture and society of developing areas, there needs to be an awareness of what Walter (1982) would characterise as a romantic ideal. Whilst it may seem to the urban citizen of an 'advanced' economy that the peasants of a developing region do in fact possess riches of a spiritual sort, in that, for example, their way of life is more 'natural', such a viewpoint overlooks the harshness of that way of life. Thus the motivation of the subsistence farmer turned hotel keeper, catering for the tourist who comes to enjoy the sunshine, is easily understood and difficult to criticise, for to criticise such an action is to deny the aspirations for advancement not only of the farmer himself, but of his family and children.

Tourism and Crime

One aspect of tourism that has attracted attention is the hypothesis that tourism generates crime. Mathieson and Wall (1982: 150) surveyed existing literature on the relationship between crime and tourism, and noted that 'The literature on crime as an externality of tourist development is not large, but most is empirically based'. McPheters and Stronge (1974) and Pizam (1978) indicate a positive correlation between tourism and crime in studies of Florida. Certainly many residents *perceive* a link between tourism and crime, for it seems to them that, as tourism increases, so too does crime (Rothman, 1978; Milman & Pizam, 1988; Lawson *et al.*, 1998). In their study of Miami, McPheters and Stronge (1978) note the relationship between increases in crime and the tourist season. Pizam and Pokela (1985) indicate that residents are highly aware of links between the 'sexualisation' of their community and drugs and organised crime due to a legalisation of gambling in an attempt to attract tourists. Certainly, in terms of Mediterranean reports, there is almost a folklore about young men on scooters stealing handbags from the shoulders of tourists, whilst in Paris the pickpockets flourish during the tourist season. Mathieson and Wall (1982) comment:

> In summary, it appears that tourism contributes to an increase in crime, especially on a seasonal basis. It does this through the generation of friction between the host population and tourists which may be mani-

> fest in criminal activities. In addition, the target for criminals is expanded and situations are created where gains from crime may be high and the likelihood of detection small. (Mathieson & Wall, 1982: 151)

Prideaux (1996) locates these types of interactions between resident community and tourists within two parameters: the destination lifecycle and the nature of the resort. He argues that, as destinations grow, so too does an ambience that makes it easier for crime to develop. As Ryan (1993) argues, tourism destinations are characterised by large movements of temporary residents, which makes it more difficult for the policing authorities to observe out-of-the-ordinary actions. However, Prideaux adds the other component: the nature of the resort. He argues that more hedonistic resorts, when compared to equally mature but more family-oriented ones, tend to have higher levels of crime. To support his contention, Prideaux provides differential crime statistics for the Queenland resorts of the Gold Coast and Sunshine Coast; the former being defined a 'hedonistic' resort and the latter a 'family' resort. There is certainly evidence that resort destinations that are characterised by bars, discos and clubs attract high levels of petty crime associated with drunkenness, and more serious crimes associated with drug taking. In June 2002 leisuretourism.com reported that Ayai Napa in Cyprus had reversed its policy on clubs. In the years immediately prior to that date, the resort had become well known for its dance club scene and club culture. However 'clubbers' were not only getting drunk, they were also attracting sellers of the drug, ecstasy. The mayor, Barbara Pericleous, therefore announced measures that included the banning of 'pub crawls', a strict enforcement of bar and club licensing hours, the deployment of undercover police to identify drug dealers, and the closure of clubs that flouted noise regulations and/or failed to take measures to combat drug dealing. In its place, the mayor was reported as wanting to attract 'nice people' and young families.

What this case tends to illustrate is a possible new theme in the intervening years since Mathieson and Wall (1982) undertook their study; namely the victim is not always the tourist. For several years since the 1980s the trade and daily press of Europe has been reporting that tourists may be the aggressors as well as the victims. For example, on 4 July 1989 the *Independent* newspaper reported that:

> The British package holiday subtly dominated the news at the weekend. There were fresh scenes of congestion at airports ... and from Majorca came reports of five Britons remanded in custody after the death of a taxi driver. (cited in Ryan, 1991a: 159)

Throughout 1988 and 1989, drunken behaviour by holidaymakers on aircraft and at Spanish destinations led to officials of the Association of

British Travel Agents (ABTA) meeting with representatives of the Spanish government to discuss means of handling the issue. In the summer of 1988, a British government minister, Tim Eggar, flew to Spain to discuss the problem further, but seemingly with little effect, as the same stories of violence were to be heard the following year. In 1989 the Spanish authorities reinforced the police force at the main resorts, not to protect the tourists from the Spanish so much as to protect the tourists against their own drunkenness, and to avert, if possible, worse cases of violence. The stories have continued with each passing year, as is easily confirmed by a search of the Internet. Two examples of writers' observations on different websites illustrate this, the first relating to an ecovillage in Ibiza and the second to a review of Amsterdam night life.

> Ibiza is an island of excess. The annual tourist invasion strains the island in many ways: Hooligan behaviour strains the nerves of the locals, drunk tourists clog the inadequate roadways, and the enormous, high-priced resorts cater to those who decadently waste water that, in summer, is in short supply. (http://www.personalchoices.org/004, June 2000)

> 54 corpses were fished out of the canals of Amsterdam last year. While about half of them were later determined to have been locals – mostly junkies and bums – the rest were drunk tourists who fell in and drowned while pissing. (www.pavementmagazine.com, June 2002)

A problem that has also emerged is 'air rage' when drunk passengers by their actions not only threaten the well being of cabin staff but also place in jeopardy the whole of the aircraft. In January 1999 the BBC (BBC, 1999) reported that 50 incidents took place at Manchester Airport in 1998, and a Disruptive Passenger Protocol is now enforced by police, airport and airline staff. Airline companies around the world have sought a clarification of law relating to jurisdiction, and generally it would appear that the defendant would be answerable in a court of the home base of the airline concerned.

The variables that are significant in these situations appear to be:

(1) tourists whose cultural norms include:
  (a) peer group cohesiveness,
  (b) intolerance of those outside their group,
  (c) values that justify behaviour patterns that include excessive drinking, indulgence in violence and casual sex where possible;
(2) perceived freedom from normal constraints;
(3) expectation of a 'good time' that conforms with their norms. Such expectations are shaped by:
  (a) perceived images of holiday destinations and companies shaped by past experience, stories and media activity – e.g. publications

such as *Beach Party: The Last Resort* (Benny Dorm (pseudonym), 1988), which confirms derogatory stereotyping – and activities such as 'happy hours' (where drinks are sold half-price) and pub crawls organised by couriers,

(b) belief that they can impose their own values on the host community and other tourists;

(4) holiday destinations that are not 'foreign' – i.e. the general milieu is in fact a familiar one to this type of tourist, and is primarily one of pubs, clubs and discos.

Studies relating to football hooliganism may be pertinent to such behaviour and, if this is the case, the stereotypes of young, low-income and uneducated groups of men would not be totally valid as a description or explanation of this phenomenon (Chittenden, 1989). If this type of crime is to be understood, reference has to be made to sets of norms, values and ethics that generate a predisposition to violent action. Ryan and Robertson (1997), from a study of students, argue that much drunken and hooligan tourist behaviour is a part of adolescence and in essence the holiday simply offers a transfer of venue for behaviour that is not uncommon every Saturday night in many city centres. Ryan and Robertson also undertook a cluster analysis that showed that much of the 'bad' behaviour emanated from just 16% of the sample, who were continually over-represented in figures relating to drug taking, hangovers, vomiting, unprotected sex and the like. The issue might be that some resorts, such as Ibiza or Ayia Napa, because of their reputation for the club scene and hedonistic life style, tend to attract higher concentrations of such people.

It should not be thought that such behaviour is restricted to young adults. Wickens (1997) records the exploits of thrill-seeking adult females. However, a combination of less-public displays of hedonistic behaviour with higher income, and that these women are able to indulge in such behaviours in locations where they are less likely to be picked up by the police, mean their cases feature less in court proceedings.

Tourist crime may take many different forms. Hamilton (1988) reports the case in which customs officers at Bristol Airport detained a holiday-maker returning from Ibiza with a suitcase of 500 Ibiza wall lizards. An endangered species, the lizards were valued at £30 each. Arguably, this is not tourism crime *per se* in that the motivation had presumably little to do with holidays, but it nonetheless indicates the opportunities that easier travel related to tourism brings.

There is one other aspect of crime that has received little attention from researchers, and that is exploitation by corporations. Indeed, within Doxey's Irridex (1975), it might be argued that one factor that generates antagonistic attitudes towards tourism is the feeling of exploitation that members of the host society might feel. Hoosie (1990) reports that a government history of the building of Cancun, the Mexican tourist resort, relates how a Mexican lawyer disguised himself as a local landowner with a casual interest in buying land in Cancun. Consequently the tourist agencies were able to buy the land at extremely low prices. In 1984, 50 acres of land at Huatulco were purchased for approximately $US3000; by 1989 the value of the same land was estimated as being about $US3.5 to 4 million. By that year, Cancun attracted more than a million visitors and earned about $US0.6 billion from tourism. The original landowners received little of this money. However, Hoosie (1990) also reported that the lessons had been learnt, and Fonatur, the Mexican tourist agency, was taken to court by the former residents of Huatulco seeking compensation for low land prices. However, in 2001 Weiner was repeating the same charges, citing the case of Xcacel (pronounced Shkah-SELL), a beach 67 miles south of Cancun, which is one of the world's last sanctuaries for green and loggerhead sea turtles, both endangered species. In 1998 a Spanish hotel company, Sol Melia, purchased the beach in a deal brokered by Mario Villanueva, who was then governor of Quintana Roo and yet, in 2001, was a fugitive, having been charged with protecting cocaine traders. Environmentalists sued to stop the company's plans for a 1400-room hotel next to the turtle sanctuary and called on the government to ban the development. In July 2001 the Environment Ministry, after a major campaign by NGOs and conservation groups, reversed its earlier decision and banned the development of the beach. This case illustrates how the already complex issues of tourism environmental planning and the need to meet the needs of many stakeholders can become yet even more confused when corruption and crime syndicates are part of the political and social fabrics of resident cultures. In such instances both corporates and residents can become embroiled in what can only be described as messy and unsatisfactory relationships.

Tourism is not only a cause of crime, but is a victim of criminal actions. Ryan (1991b, 1993) provides examples and a model of the crime/tourism relationship. He notes examples where tourism has attracted the attention of terrorist-criminal organisations who seek publicity for their aims, and in some cases require cover for money laundering or for acquisition of money through attacks, drug smuggling, and the like. For example, the Basque movement, ETA, has bombed tourist sites on a number of occasions since the 1980s and did so again on June 2002. While, for the most part the objective has not been to injure tourists, the media coverage gained during periods of peak holiday demand helps publicise ETA's demands. In the case of the 'Maoist' Shining Path guerrilla movement in the 1980s in Peru, tourist targets were more explicitly attacked as a means of undermining the government, stopping tourism policies that offered alternative employment and income to cocaine-growing in rural areas (which both funded arms purchases and caused social ills in the USA), and killing representatives of capitalist structures. It was therefore of little surprise to find that overseas visitor numbers declined from 300,000 to 30,000 in this decade.

Tourism and Prostitution

One subject that has attracted some attention from researchers is the relationship between tourism and prostitution. Thre are a number of reasons for this, including a sense of moral outrage, the international adoption of conventions against the trafficking of women and the commercial sexual exploitation of children, and the growth of feminist literature. The result has been that what was once regarded as a comparatively homogenous phenomenon of tourist patronage of prostitutes is now regarded in a multiplicity of ways. To state a number of 'truisms', first there is general repugnance that children should be sexually exploited for any reason, much less simply commercial reasons. Second the trafficking of female labour for any purpose, not simply for purposes of prostitution, is universally condemned. Third, the link between tourism and prostitution is well established. For example, within European cities such as Hamburg and Amsterdam the brothels have long been a tourist attraction, and the streets are often thronged by curious tourists who wish to see the girls.

However, the period since 1990 has seen an ever-more complex set of explanations and analyses emerging. The first period of research was broadly initiated by Christian groups in areas such as the Philippines and Thailand in a series of conferences in Penang (1974), Manila (1980), Chiang Mai (1984), Bad Boll (1988) and London (1989). It was noted that, while tour operators and agents in the tourist-generating countries showed varying degrees of openness about the nature of some of the bars in places such as Patpong, within the hotels of Bangkok itself literature was easily available for any interested tourist (Wyer *et al.*, 1988). Christian groups such as Asian Women United, a Protestant group, researched tourism in South East Asia, and arrived at high estimates of the number of women working in prostitution and in related activities such as masseuses and bar hostesses. Breen (1988) reported a finding that the number of prostitutes in South Korea may be between 600,000 and 1,000,000 in a country of 41 million; whilst one report (O'Grady, 1981) estimated that in 1985 there were approximately 500,000 prostitutes in Thailand. It is also thought that there may be as many as 100,000 'hospitality' girls in Manila. Most of these estimates date from the early 1980s, fuelled in part by speculation about the possible consequences of AIDS.

By 2002, however, some authorities were questioning the nature of the link with tourism, and the actual numbers of those involved in tourism. Aramberri (2000) in particular has questioned the 'unaccepting' estimates of numbers of prostitutes and has argued that the economic impact of sex tourism on economies like that of Thailand has been significantly overestimated. He suggests that sex tourism accounts for little more than 1% of GNP. Beddoe, Hall and Ryan (2001) report the difficulties of obtaining statistics on this issue. But, while agreeing that figures may have been overestimated, they nonetheless continue to maintain that the problem is significant and characterised by high degrees of corruption. Indeed Ryan and Hall (2001) specifically state that the trafficking of women is simply 'evil'. Yet the same authors have also supported the perspective that prostitution should be decriminalised. How can such seemingly incompatible views be sustained?

What has become evident is that tourism is not the sole cause of these wrongs. Prostitution, the trafficking of women and the abuse of children are embedded in a framework of values and social structures within the respective societies involved. These structures are ones of unequal power and income, and a combination of corruption, poverty and an unwillingness to face the issue that women and children are seen as 'inferior' all lead to a denial of human rights to women and children. From this perspective the commercial sexual exploitation of women, men and children is but part of wider problem that is also evidenced by child labour in other industries and the slavery of women for domestic and industrial work. The evidence of such practices is mounting, and as Brown (2000) clearly shows, the worst areas are not those patronised by tourists but are those used by local male populations, particularly in countries like Pakistan. Fundamentalist Islamic and Buddhist attitudes toward women have been identified by some commentators as creating a pervasive culture that at worst condones some of the practices, or does not wish them to be made public as they are 'shameful' (e.g. see Truong, 1990; Hill, 1993; Brown, 2000). In the case of the exploitation of children for commercial sexual purposes, Ryan, Hall and Beddoe (2002), as part of a report for the World Tourism Organisation, were required to analyse the situation within developed countries. It was suggested that a framework for understanding the situation specific to the commercial exploitation of children was provided by the diagram illustrated in Figure 9.5.

In short, simply trying to isolate such practices from the wider framework would, it is argued, prove ineffective. Government and non-government agencies are increasingly accepting the need to work with bodies such as Sex Workers Collectives, who generally resist the notion that sex workers are simply victims. This is a view being expressed not simply by those collectives that exist in countries such as the UK or the USA, but also in what might be regarded as developing countries (e.g. see Kempadoo & Doezema, 1998; and Kempadoo, 1999). The legal position of the members of such collectives is important in that they can claim full human rights under various legislation and international conventions. This is one reason why the claims for decriminalisation have been growing.

The reason why prostitution has become so closely associated with tourism is evident. There is the historical heritage of the effects of the Vietnam War, and further evidence from many other parts of the world. In South-East Asia, it would appear that in places such as Thailand prostitution had always existed on a larger scale than in Western European countries. Indeed, the concept of the courtesan, as evidenced by the original tradition of the *kisaeng* and *geisha*, as cultured young ladies who provided musical entertainment, allocated to such girls a respected place in their societies. However, the impetus of the wars in Korea and Vietnam in the 1950s and 1960s with first French and then American involvement reinvigorated the tradition through the provision of R & R (Rest and Recreation) facilities for the armed forces away from the battlefield. The contrast between the wealth of the foreigner and the poverty of the girls also generated a series of misconceptions and hopes amongst the prostitutes. Cohen (1982b) reports the motivations of the girls as including the hope of meeting a foreigner,

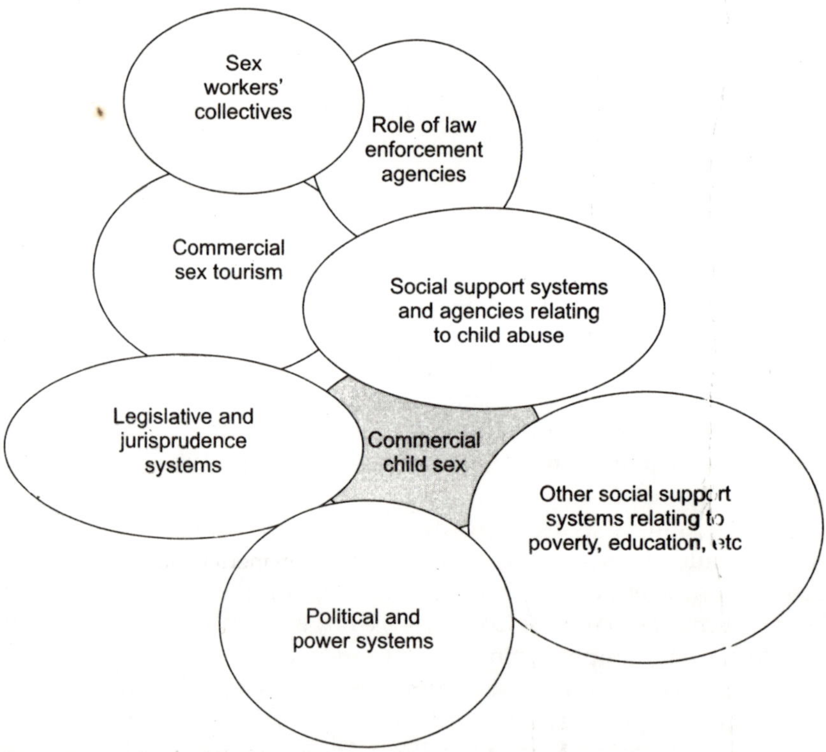

Figure 9.5 Interested groups involved in commercial child sex exploitation.

getting married, and then emigrating to an affluent Western society. However, the essential reasons for the girls entering into prostitution are in many ways no different in type (although possibly different in degree), from that of their European and American counterparts. The main reason is poverty, particularly the poverty of the rural areas from which many of the girls come. In addition, there is the need for women to maintain their children after desertion by their husbands. In this respect there is a cultural difference between Europe and many parts of Asia, in that such women, and indeed widows, are seen as no longer being eligible for marriage (Jones, 1986). With no social welfare benefit system, and if the women possess no marketable skills for use in commerce and industry, prostitution may well seem to be the only means of supporting their families. In addition, the demonstration effect, whereby only those girls who are working in the bars appear to have money, will also reduce their opposition to such activities. Indeed, as Cohen (1982b) comments, the peer group of fellow prostitutes may be the only support group that these girls possess.

Whilst there is a growing literature on the relationship between tourism and prostitution in South-East Asia, some of which is speculative, there was relatively little research into the subject in developed countries such as Britain, the USA or Australia until the last decade or so of the twentieth century. In 1991 Ryan (Ryan, 1991a) cited the work of Kinnell (1989), to tentatively suggest that the relationship between tourism and prostitution was generally weak. In work funded by the Birmingham Health Authority in the UK, Kinnell stated:

> It is evident that prostitution in Birmingham is not a service industry to visitors from outside the region who seek commercial sex because they are away from home, or as a form of tourist entertainment. Approximately 60% of clients in both data sets lived in the City of Birmingham, and 83–95% within the West Midlands Regional Health Authority boundaries. (cited by Ryan, 1991: 162)

However, whether or not because of the emergence of more liberal attitudes, more research or simply a growth of the phenomenon to new groups of clients (including women), these conclusions might now be questioned. In countries such as Australia, where legalisation has occurred, there is evidence that specific areas are successful in attracting clients. In some cities, such as Auckland in New Zealand, it has become evident that a process of licensing massage parlours has created a more open situation, and a de facto openness about sex work was, at the time of writing, being considered by New Zealand legislators in a bill to decriminalise sex work. This bill, at the time of the first reading, had overwhelming support in Parliament.

One factor that has emerged is what might be termed a liberal feminist perspective on sex work. As with many attitudes, a continuum of views may be discerned. At one extreme is a view that sex work is not simply an economically gainful form of employment, but is in fact a liberating force for some women, who nurture both their own sexuality and a sense of masculinity (see for example the work of Kruhse MountBurton, 1995, 1996). For many commentators however, a more pragmatic perspective is that sex work provides financial security for many women who would otherwise face severe financial difficulties when seeking to support families. While not a choice of work for all, it is a perfectly logical decision for many caught in low-income situations. It is at this stage that the argument for decriminalisation occurs. Decriminalisation permits sex workers to enjoy full human rights. They are not doubly penalised for poverty by being declared criminals, a situation often made all the worse by a tendency to take legal action against the generally female sex worker but not against the male client. Additionally, if sex work is decriminalised, it permits easier and open access to medical support facilities, and arguably creates an open situation that makes more difficult the exploitation of those under the age of consent.

It has also become increasingly evident that the 'predatory tourist' seeking sexual pleasures is not always male. As early as 1988, Yamba claimed that the largest group of Africans in Sweden consisted of 1500 Gambian boys 'imported' into Sweden by mature Swedish women who befriended them on holiday. As the Gambian culture tends to disapprove of sexual relations between males and older women, the boys tend to tire of their older girlfriends and seek relationships with girls of their own age. Yamba argues that the result is often that the boys are then thrown out onto the streets (Yamba, 1988). Subsequent work in the Caribbean among beach boys revealed the 'rent a dreadlock' syndrome and the practice of North American and (increasingly) European females of holidaying in the area for purposes of engaging in sexual liaisons. The term 'romance tourism' was coined to describe sexual relationships where payments were made, not by the hour, but in terms of favours and gifts, and where often both males and females would return over a number of years (e.g. see Pruitt & LaFont, 1995; Kempadoo, 1999). In some cultures it appears that males have an expectation that European females who holiday alone or in all-female groups are seeking sex and complex patterns of relationships and motives are exhibited. Cohen (1971) and Bowman (1988) recount how young Palestinian shopkeepers in East Jerusalem gossip about bargaining with wealthy European and American women for sexual favours, and then, in order to establish the required male supremacy after receiving payment, will abuse them. Within Athens, professional playboys, the 'kamakia' (or harpoons) earn money from commissions paid by owners of discos, bars, restaurants and tourist shops for taking female tourists to these outlets. On Rhodes, in 1989, the 'kamakia' formed an association whereby their members carry a card showing a negative AIDS test result; this card also entitles the holder to discounts at local cafes, bars, restaurants and discos.

It can be concluded from this short review that the relationship between prostitution and tourism is complex, and academically the analysis has been evolving from a simple perception that prostitution is criminal in purpose and therefore to be treated as a subset of the crime/tourism relationship. Nonetheless, in Prideaux's (1996) terminology, it can be perceived as part of the hedonistic tourism phenonomenon. In a sense this echoes the earlier assertion listed by Mathieson and Wall (1982: 149) that the processes of 'tourism have created locations and environments which attract prostitutes and their clients', whilst in addition the hedonistic nature of the holiday might also have a role to play. It can be noted that sex has for long been the fourth 's' (the others being 'sun, sea and sand') and sex from a romantic viewpoint has often been utilised in the selling of the holiday product. Equally, the promise, or potential, of sex in a more explicit manner is not unknown in the promotion of holiday products. Nor has it always been the tourist who has been the seeker of sexual pleasure. Another of the stereotypes of the Mediterranean has been that of the 'Latin lover'. From the research that has been undertaken it appears that the practice of prostitution differs in different areas with reference to such factors as:

(1) whether it is locals or people coming from outside the tourist zone who provide the service,
(2) whether it is a service being provided for the indigenous population within a tourist zone with some tourist participation, or
(3) whether it is primarily aimed at tourists.

Equally, not all prostitutes are drawn from poor backgrounds. In the case of the 'cool mimos' of Nairobi, it appears that several are drawn from women with university backgrounds, although a motivation is to obtain money to help finance their studies. If, therefore, there is no consistent impact related to tourism on such practices, it might be argued that there is nothing inherent in tourism per se to cause the problem, but rather that tourism might simply confirm patterns that already exist. Equally, the very flows of tourism to some areas have helped to draw attention to the problem, and may cause counter-measures to be taken against prostitution or, as in the German and Dutch cases, cause it to be regulated.

Conclusions

In looking at the potential impacts of tourism it would appear that a number of variables are important. These include:

(1) the numbers of tourists;
(2) the types of tourists and exhibited behaviours;
(3) the stage of the destination lifecycle reached and tourist development that has taken place;
(4) the differential in economic development between tourist-generating and tourist-receiving zones;
(5) the difference in cultural norms between tourist-generating and tourist- receiving zones;
(6) the physical size of the area, which affects the densities of the tourist population;
(7) the extent to which tourism is serviced by an immigrant worker population;
(8) the degree to which incoming tourists purchase properties;
(9) the degree to which local people retain ownership of properties and tourist facilities;
(10) the attitudes of government bodies;
(11) the beliefs of host communities, and the strength of those beliefs;
(12) the role of intermediaries, and the degree to which those intermediaries identify with tourists or residents;
(13) the degree of exposure to other forces of technological, social and economic change;
(14) the policies adopted with regard to tourist dispersal;
(15) the marketing of the tourist destination and the images that are created of that destination;
(16) the homogeneity of the host society;
(17) the accessibility to the tourist destination;
(18) the original strength of artistic and folkloric practices, and the nature of those traditions;
(19) the current power structures and political processes; and
(20) the equality or inequality of income existing within the resident population;
(21) the degrees of economic and cultural difference between residents and visitors.

It is possible for societies to retain patterns of life that are different from those of visitors. In this respect the Amish and traditional Mennonite communities of the USA and Canada are examples where communities, bound by a strong sense of commonality and purpose, are able to sustain their lifestyles in the very midst of what might be termed 'mainstream North American cultures'. Equally, the Navajo Indians have been able to reassert their lifestyles to the degree that they wish, albeit the discovery of raw materials on their reservations has helped the establishment of economic stability (even though the long-term questions have yet to be answered).

Cultures change because the environment within which the culture exists changes – an environment that is both physical and social. Many of the cultures studied exhibit processes of change independent of those thought to be associated with tourism, and tourism is but one means by which acculturation (borrowing from one culture by another) occurs. However, where tourism might differ from other sources (such as exposure to ideas, images portrayed by mass media and business practices) is in the fact that the source of change is there, physically, in the heart of the host society. It is this factor that has attracted attention, along with the transitory nature of many individual relationships. What may be concluded is that, whilst tourism can be a catalyst for change, the nature of the change cannot always be predicted if host societies are aware of the potential that tourism has for such change, particularly if, at an early stage, they seek to make decisions upon the volume and type of tourism they want. If, however, the host community leaves the development of tourism to outside bodies, in many cases the models of large resort complexes will emerge with the now all-too-familiar refrain of societies reacting to changes that are imposed from without. It is perhaps this factor more than many others that accounts for the differences in tourism development between such areas as, say, the Costa del Sol (with its ready access for tourists) and the Maldive Islands (where tourist flows are restricted to certain islands), or between Nepal (with its fairly open access to tourists) and Bhutan (where only limited numbers of tourists are permitted, and then only in groups). If it is said that the freedoms enjoyed by societies have the price of perpetual vigilance, this is also true of tourism.

Chapter 10

Concluding Words

The previous chapters have argued that the essential component of the tourist product is the tourist experience of a location and its people. In part, the degree of satisfaction gained from that experience relates to the expectations of the tourist, the degree of reality on which those expectations are based, the ability of the tourist to adapt to perceived realities, and the nature of the critical encounters that shape that reality. In a sense, therefore, the previous chapters have looked at three zones, as illustrated in Figure 10.1. These three zones are discussed below.

The tourist-generating zone. This is only in part a geographical entity. It is geographical in the sense that the tourist comes from a place, but that place is also a network of social and political institutions that shape patterns of thought. In addition, it is a resource bank that determines the ability of the tourist to travel.

The tourist receiving zone. Again, whilst this is obviously geographical, it, too, consists of a network of social and political institutions and resources that shape the residents' attitudes towards tourists. With reference to its geographical location, it is not simply the tourist destination itself, but the wider framework within which the zone of interaction resides, and upon which it may draw a migrant labour force and peripheral tourist attractions.

The zone of interaction and interpretation. This is physically the tourist destination zone but, as previously noted, such zones change both temporally and spatially. It is the place of interaction between the tourist and host. It is not simply a geographical entity, but also a psychological and social one that exists within a geographical space.

The tourist-generating zone is the source of demand, whilst the host zone creates a set of resources and attitudes on the part of residents within which the tourist will reside during the holiday period. These tourist inputs begin to interact with the tourist prior to the tourist's arrival, because those social and physical resources will be the basis of an attitude-formation process on the part of the tourist that helps to shape the decision to visit. Obviously, however, the manner in which those resources reach the tourist, through marketing channels and other media, and the way the tourist interprets the data received, is partially dependent on the functioning of the tourist-generating zone. As it is, Figure 10.1 simplifies the previous discussion in that it is seen from the viewpoint of the tourist. It omits, for example, the shaping of the hosts' perceptions of the tourist and the tourist-generating zone. The tourists themselves are transmitters of information about the tourist- generating zone, and their behaviours and attitudes will help shape, in turn, residents' perceptions of that zone in both its geographical and social senses. Indeed it goes further, in that tourist demands and

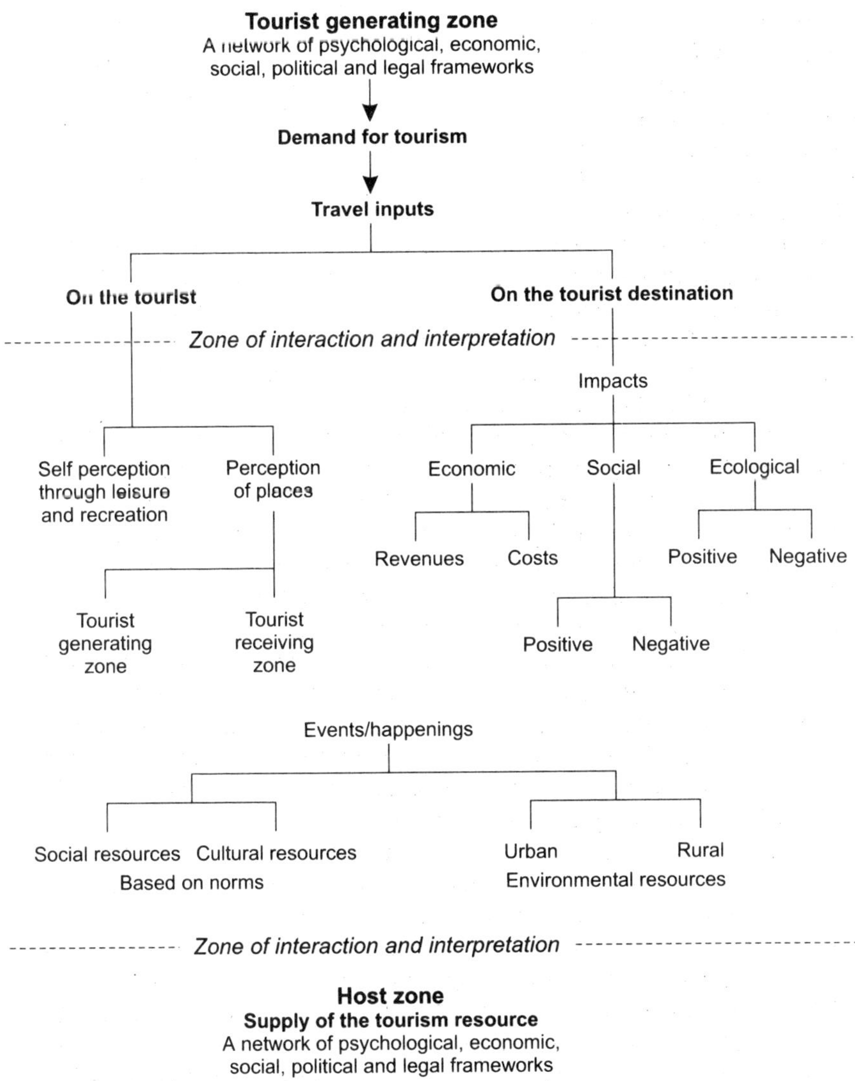

Figure 10.1 Tourism: An overall view

behaviours also help shape residents' own understanding of what constitutes the tourist-receiving zone or space. Nonetheless the diagram reinforces the primacy of the zone of interaction and interpretation that is the essence of the tourism 'product'. It also presents the vulnerability of tourism to future mega-trends that may be pessimistic in nature. The deterioration of the globe's natural environment may mean a decrease in our material standard of living and, in reaction to this, leisure policies may become guided more by responses to environmental, social and economic reforms than simply by a demand for touristic opportunity. Within this framework, the psychological framework may change in terms of the location of recreation and the role of the holiday within leisure. On the other hand, concern with environmental, stress-free living patterns may place leisure and holiday activities within a framework of stress-avoidance techniques – that is, the avoidance of both personal and environmental stress.

Schwaninger (1984, 1989) argues that the following trends are both apparent and long term:

(1) further increasing differentiation and pluralisation of demand;
(2) emergence of new specialised markets and market segments;
(3) decrease of physically and culturally passive forms of vacation in favour of more active pastimes; and
(4) a shift towards maximising individual liberty in recombining elements for custom-made holiday packages (modular product design).

Further, Schwaniger (1984, 1989) argues that the need for the non-standardisation of services arises from:

(1) the quest for self-determination and 'do-it-yourself';
(2) the advanced level of travel experience in the population that leads to a more critical and quality-orientated approach, as well as a growing sophistication and rationality of choice;
(3) an increasing desire to relate to nature;
(4) higher levels of environmental consciousness and sensitivity to the quality of life in general; and
(5) the increasing effort to learn, which often manifests itself in serious attempts to get to know foreign cultures.

All of these themes have emerged in this book, and it can be argued that these trends are not solely determined by the presence of economic growth, and thus could resist a downturn in the economic environment. Yet they all point to the growing importance of 'societal marketing' within the tourism industry. Greater segmentation of markets allied with the increasing sophistication of databases must mean that such marketing will play a greater role in the future of tourism.

However, since 1991 there are signs that some of the assumptions implicit in Schwaninger's list must be re-examined. For much of the 1980s and 1990s, tourism academics seem to have assumed that the general public shared their concerns about environmental issues, and it is certainly true that such issues have been to the forefront of public discussion. But the reality might be that there exists neither a political will nor a public willingness to change patterns of life, and that the much-vaunted 'ecotourism' and 'cultural tourism' movements are simply commodifications wherein tourists justify their explorations in terms of assuaging guilt rather than a serious concern about environmental issues. In short, to revert back to Rivers writing in 1974, there is a crisis in mobility (Rivers, 1974a, 1974b). The changing attitudes towards environmental issues are well expressed in the reluctance by some nations to fully adopt the Kyoto Convention, and there are criticisms that tourism has not just failed to deliver a more understanding world, but is part of the problem. In 2002 Die Arbeitsgemeinschaft für Nachhaltige TourismusEnwicklung (DANTE), a Pan-European network of organisations suggested that tourism had failed in fulfilling ten principles (see http://www.tourism-watch.de/dt/21.dante/content.html). These principles relate to poverty and social justice, sustainable mobility, biodiversity, water conservation, social justice and human rights. Yet one interpretation of these failings is that no one should travel, and the issue is whether that in turn would not exact a cost of its own. Such criticisms of tourism are in part a criticism of the capitalistic structures and processes of globalisation, and demonstrations against globalisation at World Trade Organisations have revealed the depth of feeling. Yet perhaps these demonstrations are reflective of an increasing desperation on the part of those who demonstrate. For the actual behaviour of the 'silent majority' simply demonstrates that people still wish to have their jet travel, their luxury hotels and their visits to natural settings under conditions that show the sights.

Finally, it must be noted that, if the nature of the tourism product is an experience of place at a particular time, with either different groups of people or alone, then any study of tourism is bound within a psychological, geographical and cultural milieu. The role of mood in the shaping of the perception of the tourist experience is important (Pearce, 1988; Yardley, 1990). The complexity of the tourist experience becomes increasingly apparent to researchers. Whilst Cohen (1979a, 1979b, 1979c) discussed the concept of authenticity in terms of a gap between perceived and 'objective' authenticity, Pearce (1988), in his work, *The Ulysses Factor,* discussed a nine-stage model of authenticity. Today the emphasis is on 'experiential authenticity' (Wang, 2000). In marketing terms the market has moved from 'market segmentation' to individualism – where each product makes a promise and the individual tourist selects what he or she wants from a range of potential experiences. The package holiday still exists, but is repackaged to meet individual need. Tourism represents a tension between the consumerism and hedonism of a society used to economic progress and the costs of that progress in terms of environmental impact and power inequalities. For optimists the missing item in this scenario, technological change, represents a means by which this tension will be solved. Transport will become more fuel-efficient, alternative sources of power such as wind and solar power are becoming more economical, and the dire forecasts of the Club of Rome about world famine have not been fulfilled. For the pessimists, the technological answers are part of the problem. Genetic modification is to be feared, a world linked by the Internet is a world of both surveillance and the immediate gratification of base wants, and higher needs of a simple nature are perceived to be replaced by empty gloss and advertising hype. Tourism, as a social phenomenon reflects all of these tensions. It can offer the life-changing cathartic moment, and the drunken hedonism of the moment. From a purely academic perspective it is these tensions and aspects that create a rich subject for research and analysis. For those concerned with the future of the world, if offers both hope and dismay. What may be stated with any degree of certainty is that it is the nature of the human condition that such tensions will continue, even as the expressions of those tensions change.

References

Adams, R. (1973) Uncertainty in nature, cognitive dissonance, and the perceptual distortion on environmental information. *Economic Geography* 49, 287–297.

Adams, P.D. and Parmenter, B.R. (1995) An applied general equilibrium analysis of the economic effects of tourism in a quite small, quite open economy. *Applied Economics* 27 (10), 985–994.

Agarwal, S. (2002) Restructuring seaside tourism: The resort lifecycle. *Annals of Tourism Research* 29 (1), 25–55.

Aguiló Perez, E. and Juaneda Sampol, C. (2000) Tourist expenditure for mass tourism markets. *Annals of Tourism Research* 27 (3), 624–637.

Aguiló, P.M., Alegre, J. and Riera, A. (2001) Determinants of the price of German tourists packages on the island of Mallorca. *Tourism Economics* 7 (1), 59–74.

Ajzen, I. (1988) *Attitudes, Personality and Behaviour.* Milton Keynes: Open University Press.

Alderson, F. (1972) *Bicycling: A History.* Newton Abbot: David and Charles.

Allen, R.L., Long, P.T., Perdue, R.R. and Kieselbach, S. (1988) The impact of tourism development on residents' perceptions of community life. *Journal of Travel Research* 27 (1), 16–21.

Allison, W.R. (1996) Snorkeler damage to coral reefs in the Maldive Islands. *Coral Reefs* 15, 215–218.

Allport, G. (1961) *Pattern and Growth in Personality.* New York: Holt, Rinehart and Winston.

Aotearoa Maori Tourism Federation (1995) Report on the current market position of Maori tourism product. Rotorua: Aotearoa Maori Tourism Federation.

Aotearoa Maori Tourism Federation (1996) Report on the current market position of Maori tourism product. Rotorua: Aotearoa Maori Tourism Federation.

Ap, J. (1995) Residents' perceptions on tourism impacts. *Annals of Tourism Research* 19 (4), 665–690.

Aramberri, J. (2000) Night market. *Annals of Tourism Research* 27 (1), 241–243.

Aramberri, J. (2001) The host should get lost: Paradigms in the tourism theory. *Annals of Tourism Research* 28 (3), 738–761.

Archer, B. (1976) Uses and abuses of multipliers. In G.E. Gearing, W.W. Swart and T. Var (eds) *Planning for Tourism Development: Quantitative Approaches* (pp. 115–132). New York: Praeger.

Archer, B. (1977) Tourism multipliers: The state of the art. *Bangor Occasional Papers in Economics* 10. Cardiff: University of Wales Press.

Archer, B.H. (1980) Forecasting demand. Quantitative and intuitive techniques. *International Journal of Tourism Management* 1 (1), 1–12 summarises this early work.

Archer, B.H. and Owen, C.B. (1971) Towards a tourist regional multiplier. *Regional Studies* 5, 289–294.

Arell, N. (2000) The evolution of tourism in the Tärna Mountains: Arena and actors in a periphery. In F. Brown and D. Hall (eds) *Tourism in Peripheral Areas* (pp.114–132). Clevedon: Channel View Publications.

Asplet, M. and Cooper, M. (2000) Cultural designs in New Zealand souvenir clothing: The question of authenticity. *Tourism Management* 21 (3), 307–312.

Baloglu, S. (1999) A path analytic model of visitation intention involving information sources, socio-psychological motivations and destination image. *Journal of Travel and Tourism Marketing* 8 (3), 81–90.

Barkham, R. (1973) Recreational carrying capacity: A problem of perception. *Area* 5, 218–222.

Barker, M., Page, S.J. and Meyer, D. (2002) Evaluating the impact of the 2000 America's Cup on Auckland, New Zealand. *Event Management* 7 (2), 79–92.

Barrett, F. (1988) Have a nice day, Boyo! *Independent*, 2 January.

Barrett, F. (1989) On the Algarve's road to ruin. *Independent*, 22 July, p. 45.

Barton, K., Booth, K., Ward, J., Simmons, D.G. and Fairweather, J.R. (1998) Visitor and New Zealand fur seal interactions. Kaikoura case study. Report No. 9/1998. Canterbury, NZ: Lincoln University Tourism Research and Education Centre.

BBC (1999) BA gives air rage 'yellow card'. On WWW at http://news.bbc.co.uk/1/hi/uk/162805.stm.

BBC News (2001) Airtours axes jobs. 27 November. On WWW at http://news.bbc.co.uk/hi/english/business/newsid_1678000/1678277.stm.

Becken, S. (2001) Energy use in the New Zealand tourism sector. Unpublished PhD thesis, Lincoln University Tourism Research and Education Centre.

Becker, C., Murrmann, K.S., Murrmann, F.K. and Cheung, W.G. (1999) A pancultural study of restaurant services expectations in the United States and Hong Kong. *Journal of Hospitality and Tourism Research* 23 (3), 235–255.

Beddoe, C., Hall, C.M. and Ryan, C. (2001) *The Incidence of the Sexual Exploitation of Children.* Melbourne: World Tourism Organisation.

Beeton, S. (1999) Visitors to National Parks: Attitudes of walkers to commercial horseback tours. *Pacific Tourism Review* 3 (1), 49–60.

Benny Dorm (pseudonym) (1988) *Beach Party: The Last Resort.* London: Hodder and Stoughton.

Bentley, T.A., Page, S.J. and Laird, I.S. (2000) Safety in New Zealand's adventure tourism industry: The client accident experience of adventure tourism operators. *Journal of Travel Medicine* 7 (5), 239–245.

Berg, P. (1990) A Green City program with a bioregional perspective: Developing the San Francisco Green City plan. In D. Gordon (ed.) *Green Cities: Ecologically Sound Approaches to Urban Space.* Montreal: Black Rose Books.

Bitner, M.J., Booms, B.H. and Tetreault, M. (1990) The service encounter: Diagnosing favorable and unfavorable incidents. *Journal of Marketing* 54, January, 71–84.

Bjorklund, R. and Philbrick, A.K. (1972) Spatial configurations of mental process. Cited in A. Mathieson and G. Wall, *Tourism: Economic, Physical and Economic Impacts* (1982) Harlow: Longmans.

Black, J. (1992) *The British Abroad. The Grand Tour in the Eighteenth Century.* Stroud: Sutton Publishing.

Blake, B. and Beecher, A. (1992) *The New Key to Costa Rica.* Costa Rica: Ulysses Press.

Bland, R. (1987) Low pay in the Cornish tourism industry. *Independent*, 14 July, Letters page.

Boniface, P. (2001) *Dynamic Tourism.* Clevedon: Channel View Publications.

Boorstin, D.J. (1961) *The Image: Guide to Pseudo-Events in America.* New York: Harper and Row.

Boorstin, D.J. (1962) *The Image or What Happened to the American Dream.* Harmondsworth: Pelican Books.

Bordieu, P. (1978) Sport, status and style. *Sport History Review* 30 (1), 1–26.

Boswell, J. (1766/1955) *The Private Papers of James Boswell. Boswell on the Grand Tour: Italy, Corsica, France 1765–66* (F. Brady and F. Pottle, eds). London: William Heinemann.
Bowler, I. and Warburton, P. (1986) An experiment in the analysis of cognitive images of the environment: The case of water resources in Leicestershire. *Occasional Papers* 14. Leicester: Leicester University Geography Department.
Bowman, G. (1988) Impacts of tourism. Paper from the Conference on the Anthropology of Tourism (T. Selwyn, ed.). London: Froebel College.
Breen, M. (1988) Olympics fuel a dream more potent than fear of AIDS. *Guardian*, 26 July.
Brown, F. (1998) *Tourism Reassessed: Blight or Blessing?* Oxford: Butterworth-Heinemann.
Brown, L. (2000) *Sex Slaves: The Trafficking of Women in Asia.* London: Virago Press.
BTA (1996) Tourism intelligence reports (October). London: British Tourist Authority.
BTA (1997) Tourism intelligence reports (October). London: British Tourist Authority.
BTA (2001) A summary analysis of how markets (by purpose of visit) performed during and after the Gulf (1991) and Libyan (1986) conflicts. London: British Tourist Authority.
Brownrigg, M. and Greig, M.A. (1976) Tourism and regional development. *Speculative Paper* 5. Edinburgh: University of Edinburgh, Fraser of Allander Institute.
Buhalis, D. (2000) Relationships in the distribution channel of tourism: Conflicts between hoteliers and tour operators in the Mediterranean region. *International Journal of Hospitality & Tourism Administration* 1 (1), 113–139.
Buhalis, D. (2001) Tourism in Greece: Strategic analysis and challenges. *Current Issues in Tourism* 4 (5), 440–480.
Burgan, B. and Mules, T. (1992) Economic impact of sporting events. *Annals of Tourism Research* 19 (4), 700–711.
Burgan, B. and Mules, T. (2001) Reconciling cost–benefit and economic impact assessment for event tourism. *Tourism Economics* 7 (4), 321–330.
Burkhart, A. and Medlik, S. (1974) *Tourism, Past, Present and Future.* London: Heinemann.
Burns, J.P.A., Hatch, J. and Mules, T.J. (1986) *The Adelaide Grand Prix: The Impact of a Special Event.* Adelaide: University of Adelaide, Centre for South Australian Economic Studies.
Butler, R. (1980) The concept of a tourism area cycle of evolution. *Canadian Geographer* 24 (1), 5–12.
Butynski, T.M. and Kalina, J. (1998) Gorilla tourism: A critical look. In E.J. Milner-Gullard and R. Mace (eds) *Conservation of Biological Resources* (pp. 82–91). Oxford: Blackwell.
Buzard, J. (1993) *The Beaten Track.* Oxford: Oxford University Press.
Cai, L.A., Hu. B. and Feng, R. (2001) Domestic tourism demand in China's urban centres: Empirical analyses and marketing implications. *Journal of Vacation Marketing* 8 (1), 64–74.
Carbyn, L.N. (1974) Wolf population fluctuations in Jasper National Park, Alberta, Canada. *Biological Conservation* 6 (2), 94–101.
Caribbean Tourism Research Centre (1984) *A Study of Linkages Between Tourism and Local Agriculture.* Barbados: Caribbean Tourism Research Centre.
Carlyle, T. (1843/1981) *Past and Present.* Oxford: Clarendon Press.

Cater, E. (1988) The development of tourism in the least developed countries. In B. Goodall and G. Ashworth (eds) *Marketing in the Tourism Industry.* London: Croom Helm.

Ceballos-Lascurain, H. (1987). Estudio de prefactibilidad socioeconómica del turismo ecológico y anteproyecto arquitectónico y urbanístico del Centro de Turismo Ecológico de Sian Ka'an, Quintana Roo. Unpublished study conducted for SEDUE, Mexico.

Cessford, G. (2002) Devising a visitor satisfaction monitoring system. Paper from the Eco-tourism: Mountains and Natural Areas Conference, Otago University, 27–29 August.

Chadwick, R.A. (1981) Some notes on the geography of tourism: A comment. *Canadian Geographer* 25 (2), 191–197.

Cheong, R., Williams, P., Hobson, J.S.P (1995) The virtual threat to travel and tourism: Virtual reality and tourism, fact or fantasy? *Tourism Management* 16 (6), 417–427.

Chittenden, M. (1989) Drink, fight, drop: It's summertime in Spain. *Sunday Times,* 30 July.

Choy, D. (1995) The quality of employment. *Tourism Management* 16 (2), 129–138.

Christaller, W. (1964) Some considerations of tourism location in Europe: The peripheral regions, underdeveloped countries, recreation areas. *Papers of the Regional Science Association* 12, 95–105.

Clark, P.J. and Evans, F.C. (1955) On some aspects of spatial patterns in biological populations. *Science* 121, 101–119.

Clark, R.N. and Stankey, G.H. (1979) The recreation opportunity spectrum: A framework for planning, management and research. General Technical Report PNW-98. Oregon: Department of Agriculture, Pacific Northwest Forest and Range Experiment Station.

Clarke, J. (1997) A framework of approaches to sustainable tourism. *Journal of Sustainable Tourism* 5 (3), 224–233.

Clift, S. and Grabowski, P. (1997) *Tourism and Health: Risks, Research and Responses.* London: Pinter.

Clift, S. and Page, S.J. (1996) *Health and the International Tourist.* London: Routledge.

Cohen, E. (1971) Arab boys and tourist girls in a mixed Jewish–Arab community. *International Journal of Comparative Sociology* 12, 217–233.

Cohen, E. (1972) Towards a sociology of international tourism. *Social Research* 39 (1), 164–182.

Cohen, E. (1974) Who is a tourist? A conceptual classification. *Sociological Review* 22, 527–553.

Cohen, E. (1979a) Phenomenology of tourist experiences. *Sociology* 13, 179–201.

Cohen, E. (1979b) Rethinking the sociology of tourism. *Annals of Tourism Research* 6 (1), 18–35.

Cohen, E. (ed.) (1979c) Sociology of tourism. *Annals of Tourism Research* 6 (1), 17–194.

Cohen, E. (1982a) Marginal paradises. *Annals of Tourism Research* 9 (2), 190–227.

Cohen, E. (1982b) Thai girls and Farang men: The edge of ambiguity. *Annals of Tourism Research* 9 (3), 403–428.

Cohen, E. (1987) The tourist as victim and protege of law enforcing agencies. *Leisure Studies* 6 (2), May, 181–198.

Cohen, J.H. (2001) Textile, tourism and community development. *Annals of Tourism Research* 28 (2), 378–398.

Cohen N. (1989) Pennine Way to put down carpet against erosion. *Sunday Times,* 1 September.

Collinge, M. (1988) *The Size of the Opportunity.* Proceedings of Waterside 2000. International Congress on the Rejuvenation and Development of Waterfronts (pp. 10–19). Bristol: Bristol City Council.

Conference Board of Canada (1990) *The Impact of GST on Tourism in Canada.* Ottawa: Tourism Canada

Cook, T. (1872/1998) *Letters from the Sea and from Foreign Lands, Descriptive of a Tour Round the World.* Reprinted 1998. London: Routledge/Theommes Press and the Thomas Cook Archives.

Cooper, A. and Wilson, A. (2002) Extending the relevance of TSA research for the UK: General equilibrium and spillover analysis. *Tourism Economics* 8 (1), 7–37.

Cooper, C.P. (1981) Spatial and temporal patterns of tourist behaviour. *Regional Studies* 15 (5), 359–371.

Cooper, C., Fletcher, J., Gilbert, D. and Wanhill, S. (1993) *Tourism: Principles and Practice.* London: Pitman Publishing.

Cooper, C.P. and Jackson, S. (1989) Destination lifecycle: The Isle of Man case study. *Annals of Tourism Research* 16 (3), 377–398.

Cossar, J., Reid, D., Fallon, R., Bell, E., Riding, M., Follett, E., Dow, B., Mitchell, S. and Grist, N. (1990) A cumulative review of studies on travelers, their experiences of illness and the implications of these findings. *Journal of Infection* 21 (1), 27–42.

Countryside Commission (1989) *Forests for the Community* (CCP 270). Manchester: Countryside Commission Publications.

Coventry, N. (2002a) Defending research gap. *Inside Tourism* 396, 4 April.

Coventry, N. (2002b) TNZ refreshingly blunt with industry! *Inside Tourism* 398, 18 April.

Craik, J. (2001) Cultural tourism. In N. Douglas, N. Douglas and R. Derrett (eds) *Special Interest Tourism* (pp. 113–139). Brisbane: John Wiley and Sons.

Crabtree, A, O'Reilly, P. and Worboys, G. (2002) Setting a worldwide standard for ecotourism: Sharing expertise in ecotourism certification, developing an international ecotourism standard. Quebec: World Ecotourism Summit.

Crang, M. (1999) Knowing, tourism and practices of vision. In D. Crouch (ed.) *Leisure/Tourism Geographies: Practices and Geographical Knowledge* (pp. 238–256). Durham: University of Durham.

Crawshaw, C. and Urry, J. (1997) Tourism and the photographic eye. In C. Rojek and J. Urry (eds) *Touring Cultures: Transformations of Travel and Theory* (pp. 176–195). London: Routledge.

Crompton, J. (1979) Motivations for pleasure vacations. *Annals of Tourism Research* 6 (4), 408–424.

Crompton, J. and McKay, S.L. (1994) Measuring the economic impact of festivals and events: Some myths, misapplications and ethical dilemmas. *Festival Management and Event Tourism* 2 (1), 33–43.

Crouch, G. (1992) Effect of income and price on international tourism. *Annals of Tourism Research* 19 (4), 643–665.

Csikzentmihalyi, M. (1975) *Beyond Boredom and Anxiety.* San Francisco, CA: Josey-Bass.

Csikszentmihalyi, M. and Csikszentmihalyi, I.S. (1988) *Optimal Experiences: Psychological Studies of Flows of Consciousness.* New York: Cambridge University Press.

Cullen, R. (1986) Himalayan mountaineering expedition garbage. *Environmental Conservation* 13 (4), 293–297.

Dallington, R. (1605?) *A Method for Travill. Shewed by taking the view of France. As it sttoode in the yeare of our Lord 1598.* London.

Daniel, Y.P. (1996) Tourism dance performances: Authenticity and creativity. *Annals of Tourism Research* 23 (4), 780–797.

Dann, G. (2000) Overseas holiday hotels for the elderly: Total bliss or total institution. In M. Robinson, P. Long, N. Evans, R. Sharpley and J. Swarbrooke (eds) *Reflections on International Tourism: Motivations, Behaviour and Tourist Types* (pp. 83–94). Sunderland: University of Northumbria/Business Education Books.

Davies, B. and Mangan, J. (1992) Family expenditure on hotels and holidays. *Annals of Tourism Research* 19 (4), 691–699.

Davison, J. (1989) Strife begins at 40 for the jaded package. *Sunday Times*, 3 September, p. A11.

De Beer, E.S. (1975) The literature of travel in the seventeenth century. *Annual Report of Hakluyt Society* 1–6.

De Kadt, E. (1979) *Tourism: Passport to Development*. New York: Oxford University Press.

Dearden, P. (1989) Towards serving visitors and managing our resources. Paper in Proceedings of a North American Workshop on Visitor Management in Parks and Protected Areas, University of Waterloo Tourism Research and Education Centre, February 14–17.

Dearden, P. and Rollins, R. (1990) Planning and management of parks and protected areas in Canada: The future. Paper delivered at the 6th Canadian Congress on Leisure Research, University of Waterloo.

Debbage, K. (1991) Spatial behavior in a Bahamian resort. *Annals of Tourism Research* 18 (2), 251–268.

Delaney, J. (1999) *Geographic Information Systems: An Introduction*. Melbourne: Oxford University Press.

Dellaert, B.G.C., Ettema, D.F. and Lindh, C. (1998) Multi-faceted tourist travel decisions: A constraint-based conceptual framework to describe tourists' sequential choices of travel components. *Tourism Management* 19 (4), 313–320.

Denis, D.H. (1989) Attitudes towards holiday destinations. Unpublished paper, University of Saskatchewan College of Commerce.

Denzin, N.K. and Lincoln, Y.S. (1994) *Handbook of Qualitative Research*. Thousand Oaks: Sage Publications.

Department for Culture, Media and Sport (1999) *Tomorrow's Tourism: A Growth Industry for the New Millennium*. London: Department for Culture, Media and Sport.

DOE (1980) *Development Control Policy and Practice*. Circular 22/80. London: HMSO.

DOE (1987) *Awards of Costs and Planning Procedures*. Circular 2/87. London: HMSO.

Downward, P. and Lumsden, L. (2000) The demand for day-visits: An analysis of visitor spending. *Tourism Economics* 6 (3), 251–261.

Doxey, G.V. (1975) A causation theory of visitor-resident irritants: Methodology and research inference. Paper given at 6th Travel Research Association Conference, San Diego.

Draper, D. (1997) Touristic development and water sustainability in Banff and Canmore, Alberta, Canada. *Journal of Sustainable Tourism* 5 (3), 183–212.

DTLR (2002) *Decision to Approve the Heathrow Terminal Five and Associated Planning Applications*. Department of Transport, Local Government and the Regions (UK).

Duffus, D.A. and Dearden, P. (1990) Non-consumptive wildlife-oriented recreation: A conceptual framework. *Biological Conservation* 53 (3), 213–231.

Duffy, R. (2002) *A Trip Too Far: Ecotourism, Politics and Exploitation*. London: Earthscan Publications.

Dunn, W. and Goldsworthy, A. (1997) Report and recommendations on the Port Phillip Bay commercial dolphin swim tours. Report to the Department of Natural Resources and Environment, Victorian Government, Victoria, Australia.

Dunn, W. and Goldsworthy, A. (1998) Report and recommendations on the Port Phillip Bay commercial dolphin swim tours. Report to the Department of Natural Resources and Environment, Victorian Government, Victoria, Australia.

Dunn, W. and Goldsworthy, A. (2000) Behavioural responses of bottlenose dolphins (*Tursiops truncatus*) to dolphin swim tour vessels in southern Port Phillip Bay, Victoria. Poster presentation at Australian Marine Science Association Conference, Sydney.

Durrell, G (1989) Impressions in the sand: Corfu. *Sunday Times* colour magazine, 2 July.

Dwyer, L. (2000) Economic contribution of tourism to Andhra Pradesh, India. *Tourism Recreation Research* 25 (3), 91–102.

Dwyer, L. and Forsyth, P. (1998) Economic significance of cruise tourism. *Annals of Tourism Research* 25 (2), 393–415.

Dwyer, L., Forsyth, P., Madden, J. and Spurr, R. (in press) Economic impacts of inbound tourism under different assumptions about the macroeconomy. *Current Issues in Tourism.*

Dyos, H.J. and Aldcroft, D.H. (1969) *British Transport: An Economic Survey.* Leicester: Leicester University Press.

Echtner, C.R. and Ritchie, J.B.R. (1991) The meaning and measurement of destination image. *The Journal of Tourism Studies* 2 (2), 2–12.

Eckert, R.E. Jr, Wood, M.K., Blackburn, W.H. and Petersen, F.F. (1979) Impacts of off-road vehicles on infiltration and sediment production of two desert soils. *Journal of Range Management* 32, 394–397.

Economist Intelligence Unit (1979) International tourism development forecasts to 1990. *Special Report* 62. London: EIU.

ECTWT (1986) *Third World People and Tourism: Approaches to a Dialogue.* Tonbridge: ECTWT and Third World Tourism Ecumenical European Net.

Edwards, J. (1987) The UK heritage coast: An assessment of the ecological impacts of tourism. *Annals of Tourism Research* 14 (1), 71–87.

Edwards, P. (1998) Leisure and value for time. In WTO *Changes in Leisure Time: The Impact on Tourism* (pp. 145–151). Madrid: World Tourism Organisation.

Elroy, J. and Alburqueque, L. (1986) The tourism demonstration effect in the Caribbean. *Journal of Travel Research* 25 (2), 31–34.

Elson, R. (1976) Activity space and recreational spatial behaviour. *Town Planning Review* 47, 241–255.

Emery, F. (1981) Alternative futures in tourism. *International Journal of Tourism Management* 2 (1), 49–67.

Espiner, S.R. (2001) Visitor perception of natural hazards at New Zealand tourism attractions. *Pacific Tourism Review: An Interdisciplinary Journal* 4 (4), 179–200.

Espiner, S. (2002) The phenomenon of risk and its management in natural resource recreation and tourism settings: A case study of Fox and Franz Josef Glaciers, Westland National Park, New Zealand. Unpublished PhD thesis, Lincoln University.

ETB (1992) Software program: Applications of the Huff Spatial Model for forecasting numbers and cash flows attending sports and other recreational centres. London: English Tourist Board.

European Commission (2000a) Developing a new bathing water policy. Communication from the Commission to the European Parliament and the Council. COM (2000) 860 Brussels: EU. On WWW at http://europa.eu.int/comm/environment/docum/00860_en.htm.

European Commission (2000b) Council directive on bathing water quality. 76/160/EEC, subsequently revised in COM (2002) 581. Brussels: EU.

Evans, T.R. (1993) Residents' perceptions of tourism in New Zealand communities. Unpublished masters thesis, University of Otago, New Zealand.

Fagan, D. (1989) Cheap, exotic outpost of 70s, Phuket is now a tourist hotspot. *Toronto Globe and Mail*, 19 December, p. B23.

Fairgray, D. (2001) Introduction to the international tourism forecasts to New Zealand. Presentation at the 4th New Zealand Tourism and Hospitality Research Conference, Auckland University of Technology, 7 December.

Fairweather, J.R. and Swaffield, S.R. (2001) Visitor experiences of Kaikoura, New Zealand: An interpretative study using photographs of landscapes and Q method. *Tourism Management* 22 (3), 219–228.

Farvar, M.T. (1984) *The Careless Technology: Ecology and International Development.* Record of the Conference on the Ecological Aspects of International Development convened by the Conservation Foundation and the Centre for Biology of Natural Systems, Washington University, December 8–11.

Farver J.A.M. (1984) Tourism and employment in the Gambia. *Annals of Tourism Research* 11 (2), 249–265.

Fennell, D. and Eagles, P. (1990) Ecotourism in Costa Rica: A conceptual framework. *Journal of Parks and Recreational Administration* 8 (1), 23–34.

Fines, K.D. (1968) Landscape evaluation: A research project in east Essex. *Regional Studies* 2 (1), 41–55.

Fishbein, M. (1967) *Readings in Attitude Theory and Measurement*. New York: John Wiley and Sons.

Flook, A. (2001) The changing structure of international trade in tourism services, the tour operators perspective, Geneva, 22 February. On WWW at http://www.wto.org/english/tratop (April 12, 2002).

Forster, E.M. (1908/1988) *Room with a View.* New York: Bantam Classics.

Frechtling, D. (1996) *Practical Tourism Forecasting*. Oxford: Butterworth Heinemann.

Freeman, D. and Sultan, E. (1997) The economic impacts of tourism in Israel: A multi-regional input–output analysis. *Tourism Economics* 3 (4), 341–360.

Fussell, P. (1982) *Abroad: British Literary Travelling Between the Wars.* New York: Oxford University Press.

Galicia, E. and Baldassarre, G.A. (1997) Effects of motorised tour boats on the behaviour of non-breeding American flamingos in Yucatan, Mexico. *Conservation Biology* 1 (5), 1159–1165.

Gallarza, M.G., Saura, I.G. and García, H.C. (2002) Destination image: Towards a conceptual framework. *Annals of Tourism Research* 29 (1), 56–78.

Getz, D. (1997) *Event Management and Event Tourism*. New York: Cognizant Communications.

Getz, D. (2000) *Explore Wine Tourism: Management, Development and Destinations.* New York: Cognizant Communications.

Getz, D. and Jamal, T.B. (1997) The environment-community symbiosis: A case for collaborative tourism planning. *Journal of Sustainable Tourism* 2 (3), 152–173.

Gibson, H. and Yiannakos, A. (2002) Tourist roles: Needs and the lifecourse. *Annals of Tourism Research* 29 (2), 358–383.

Glyptis, S. (1981) People at play in the countryside. *Geography* 66 (4), 277–285.

Gove, M. (2001) Breed or die out, *The Times*, 15 November, 2nd section, pp.2–3.

Granger, W. (1990) Naturalizing existing parklands. In D. Gordon (ed.) *Green Cities: Ecologically Sound Approaches to Urban Space*. Montreal: Black Rose Books.

Green Globe 21 (2001) The news, November 2. On WWW at www.Green-Globe.com.

Greenwood, D.J. (1977) Culture by the pound: An anthropological perspective on tourism as cultural commodization. In V.L Smith (ed.) *Hosts and Guests: An Anthropology of Tourism*. Philadelphia: University of Pennsylvania Press.

Gregory, C. (1989) Life-blood of the nation's treasures. *Independent*, 13 May.

Guest, P. (1988) The American Dream that came true, at a price. *Independent*, 24 December.

Guitart, C. (1982) UK charter flight package holidays to the Mediterranean: A statistical analysis. *Tourism Management* 3 (1), March, 16–39.

Gunn, C. (1979) *Tourism Planning*. New York: Rusak.

Gyte, D.M. (1988) Repertory grid analysis of images of destination: British tourists in Mallorca. *Trent Working Papers in Geography*. Nottingham: Nottingham Polytechnic.

Hall, C.M. (2000) Rethinking collaboration and partnership: A public policy perspective. In B. Bramwell and B. Lane (eds) *Tourism Collaboration and Partnerships: Politics, Practice and Sustainability* (pp. 143–158). Clevedon: Channel View Publications.

Hall, C.M. and Jenkins, J.M. (1995) *Tourism and Public Policy*. London: Routledge.

Hall, C.M. and Page, S.J. (1999) *The Geography of Tourism and Recreation: Environment, Place and Space*. London: Routledge.

Hall, E.T. (1984) *The Dance of Life: The Other Dimension of Time*. New York: Doubleday.

Hallenstein, D. (1989) Scientists wring their hands as algae tide grows. *Sunday Times*, 16 July, p. A21.

Hamilton, A. (1988) Tourist had 500 lizards in his luggage. *Independent*, 17 December.

Hammitt, W.E. and Cole, D.N. (1987) *Wild-life Recreation: Ecology and Management*. New York: Wiley Interscience.

Hammitt, W.E. and Cole, D.N. (1998) *Wild-life Recreation: Ecology and Management* (2nd edn). New York: Wiley.

Hanna, M. (1976) *Tourism Multipliers in Britain*. London: London.

Hansen, C. and Jensen. S. (1996) The impact of tourism on employment in Denmark: Different definitions, different results. *Tourism Economics* 2 (4), 283–302.

Hartley, E.A. (1976) Man's effects on the stability of alpine and sub-alpine vegetation in Glacier National Park, Montana. PhD dissertation, Duke University, North Carolina.

Hawkins, J.P. and Roberts, C.M. (1993) Effects of recreational scuba diving on coral reefs: Trampling on reef flat communities. *Journal of Applied Ecology* 30 (1), 25–30.

Haywood, K.M. (1992) Revisiting resort cycle. *Annals of Tourism Research* 19 (2), 351–354.

Healy, R.G. (1994) 'Tourist merchandise' as a means of generating local benefits from eco-tourism. *Journal of Sustainable Tourism* 2 (3), 137–151.

Henshall-Momsen, J. (1986) Recent changes in Caribbean tourism with special reference to St Lucia and Montserrat. *Trent University Occasional Paper* 11. Ontario: Trent University.

Heredotus. (465?/1954) *The Histories* (A. de Sélincourt, trans.). Harmondsworth: Penguin Classics.

Hernandez, S.A., Cohen, J. and Garcia, H.L. (1996) Residents' attitudes toward an instant resort enclave. *Annals of Tourism Research* 23 (4), 755–780.

Heron, R.P. (1989) *Community Leisure and Cultural Vitality.* Rotterdam: Stichting Recreatie.

Heron, R.P. (1990) The institutionalization of leisure: Cultural interpretation. Paper given at 6th Canadian Congress on Leisure Research, University of Waterloo.

Hewson, D. (1989) The crackdown on the Costas. *Sunday Times,* 18 March.

Hibbert, C. (1987) *The Grand Tour.* London: Channel 4 TV/Thames Methuen.

Higham, J.E.S. (1998) Tourists and albatrosses: The dynamics of tourism at the Northern Royal Albatross Colony, Taiaroa Head, New Zealand. *Tourism Management* 19 (6), 521–533.

Higham, J.E.S. (2001) Managing ecotourism at Taiaroa Royal Albatross Colony. In M. Shackley (ed.) *Flagship Species: Case Studies in Wildlife Tourism Management* (pp. 17–30). Burlington, VT: The International Ecotourism Society.

Higham, R. (1960) *Britain's Imperial Air Routes 1918–1939*. London: Foulis and Co.

Hill, C. (1993) Planning for prostitution: An analysis of Thailand's sex industry. In M. Tushen in and B. Halcomb (eds) *Women's Lives and Public Policy: The International Experience* (pp. 133–143). Westport: Greenwood Press.

HMSO (1969) *Development of Tourism Act.* London: HMSO.

HMSO (1987) A vision for England. *Employment Gazette,* May, 233–237.

Hobson, J.S.P. and Williams, P. (1997) Virtual reality: The future of leisure and tourism? *World Leisure & Recreation* 39 (3), 19–22.

Hobson, P.J.S. and Christensen, M. (2001) Cultural and structural issues affecting Japanese tourist shopping behaviour. *Asia Pacific Journal of Tourism Research* 6 (1), 37–45.

Hollinshead, K. (1999) Surveillance of the worlds of tourism: Foucault and the eye-of-power. *Tourism Management* 20 (1), 7–23.

Holmes, D.O. and Dobson, H.E.M. (1976) *Ecological Carrying Capacity Research: Yosemite National Park, Part 1: The Effects of Human Trampling and Urine on Sub alpine Vegetation, and Survey of Past and Present Backcountry Use.* Berkeley: California University.

Honey, M. (1999) *Ecotourism and Sustainable Development: Who Owns Paradise?* Washington, DC: Island Press.

Hoosie, L. (1990) Gringos in paradise. *Business Magazine, Toronto Globe and Mail,* February, pp. 65–70.

House of Commons Education and Employment Committee (1999). Second report: Part-time working (Vol. 1). Report and Proceedings of the Committee, Session 1998–1999. London: The Stationery Office.

Hovinen, G. (1981) A tourist cycle in Lancaster County, Pennsylvania. *Canadian Geographer* 3: 283–286.

Hovinen, G. (2002) Revisiting the destination life cycle model. *Annals of Tourism Research* 29 (1), 209–230.

Huff, D.L. (1966) A programmed solution for approximating an optimum retail location. *Land Economics* 42: 293–303.

Huybers, T. and Bennett, J. (2000) Impact of the environment on holiday destination choices of prospective UK tourists: Implications for Tropical North Queensland. *Tourism Economics* 6 (1), 21–46.

IMS (1988) *Productivity in the Leisure Industry.* London: Institute of Manpower Studies.

Inglis, F. (2000) *The Delicious History of the Holiday.* London and New York: Routledge.

Irving, G.R. (1999) The tourism health interface in New Zealand: Can the health promotion model be applied? Unpublished PhD Thesis, Massey University Department of Management Studies, Auckland.

Institute of Regional Planning and Regional Sciences (1999) *Tourism, Nature Conservation and Development in the Region of Languedoc-Roussillon (Carcassonne, Canal du Midi, Corbières, Nature Park of Haut Languedoc, Leucate, Port-Vendres).* Hanover: Institute of Regional Planning and Regional Sciences, University of Hanover.

Iso-Ahola, S.E. (1982) Towards a social psychology of tourism motivation: A rejoinder. *Annals of Tourism Research* 9, 256–261.

IUCN (The World Conservation Union) (1998) Introduction of non-native species in the Antarctica Treaty Area: An increasing problem. Paper presented to the XXII ATCM Tromso, Norway, May.

Jackman, B. (1988) Quality of the North Sea coastline. *Sunday Times* colour magazine, 11 June.

Jackson, E. and Dunn, E. (1987) *Ceasing Participation in Recreation Activities: An Analysis of Data from the 1984 Public Opinion Survey.* Edmonton: Alberta Recreation and Parks.

Jackson, E. and Dunn, E. (1988) Integrating ceasing participation with other aspects of leisure behavior. *Journal of Leisure Research* 20 (1) 31–45.

Jacobsen, T and Kushcan, J.A. (1986) Alligators in natural areas: Choosing conservation policies consistent with local objectives. *Biological Conservation* 36, 181–196.

Jafari, J. (1981) The unbounded reaches of leisure, recreation: Tourism in the paradigms of play. Paper from 31st AIEST Annual Conference. AIEST vol. 22. Berne, Switzerland.

Jafari, J. (1982) Understanding the structure of tourism. Paper from 32nd AIEST Annual Conference. AIEST vol. 23. St Gallen, Switzerland.

Jamal, A., 2002, Clean up Australia day: Four tonnes of rubbish collected. Press release from the Mayor's Office, Waverley District Council, 22 March.

Jamal, T.B. and Getz, D. (1995) Collaboration theory and community tourism planning. *Annals of Tourism Research* 22 (1), 186–204.

Jamal, T.B. and Getz, D. (1999) Community roundtables for tourism-related conflicts: The dialectics of consensus and process structures. *Journal of Sustainable Tourism* 7 (3/4), 290–313.

Jamal, T.B. and Hollinshead, K. (2001) Tourism and the forbidden zone: The underserved power of qualitative inquiry. *Tourism Management* 22 (1), 63–82.

James, H. (1908/1988) *Portrait of a Lady* (N. Bradbury, ed.). Oxford: Oxford University Press.

James, C. (2002) Forestry code to speed resource consents. *New Zealand Herald*, Business section, 19 February.

Jenkins, A. (2001) The meaning of life. *The Times Magazine*, 24 November, pp. 34–38.

Johnstone, I.M., Coffey, B. and Howard-Williams, C (1985) The role of recreational boat traffic in interlake dispersal of macrophytes: A New Zealand case study. *Journal of Environmental Management* 20 (4), 263–279.

Jones, D.R.W. (1986) Prostitution and tourism. *Occasional Paper* 11. Ontario: Trent University, Department of Geography .

Kahn, R.F. (1972) *Selected Essays in Employment and Growth.* Cambridge: Cambridge University Press.

Kane, E.J. (1974) *Economic Statistics and Econometrics: An Introduction to Quantitative Economics.* New York: Harper and Row.

Kariel, H.G. and Kariel, P.E. (1972) *Explorations in Social Geography.* London: Addison-Wesley Publishing Company.
Katselidis, K. and Dimopoulos, D. (2000) The impact of tourist development on loggerhead nesting activity at Daphni beach, Zakynthos, Greece. In F.A. Abreu-Grobois, R.Biseno-Duenas, R.Marquez-Millan and L.Sarti-Martinez (eds) Proceedings of the 18th International Sea Turtle Symposium (pp. 75–77). NOAA Technical Memorandum NMFS-SEFSC-436.
Kay, T. and Jackson, G. (1990) The operation of leisure constraints. Paper given at 6th Canadian Congress on Leisure Research, University of Waterloo.
Kelly, G.A. (1955) *The Psychology of Personal Constructs.* Norton: New York.
Kempadoo, K. (1999) Continuities and change: Five centuries of prostitution in the Caribbean. In K. Kempadoo (ed.) *Sun, Sex, and Gold: Tourism and Sex Work in the Caribbean* (pp. 3–36). Lanham: Rowman and Littlefield.
Kempadoo, K. and Doezema, J. (eds) (1998) *Global Sex Workers: Rights, Resistance and Redefinition*. London: Routledge.
Keynes, J.M. (1936) *The General Theory of Employment, Interest and Money.* London: MacMillan.
Kermath, B.M and Thomas, R.N. (1992) Spatial dynamics of resorts: Sosúa, Dominican Republic. *Annals of Tourism Research* 19 (2), 173–190.
Kim, S. and Littrell, M.A. (2001) Souvenir buying intentions for self versus others. *Annals of Tourism Research* 28 (3), 638–657.
Kinnell, H. (1989) Prostitutes, their clients and risks of HIV Infection in Birmingham. Occasional paper. Birmingham: Central Birmingham Health Authority.
Ko, T.G. (1999) The issues and implications of escorted shopping tours in a tourist destination region: The case study of Korean package tourists in Australia. *Journal of Travel and Tourism Marketing* 8 (3), 71–80.
Koutsoyiannis, A. (1975) *Modern Microeconomics*. London: MacMillan Press.
Krippendorf, J. (1987) *The Holidaymakers.* Oxford: Heinemann.
Kruhse Mount-Burton, S. (1995) Sex tourism and traditional Australian male identity. In M-F. Lanfant, J.B. Allcock and E.M. Bruner (eds) *International Tourism: Identity and Change*. London: Sage.
Kruhse Mount-Burton, S. (1996) The contemporary client of prostitution in Darwin, Australia. Unpublished PhD thesis, Griffith University, Queensland.
Krut, I. and Gleckman, H. (1998) *ISO 14001: A Missed Opportunity for Sustainable Global Industrial Development*. London: Earthscan.
Kulendran, N. and Witt, S.F. (2001) Cointegration versus least squares regression. *Annals of Tourism Research* 28 (2), 291–311.
Landals, M. and Scotter, G.W. (1974) An ecological assessment of the summit area, Mount Revelstoke National Park. Unpublished report, Canadian Wildlife Service, Edmonton, Alberta.
Law, R. (2000) Back-propagation learning in improving the accuracy of neural network based tourism demand forecasting. *Tourism Management* 21 (4), 331–340.
Lawson, F. and Bond-Bovy, M. (1977) *Tourism and Recreational Development*. London: Architectural Press.
Lawson, R., Williams, J. Young, T. and Cossens, J. (1998) A comparison of residents' attitudes towards tourism in 10 New Zealand destinations. *Tourism Management* 19 (3), 247–256.
Lea, J. (1988) *Tourism and Development in the Third World.* Routledge, London.
Leopold, D. (1969) Landscape aesthetics. *Natural History* 78, 36–45.

Leung, Y-F. and Marion, J.L. (1996) Trail degradation as influenced by environmental factors: A state of knowledge review. *Journal of Soil and Water Conservation* 51, 131–136.

Leung, Y-F. and Marion, J.L. (1999) Assessing trail conditions in protected areas: Application of a problem assessment method in Great Smoky Mountains National Park, USA. *Environmental Conservation* 26 (4), 270–279.

Lever, A. (1987) Spanish tourist migrants: The case of Lloret de Mar. *Annals of Tourism Research* 14 (4), 449–470.

Lewis, B. and Outram, M. (1986) Customer satisfaction with package holidays. In B. Harris (ed.) *Are They Being Served.* London: Philip Allen.

Liddle, M. (1997) *Recreation Ecology.* London: Chapman and Hall

Liddle, M.J. and Scorgie, H.R.A. (1980) The effect of recreation on freshwater plants and animals: A review. *Biological Conservation* 17, 183–206.

Lim, C. and McAleer, M. (2002) Time series forecasts of international travel demand for Australia. *Tourism Management* 23 (4), 389–396.

Lindberg, K. and Johnson, R.L. (1997) Modelling resident attitudes toward tourism. *Annals of Tourism Research* 24 (2), 402–424.

Liu, J.C., Sheldon, P. and Var, T. (1986) A cross-cultural approach to determining resident perception of the impact of tourism on the environment. Conference proceedings (W. Benoy Joseph, ed.). Cleveland, OH. Cleveland State University, Academy of Marketing Science.

Loker-Murphy, L. (1996) Backpackers in Australia: A motivation-based segmentation study. *Journal of Travel and Tourism Marketing* 5 (4), 23–46.

Long, P.T. and Nuckolls, J.S. (1994) Organising resources for rural tourism development: The importance of leadership, planning and technical assistance. *Tourism Recreation Research* 19 (2), 19–34.

Long, P.T., Perdue, R.R. and Allen, L. (1990) Rural resident tourist perceptions and attitudes by community level of tourism. *Journal of Travel Research* 28 (3), 3–9.

Loukissas, P.J. (1982) Tourism's regional development impacts: A comparative analysis of the Greek islands. *Annals of Tourism Research* 9 (4), 523–541.

Lovingood, P.E. and Mitchell, L.S. (1978) The structure of public and private recreational systems: Columbia, South Carolina. *Journal of Leisure Research* 10 (1), 21–36.

Low Pay Unit (1986) *Low Pay and Minimum Wages.* London: Low Pay Unit/ Economic and Social Justice.

Lull, H.W. (1959) Soil compaction on forest and range lands. *USDA Forest Service Miscellaneous Publication* 768. Washington, DC: USDA Forest Service.

Lundtorp, S. and S. Wanhill. (2001) The resort lifecycle theory: Generating processes and estimation. *Annals of Tourism Research* 28 (4), 947–964.

Lunn, N.J. (2001) Arctic tourism: Polar bears and the Churchill experience. In M. Shackley (ed.) *Flagship Species: Case Studies in Wildlife Tourism Management* (pp. 91–98). Burlington, VT: The International Ecotourism Society.

Lynch, K. (1960) *The Image of the City.* Cambridge, MA. MIT Press.

Lyon, A. (1998) The impact of tourist feedings of saltwater crocodiles (*Crocodylus porosus*): A study of the Jumping Crocs Cruise. Unpublished MSc thesis, Northern Territory University, Darwin.

Lyon, T. (1999) Making special events special. *The Cyber-Journal of Sport Marketing.* October. On WWW at www.cjsm.com/default.htm .

MacCannell, D. (1976) *The Tourist: A New Theory of the Leisure Class.* New York: Schocken Books.

MacNaught, T.J. (1982) Mass tourism and the dilemmas of modernisation in Pacific Island communities. *Annals of Tourism Research* 9, 359–381.

Mader, U. (1988) Tourism and the environment. *Annals of Tourism Research* 15 (2), 274–277.

Male, K. (2001) *Good Old Kiwi Baches, and a Few Cribs Too*. Auckland: Tandem Press.

Markwell, K. (1998) Taming the 'chaos of nature': Cultural construction and lived experience in nature-based tourism. Unpublished PhD dissertation, University of Newcastle, Australia.

Marsh, J.S. (1986) Advertising Canada in Japan and Japanese tourism in Canada. In *Canadian Studies of Parks, Recreation and Tourism in Foreign Lands.* Ontario: Trent University, Department of Geography.

Marshall Macklin Monoghan Consulting Group. (1980) *Tourism Development Strategy: Collingwood-Midland-Orillia Zone.* Toronto, ON: Ministry of Tourism and Recreation.

Martin, C. and Witt, S. (1987) Tourism demand forecasting models: A choice of appropriate variable to represent the tourist's cost of living. *Tourism Management* 8 (3), 233–246.

Martin, C. and Witt, S. (1988) Substitute prices in models of tourism demand. *Annals of Tourism Research* 15 (2), 255–268.

Martin, C. and Witt, S. (1989) Forecasting tourism demand: A comparison of the accuracy of several quantitative methods. *International Journal of Forecasting* (5) 1, 1–13.

Maslow, A. (1943/1970) *Motivation and Personality* (2nd edn). New York: Harper.

Mathieson, A. and Wall, G. (1982) *Tourism, Economic, Physical and Social Impacts.* Harlow: Longmans.

Mason, C.F. (1991) *Biology of Freshwater Pollution* (2nd edn). Colchester: Longman Scientific and Technical.

Master, H. and Prideaux, B. (2000) Culture and vacation satisfaction: A study of Taiwanese tourists in South East Queensland. *Tourism Management* 21 (5), 445–449.

Mayo, E.J. and Jarvis, L.P. (1986) Objective distance vs. subjective distance and the attraction of the far off destination. Conference proceedings (W. Benoy Joseph, ed.). Cleveland, OH: Cleveland State University, Academy of Marketing Science.

Mayo, E.J. and Jarvis, L.P. (1981) *The Psychology of Leisure Travel*. Boston, MA: CBI Publishing Co.

Mazanec, J. (1981) The tourism/leisure ratio: Anticipating the limits to growth. *Tourist Review* 36 (4), 2–12.

Mazanec, J.A. (2002) Tourists' acceptance of Euro pricing: Conjoint measurement with random coefficients. *Tourism Management* 23 (3), 245–255.

Mazzocchi, M. and Montini, A. (2001) Earthquake effects on tourism in Central Italy. *Annals of Tourism Research* 28 (4), 1031–1046.

McCleary, W.K., Choi, M.B. and Weaver, A.P. (1998) A comparison of hotel selection criteria between US and Korean business travelers. *Journal of Hospitality and Tourism Research* 22 (1), 25–38.

McCool, S.F. and Cole, D.N. (1997) Experiencing limits of acceptable change: Some thoughts after a decade of implementation. In S.F. McCool and D.N Cole (eds) Proceedings from a Workshop on Limits of Acceptable Change and Related Planning Processes: Progress and Future Directions, University of Montana's Lubrecht Experimental Forest, Missoula, Montana May 20–22, 1997 (pp. 72–78) (General technical Report INT-GTR-371) Ogden, UT: US Department of Agriculture Forest Service, Rocky Mountain Research Station.

McFeters, G.A., Barry, J.P. and Howington, J.P. (1993) Distribution of enteric bacteria in Antarctica seawater surrounding a sewage outfall. *Water Research* 27, 645–650.

McGibbon, J. (2000) *The Business of Alpine Tourism in a Globalising World. An Anthropological Study of International Ski Tourism in the Village of St Anton am Arlberg in the Tirolean Alps.* Rosenheim: Vetterling Druck.

McKercher, B. (1993) Some fundamental truths about tourism: Understanding tourism's social and environmental impacts. *Journal of Sustainable Tourism* 1 (1), 6–16.

McKercher, B. and du Cros, H. (2002) *Cultural Tourism: The Partnership Between Tourism and Cultural Heritage Management.* New York: The Haworth Hospitality Press.

McKenzie, C. (1989) Yellowstone: Green once more. *Toronto Globe and Mail,* 21 October.

McPheters, L.R. and Stronge, W.B. (1974) Crime as an environmental externality of tourism. *Land Economics* 50, 288–292.

Medlik, S. (1985) *Productivity and Tourism: Study for the Confederation of British Industry.* London: CBI.

Medlik, S., (1988) *Tourism and Productivity.* London: British Tourist Authority/English Tourist Board.

Middleton, V.T.C. (1988) *Marketing of Travel and Tourism.* Oxford: Heinemann Professional Publishing.

Mill, R.C. and Morrison, A.M. (1985) *The Tourist System: An Introductory Text.* Englewood Cliffs, NJ: Prentice Hall.

Miller, P. and Robbins, T. (2001) Lost album reveals first holiday snaps. *Sunday Times,* 18 November, p. 20.

Miller, R.R. (2002) Extending the relevance of TSA research for the UK: General equilibrium and spillover analysis. *Tourism Economics* 8 (1), 5–6.

Milligan, J. (1989) Migrant workers in the Guernsey hotel industry. Unpublished thesis, Nottingham Business School, Nottingham Polytechnic.

Milliken, R. (1989) Sun, sand and sewage at Australia's most famous playground. *Independent,* 14 July.

Milman, A. and Pizam, A. (1988) Social impacts of tourism on Central Florida. *Annals of Tourism Research* 15 (2), 191–205.

Miossec, J.M. (1976) Un modele de l'espace touristique. Quoted in D. Pearce *Tourist Development* (1981). Harlow: Longman.

Moorcock, M. (2000) *The Dancers at the End of Time.* Stone Mountain, GA: White Wolf Publishing.

Morgan, K. (2001) Rainforest tourism in Peru's Tambopata Region: Positive benefits for peccaries? In M. Shackley (ed.) *Flagship Species: Case Studies in Wildlife Tourism Management* (pp. 39–50). Burlington, VT: The International Ecotourism Society.

Morgan, S. (1821) *Italy* (3 volumes). London.

Morisita, M. (1957) A new method for the estimation of density by the spacing method. *Seiro-seita* 7, 134–144.

Morley, C. (2000) Demand modelling methodologies: Integration and other issues. *Tourism Economics* 6 (1), 5–19.

Morris, J. (1987) Sick of the tourist roller-coaster. *Independent,* 9 December.

Mosisch, T.D. and Arthington, A.H. (1998) The impacts of power boating and water skiing on lakes and reservoirs. *Lakes and Reservoirs: Research and Management* 3 (1) 1–17.

Mules, T. (2000) Globalisation and the economic impacts of tourism. In B. Faulkner, G. Moscardo and E. Laws (eds) *Tourism in the 21st Century: Lessons from Experience* (pp. 312–327). London: Continuum.

Murphy, P.E. (1978) Preferences and perceptions of urban decision-making groups: Congruence or conflict? *Regional Studies* 12, 749–759.

Murphy, P.E. (1983a) *Tourism in Canada: Selected Issues and Options*. British Columbia: University of Victoria, Department of Geography.

Murphy, P.E. (1983b) Perceptions and attitudes of decision making groups in tourism centres. *Journal of Travel Research* 21 (3), 8–12.

Murphy, P.E. (1985) *Tourism: A Community Approach*. New York: Methuen.

MVA (1987) *Meewasin Valley Authority Development Plan, 1987–1992*. Saskatoon: Meewasin Valley Authority.

Myers, N. (1972) National parks in savannah Africa. *Science* 178, 1255–1263.

National Office of Statistics (2001) *Population Trends* 106, Winter. London: National Office of Statistics.

Newsome, D., Moore, S.A. and Dowling, R.K. (2001) *Natural Area Tourism: Ecology, Impacts and Management*. Clevedon: Channel View Publications.

Niedercom, J.H. and Bechdoldt, B.V. (1966) An economic derivation of the 'gravity law' of spatial interaction. *Journal of Regional Science* 9, 273–282.

North, R. (1989) Scorched earth plan to get back to nature. *Independent*, 23 January, p. 11.

Norton, W. (2000) *Cultural Geography: Themes, Concepts, Analyses*. Ontario: Oxford University Press.

Nova (1990) Poison in the Rockies. Transcript from PBS program broadcast on 29 May.

Nugent, T. (1749) *Grand Tour Containing an Exact Description of Most of the Cities, Towns and Remarkable Places of Europe*. London.

NZPA (2002) Hold call on whale watching. New Zealand Press Association, 11 March.

O'Connell, E. (2002) Male fish fertility affected by endocrine disrupting substances. London: UK Environment Agency.

Office of the Deputy Prime Minister (2001) *Planning: Delivering a Fundamental Change*. Green Paper. London: Office of the Deputy Prime Minister.

O'Grady, R. (1981) *Third World Stopover*. Geneva: World Council of Churches.

Oh, H. (2001) Revisiting importance-performance analysis. *Tourism Management* 22 (6), 617–627.

Ovid (Publius Ovidius Naso) (6?/1965) *Ars Amatoria* (B.P. Moore, trans.). London: The Folio Society.

Page, S.J., Bentley, T.A., Meyer, D. and Chalmers, D.J. (2001) Scoping the extent of tourist road safety: Motor vehicle transport accidents in New Zealand 1982–1996. *Current Issues in Tourism* 4 (6), 503–526.

Page, S.J. and Thorn, K. (1997) Towards sustainable tourism planning in New Zealand: Public sector planning responses. *Journal of Sustainable Tourism* 5 (1), 59–77.

Pamment, M. (2001) Lifestyle and relax. *Sunday Times* style supplement, 18 November, pp. 47–48.

Parasuraman, A., Zeithaml, V.A. and Berry, L.L. (1985) A conceptual model of service quality and its implications for future research. *Journal of Marketing* 49 (4), Fall, 41–50.

Parasuraman, A., Zeithaml, V.A. and Berry, L.L. (1991) Refinement and reassessment of the SERVQUAL scale. *Journal of Retailing* 67 (Winter), 420–450.

Parasuraman, A., Zeithaml, V.A. and Berry, L.L (1994a) Alternative scales for measuring service quality: A comparative assessment based on psychometric and diagnostic criteria. *Journal of Retailing* 70 (3), 201–230.

Parasuraman, A., Zeithaml, V.A. and Berry, L.L (1994b) Moving forward in service quality research: Measuring different customer-expectation levels, comparing alternative scales, and examining the performance-behavioural intentions link. *Marketing Science Institute Working Paper* 94–114, September.

Parasuraman, A., Zeithaml, V.A. and Berry, L.L (1994c) Reassessment of expectations as a comparison standard in measuring service quality: Implications for further research. *Journal of Marketing* 58 (January), 111–124.

Parker, S. (1971) *The Future of Work and Leisure*. New York: Praeger.

Parks Canada (1959) *Planning Considerations: Prince Albert National Park*. Report number 7 2-31959. Ottawa: Parks Canada.

Parks Canada (1988) *Land Use Classifications*. Ottawa: Parks Canada.

Parks, G.B. (1951) Travel as education. In R.E. Jones (ed.) *The Seventeenth Century: Studies in the History of English Thought and Literature from Bacon to Pope* (pp. 45–53). London: Oxford University Press.

Pearce, D.G. (1981) *Tourist Development*. Harlow: Longmans.

Pearce, D. (1995) *Tourism Today: A Geographical Analysis*. Harlow: Longmans.

Pearce, P.L. (1982a) Perceived changes in holiday destinations. *Annals of Tourism Research* 9 (2), 145–164.

Pearce, P.L. (1982b) *The Social Psychology of Tourist Behaviour*. Oxford: Pergamon Press.

Pearce, P.L. (1988) *The Ulysses Factor: Evaluating Visitors in Tourist Settings*. New York: Springer-Verlag.

Pearce, P.L., Moscardo, G. and Ross, G.F. (1996) *Tourism Community Relationships*. Oxford: Pergamon.

Pennings, J. (1976) Leisure correlates of working conditions. Unpublished paper, Carnegie-Mellon University, Graduate School of Industrial Administration

Petri, K.L., Billo, R.E. and Bidanda, B. (1998) A neural network process model for abrasive flow machining operations. *Journal of Manufacturing Systems* 17 (1), 52–64.

Pettifer, J. (1987) *Diamonds in the Sky*. Channel 4 TV.

Pfäfflin, G.F. (1987) Concern for tourism: European perspective and response. *Annals of Tourism Research* 14, 576–588.

Phillips, A. (1988) *The Countryside as a Leisure Product*. Proceedings of the Conference in Rural Tourism. London: English Tourist Board.

Pielo, E.C. (1959) The point-to-point distances in the study of patterns of plant populations. *Journal of Ecology* 47, 607–612.

Pike, S. (2002) Positioning as a source of competitive advantage: An investigation of Rotorua's position as a domestic short break holiday destination. Unpublished PhD thesis, Department of Tourism Management, The University of Waikato.

Pike, S. (2001) Destination positioning: Importance-performance analysis of short break destinations. Poster presentation. Travel and Tourism Research Association Convention, Fort Myers, FL. June.

Pizam, A. (1978) Tourism impacts: The social costs to the destination community as perceived by its residents. *Journal of Travel Research* 16 (4), 8–12.

Pizam, A. and Pokela, J. (1985) The perceived impact of casino gambling on a community. *Annals of Tourism Research* 12 (2), 147–166.

Plog, S.C. (1977) Why destinations rise and fall in popularity. In E.M. Kelly (ed.) *Domestic and International Tourism* (pp. 26–28). Wellesley, MA: Institute of Certified Travel Agents.

Plog, S. (2002) The power of psychographics and the concept of venturesomeness. *Journal of Travel Research* 40 (Feb), 244–251.
Price Waterhouse Cooper (2000) *The Economic Impacts of Tourism in Northland.* Auckland: Price Waterhouse Cooper.
Prideaux, B. (1996) The tourism crime cycle: A beach destination case study. In A. Pizam and Y. Mansfeld (eds) *Tourism, Crime and International Security Issues* (pp. 59–76). Chichester: Wiley.
Pruitt, D. and LaFont, S. (1995) For love and money: Romance tourism in Jamaica. *Annals of Tourism Research* 22 (2), 419–440.
Purcell, L. (2002) *Black Chicks Talking.* Sydney: Hodder Headline.
Quayson, J. and Var, T. (1982) A tourism demand function for the Okanagan, BC. *Tourism Management* (3) 2, 108–115.
Rae, J.B. (1968) *Climb to Greatness: The American Aircraft Industry 1920–1960.* Cambridge, MA: MIT Press.
Ragan, L. (1989) Despair in the Dales on visitor onslaught. *Yorkshire Evening Post*, 28 March, p. 28.
Reed, M.G. (1997) Power relations and community-based tourism planning. *Annals of Tourism Research* 24 (3), 566–591.
Reilly, W.J. (1931) *The Law of Retail Gravitation.* New York: Putnam Press.
Renton, A. (1989) At loggerheads with the turtle. *Independent*, 5 August, p. 39.
Reisinger, Y. and Turner, L. (1997) Tourist satisfaction with hosts: A cultural approach comparing Thai tourists and Australian hosts. *Pacific Tourism Review* 1 (2), 147–159.
Reisinger, Y. and Turner, L. (1998) Cross cultural differences in tourism: A strategy for tourism marketers. *Journal of Travel and Tourism Marketing* 7 (4), 79–106.
Reusberger, B. (1977) This is the end of the game. *New York Times Magazine* 40 (3), 38–43.
Reynolds, W.H. (1985) The role of the consumer in image building. *California Management Review* 7 (1), 69.
Richards, G. (1972) Tourism and the economy: An examination of methods for evaluating the contribution and effects of tourism in the economy. Unpublished PhD thesis, University of Surrey.
Richardson, J.I. (1999) *A History of Australian Travel and Tourism.* Melbourne: Hospitality Press.
Richins, H. (1996) Setting an international precedent: Ecotourism in Australia. *Visions in Leisure and Business* 15 (1), pp.27–42.
Rickard, W.E. and Brown, J. (1974) Effects of vehicles on Arctic Tundra. *Environmental Conservation* 1, 55–62.
Riley, R. (1994) Movie-induced tourism. In A.V. Seaton, C.L. Jenkins, R.C. Wood, P.U.C. Dieke, M.M. Bennett, L.R. MacLellan and R.Smith (eds) *Tourism: The State of the Art* (pp. 453–459). Chichester: Wiley.
Riley, M., Ladkin, A. and Szivas, E. (2002) *Tourism Employment: Analysis and Planning.* Clevedon: Channel View Publications.
Riley, S. and Palmer, J. (1975) Of attitudes and latitudes: A repertory grid study of perceptions of seaside resorts. *Journal of the Market Research Society* 17 (2), 74–89.
Ritchie, J.B.R. (1981) Leisure, recreation, tourism: A North American perspective. Paper from 31st AIEST Annual Conference. AIEST, vol. 22. Berne, Switzerland.
Ritchie, J.B.R. (1988) Consensus policy formulation in tourism: Measuring resident views via survey research. *Tourism Management* 9 (3), 199–212.

Ritchie, B.W. (1996) How special are special events? The economic impact and strategic development of the New Zealand masters games. *Festival Management and Event Tourism* 4 (3/4), 117–126.
Ritchie, J.R. and Zins, M. (1978) Culture as a determinant of the attractiveness of a tourist region. *Annals of Tourism Research* 5 (2), 252–270.
Rivers, P. (1974a) *The Restless Generation: A Crisis in Mobility*. London: Davis Pointer.
Rivers, P. (1974b) Unwrapping the African tourist package. *Africa Report* 19 (2), 12–16.
Rodale, R. (1989) Editorial. *Prevention* 39, September, p 27.
Rolfe, E. (1964) Analysis of a spatial distribution of neighbourhood parks in Lansing: 1920–1960. *Papers of the Michigan Academy of Science, Arts and Letters* 50, 479–491.
Rojek, C. (1993) *Ways of Escape: Modern Transformations in Leisure and Travel*. Basingstoke: MacMillan.
Ropponen, P.J. (1976) Tourism and the local population. In *Planning and Development of the Tourist Industry in the ECE Region* (pp. 104–109). New York: UN Economic Commission for Europe.
Ropponnen, R. (1968) *Die Kralt*. Helsinki: Russlands.
Ross, G.F. (1994) *The Psychology of Tourism*. Melbourne: Hospitality Press.
Rothman, R.A. (1978) Residents and transients: Community reaction to seasonal visitors. *Journal of Travel Research* 16 (3), 8–13.
Rubenstein, D. (1989) Cycling in the 1890s. *Victorian Studies* 21, 47–71.
Rudney, R. (1980) The development of tourism on the Côte d'Azure: An historical perspective. In D.E. Hawkins, E.L. Shafer and J.M. Rovelstad (eds) *Tourism Planning and Development Issues*. Washington, DC: George University Washington Press.
Russel, J.A., Ward, L.M. and Pratt, G. (1981) Affective quality attributed to environments: A factor analytic study. *Environment and Behaviour* 13 (3), 259–288.
Russell, R. and Faulkner, B. (1998) Destination life cycle in Coolangatta. An historical perspective on the rise, decline and rejuvenation of an Australian Seaside Resort. In E. Laws, B. Faulkner and G. Moscardo (eds) *Embracing and Managing Change in Tourism: International Case Studies* (pp. 95–115). London: Routledge.
Russell, R. and Faulkner, B. (1999) Movers and shakers: Chaos makers in tourism development. *Tourism Management* 20 (4), 411–423.
Ryan, C. (1989) *Attitudes Towards Tourism by Nottingham Citizens*. Report for Nottingham Tourism Development Action Programme, Nottingham Business School, Nottingham Polytechnic.
Ryan, C. (1991a) *Recreational Tourism: A Social Science Perspective*. London: Routledge.
Ryan, C. (1991b) Tourism, terrorism and violence: The risks of wider world travel. *Conflict Study* 244. London: Research Institute for the Study of Conflict and Terrorism.
Ryan, C. (1993) Tourism and crime: An intrinsic or accidental relationship? *Tourism Management* 14 (3), 173–183.
Ryan, C. (1996a) Linkages between holiday travel risk and insurance claims: Evidence from New Zealand. *Tourism Management* 17 (8), 593–602.
Ryan, C. (1996b) Economic impacts of small events: Estimates and determinants, a New Zealand Example. *Tourism Economics* 4 (4), 339–352.
Ryan, C. (1997) Maori and tourism: A relationship of history, constitutions and rites. *Journal of Sustainable Tourism* 5 (4), 257–279.

Ryan, C. (1997b) Rafting in the Rangitikei, New Zealand: An example of adventure holidays. In D. Getz and S.J. Page (eds) *The Business of Rural Tourism: International Perspectives* (pp. 162–190). London: International Thomson Business Press.

Ryan, C. (1998a) The travel career ladder: An appraisal. *Annals of Tourism Research* 25 (4), 936–957.

Ryan, C. (1998b) Dolphins, Marae and canoes: Eco-tourism in New Zealand. In E. Laws, B. Faulkner and G. Moscardo (eds) *Embracing and Managing Change in Tourism: International Case Studies* (pp. 285–306). London: Routledge.

Ryan, C. (1999a) From the psychometrics of SERVQUAL to sex: Measurements of tourist satisfaction. In A. Pizam and Y. Mansfield (eds) *Consumer Behavior in Travel and Tourism* (pp. 267–286). Binghamtom, NY: Haworth Press.

Ryan, C. (1999b) The use of a spatial model to assess conference market share: A New Zealand example. *International Journal of Tourism Research* (formerly *Progress in Tourism and Hospitality Research*) 1 (1), 49–53.

Ryan, C. (1999c) Some dimensions of Maori involvement in tourism. In M. Robinson and P. Boniface (eds) *Tourism and Cultural Conflict* (pp. 229–245). Wallingford: CABI Publishing.

Ryan, C. (2000a) Tourist behaviour research: The role of 'I' and neural networks. In B. Faulkner, G. Moscardo and E. Laws (eds) *Tourism in the 21st Century: Lessons from Experience* (pp. 247–265). London: Continuum Books.

Ryan, C. (2000b) Australian tourists and their interest in wildlife based tourism attractions. In R. Robinson, P. Long, N. Evans, R. Sharpley and J. Swarbrooke (eds) *Motivations, Behaviour and Tourists Types: Reflections on International Tourism* (pp. 341–356). Sunderland: Business Education Publishers.

Ryan, C. (2001a) Entertainment, globalisation and mutant messages: The search for edutainment and tourism based on indigenous peoples' culture. A paper prepared for the 2001 Conference of the International Academy for the Study of Tourism. Macau: Institute of Tourism.

Ryan, C. (2001b) Saltwater crocodiles: A North Australian tourist icon. In M. Shackley (ed.) *Flagship Species: Case Studies in Wildlife Tourism Management* (pp. 5-16). Burlington, VT: The International Ecotourism Society.

Ryan, C. (2002a) Motives, behaviours, body and mind. In C. Ryan (ed.) *The Tourist Experience: A New Introduction* (pp. 27–57). London: Continuum.

Ryan, C. (2002b) Tourism is the edge: An essay in liminalities and marginalities. Keynote paper in Proceedings of the12th International Research Conference of the Council of Australian Universities in Tourism and Hospitality Education (C. Pforr, ed.). Freemantle: Council of Australian Universities in Tourism and Hospitality Education.

Ryan, C. (2002c) Tourism and cultural proximity: Examples from New Zealand. *Annals of Tourism Research* 29 (4), 952–971.

Ryan, C. (2002d,) 'The time of our lives' or time for our lives: An examination of time in holidaying. In C. Ryan (ed.) *The Tourist Experience* (pp. 201–212). London: Continuum.

Ryan, C. (2002e) From motivation to assessment. *The Tourist Experience* (pp. 58–77). London: Continuum.

Ryan, C. (2003) The silent voice of the father: An examination of father–child interaction on holidays. Conference paper, Council of Australian Universities in Tourism and Hospitality Education Annual Conference, Southern Cross University, NSW.

Ryan, C. (in press a) Review of *Dynamic Tourism* by P. Boniface. *Tourism Management*.

Ryan, C (in press b) Risk acceptance in adventure tourism: A contextual review. In S.J Page and J. Wilks (eds) [title unconfirmed].
Ryan, C. and Cave, J. (2002) *Perceptions of Auckland*. Report commissioned by Tourism Auckland, Department of Tourism Management, Waikato University, New Zealand.
Ryan, C. and Cliff, A. (1996) Users and non-users on the expectation items of the ServQual scale. *Annals of Tourism Research* 23 (4), 931–934.
Ryan, C. and Cliff, A. (1997a) Do travel agencies measure up to customer expectation? An empirical investigation of travel agencies' service quality as measured by SERVQUAL. *Journal of Travel and Tourism Marketing* 6 (2), 1–32.
Ryan, C. and Connor, M. (1981) *Tourism in Markel Harborough*. Lincoln. East Midlands Tourist Board.
Ryan, C. and Crotts, J. (1997) Carving and tourism: A Maori perspective. *Annals of Tourism Research* 24 (4), 898–918.
Ryan, C. and Evans, T. (2002) The economic impact of tourism on the Rangitikei Region of New Zealand. Unpublished report, Department of Tourism Management, The University of Waikato Management School, Hamilton, New Zealand.
Ryan, C. and Groves, J. (1987) Attitudes of cruise line holidaymakers. Working paper, Nottingham Business School, Nottingham Polytechnic.
Ryan, C. and Hall, C.M. (2001) *Sex Tourism: Marginal People and Liminalities*. London: Routledge.
Ryan, C. and Harvey, K. (2000) Who likes saltwater crocodiles? An analysis of socio-demographics of those viewing tourist wildlife attractions based on saltwater crocodiles. *Journal of Sustainable Tourism* 8 (5), 426–433.
Ryan, C., Hughes, K. and Chirgwin, S. (2000) The gaze, spectacle and eco-tourism. *Annals of Tourism Research* 27 (1), 148–163.
Ryan, C. and Huyton, J. (2000) Who is interested in Aboriginal tourism in the Northern Territory, Australia? A cluster analysis. *Journal of Sustainable Tourism* 8 (1), 53–88.
Ryan, C. and Huyton, J. (2002) Tourists and aboriginal people. *Annals of Tourism Research* 29 (3), 631–647.
Ryan, C. and Lockyer, T. (2001) An economic impact case study: The South Pacific Masters' Games. *Tourism Economics* 7 (3), 267–276.
Ryan, C. and Mo, X. (2001) Chinese visitors to New Zealand: Demographics and perceptions. *Journal of Vacation Marketing* 8 (1), 13–27.
Ryan, C. and Mohsin, A. (2001) Backpackers: Attitudes to the 'outback'. *Journal of Travel and Tourism Marketing* 10 (1), 69–92.
Ryan, C. and Richardson, M. (1983) The use of swimming pools in Broxtowe: An application of gravitational theory. Unpublished paper, Nottingham Business School, Nottingham Polytechnic.
Ryan, C. and Rippey, N. (2000) Perceived and actual usage patterns of Rotorua Airport. Unpublished report, Department of Tourism Management, The University of Waikato.
Ryan, C. and Robertson, E. (1997) New Zealand student-tourists: Risk behaviour and health. In S. Clift and P. Grabowski (eds) *Tourism and Health: Risks, Research and Responses* (pp. 119–138). London: Pinter.
Ryan, C. and Saward, J., 2003, Can zoos be an alternative to wildlife viewing in natural settings? An examination of Visitor Perceptions at Hamilton Zoo, New Zealand. Paper presented in refereed paper proceedings of the 2003 Council of Australian Universities in Tourism and Hospitality Education Conference, Coffs Harbour, Southern Cross University. Canberra: Bureau of Tourism Research.

Ryan, C., Scotland, A. and Montgomery, D. (1998) Resident attitudes to tourism development: A comparative study between the Rangitikei, New Zealand and Bakewell, United Kingdom. *Progress in Tourism and Hospitality Research* 4 (2), 115–130.

Ryan, C. and Sterling, S. (2001) Visitors to Litchfield National Park, Australia: A typology based on behaviours. *Journal of Sustainable Tourism* 9 (1), 64–75.

Ryan, C. and Wheeller, B. A. (1982) Visitors to Nottingham Castle. Report for Nottingham City Council, Nottingham Business School, Nottingham Polytechnic.

Ryan, D. (2001) What women want. *Sunday Times* travel supplement, 18 November, pp. 1–2.

Saleh, F. and Ryan, C. (1990) Service quality in hotels: Servqual revisited. Paper presented for *Tourism Research in the 1990s* (pp. 313–328). Durham: University of Durham.

Sarbin, H. B. (1981) *The Traveller: 1981 and Beyond*. Published remarks before the World Hospitality Congress, Boston, MA, 11 March.

Sax, J.L. (1980) *Mountains Without Handrails: Reflection on National Parks*. Ann Arbor, MI: University of Michigan Press.

Schwaninger, M. (1984) Forecasting leisure and tourism. *Tourism Management* 5 (4), 250–257.

Schwaninger, M. (1989) Trends in leisure and tourism for 2000–2010. In S. Witt and L. Mountiho (ed.) *Tourism Management and Marketing Handbook*. Hemel Hempstead: Prentice Hall.

Seakhoa-King, A. (2002) Qualitative data collection in tourism research: Practical issues and challenges. Paper presented at Tourism Research 2002 Conference, Welsh School of Hospitality, Tourism and Leisure Management, University of Wales Institute.

Searle, R. (1989) Banff National Park. *Borealis* 1 (2), 9–12.

Seaton, A.V. (2000) Battlefield tourism on the Somme and in Flanders. *Tourism Recreation Research* 25 (3), 63–78.

Seddighi, J.R. and Shearing, D.F. (1997) The demand for tourism in North-East England with special reference to Northumbria: An empirical analysis. *Tourism Management* 18 (8), 499–512.

Sessa, A. (1988) The science of systems for tourism development. *Annals of Tourism Research* 15 (2), 219–235.

Shackley, M. (1992) Manatees and tourism in southern Florida: Opportunity or threat. *Journal of Environmental Management* 34, 257–265.

Shackley, M. (1996) *Wildlife Tourism*. London: Routledge.

Shackley, M. (2001a) *Flagship Species: Case Studies in Wildlife Tourism Management*. Burlington, VT: The International Ecotourism Society.

Shackley, M. (2001b) Managing a marine ecotourism destination: The case of Stingray City. In M. Shackley (ed.) *Flagship Species: Case Studies in Wildlife Tourism Management* (pp. 31–38). Burlington, VT: The International Ecotourism Society.

Sharpley, R. (1994) *Tourism, Tourists and Society*. Huntingdon: Elm Press.

Sharpley, R. and Craven, B. (2001) The 2001 foot and mouth crisis: Rural economy and tourism policy implications, a comment. *Current Issues in Tourism* 4 (6), 527–537.

Shaw, S. (1990) Where has all the leisure gone? The distribution and redistribution of leisure. Keynote paper presented at the 6th Canadian Congress on Leisure Research, University of Waterloo.

Sheridan, M. (1989) Emergency status for Italy's algae problem. *Independent*, 19 July.

Simmons, D. and Forer, P. (1996) Demand, supply and capacities: A research framework for tourism planning. In G. Kearsley (ed.) *Towards a More Sustainable Tourism: Proceedings of Tourism Down Under II* (pp. 343–356). Dunedin: Centre for Tourism, Otago University.

Sickle, K. van and Eagles, P.F.J. (1998) Budgets, pricing policies and user fees in Canadian parks' tourism. *Tourism Management* 19 (3), 225–235.

Sinclair, M.T. (1981) The theory of the Keynesian income multiplier and its applications to tourist expenditure in Malaga. Unpublished PhD thesis, Reading University.

Sinclair, M.T. and Sutcliffe, C.M.S. (1982) Keynesian income multipliers with first and second round effects: An application to tourism expenditure. *Oxford Bulletin of Economics and Statistics* 44 (4), 321–338.

Sinclair, M.T. and Stabler, M. (1997) *The Economics of Tourism*. London: Routledge.

Sinclair, M.T., Clewer, A. and Pack, A. (1990) Hedonic prices and the marketing of package holidays: The case of tourism resorts in Malaga. In G.J. Ashworth and B. Goodall (eds) *Marketing Tourism Places* (pp. 85–103). London: Routledge.

Smale, B.J.A. and Nykiforuk, C.I.J. (2001) Tourist generating regions in Canada: Factors associated with travel patterns and tourist behaviour. In *Tourism Satellite Account (TSA) Implementation Project: Enzo Paci Papers on Measuring the Economic Significance of Tourism* (Vol. 1, pp. 155–172). Madrid: World Tourism Organisation.

Smith, M. (1988) Plastic enemy within the sea. *Independent*, 14 November, p. 17.

Smith, R. (1992) Beach resort evolution: Implications for planning. *Annals of Tourism Research* 19 (2), 304–322.

Smith, S.L.J. (1983) *Recreation Geography*. Harlow: Longmans.

Smith, S.L.J. (1989) *Tourism Analysis: A Handbook*. Harlow: Longmans.

Smith, S.L.J. (1990) A test of Plog's allocentric/psychocentric model: Evidence from seven nations. *Journal of Travel Research* 28 (4), 40–43

Smith, S.L.J. (1995) The tourism satellite account: Perspectives of Canadian tourism associations and organisations. *Tourism Economics* 1 (3), 225–245.

Smith, S.J. and Wilton, D. (1997) TSAs and the WTTC/WEFA methodology: Different satellites or different planets? *Tourism Economics* 3 (3), 249–264.

Smith, V.L. (1977a) Eskimo tourism: Micro models and marginal men. In V.L. Smith, *Hosts and Guests: The Anthropology of Tourism* (pp. 51–70). Philadelphia: The University of Pennsylvania Press.

Smith, V.L. (1977b) *Hosts and Guests: The Anthropology of Tourism*. Philadelphia: University of Pennsylvania Press.

Smith, V.L. (1994) Privatization in the Third World: Small-scale tourism enterprises. In W. Theobald (ed.) *Global Tourism: The Next Decade* (pp. 163–173). Oxford: Butterworth Heinemann.

Smith, V.L. (1989) *Hosts and Guests: The Anthropology of Tourism* (2nd edn). Philadelphia: University of Pennsylvania Press.

Smith, V.L. (2000) Space tourism: The 21st century 'frontier'. *Tourism Recreation Research* 25 (3), 5–16.

Smith, V.L. and Brent, M. (2001) *Hosts and Guests Revisited: Tourism Issues of the 21st Century*. New York: Cognizant Communications.

Soane, J.V.N. (1993) *Fashionable Resort Regions: Their Evolution and Transformation with Particular Reference to Bournemouth, Nice, Los Angeles and Wiesbaden*. Wallingford: CAB International.

Sohn, I. (1986) *Readings in Input–Output Analysis: Theory and Applications*. New York: Oxford University Press.

Soisson, J-P. (1979) The tourism satellite account: Presentation of accounting tables and of the first estimation of domestic tourism expenditure 'Regards sur l'économie du tourisme' 24, fourth quarter 1979, France. Reproduced in *The Tourism Satellite Account as an Ongoing Process: Past, Present and Future Developments*. 2001. Madrid: World Tourism Organisation.

South Australia Tourist Commission (1986) *1987–1989 South Australian Strategic Tourism Plan*. Adelaide: South Australia Tourist Commission.

Sprawson, C. (1992) Everything going swimmingly. *The Independent Weekend*, 23 May, p. 29.

Stankey, G.H., Cole, D.N., Lucas, R.C., Petersen, M.E. and Frissell, S. (1985) *The Limits of Acceptable Change (LAC) System for Wilderness Planning*. (General Technical Report INT-176) Ogden, UT: United States Department of Agriculture (Forest Service), Intermountain Forest and Range Experiment Station.

Starke, M. (1820) *Travels on the Continent: Written for the Use of and Particular Information of Travellers*. London.

Statistics New Zealand (2001) *Tourism Satellite Accounts*. Wellington: Statistics New Zealand.

Stewart, J.Q. (1948) Demographic gravitation: Evidence and applications. *Sociometry* 11 (1), 31–58.

Summary, R. (1987) An estimation of tourism demand by multivariate regression analysis: Evidence from Kenya. *Tourism Management* 8 (4), 317–322.

Tahana, N. and Oppermann, M. (1998) Maori cultural performances and tourism. *Tourism Recreation Research* 23 (1), 23–30.

Taylor, J. (2001) Authenticity and sincerity in tourism. *Annals of Tourism Research* 28 (1), 7–26.

Teas, R.K. (1993) Consumer expectations and measurement of perceived service quality. *Journal of Professional Services Marketing* 8 (2), 35–54.

Teas, R.K. (1994) Expectations as a comparison standard in measuring service quality: An assessment of a reassessment. *Journal of Marketing* 58, 132.

Thomas, W. (1549/1961) *The History of Italy. A Book Exceeding Profitable to be Read Because it Entreath of the State of Many and Divers Commonwealths How they Have Been and Now be Governed*. Reprinted in G.B. Parks (ed.) *Folger Documents of Tudor and Stuart Civilisation*, 1961. New York: Cornell University.

Thomas, B. and Townsend, A. (2001) New trends in the growth of tourism employment in the UK in the 1990s. *Tourism Economics* 7 (3), 295–310.

Tobin, G.A. (1974) The bicycle boom of the 1890s. *Journal of Popular Culture* 8, 838–849.

Toffler, A. (1970) *Future Shock*. Random House, New York.

Toflller, A. (1981) *The Third Wave*. Benton, New York.

Tourism Forecasting Council (2001) *Forecast, February 2001*. Commonwealth Department of Industry, Science and Resources. On WWW at http://www.tourism.gov.au.

Town of Canmore (1995) *Social Planning Goals and Economic Development Strategy*. Canmore, Alberta: Town of Canmore.

Towner, J. (1984) The European Grand Tour, c1550–1840: A study of its role in the history of tourism. Unpublished doctoral thesis, University of Birmingham.

Towner, J. (1985) The Grand Tour: A key phase in the history of tourism. *Annals of Tourism Research* 12 (3), 297–333.

Towner, J. (1996) *An Historical Geography of Recreation and Tourism in the Western World: 1540–1940*. Chichester: John Wiley and Sons.

Travis, A.S. (1982) Physical impacts: Trends affecting tourism, managing the environmental and cultural impacts. *Tourism Management* 3 (4), December, 256–262.

Trollope, J. (2001) Women travelling alone. *Sunday Times* travel supplement, October.

Truong, T-D. (1990) *Sex, Money and Morality: Prostitution and Tourism in South-east Asia.* London: Zed Books.

Tsai, M., Ryan, C. and Lockyer, T. (2002) Culture and evaluation of service quality: A study of the service gaps in a Taiwanese setting. *Asia Pacific Journal of Tourism Research* 7 (2), 8–19.

Tsartas, P. (1992) Socioeconomic impacts of tourism on two Greek islands. *Annals of Tourism Research* 19 (3), 516–533.

Turner, L. and Ash, J. (1975) *The Golden Hordes: International Tourism and the Pleasure Periphery.* London: Constable.

Tuting, L. (1989) Trekking tourism in Nepal (Trans. by R. Heard from 'Tourismus und Okologie'). *Okozid* 5.

Turner, L.W. and Witt, S.F. (2001) Factors influencing demand for international tourism: tourism demand analysis using structural equation modelling revisited. *Tourism Economics* 7 (1), 21–38.

UKEA (2001) *The Fate and Behaviour of Steroid Oestrogens in Aquatic Systems* (P2-162/TR, September). London: UK Environment Agency.

UNEP (2002) *Sustainable Tourism Development.* New York: United Nations Environment Programme. On WWW at www.unep.org.

United Nations (1963) Conference on Tourism and International Conference, Rome. See http://www.international.icomos.org/publications/ 93touris19.pdf.

Urry, J. (1990) *Tourist Gaze: Travel, Leisure and Society.* London: Sage Publications.

Urry, J. (2000) The global media ,and cosmopolitanism. Paper presented at Transnational Amercia Conference, Bavarian American Academy, Munich, June. On WWW at www.comp.lancaster.ac.uk/sociology/soc056ju.html.

van der Zande, van der Ter Keurs, W.J. and van der Weijden, W.J. (1980) The impact of roads on the densities of four bird species in an open field habitat: Evidence of a long distance effect. *Biological Conservation* 18: 299–321.

Vaughan, D.R. (1986) *Estimating the Level of Tourism-related Employment: An Assessment of Two Non-survey Techniques.* London: BTA/ETB Research Services.

Victurine, R. (2000) Building tourism excellence at the community level: Capacity building for community based entrepreneurs in Uganda. *Journal of Travel Research* 38 (3), 221–229.

Voelkl, J. and Ellis, G. (1990) Use of criterion scaling in the analysis of experience sampling data. Proceedings of 6th Canadian Congress of Leisure Research. Ontario: Ontario Research Council on Leisure.

Vukonic, B. (1996) *Tourism and Religion.* Oxford: Pergamon.

Waiser, B. (1989) *Saskatchewan's Playground.* Saskatoon: Fifth House Publishers.

Wagner, J.E. (1997) Estimating the economic impacts of tourism. *Annals of Tourism Research* 24 (3), 592–608.

Wallace, A.F.C. (1956) Revitalisation movements. *American Anthropologist* 58, 265.

Walpole, M.J. and Goodwin, H.J. (2000) Local economic impacts of dragon tourism in Indonesia. *Annals of Tourism Research* 27 (3), 559–576.

Walter, J.A. (1982) Social limits. *Leisure Studies* 1 (September), 295–304.

Walmesley, D.J. and Jenkins, J. (1992) Tourism cognitive mapping of unfamiliar environments. *Annals of Tourism Research* 19 (3), 268–286.

Walton, J.K. (1983) *The English Seaside Resort: A Social History, 1750–1914.* Leicester: Leicester University Press.
Walther, F.R. (1969) Flight behaviour and avoidance of predators in Thompson's Gazelle (*Gazella Thomsoni* Guenther 1884) *Behaviour* 34, 184–221.
Wang, N. (2000) *Tourism and Modernity: A Sociological Analysis.* Oxford: Pergamon.
Ward, J., Burns, B., Johnson, V., Simmons, D.G. and Fairweather, J. (2000) Interactions between tourists and the natural environment: Impacts of tourist trampling on geothermal vegetation and tourist experiences at geothermal sites in Rotorua; Rotorua case study. Report No 16/2000. Canterbury: Lincoln University Tourism Research and Education Centre.
Waring, M. (1988) *Counting for Nothing: What Men Value and What Women are Worth.* Wellington, NZ: Allen & Unwin/Port Nicholson Press.
Waverley District Council (1999) *Building and Development Report: July.* Sydney: Waverley District Council.
Wearing, B. and Wearing, S. (1996) Refocusing the tourist experience: The flâneur and the chorister. *Leisure Studies* 15, 229–243.
Weaver, D. (2001) *Ecotourism.* Melbourne: Wiley.
Webster, B. and Hurst, G. (2001) Business and unions hail 'jobs bonanza'. *The Times,* 21 November, p. 27.
Weiner, T. (2001) Saving the coast of Mexico from 'Cancuning': Greed still trumps the environment. *The Associated Press,* 12 January.
Wells, S. (1991) A proposal for a satellite account and information system for tourism. Discussion paper delivered at the International Conference on Travel and Tourism Statistics in Ottawa, 26 June.
Weyerhaeuser Canada (1989) *Forests for Everyone: Today and Tomorrow.* Prince Albert: Weyerhaeuser Canada Ltd.
Wheeller, B.A. (1990) Alternative tourism. Paper presented at the Tourism Research into the 1990s, University of Durham, Durham.
Wheeller, B. (1993) Sustaining the ego. *The Journal of Sustainable Tourism* 1 (2) 121–130.
Wheeller, B.A. (1997) Here we go, here we go, here we go eco. In M.J. Stabler (ed.) *Tourism and Sustainability: Principles to Practice* (pp. 39–50) Wallingford: CAB International.
White, P.E. (1974) The social impact of tourism on host communities: A study of language change in Switzerland. *Research Paper* 9. Oxford: Oxford University School of Geography.
Whysall, P. (1974) The changing pattern of retail structure of Greater Nottingham. Unpublished PhD thesis, University of Nottingham, Nottingham.
Wickens, E. (1997) Licensed for thrills: Risk taking and tourism. In S. Clift and P. Grabowski (eds) *Tourism and Health: Risks, Research and Responses* (pp. 151–164). London: Pinter.
Wilderness Act (1964) Wilderness Act of September 3. (P.L 88–577, 78 Stat. 890; 16 USC 1 1 21 (note), 1 1 31-1136), section 2c.
Wilks, J., Watson, B. and Faulks, J. (1999) International tourists and road safety in Australia: Developing a national research and management programme. *Tourism Management* 20 (6), 645–654.
Williams, J. and Lawson, R. (2001) Community issues and resident opinions of tourism. *Annals of Tourism Research* 28 (2), 269–290.
Williams, S. (1998) *Tourism Geography.* London: Routledge.
Wilson, R. (1989) Changing markets of the English seaside resort. Unpublished thesis, Nottingham Business School, Nottingham Polytechnic.

Withey, L. (1998) *Grand Tours and Cook's Tours. A History of Leisure Travel, 1750 to 1915*. London: Arum Press.

Witt, C.A. and Wright, P. (1990) Tourism motivation, life after Maslow. Paper from *Tourism Research into the 1990s*. Durham: University of Durham Department of Economics.

Witt , C.A and Witt, S.F. (1994) Demand elasticities. In S.F. Witt and L. Moutinho (eds) *Tourism Marketing and Management Handbook* (2nd edn, pp. 521–529). Hemel Hempstead: Prentice Hall International.

Witt, S.F. (1978) The demand for foreign holidays. Unpublished PhD thesis, Bradford University.

Witt, S.F. (1992) Tourism Forecasting: How well do private and public sector organizations perform? *Tourism Management* 13 (1), 79–84.

Witt, S.F. and Martin C. (1987) Deriving a relative price index for inclusion in international tourism demand estimation models. *Journal of Travel Research* 25 (3), 38–40.

Witt, S.F. and Mountiho, L. (eds) (1989) *Tourism Management and Management Handbook*. London: Prentice Hall.

Witt, S.F. and Martin, C. (1989) Forecasting tourism demand: A comparison of the accuracy of several quantitative methods. *International Journal of Forecasting* 5 (1), 1–13.

Wood, P. and Treadwell, J. (1999) The New Zealand bach: Fact or fiction. Presented to the New Zealand Institute of Architects in Dunedin, October.

Wordsworth, W. (1888/1999) *The Complete Poetical Works of William Wordsworth* Reprinted 1999. New York: Bartleby.Com.

WTO (1982a) *Review of Governmental Policies on Environmental Impacts of Tourism*. Madrid: World Tourism Organisation.

WTO (1982b) *Risks of Saturation, or Tourist Carrying Capacity Overload in Holiday Destinations*. Madrid: World Tourism Organisation.

WTO (1983) *Workshop on Environmental Aspects of Tourism*. World Tourism Organisation, Madrid.

WTO (1991) *World Directory of Documentation Resources and Systems for the Travel and Tourism Sector*. Madrid: World Tourism Organisation.

WTO (1998) *Yearbook of Tourism Statistics* (Vol. 1, 50th edn). Madrid: World Tourism Organisation.

WTO (1999) *Changes in Leisure Time: The Impact on Tourism* (1999). Madrid: World Tourism Organisation.

WTO (2001a) *Compendium of Tourism Statistics* (2001 edn). Madrid: World Tourism Organisation.

WTO (2001b) *The Tourism Satellite Account As an Ongoing Process: Past, Present and Future Developments*. Madrid: World Tourism Organisation.

WTTC, WTO and the Earth Council (1996) *Agenda 21 for the Travel and Tourism Industry: Towards Environmental Sustainable Development*. On WWW at http://www.wttc.org/agenda21.htm

WTTC (World Travel and Tourism Council) (1997) Rejoinder. *Tourism Economics* 3 (3), 281–288.

WTTC (2001) *Tourism Satellite Accounting Research, Estimates and Forecasts for Government and Industry*. London: World Travel and Tourism Council.

Wynn, R.F. and Holden, K. (1974) *An Introduction to Applied Econometric Analysis*. London: MacMillan..

Yamba, B. (1988) Swedish Women and the Gambia. Paper from the Conference on the Anthropology of Tourism (T. Selwyn, ed.). London: Froebel College.

Yardley, J. (1990) The role of mood in measuring levels of satisfaction with recreational participation. Paper at the 6th Canadian Congress on Leisure Research, University of Waterloo, South Ontario.
Yiannakos, A. and Gibson, H. (1992) Roles tourists play. *Annals of Tourism Research* 19 (2), 287–303.
Young, B. (1983) Touristization of traditional Maltese fishing-farming villages. *Tourism Management* 4 (1), March, 35–41.
Yu, X. and Weiler, B. (2001) Mainland Chinese pleasure travelers to Australia: A leisure behavior analysis. *Tourism, Culture and Communication* 3 (2), 81–92.
Yuksel, A. and Yuksel, F. (2001) Measurement and management issues in customer satisfaction research: review, critique and research agenda: Part 1. *Journal of Travel and Tourism Marketing* 10 (4), 47–80.
Zhang, H.Q. and Heung, V.C.S. (2001) The emergence of the mainland Chinese outbound travel market and its implications for tourism marketing. *Journal of Vacation Marketing* 8 (1), 7–12.
Zhi Hua Wang and Ryan, C. (1998) New Zealand retailers' perceptions of some tourists' negotiation styles for souvenir purchases. *Tourism, Culture and Communication* 1 (2), 139–152.
Zipf, G.K. (1946) The PIP2/D hypothesis: An inter-city movement of persons. *American Sociological Review* 11, 677–686.
Zuzanek, J. and Mannell, R. (1983) Work leisure relationships from a sociological and social psychological perspective. *Leisure Studies* 2 (September), p. 327.

Index